CHILDHOOD AND ADOLESCENCE IN ANGLO-SAXON LITERARY CULTURE

Childhood and Adolescence in Anglo-Saxon Literary Culture

EDITED BY SUSAN IRVINE
AND WINFRIED RUDOLF

UNIVERSITY OF TORONTO PRESS
Toronto Buffalo London

Toronto Buffalo London
www.utorontopress.com

ISBN 978-1-4875-0202-7

Library and Archives Canada Cataloguing in Publication

Childhood and adolescence in Anglo-Saxon literary culture / Susan Irvine, Winfried Rudolf, editors.

(Toronto Anglo-Saxon series; 28)
Includes bibliographical references and index.
ISBN 978-1-4875-0202-7 (hardcover)

1. English literature – Old English, ca. 450–1100 – History and criticism. 2. Children in literature. 3. Adolescence in literature. 4. Families in literature. I. Irvine, Susan (Susan Elizabeth), editor II. Rudolf, Winfried, editor III. Series: Toronto Anglo-Saxon series ; 28

PR173.C45 2018 829'.093523 C2017-904923-2

University of Toronto Press gratefully acknowledges the financial assistance of the Centre for Medieval Studies, University of Toronto, the English Department at University College London, and the University of Göttingen in the publication of this book.

University of Toronto Press acknowledges the financial assistance to its publishing program of the Canada Council for the Arts and the Ontario Arts Council, an agency of the Government of Ontario.

Canada Council for the Arts
Conseil des Arts du Canada

Funded by the Government of Canada
Financé par le gouvernement du Canada

Contents

Acknowledgments

We would like to thank the contributors to the volume for their good will and patience throughout, and our colleagues at UCL and Göttingen respectively for their interest and support. We would also like to thank Andreas Lemke, Paul Langeslag, Julia Josfeld, Sandra Schütz and Christy Hosefelder for helping to organise the conference in Göttingen in 2014, an event that gave contributors an opportunity to engage in dialogue with each other and with wider audiences about the volume's topic. The conference was sponsored in part by the Universitätsbund Göttingen whose support we would like to acknowledge. Oliver Bock and Victoria Symons were helpful with the final stages of preparation. Finally, we would like to thank the Centre for Medieval Studies at the University of Toronto, the Department of English at UCL, and the University of Göttingen for contributing to the publication costs of this volume.

Susan Irvine and Winfried Rudolf

Abbreviations

ACMRS	Arizona Centre for Medieval and Renaissance Studies
ASE	*Anglo-Saxon England*
ASPR	Krapp, George P., and Elliot V.K. Dobbie, ed., The Anglo-Saxon Poetic Records, 6 vols. (New York: Columbia University Press, 1931–42)
BAR	British Archaeological Reports
BT(S)	Bosworth, Joseph, *An Anglo-Saxon Dictionary. Based on the Manuscript Collections of the Late Joseph Bosworth.* Ed. Thomas Northcote Toller and Alistair Campbell. Oxford: Oxford University Press, 1838–1972 (London: Longman, 1838; ed. Toller, 1882–98; Toller's Supplement, 1921; reprinted 1966; Campbell's *Enlarged Addenda and Corrigenda to the Supplement*, 1972)
CCSL	Corpus Christianorum Series Latina
DOE	*Dictionary of Old English: A to G online*, ed. Angus Cameron, Ashley Crandell Amos, Antonette diPaolo Healey et al. (Toronto: Dictionary of Old English Project, 2007)
EETS	Early English Text Society
os	original series
ss	supplementary series
JEGP	*Journal of English and Germanic Philology*
JML	*The Journal of Medieval Latin*
MED	*The Middle English Dictionary Online*. June 2016. University of Michigan (accessed August 2016)
MGH	Monumenta Germaniae Historica
NM	*Neuphilologische Mitteilungen*
N&Q	*Notes and Queries*

PL	Patrologia Latina, ed. J.P. Migne, 221 vols. (Paris, 1844–64), cited by volume and column number
OED	*The Oxford English Dictionary Online*. June 2016. Oxford University Press (accessed August 2016)
RES	*The Review of English Studies*
SELIM	*Sociedad Española de Lengua y Literatura Inglesa Medieval*
UTP	University of Toronto Press

CHILDHOOD AND ADOLESCENCE IN ANGLO-SAXON LITERARY CULTURE

Introduction

SUSAN IRVINE AND WINFRIED RUDOLF

During the past decades scholarship on Anglo-Saxon literature and culture has seen a number of remarkable publications in the field of gender studies. These examinations have opened up a whole new range of perspectives on the lives, roles, and self-definitions of fully grown men and women in early England. In comparison, the Anglo-Saxon child still seems to stand in the shade, where it continues to lead, in Mathew Kuefler's terms, "a wryed existence."[1] One reason for this relative lack of interest in Anglo-Saxon childhood may be the near silence of children in early medieval literature; another may be the fact that literary production and its criticism, both past and present, remain largely a matter of adults. Although children play only minor roles in Anglo-Saxon texts and therefore have kindled hardly any contemporary scholarly debate, recent years have shown a gradually growing interest in their fates, not least in the wake of the emerging field of the literary study of ageism.[2] The majority of research, however, has

1 Mathew S. Kuefler, "'A Wryed Existence,'" 823–34. In the term "wryed" Kuefler is quoting a far-fetched translation by Michael Alexander of the phrase "bi me ful geomorre" (literally: "about myself, the very sad [feminine] one") in line 1 of the Old English poem *The Wife's Lament*; see the bilingual edition by Alexander, *The Earliest English Poems*, 108–9. The word encapsulates notions of protection as well as the Anglo-Saxon child's covered-up existence.

2 The editors of this volume were first drawn to the topic of childhood in the year 2005, when the International Medieval Congress in Leeds declared "Youth and Age" as its special thematic strand. The result was a first enquiry into the rich tradition of the *oblatus mortus* theme in Old English homilies; see Winfried Rudolf, "The Source and Textual Identity of 'Homily' Napier XXXI – Ælfric and the *Munuccild* of Saint-Maurice d'Agaune," 607–22. After organising related sessions at the 48th and 49th International Congress on Medieval Studies at Kalamazoo, MI, in the years 2013 and 2014, followed

been provided by historians and is dedicated to the later Middle Ages.[3] One major aim of this book is to expand the interest to earlier centuries of the period by starting new discussions about the representations of children and their education through Old English texts, as well as to reassess the controversial concept of Anglo-Saxon childhood. We hope that the range of texts and subjects covered by this volume will raise a sustained interest in the topic and finally allow the Anglo-Saxon child to step into the light.

When we look closely at the vocabulary denoting the child in Old English texts, it does in fact already stand out. The range of different terms for Anglo-Saxon children and adolescents clearly distinguishes them from older members of the population.[4] While the variety of words known from written sources does not match that of modern English (kid, mite, moppet, nipper, offspring, urchin, whippersnapper, to name but a few), these words are of no less interest. Alongside the more common usages – *bearn*, *cild*, *lytling*, for example – occur colourful and curious words such as *magotimber*, *umbor*, and *wencel*. Of these, *umbor* is arguably the most intriguing. It is attested just three times in the surviving corpus of Old English, once in the poem *Maxims I* and twice in *Beowulf* (lines 46b and 1187a) as part of the adjectival compound *umborwesende*.[5] Its origin is uncertain: it has been linked both to Gothic *wamba* (womb) and to Latin *umbo* (the boss or buckle of a shield).[6] Since the Latin word *umbo* was also used to refer to the

---

by an international symposium on the topic in Göttingen in June 2014, the editors were overwhelmed by the size of the audiences at these events and very pleased to learn that the Richard Rawlinson Centre for Anglo-Saxon Studies and Manuscript Research at Western Michigan University had decided to declare "Childhood and Adolescence in Early Germanic Culture" as its major topic, with two sessions being held at the 50th ICMS in 2015.

3 See, for example, the comprehensive studies by Nicholas Orme, *Medieval Children*, and Shulamith Shahar, *Childhood in the Middle Ages*. Notable studies by historians of the early Middle Ages are Mary Martin McLaughlin, "Survivors and Surrogates: Children and Parents from the Ninth to the Thirteenth Centuries," 20–124; and Janet Nelson, "Parents, Children, and the Church in the Earlier Middle Ages," 81–114.

4 See Jane Roberts and Christian Kay with Lynne Grundy, *A Thesaurus of Old English*, sections 02.03.01.02–05 and 02.03.02.02, and online at http://oldenglishthesaurus.arts.gla.ac.uk/. See also Sally Crawford, *Childhood in Anglo-Saxon England*, 44–6.

5 On the possibility that *umborwesende* may be two separate words, see, for example, Alfred Bammesberger, "Wealhtheow's Address to Beowulf (*Beowulf*, Lines 1226b–7)," 455–7, at 457.

6 See Hans Schabram, "Bemerkungen zur Etymologie von ae. *umbor* 'Kind,'" 403–14; Hilding Bäck, *The Synonyms for "Child," "Boy," "Girl" in Old English*, 78.

navel, the latter is perhaps more plausible than it might initially seem when the link between the navel and the nourishment of the child in the uterus is taken into account.[7] Fittingly, the Old English term *cild* – direct cognate to the most frequently used Modern English *child* – has a widely accepted etymological relation to Gothic *kilþei* (belly, womb; with Gothic *inkilþo* meaning "pregnant").[8] These words remind us that the child begins life as a physical protuberance and alert us to the way in which visible differences from adulthood (most obviously the child's relative smallness) might contribute to defining the idea of childhood.[9] At the same time these coinages foreground the notion of childhood as a dynamic process of growing and stepping forward into this world, therefore offering us a first tantalising glimpse into the Anglo-Saxon perspective on the younger generation.

A dynamic view of childhood, opposite to binary distinctions between the immature and the mature, is essential to any kind of research on the topic, because stages in human development remain as transitional and individual as the semantic layering of words. Although defining moments in the biological life cycle of a human being (such as primary and deciduous dentation, menstruation, breaking of voice, or growing a beard) are anthropological constants, their occurrence can vary from person to person. In the same way Old English childhood terminology, such as *cildhad* (childhood) or *cnihthad* (the period between childhood and manhood, boyhood), can only vaguely correspond to these phenotypic demarcations; they can equally relate to (sometimes changing) Anglo-Saxon social and legal concepts, or even extend into the realm of metaphor. The same is true of the Latin coinages *infantia*, *pueritia*, and *adolescentia* famously introduced by Isidore in his *Etymologiae*, the indispensable compendium of every good medieval library.[10] Clear-cut as Isidore's definitions may seem,

---

7 The two meanings are linked by Isidore of Seville: "The navel (*umbilicus*) is the centre of the body, so called because it is a 'protuberance of the belly' (*umbus illiorum*). Whence also the place in the middle of a shield is called 'boss' (*umbo*), from which it hangs, for the infant hangs from it in the uterus and it is also nourished from it." Stephen A. Barney, W.J. Lewis, J.A. Beach, and Oliver Berghof, trans., *The Etymologies of Isidore of Seville*. The Germanic and the Latin explanations are perhaps not mutually exclusive, since both denote a kind of protuberance.

8 Schabram, "Etymologie von ae. *umbor*," 409.

9 See Crawford, *Childhood in Anglo-Saxon England*, xv: "In biological terms, children are quite simply not adults."

10 Isidore, *Etymologiae*, XI.ii, "De aetatibus hominum," ed. Lindsay, 1: n.p.

they did not find unanimous acceptance among medieval scholars, who may vary their usage according to their individual experience.[11] Still, common to all semantic angles taken at the terminology is the identification of childhood as a transitional phase that should entail the development of physical, sensual, and intellectual abilities and ultimately lead to a state of greater maturity and experience of the individual. This early period of development requires the support of other human beings, which provides the essential social dimension to the human experience that defines our species. Views on this stage of social dependence as well as related notions of immaturity can differ with age: children themselves realise their own childhood primarily through the various individual deficits they urgently seek to overcome, while adults often reminisce on the joys of innocent carelessness, capacity for enthusiasm, physical and mental agility, emotional care, and seemingly boundless opportunities of their young years.

The child's quality of an undefiled mind, paired with the gift of effortless perception, creates fundamental tensions within the moral framework of the Christian Middle Ages and its theology of sin. Although medieval scholars (including famous Anglo-Saxons such as Bede) celebrate children's impartial acceptance of Christian teachings and the perceptiveness of the infant brain, they likewise identify a central contradiction between childish boisterousness and virtuous behaviour, the latter of which inevitably calls for the education of specific normative principles.[12] In his influential and often quoted *Confessiones*, for example, Augustine remembers his own childhood as a time during which he was a fundamentally different person with regard to the norms of good conduct.[13] His retrospective is far from

11 For the contrasting views see Andreas Lemke, "*Puer* and *pueritia* in Bede's *Historia ecclesiastica gentis Anglorum*," 153–69, as well as his and Joyce Hill's contributions to this volume.

12 This contradiction finds an interesting manifestation in the widespread European tradition of the boy-bishop's feast; see Tanja Skambraks, *Das Kinderbischofsfest im Mittelalter*, in which a carnivalesque element of temporary social deregulation provides a forceful symbolic reminder of the purity and innocence a prelate should strive for.

13 Augustine, *Confessions*, trans. Chadwick, 6–18. The work is cited extensively by Anglo-Saxon scholars such as Bede, Alcuin, and Byrhtferth; see Michael Lapidge, *The Anglo-Saxon Library*, 232 and 282. At least five manuscripts containing the work from the late Anglo-Saxon period survive; see Helmut Gneuss and Michael Lapidge, *Anglo-Saxon Manuscripts: A Bibliographical Handlist of Manuscripts and Manuscript Fragments Written or Owned in England up to 1100*, nos. 163, 434, 456.8, 603, 697.

nostalgic, since he does not look back on his childhood as a time of carefree light-heartedness, but rather as a period of wayward and disorganised indolence of which he feels deeply ashamed. This shame is enhanced through Augustine's adult role as proficient scholar and teacher, who fully realises his former ignorance and lack of resolution as an obstacle to his own spiritual enlightenment. No matter if Augustine's account of childhood memories is simply a rhetorical trick by whose means he wishes to discipline his Christian audience, or indeed a heartfelt emotion: he expresses a specific sentiment about his formative years as a human being, albeit this sentiment may differ profoundly in its nature from present-day forms of childhood nostalgia. Augustine acknowledges various weaknesses of the infant body, but admits that adults allow the capricious expression of desire in children, whereas the same things would not be tolerated in adults.[14] In doing so, he identifies childhood as a set period with its own social regulations and pedagogical implications for the Christian Middle Ages and articulates a strongly negative sentiment about it.

Augustine's teachings, influential as they were during the entire Middle Ages, pose more questions to the modern scholar than they answer. This is certainly true for the still hotly disputed issues of whether and how medieval childhood was perceived, both as a distinct period and a sentiment. It is now well over half a century since Philippe Ariès published his influential book *L'enfant et la familiale sous l'Ancien Régime*.[15] His startling and controversial claim that "in medieval society the idea of childhood did not exist" has also permeated the subsequent discussions of Anglo-Saxon childhood.[16] By this claim, Ariès meant not that affection for children was lacking, but rather that in the medieval period, unlike in modern society, children were viewed as having no distinctive nature of their own, and there was no set of expectations about what was to constitute childhood; children were seen essentially as miniature adults.[17] The conventional "ages of life," he argued – "childhood, puerility, adolescence, youth, senility, old age" – acted in the Middle Ages as scientific categories that were "purely

14 Augustine, *Confessions,* I.11.

15 Philippe Ariès, *L'enfant et la familiale sous l'Ancien Régime*, trans. Robert Baldick, *Centuries of Childhood.*

16 Ariès, *Centuries of Childhood*, 125.

17 Ibid., 31 and 125; cf. Barbara Greenleaf, *Children Through the Ages: A History of Childhood*, 63, who refers to the tradition of seeing the child "as a miniature adult."

theoretical."[18] For Ariès, and other scholars such as Lloyd de Mause and Lawrence Stone who have built on his approach, it is only long after the Middle Ages that we see the kind of sentimental attitude towards childhood that would eventually culminate in the child-centred world of modern societies, especially in the West.[19]

Ariès's denial of any concept of childhood in the medieval period has been vigorously contested by other scholars. His pictorial evidence, for example, has been shown to be unrepresentative, taking insufficient account of the influence of theology on pictures of the baby Jesus, and of other more naturalistic portrayals of children in medieval art.[20] Moreover his view that the high rate of infant mortality in the medieval period affected people's readiness to invest emotionally in their children has been challenged.[21] Linda Pollock brought into question the methods of reconstructing thoughts and feelings used by Ariès and his followers, recommending the case-by-case study of actual child-parent relationships.[22] Along these lines, a strong case for the existence of a concept of childhood in the High and Late Middle Ages was put forward by Shulamith Shahar, who argued from a range of manuals relating to childhood, and other textual sources, that "parents invested both material and emotional resources in their offspring."[23] Early childhood (*infantia*) in the medieval period, she suggests, is particularly bound up with growing and playing, whereas for *pueritia* (often believed to start from the age of seven) the defining feature is education. Shahar's work has established new ways of identifying and defining the concept of childhood in relation to the Middle Ages. The focus of her work, however, is firmly on the twelfth century onwards. Recent studies, such as the one offered by John Clarke, have re-established some of Ariès's ideas, declaring the current notion of childhood as a modern invention,

---

18 Ariès, *Centuries of Childhood*, 17 and 29. On the origin of the conventional ages of life, see, for example, Shahar, *Childhood in the Middle Ages*, 264 n. 3.

19 Lloyd deMause, ed., *The History of Childhood*; Lawrence Stone, *The Family, Sex and Marriage in England 1500–1800.*

20 See, for example, Ilene H. Forsyth, "Children in Early Medieval Art: Ninth through Twelfth Centuries," 31–70.

21 Ariès, *Centuries of Childhood*, 37: "people could not allow themselves to become too attached to something that was regarded as a probable loss." The view has been challenged by, for example, Barbara Hanawalt, *The Ties That Bound*, 184–7.

22 Linda Pollock, *Forgotten Children: Parent-Child Relations 1500–1900.*

23 Shahar, *Childhood in the Middle Ages*, 1.

essentially a social construct, driven by the rise of educational systems.[24] Such systems, as Clarke argues, would depend on political, economic, and socio-historic circumstances and on the nation as a whole, and therefore only emerge from the seventeenth century onwards.

The debate remains a complex one, not least because it emerged in Western societies and primarily assesses Western cultures from within these cultures. Yet it is fair to say after the last half-century that its central controversy reveals fundamental cultural differences in the academic and non-academic understanding of the term and concept of "childhood": for Ariès, the experience seems to involve state-regulated education, protection, and a kind of emotional care as encountered within the modern Western family and therefore generates a sentiment circumscribing a perceptible otherness of the early phase of a person's life. Within such strongly social parameters it is understandable that this concept of childhood is conditioned by the recognition of children's rights to such a form of upbringing. Others, partly because of a cultural misunderstanding of the bold Gallic rhetoric of Ariès's claim,[25] may have overemphasised their criticism of it by all too quick assumptions of direct correspondences between medieval *thens* and the *now*. Between these opposites this volume is seeking for better answers to the notion of childhood during the Anglo-Saxon period, for the first time based on a range of Old English and Anglo-Latin texts, anchored in the extant systems of education and the social, political, and religious contexts of this time. In doing so, it treats "childhood" first and foremost as a pragmatic term that addresses the typical formative experiences connected to the basic needs of the youngest individuals within Anglo-Saxon society in order to secure their survival as adults, such as the key concepts of protection, nourishment, and education (no matter how institutionalised or not). This volume therefore assumes a range of childhoods within different social strata, varying in degrees of care and exploitation, emotional attachment and ludic freedom, need for obedience and punishment, just as their expressions in literature can differ significantly from each other, depending on author, patron, and wider audience. Since there is no reason to assume that any of the sources analysed here was

24 John Clarke, "The Origins of Childhood: In the Beginning …," 3–13.

25 On the specifics of academic language and its claims in the Gallic context, see Johan Galtung, "Struktur, Kultur und intellektueller Stil. Ein vergleichender Essay über sachsonische, teutonische, gallische und nipponische Wissenschaft," 151–96, at 172–6.

composed by a child, the texts necessarily provide a repertoire of various child-adult relationships, between authors and the children they present in their texts, between parents and their offspring, between siblings, and between teachers and their pupils. Many of these relationships have remained relatively unexplored in Old English literature, not least the sensitive areas of the emotional attachment of adults to children, generational conflict, or the political and social constraints on education. The collection of essays presented here directly addresses this scholarly neglect.

To date, scholarship on the central topic of this book has been largely confined to studies focusing on historical and archaeological evidence, among which Sally Crawford's book *Childhood in Anglo-Saxon England* has been by far the most influential. With relatively little attention paid since the publication of her book to wider aspects of the subject, important questions about perceptions of childhood and adolescence in the Anglo-Saxon period remain unanswered. Was there a separate childhood world in Anglo-Saxon England? If so, to what extent was it defined by its own objects, texts, and spaces? What did the Anglo-Saxon church and a culture of scriptural learning contribute to a concept of childhood? How far can the idea of childhood be seen to reflect the actual treatment of children and their development into adolescents? This volume addresses such questions from the perspective of literary studies in particular. The essays draw on the many kinds of evidence – literary, linguistic, onomastic, palaeographical, and historical – provided by texts, while taking fully into account new advances in other areas of research such as social history, medicine, or archaeology. They study these textual representations of the child with a careful attention to the particular characteristics of Anglo-Saxon culture, focusing on aspects such as kinship and community, conversion and pagan survivals, Christian education and monastic reform, or kingship and wisdom.

Any study of childhood and adolescence in Anglo-Saxon England must confront the fact that the voices of children and adolescents themselves are rarely heard, or at least can rarely be identified. Almost all texts representing children are written retrospectively, with adults drawing on historical sources and memories (whether their own or those of others) to depict the younger members of society. This retrospective happens from the vantage point of adult experience and it can bring about a variety of emotions about childhood, such as nostalgia, shame, loneliness, or gratitude. Apart from these sensuous influences that come with the subtly distinct processes of memory, recollection, and remembrance, literary accounts of childhood – potentially more attractive to child audiences than other topics – are prone to include pedagogical or even ideological agendas created by grown-ups. They often do so whilst attempting to rewrite an adult person's actual biography. The literary perspective of adults cannot therefore be assumed to be a reliable guide into a child's world. Moreover, although textual accounts can provide important evidence for conceptions of childhood in the period, they cannot be assumed to reflect accurately the socio-historical reality of Anglo-Saxon childhood and adolescence. This is perhaps especially true for cultures that are profoundly religious and in which textual production serves, among other things, as expression of the educational supremacy of religious institutions. Negotiating the potential gap between these inevitably biased literary representations and a child's everyday existence in Anglo-Saxon England is all the more complicated when so little is known of the latter. Nevertheless, working from the evidence we have in text and artefact, this book carefully attempts to gauge the width of this potential gap and fill this space at least with incentives for a debate that is overdue.

This volume takes full account of the multilingual nature of textual production in Anglo-Saxon England and its generic variety, and it is fully aware of the indebtedness of Old English literature to a variety of European sources, therefore attempting to crystallise specific Anglo-Saxon notions of childhood by comparison with those sources. The contributors draw on texts written in both English and Latin, and belonging to a range of genres including historiography, biblical and heroic poetry, riddles, legal documents, elegies, wisdom literature, philosophical prose, saints' lives and homilies. Within and across these linguistic and generic boundaries, various themes emerge as pivotal in the consideration of the world of children and adolescents in Anglo-Saxon England: the contexts and processes of learning and education; the societal bonds (or breakdown of bonds) between the young and their peers, parents, or foster-parents; the role of religious rhetoric. These themes will be seen to interact and overlap throughout the volume, setting up a complex network of links between different texts and encouraging dialogues across essays.

The volume begins with an opening address by Sally Crawford in which she explores the history of approaches to childhood from her perspective as an archaeologist, offering a theoretical underpinning for the collection as a whole. She invites readers to think about the range of kinds of evidence that might be brought to bear, and to evaluate them outside modern concepts of childhood. She argues that a reassessment of how material culture and spaces were accessed by children differently over time can enhance our understanding of Anglo-Saxon perceptions of childhood.

Her text provides a useful platform for the literary explorations offered by the remaining essays.

Following Crawford's introductory remarks, the volume is ordered alongside the development of the child – from its conception and birth through to the stages of higher education and open challenging of their parents and teachers. This structure is intended to help readers negotiate their way around a collection of essays whose primary intention is to reassess the evidence from as wide a textual basis as is available. The boundaries between these single essayistic steps as well as between the literary genres chosen should be considered as flexible, which is why cross-references will be highlighted whenever they occur.

Leonard Neidorf's essay assesses the considerations governing parents' name-giving decisions in Anglo-Saxon England. Drawing primarily on onomastic data derived from the *Northumbrian Liber Vitae*, he argues that ethnic names referring to the original Anglo-Saxon tribes are gradually replaced by names that manifest the idea of "Angelcynn," thus representing a fundamental change in the expectations that Anglo-Saxon parents would have in the social advantages of a given name.

Protection and welfare of the young child is the concern of the Old English homiletic addresses studied by Winfried Rudolf. He analyses the Anglo-Saxon church's intrusion into the domestic matters of conception, birth, and nursing of children, revealing how preachers aim to protect children from fates such as abandonment and (careless) infanticide. Political and religious interests can be seen to coincide in these texts, although they may occasionally concur with traditions of folklore, while pastoral control over parental protection, education, and punishment of small children is also achieved by means of exploiting the helplessness and innocence of children as a rhetorical tool.

Shu-han Luo takes as her subject the Old English *Riddles* of the Exeter Book, seeing them as expressions not only of fascination with gestation and growth, but also of nostalgia through their keen awareness of transience. Luo traces the different kinds of evidence offered by the *Riddles* for how Anglo-Saxons conceptualised the joys and dangers of the childhood world, excavating, among other things, the appeal of these themes in the Anglo-Saxon classroom as well as the rarely addressed aspect of emotional attachment between siblings and their separation through untimely loss.

Stacy Klein's essay focuses on the representations of parenting and childhood in *Fortunes of Men*, as well as in Old English wisdom literature more generally. Klein argues that images of parental anxiety and of children as fragile beings are used by the poet of *Fortunes* to explore ways of achieving a productive life within an apparently chaotic social world. The linguistic refrains and repetitive formal structures of the poem, Klein suggests, can be linked to the patterns underlying human development and parental care. Such patterns reflect a human commitment to shaping one's role in society, itself in turn a sign of the ultimate order that a caring deity imposes on the world.

Andreas Lemke examines children as ideal converts in Bede's *Historia ecclesiastica gentis Anglorum*. Focusing on several key episodes featuring children, Lemke argues that children are used as a didactic tool by Bede, who highlights their innocence, love of God, and moral authority in order to encourage readers to recognise themselves as children of God and as a new generation of the faithful within a divine plan of salvation history.

Closely analysing the traditional elements of hagiographical narrative, Joyce Hill evaluates the range of childhood motifs in the lives of a number of English saints, focusing in turn on saints whose childhoods mark them out for later sanctity (Cuthbert, Guthlac, Wilfrid, Dunstan, Æthelwold, and Oswald), female saints such as Æthelthryth (where childhood is only mentioned in passing), and the child saints Rumwold and Kenelm. She shows that aspects of childhood and adolescence contributed significantly to the narrative paradigm of saintliness, and suggests that contemporary conditions of childhood and adolescence might have been reflected in the differences between individual saints, thus appealing to a variety of audiences.

Andy Orchard focuses on the witty riddle-dialogue by Alcuin known as the *Disputatio Pippini cum Albino* and the educational practices it demonstrates. In addition to offering a new text and translation of the *Disputatio*, the essay points to a wealth of interaction between this work and a range of related texts, identifying the particular didactic contributions made by Alcuin. It discusses the catenary principle underlying the work's structure, and raises questions about the extent to which this might be a valuable guiding principle of medieval dispute and literary composition within a pedagogical context.

The focus in Susan Irvine's essay is on representations of foster-parenting in the Old English *Boethius*. This specific parent-child relation serves as a fascinating rhetorical simile for the connection between the allegorical Wisdom and Mod in this remarkably independent translation. It is informed by a literary tradition in which fostering is perceived as fraught with danger, and this idea is enhanced by further depictions of intergenerational conflict within the *Boethius* itself. The idea of education as an inevitable field of interaction between different generations, Irvine suggests, particularly informs the work's representation of foster-relationships.

Such relationships are also at the centre of Richard North's essay, which examines Hrothulf's and Beowulf's childhoods as they are represented in the epic poem *Beowulf*. North argues that the poet seeks deliberately to compare Hrothulf's childhood with Beowulf's through their common fate as foster-sons, arguing that the latter's privations as a child set Beowulf up as the better king, in spite of causing an inferiority complex that may ultimately be responsible for the tragic end of the hero.

In his contribution, Daniel Anlezark pays special attention to the relation between youth and education in a comparison of the three holy youths (from the Book of Daniel) as depicted in the Old English poems *Daniel* and *Azarias* with those in Aldhelm's *De virginitate*. Anlezark examines precisely how the age of the youths is defined and characterised in these texts, and then considers their representation as "wise youths" (in *Daniel* in particular) in relation to contexts of generational conflict and reform in Anglo-Saxon England. In contrast to a number of other contemporary literary sources, spiritual wisdom is shown here to be a quality independent of age, thus questioning established concepts of authority in education in relation to the knowledge that is handed on.

Andrew Rabin's essay on parent-child litigation, finally, examines ways in which conflicts of interest between parents and children might play out in legal disputes. Focusing on specific legal cases (but bearing in mind that the dispute narratives may not themselves be entirely reliable witnesses), Rabin shows how their progress reveals the types of strategies available to those, such as women and children, with only limited rights in an Anglo-Saxon courtroom. Within the context of Christian values, Rabin's exemplary study of a son challenging his mother in court exposes fundamental issues about the expected behaviour of children and the undeniable overlaps between secular and ecclesiastical legislation.

The range of evidence presented in these essays promises valuable points of contact for a number of related fields of research, as much as it may provoke and confound the modern reader with a fresh take on an important yet neglected field of research. Our aim is to invite the thorough reconsideration of questions about how childhood and adolescence were conceived in the early Middle Ages from a number of different perspectives. Although we envisage that the volume will provide some answers to those questions, we particularly hope that it will prompt further debate and research in an area whose implications for our understanding of early medieval culture and society are becoming increasingly evident.

1 Childhood and Adolescence: Interdisciplinary Approaches to the Archaeological and Documentary Evidence

SALLY CRAWFORD

The study of childhood in the past is, today, a well-established discipline, and over the last few decades there has been a steady stream of publications on the history, archaeology, and literature of medieval childhood.[1] Childhood studies is one of the most active areas in academia today, supported by dedicated international journals such as the *Journal of the History of Childhood and Youth* and the interdisciplinary *Childhood in the Past: An International Journal.* Childhood is common to all human societies, but the definition of childhood varies from culture to culture. How children experience childhood, how they interact with the material culture around them, how they are educated, and expectations of their roles and activities within their cultures are all subject to change, variation, negotiation, and coercion. Childhood is, in this sense, a cultural construct, and its study offers an important and informative key to understanding society in the past. When I began my doctoral research in 1986, there was little awareness of childhood as a separate, distinct, and meaningful area of study. My intention in looking at Anglo-Saxon childhood and material culture was to test prevalent theories in the archaeological interpretation of mortuary ritual through the lens of children's interments in the furnished burial ritual of the fifth to seventh centuries.[2] By looking at the way juveniles were treated in the burial record, and comparing and contrasting the physical and material investment in their burials with those of adult males

1 For a survey of the literature, see Sally Crawford, "Medieval and Anglo-Saxon Childhoods," *Oxford Bibliographies*, http://www.oxfordbibliographies.com/view/document/obo 9780199791231/obo-9780199791231-0091.xml.

2 Sally Crawford, *Age Differentiation and Related Social Structure.*

and females, I hoped to be able to tease out the vocabulary of the burial ritual, and to understand, in a more nuanced way, the extent to which the furnished inhumation burial ritual reflected or symbolised personal, ascribed, theoretical, or age- and gender-related status in the individual.

The first problem I encountered in this study was that the integral and fundamental part that children play in the structuring of cultural, political, ritual, and economic social interactions had not registered at all in Anglo-Saxon archaeology in the 1980s. Children were completely absent in analyses of pre-Christian excavated settlements apart from occasional reports of infant bones, there was minimal investigation of the relationship between age and the furnished burial ritual, and the relative lack of infants in the burial record had not been the focus of a specific study. Part of the "invisibility" of childhood in the archaeological record was that site formation was assumed to be a record of adult cultural behaviours.[3] There was no discourse of childhood in archaeology until the innovative and groundbreaking essay by Grete Lillehammer that appeared in 1989, which laid the foundation of the discipline.[4] Lillehammer argued that a study of childhood was not just about understanding the education of the youngest members of communities, but that the study would also oblige historians to rethink fundamental issues and to reflect carefully on current practice and assumptions – about identity, acculturation, and adaptation.[5]

The invisibility of early medieval childhood in the past was not limited to archaeology: before 1990 there was very little on childhood in Anglo-Saxon England at all, Mathew Kuefler's work on attitudes to children in the documentary sources marking the first modern scholarly investigation of the subject.[6] Children were a "mute group," like the poor before economic historians began to problematise poverty, or women before feminists began to draw attention to gender as a cultural construct.[7] Anglo-Saxon children and childhood were treated as almost ahistorical, apparently existing outside the framework of social, political, and economic change and development, so that there was an embedded assumption, certainly in

3 Mary Lewis, *The Bioarchaeology of Children*, 9.

4 Grete Lillehammer, "A Child is Born: The Child's World in an Archaeological Perspective," 91–105.

5 Ibid., 93.

6 Mathew Kuefler, "'A Wryed Existence': Attitudes toward Children in Anglo-Saxon England," 823–34.

7 For mute group theory and feminism, see Edwin Ardener, "Belief and the Problem of Women," 1–17.

the furnished inhumation cemetery reports, which offered the most accessible route to childhood through the burials and bodies of children, that modern and Anglo-Saxon ideas about childhood could be mapped on to each other.[8]

This embedded assumption that "childhood" was a simple concept, universally understood and requiring little definition, became immediately apparent when I tried to compare the numbers of children buried in different excavated cemeteries. One of the fundamental problems I encountered when I tried to understand early Anglo-Saxon burial practice as it applied to children was the weak and confusing terminology associated with the subject. What was a "child" in one site report was an "adolescent" or "young adult" in another, and the upper age range at which a skeleton was described as a "child" at the time of death differed widely between site reports. There was no clear idea of what a "child" was, and there was little awareness that a chronological or biological determination of age might be different from a social and cultural one.[9]

Part of the problem was that "childhood" is a loaded term, full of deeply seated, culturally constructed, unconscious layers of meaning, which were being applied to the evidence, colouring interpretations and informing interpretations of the burial ritual.[10] A plan of the cemetery site at Berinsfield, Oxfordshire, for example, was published showing the link between weapon burials and epigenetic traits. The key distinguishes several groups – male adults with and without weapons, juveniles with and without weapons, and female adults.[11] The "juvenile" category extended from neonate to sixteen years of age. The only two juveniles with weapons shown in this plan were a sixteen-year-old with a spear and shield, and an eleven- to twelve-year-old with a spear. Neither of these two males was in the same age category as infants from an Anglo-Saxon perspective, as both the ritual itself and early Anglo-Saxon law codes make clear: both were at an age to take on young male adult roles. The term "juvenile" in this context refers to biological development, which is irrelevant to the social meaning of the weapon. Osteoarchaeologist Rebecca Gowland argued

---

8 Sally Crawford, "When Do Anglo-Saxon Children Count?," 17–24.

9 Ibid.

10 Joanna Sofaer Derevenski, "Material Culture Shock: Confronting Expectations in the Material Culture of Children," 3–16, at 11.

11 Angela Boyle, Anne Dodd, David Miles, and Andrew Mudd, *Two Oxfordshire Anglo-Saxon Cemeteries: Berinsfield and Didcot*, fig. 12, 71.

that our cultural reactions to the word even impinge on the apparently scientific and neutral analysis of children's skeletons. She has suggested that, for the purposes of thinking effectively about Anglo-Saxon childhood, it would be better to drop the use of the words "child," "infant," "adolescent," and "sub-adult" altogether, and to focus instead on simple chronological age groupings. Equally, rather than trying to map biological age onto semantically loaded terms, she argued that it might be more useful to think about cultural age markers and activity thresholds across the life course.[12] Does the same problem – modern cultural assumptions blocking an understanding of the Anglo-Saxon construct of childhood – apply in studies of Old English texts? I think the answer is a distinct "yes." Old English textual references to children are habitually translated directly into the modern equivalent term (with all the embedded modern cultural reactions to the word that that entails), without any discussion about what those terms actually meant to the original writers and audiences, or of what kind of age group those terms were applied to. By the same token, are Anglo-Saxon adults (because they are not specifically categorised as children in Old English texts) biologically or chronologically in a group that we would today view as adult? If we have not had a conversation about the age at which a child is perceived as an adult in different cultural contexts – textual, art historical, poetic, archaeological – then we are failing to grasp some fundamental issues of social and identity construction in Anglo-Saxon England.

Children, in Anglo-Saxon archaeology, have rarely been identified as agents. They have not been ascribed an active role in creating anything at all in the archaeological record unless there is an irrefutable reason to connect them with the material culture, such as a fingerprint on a clay oven,[13] and they have not been considered as potential writers or authors of texts or artwork unless those texts appear to be practice pieces, or were written specifically in the context of an educational environment.[14]

---

12 Rebecca Gowland, "Ageing the Past: Examining Age Identity from Funerary Evidence," 143–55, at 143.

13 An example of a (probable) child's handprint was found during excavations at Sedgeford, Norfolk in 2015, leading to interest from the local press: http://www.edp24.co.uk/news/anglo_saxon_handprint_uncovered_in_sedgeford_dig_in_west_norfolk_1_4165736.

14 For some material hints at the scribal training of children, see the discussion of "writ þus" marginalia by Kenneth Sisam, "Marginalia in the Vercelli Book," 109–18, at 110–12.

Recently, children's intersection with the archaeological record and their engagement with their environment has been the subject of new theoretical approaches. In particular, there has been a reconsideration of the lack of apparent evidence for children's agency and activities in Anglo-Saxon settlement excavations compared to the impact children's play must have had on the material culture of Anglo-Saxon settlements, and a recognition that some of the archaeology from settlements must reflect children's interaction with their living spaces.[15] Children do touch and move the objects around them: why is this not visible in the archaeological evidence? Play is part of the human life course: people of all ages play, but as Katie Hemer and Dawn Hadley assert, it is "uncontroversial to identify it as an important aspect of childhood and an activity in which children are the principal participants."[16]

Children grow and change from birth to the points at which they are incorporated into the adult world, and their ability to engage with, and manipulate, the objects around them, physically and mentally, also changes. As children develop, they incorporate, transform, and dispose of the material culture with which they come into contact in different ways and for variable periods. Equally, the act of engagement with material culture will have a transformative effect on the growing child as contact with physical objects embodies knowledge and sets up communities of practice.[17] Through child agency, an object can be transformed into a toy for periods of time ranging from the whole use-life of an object, for a few moments, or on a repeated basis. Identifying artefacts as "toys" will inevitably be bogged down in a quagmire of difficulties and problems if the approach is through the "purpose" of the toy. Is a toy designed to educate a child the

15 Sally Crawford, "Spinning Yarns and Weaving Futures: Female and Juvenile Spaces in Early Anglo-Saxon Settlements," 111–22; Sally Crawford, "The Archaeology of Play Things: Theorizing a Toy Stage in the 'Biography' of Objects," 55–70; and for later medieval settlements Carenza Lewis, "Children's Play in the Later Medieval English Countryside," 86–108.

16 Dawn Hadley and Katie Hemer, "Introduction: Archaeological Approaches to Medieval Childhood, c. 500–1500," 1–25, at 13; Crawford, "Archaeology of Play Things," 56; and Jane Eva Baxter, *The Archaeology of Childhood: Children, Gender and Material Culture*, 62.

17 See, for example, Joanna Sofaer and Sandy Budden, "Many Hands Make Light Work: Embodied Knowledge at the Bronze Age Tell at Szazhalombatta," 117–27, at 118; and more generally Willeke Wendrich, ed., *Archaeology and Apprenticeship: Body Knowledge, Identity, and Communities of Practice*.

same as a toy used for "play"? Is a child, imitating adult behaviours – using a wooden spoon to mix a cake batter, for example – using the object as a toy, or as a tool? Are miniature artefacts media for inculcating children into the adult world, and therefore adult tools rather than children's toys? These questions, which have dominated discourse of children's material culture, are in many ways an adult-centred distraction from a discussion of important aspects of the agency of the child in the use and manipulation of its own separate domain: child object-play.[18] Furthermore, they hamper wider understanding of the importance of children's daily engagement with material culture and the sensory environment (including listening to stories and writing documents) for embodying knowledge and creating the adult of the future; and the opportunity offered by the play/ontology nexus to control and establish social power structures: when King Alfred commented on preventing children taking coins and playing with them (even though they would eventually inherit their parents' wealth), he is describing a specific childhood where the tangible material culture that shaped the child's idea of itself and its idea of "normal" included a detailed knowledge of the appearance of coins, coupled with a perception that coins were exclusive to the (elite) adult domain and not accessible for play.[19]

Spaces may also be appropriated and transformed for play, and where children played in the medieval period has begun to be considered from an archaeological perspective.[20] Carenza Lewis reviewed and reinterpreted medieval English settlement archaeology from the standpoint that children's play should leave some trace in the archaeological record. While she acknowledges that alternative explanations for the pits, post-holes, and stake-holes she suggests as traces of children's games might have other interpretations, nonetheless she rightly insists that a non-child explanation should not be privileged over a child-centred interpretation, and that reviewing the archaeology with a child-centred perspective provides "a much-needed shock to our established ways of thinking as we realise how completely we have wiped the sticky fingerprints of children off our views

18 Sofaer Derevenski, "Material Culture Shock," 3–15; Crawford, "Archaeology of Play Things."

19 Henry Sweet, ed., *King Alfred's West-Saxon Version of Gregory's Pastoral Care*, 2:391.

20 Mark Hall, "'Merely Players'? Playtime, Material Culture and Medieval Childhood," 39–56, at 39.

of the past."[21] Furthermore, children's use of play spaces and access to space within settlements relates to socialisation practices within society: children's experiences have a role in social reproduction.[22] Much of this experience will be closely related to the home and the domestic environment: "what occurs within the domestic sphere will have very strong effects on the types of cultural knowledge that are imparted to children."[23] The relevance of children's experiences, and where they take place, in social reproduction, in embodying knowledge, and in creating social imaginaries, alerts us also to the importance of recognising where such experiences are being manipulated or controlled in an exercise of social power, both in the archaeological evidence (change in settlement location or spatial layout, for example) or in the documentary sources.[24]

Anglo-Saxon written sources do provide clear evidence of children's play and play spaces being contested areas, most strikingly in the example of St Cuthbert's childhood. The anonymous early eighth-century writer of Cuthbert's prose *vita* described an eight-year-old Cuthbert playing with his friends at highly physical and competitive games. The games, at which Cuthbert excels, were interrupted by a small child who called out to Cuthbert to "leave this foolish play" because "these unnatural tricks done to show off your agility are not befitting to you or your high office."[25] The anonymous *vita* does not offer a commentary on this part of the incident, but Bede, in his prose version of the life, makes an explicit connection between the child's admonition to Cuthbert and the New Testament: it is time for Cuthbert to put aside "childish things" and "vain play"; to make the transition between childhood and adulthood.

Cuthbert was not an adult at this time, of course: in fact the anonymous *vita* is at pains to make it clear that Cuthbert has only just begun the transition from infant to boy in the cultural terms of the writer. Cuthbert's normative play, as an eight-year-old, in a play space with his contemporaries, was being contested in this incident. Why might Old English childhoods have been arenas for debate? A closer look at the Cuthbert episode,

21 Lewis, "Children's Play," 105.

22 Sally Smith, "The Spaces of Late Medieval Peasant Childhood: Children and Social Reproduction," 57–74, at 58–9.

23 Ibid., 64.

24 Ibid., 62.

25 Bertram Colgrave, ed., *Two Lives of St Cuthbert*, 65: "relinque uanitatem ioci amare … hec tibi et tuo gradui contraria nature propter agilitatem non conueniunt."

particularly in the context of recent developments both in childhood studies and in archaeological method and theory, sheds some important light on the issue of early conversion-period childhoods.

Much research into the archaeology of childhood in the past has been on understanding childhood as an agent for social reproduction.[26] Childhood engagement with space, material culture, and daily practices helps to create and perpetuate ideas of identity, belonging, and social memory.[27] But when society is undergoing change and social norms are being reconstructed, childhood and childhood memories become contested spaces. The value of youthful memory to the creation of the new Christian elite in Anglo-Saxon England is evident in the hagiographic sources. Miracle stories and events in saints' lives are authenticated and validated by the memories of old people who were young at the time of the miracle.[28] Children's experiences are central to the building of social memories; the child's intervention in Cuthbert's play is part of the manipulation of social memory – for Cuthbert, who will no longer be part of the group of boys who play boisterous games, but also for the audience of the *vita*, who learn together from the text and create a collective memory of "proper" games for a monastic community.[29]

Though little is known about Cuthbert's lineage, his competitive and physical early childhood play, as described by the anonymous monk and Bede, put him on a trajectory to become a specific kind of high-status secular adult in his society.[30] The physical prowess ascribed to the eight-year-old Cuthbert is particularly significant in this context. Advances in the chemical analyses of Anglo-Saxon skeletons have allowed researchers to focus more and more precisely on anatomical changes in the body caused by environmental factors, such as physical activity, in combination with diet.[31] Early law codes indicate that higher-status children had access

---

26 Kathryn Kamp, "Where Have All the Children Gone? The Archaeology of Childhood," 1–34; Baxter, *Archaeology of Childhood*; Sofaer Derevenski, "Material Culture Shock."

27 See especially Smith, "Spaces of Late Medieval Peasant Childhood."

28 Catherine Cubitt, "Memory and Narrative in the Cult of Early Anglo-Saxon Saints," 29–66, at 36.

29 Ibid., 32, 36.

30 Benedicta Ward, "The Spirituality of St Cuthbert," 65–76, at 67.

31 Karen Privat, Tamsin O'Connell, and Michael Richards, "Stable Isotope Analysis of Human and Faunal Remains from the Anglo-Saxon Cemetery at Berinsfield, Oxfordshire: Dietary and Social Implications," 779–90.

to a higher quality of food, and this is reinforced by, for example, analysis of isotope evidence in early Anglo-Saxon skeletons and by the height difference between those in the cemeteries buried with weaponry, and those without.[32] Analysis of the stable isotope evidence from skeletons at the furnished inhumation cemetery at Berinsfield, Oxfordshire, coupled with analysis of the grave goods suggested that the "wealthy upper class had distinctive dietary habits," and what is more, males over the age of thirty typically ate the lower-status diet.[33] Diet and childhood activities/training have an impact on the physical shape and motor skills of the adult: throughout childhood, the physical actuality of the body is negotiated and manipulated through nutrition, activity, and environment – body and social identity are interwoven.[34] There is surprisingly little in the textual discussions of Anglo-Saxon childhood that relates to children's diets, though getting food into the little blighters is one of the biggest daily concerns of any parent or caregiver. Recent scholarship has highlighted the extent to which eating was a culturally constructed activity. It helped to fix people in their social place. Access to food and the material culture of food – bowls, glasses, cutlery – was linked to aspects of social control, social cohesion, and social identity.[35] With the advent of Christianity, there came a need to redefine what a "normal" high-status adult body looked like, seen most clearly in the *vita* of St Guthlac, where the bulky, muscular strength of traditional Anglo-Saxon secular heroes, exemplified by Beowulf, was carefully restyled into mental, spiritual strength in a fasting, abstemious saint's body.[36] By warning Cuthbert away from games of physical strength when he was still young enough to have his physical form remodelled by

---

32 For the links between diet and social identity, see Bradley Hull and Tamsin O'Connell, "Diet: Recent Evidence from Analytical Chemical Techniques," 667–87. For links between access to food and status, see also Sally Crawford, "Food, Fasting and Starvation: Food Control and Body Consciousness in early Anglo-Saxon England," 99–107.

33 Privat, O'Connell, and Richards, "Stable Isotope Analysis," 788.

34 For research on the relationship between diet, culture, and health, see, e.g., Philip Schofield, "Medieval Diet and Demography," 239–53. See also Roberta Gilchrist, "Archaeological Biographies: Realizing Human Lifecycles, Courses and Histories," 325–8.

35 Christina Lee, *Feasting the Dead: Food and Drink in Anglo-Saxon Burial Rituals*; Marjorie Brown, "The Feast Hall in Anglo-Saxon Society," 1–13; Allen Frantzen, *Food, Eating and Identity in Early Medieval England*. Also Crawford, "Food, Fasting and Starvation," 99–101.

36 The ramifications of monastic life on monastic bodies and the potential challenge to masculinity are discussed in Crawford, "Food, Fasting and Starvation," 102–5.

different activities, Cuthbert's divinely inspired childish messenger also ensured that the boy would not grow into a muscular, Beowulfian adult. The *vita* is making a profound point about what kind of body the holy adult would need, and therefore what kind of childhood activities would be best for the creation of that body – a body that was a reversal of the pre-Christian ideal in which high-status masculinity was associated with consumption (of food and of resources) leading to physical bulk, and in which low status was associated with the limited childhood diet, which would lead to thin, weaker, smaller adults. Furnished seventh-century cemeteries illustrate a strong correlation between masculine high status and displays of food and weaponry. This is particularly visible in the Mound 1 ship burial at Sutton Hoo, dating to the early seventh century, but it finds widespread expression across Anglo-Saxon England. Mortuary archaeology also indicates that male high-status children were capable of representing warrior attributes from their early teens.[37] The hagiographer's negative attitude towards Cuthbert's childhood activity effectively contested secular play in a way that would promote a different kind of elite adult male body, an attitude which may also lie behind Bishop John of Beverley's reported lack of enthusiasm towards his young acolytes when they wanted to have a horse race.[38] His displeasure may not have been directed at play per se, but at play that represented a challenge to reframing elite Christian childhood training away from developing the warrior physique, and towards stamina, fasting, and self-denial.[39]

Read in the context of the archaeological records, Anglo-Saxon hagiography also offers evidence of direct challenges to cultural norms embedded in childhood memories. When the adult St Æthelthryth developed a tumour on her neck, Bede reports that she reflected that it was a penance for having worn necklaces in her youth in "needless vanity."[40] The

37 Sally Crawford, *Childhood in Anglo-Saxon England*, 157–8.

38 Bertram Colgrave and Roger A.B. Mynors, eds. and trans., *Bede's Ecclesiastical History of the English People*, v.6.

39 Some prescriptions in Old English homilies and penitentials explicitly exclude children from fasting, but the Penitentials also include fasting as a punishment: see for example the *Scriftboc*, where sexual transgressions by *lytel cniht* (small boys) is punishable by between five and fifteen days of fasting. Oxford, Bodleian Library, MS Junius 121, s. xi, fol. 88b; Robert Spindler, ed., *Das altenglische Bussbuch (sog. Confessionale Pseudo-Egberti)*, 177:7a.

40 Colgrave and Mynors, *Bede's Ecclesiastical History*, iv.19 ("ut sic absoluar reatu superuacuae leuitatis," 396–7).

archaeological evidence suggests a much more nuanced and politically powerful message in this rejection of her youthful necklaces. If male high status was illustrated in the furnished burial ritual through weaponry and feasting equipment, for females the defining objects were strings of beads, brooches, and other costume elements. More significantly, though, analysis of the archaeological evidence indicates that such costume items were of far more importance in younger women's graves than in those of older women. In excavations at a later seventh-century cemetery at Westfield Farm, Ely, the grave of a ten- to twelve-year-old included a necklace in situ, consisting of a central gold cruciform pendant, a gold and garnet cabochon pendant, and one gold and six silver bullae pendants.[41] Not far away, excavations of another later seventh-century cemetery, plausibly identified as a Christian burial ground, at Trumpington, outside Cambridge, included the elite bed-burial of a woman aged about sixteen at the time of death, whose grave goods included a gold and garnet pectoral cross, though this one was designed to be stitched onto clothing, and the patterns of wear indicated that it had been worn in this way.[42]

In fact, the later seventh century saw a shift in age and gender patterns, with younger, teenage females like these more likely to be buried with such rich assemblages than older women.[43] This period saw other gender and age changes in the burial record, including age-related distinctions in women's costumes disappearing, and a shift of more valuable textiles to men's graves. Changes in burial ritual represented a fundamental shift in the pattern of social organisation and the creation of the new Christian elite.[44]

As a high-status female, St Æthelthryth, like the Westfield cemetery girl, may have been wearing ostentatious displays of gold and garnet beads from her very early teens. As the burial evidence indicates, these beads were not intended as an indication of fashion, or as a trivial embellishment. They were a clear signal of social, economic, and political status. When an aged St Æthelthryth rejected the necklaces she had worn in her youth

41 Sam Lucy et al., "Burial of a Princess? The Anglo-Saxon Cemetery at Westfield Farm, Ely," 81–141; Sam Lucy, "Gender and Gender Roles," 688–703, at 688–9.

42 http://www.cam.ac.uk/research/news/mystery-of-anglo-saxon-teen-buried-in-bed-with-gold-cross.

43 Helen Geake, *The Use of Grave Goods in Conversion-Period England, c. 600–850*, 128–9; Nick Stoodley, "Burial Rites, Gender and the Creation of Kingdoms: The Evidence from Seventh Century Wessex," 99–107.

44 Lucy, "Gender and Gender Roles," 698.

she may also have been making a political statement separating her adult identity from the culture of her troubled childhood.

Another early saint linked to a necklace is St Hilda. According to Bede, St Hilda's mother had a vision before her birth of a necklace that would spread light.[45] St Hilda's childhood involved forced displacement from home, family upheaval, threat, and a time of rapid change in wider social organisation. She was an infant when her father was murdered. By the time she was two, she was living at the court of King Edwin of Northumbria. She was thirteen at the time of his (and, of necessity, her) conversion to Christianity. As the seventh-century archaeological cemetery evidence indicates, the early teenage years were crucial in the formation of, and the statement of, ritual gender, status, and identity in the Anglo-Saxon world. At the moment of her conversion, aged thirteen, St Hilda had the option of displaying the jewellery traditionally worn by her female ancestors – the paired brooches with their festoons of beads that signified tribal affiliation – or the newer style of gold and garnet necklaces associated with the Christian Kentish/Merovingian princess Æthelburg, Edwin's wife. What St Hilda wore around her neck – whether a necklace reflecting the tribal allegiances of her mother or of her murdered father, or one announcing a politically astute liaison with the new Frankish/Kentish Christian power group at court – would have been significant. Archaeology enables us to access the real political nuances behind the story of the vision of a necklace that symbolised St Hilda, as recorded by Bede, and to begin to approach the way in which the original audience of this story would have understood the deeper ramifications of St Hilda's necklace, its relationship to her politically difficult childhood, and her life within the early Christian church in England.

St Hilda's childhood involved enforced movement from court to court. As Sally Smith has argued for the later medieval period, the childhood upheaval involved in resettlement may have profound effects on later adulthood, and may be seen as a way of coercing or emphasising power relationships.[46] It is part and parcel of our understanding of Anglo-Saxon society that elite children, at least, might experience more than one home in their lives, if they were sent to be fostered, for example. Old English literature has much on movement and migration, including children taken from

45 Colgrave and Mynors, *Bede's Ecclesiastical History,* iv.23.
46 Smith, "Spaces of Late Medieval Peasant Childhood."

homes to be slaves, movement for purposes of pilgrimage or miracle cures, movement from home to monastery, and forced migration at times of famine or war.[47]

The results of stable isotope analysis on skeletal material from excavated cemeteries are offering a new opportunity to think about the extent to which burial communities represented stable local populations, with a shared history incorporating the same landscapes and settlements over generations, or included migrant families, adults, or children.[48] Recent analysis of stable isotope information looking at strontium and oxygen ratios in seventy-eight skeletons buried at the elite seventh- to ninth-century cemetery at Bowl Hole, Bamburgh, Northumberland, shows a mixed population of locals and individuals from a range of locations. Of the group of males and females ranging in age from subadult to adult, only seven were local, with nine individuals coming from Northern England or Southern Scotland, twenty-three from Western Scotland or Ireland, and twenty-eight from Southern England or Northern Europe. The values of twelve skeletons fell outside the range for the United Kingdom, and this included individuals with probable childhood origins in Scandinavia and the southern Mediterranean or North Africa. This cemetery, closely associated with the royal settlement at Bamburgh and in use during Bede's lifetime, shows the influence of religious and political centres on migration, bringing in non-local populations either voluntarily for trade or religious purposes, or perhaps involuntarily as exiles or hostages.[49] What was the impact of these significant migrations on children's perceptions of themselves, their heritage, and their culture as they grew up in Bede's Anglo-Saxon England, and how did the presence of child migrants impact on local cultures?

A recent study of infant mortuary ritual in the early Anglo-Saxon period by Duncan Sayer postulates another cause of migration operating in earlier Anglo-Saxon England. His research argues that there are greater numbers of infant burials under the age of five in the larger Anglo-Saxon inhumation cemeteries (which he identifies as central tribal burial grounds) than in the smaller cemeteries, which seem to represent the dead

47 Hadley and Hemer, "Introduction: Archaeological Approaches," 12.

48 Dawn Hadley and Katie Hemer, "Microcosms of Migration: Children and Early Medieval Population Movement," 63–78.

49 Sarah Groves et al., "Mobility Histories of 7th–9th Century AD People Buried at Early Medieval Bamburgh, Northumberland, England," 462–76.

of family communities away from the tribal heartland.[50] Drawing on early Old English law codes for corroborative evidence, Sayer postulates that the mother and the mother's lineage were the key family in children's upbringing up to the age of five, after which the father and the father's family would take precedence in making decisions about children's lives. Sayer argued that pregnant women would travel from their husband's homes back to their own tribal heartlands to give birth, both for the benefit of having their own female kin with them at the time of birth, and to establish kinship between the new baby and its maternal tribal affiliation through its place of birth.

If Sayer's theory is correct, then we need to pay closer attention to the political, familial, and economic contexts in which children are mentioned in the earliest Old English texts. It would provide a cultural context, for example, to the story of St Wilfrid's encounter with a dead infant.[51] The mother brought her dead baby son Eodwald to Wilfrid, hoping for a cure. Wilfrid gave life to the baby, and asked in return that the boy be given to him when he reached the age of five. The mother, the story relates, was reluctant to give up the child and tried to hide among the British. In the context of Sayer's theory, it is interesting that there is no suggestion of any paternal rights or contracts being set aside or contradicted in this story: the sole agent and decision-maker in the infant child's future is the mother. When the child reached five, Wilfrid, as the child's spiritual father, exercises his (secular?) paternal right to take charge of the child's future. In this context, what is to be made of Edwin's declaration that his newly born infant daughter Eanflaed would be dedicated to the church if he was successful in his battle with king Cwichelm?[52] By reporting this as Edwin's decision (rather than that of his Christian, Frankish wife), is Bede signifying a rupture with old tribal customs, expressing new power relations between the church, gender, and childhood?

When children's presence in the documentary and archaeological evidence is evaluated outside modern concepts of childhood, even very familiar references to childhood, such as those discussed in this chapter, offer a deeper insight into Anglo-Saxon culture. New thinking in medieval archaeology is beginning to look beyond the obviously child-related artefact

---

50 Duncan Sayer, "'Sons of Athelings Given to the Earth': Infant Mortality within Anglo-Saxon Mortuary Geography," 83–109.

51 Bertram Colgrave, ed., *The Life of Bishop Wilfrid by Eddius Stephanus*, 41.

52 Colgrave and Mynors, *Bede's Ecclesiastical History*, ii.9.

or juvenile burial, to think more radically about why children appear to be invisible in the wider archaeological and documentary record, and to reflect more carefully on methodologies for identifying the "sticky fingers" of childhood in the past. The logic of numbers insists that archaeologists are failing to see what must be present in the archaeological record: the total number of Anglo-Saxon children had to be considerably larger than the total number of adults, and their traces must be present in the material culture of the period. This rethinking by archaeologists is about trying to escape our conditioned ways of viewing the world. Toys have been rethought as a concept, rather than as an object: children transform, revalue, and reassign objects; children use spaces in fluid and seasonal ways; settlements change, adapt, and evolve to accommodate and incorporate different life stages. Seen in these terms, changes in the ways in which children accessed material culture and spaces, and interacted, physically and emotionally, with their environments, offer crucial insights into childhood as a contested place – an arena in which the identities, ideologies, memories, and even bodies of adults are shaped. Archaeology as a discipline is becoming inclusive of, not exclusive of, children.

Surviving written evidence from the period is also open to re-evaluation from a child-centred perspective. There are extant texts that might have been written for use as educational tools for children in monastic settings, which may be described as "schoolbooks," but training in literacy was not limited to children, and young readers would start learning texts such as the Psalter, which they would continue to study into adulthood.[53] However, just as the absence of objects that can be described as "toys" in the archaeological record is not an indication that Anglo-Saxon children did not play with objects, in the same way the difficulty of identifying texts written specifically for children does not mean that children were not able to access texts, be influenced by them, and have an influence on Old English literature and the settings in which that literature was performed. There is good evidence that children listened when texts were read out in public, and Anglo-Saxon writers acknowledged that what children heard had an impact on their later adult careers. The writer of St Guthlac's *vita*, for example, drew attention to the influence of heroic poetry he heard in the hall on Guthlac's actions as a young adult.[54] If Anglo-Saxon children

53 See Scott Gwara, "Anglo-Saxon Schoolbooks," 507–25, for a discussion of books used in Anglo-Saxon monastic classrooms.
54 Bertram Colgrave, ed., *Felix's Life of St Guthlac*, 16.

listened to heroic poetry, then these works will have helped to form and inform children's understanding of the wider world, and will have been part of a social commonality of experience. Stories heard in childhood lay down paths for thinking about, and enacting, cultural norms – directing and ratifying prejudices, creating social imaginaries of the present and social memories of the past, organising the world, and directing ways of behaving towards others.[55] So such tales mattered, not just for adults, but also for the children who were part of the audience.

Those who listened to Old English texts may also be looked at anew within the contexts of their identities in a child-centred world. Anglo-Saxon audiences had social and familial identities as grandparents, parents, foster-parents, carers, siblings, sons, and daughters. All Old English listeners may be situated within their consciousness of social identity in the context of their families and children. From this perspective, literature also provided information and directions about how to raise children, and identified "normal" and "abnormal" child-rearing practices, including, in *Beowulf* for example, how to protect a family, how to control an inheritance, and who to trust.[56] Fathers, mothers, and families play a hugely important role in *Beowulf*, of course, offering the listener a range of examples from which to extract guidance on the consequences of family dynamics.[57] Childhoods, over and again in *Beowulf*, are shown to have an impact on adult life chances and behaviours, and, in the case of elite families, on political and dynastic histories.[58] Who, in *Beowulf*, has a childhood most aspirational for the listeners? What was the audience to learn about the consequences – in the case of *Beowulf* located in a nostalgic social past – of inadequate fathers, single mothers, family migrations, and ill-conceived kinship bonds on children's prospects?

Our understanding of Old English texts is enriched by viewing them as relevant to the construction of Anglo-Saxon childhood, as the many thought-provoking contributions to the Göttingen conference, out of

---

55 Charles Taylor, *Modern Social Imaginaries*, 23.

56 Crawford, "Anglo-Saxon Children," 125–6.

57 See for example Mary Dockray-Miller, *Motherhood and Mothering in Anglo-Saxon England*, 77–116.

58 Raymond Tripp Jr, "Did Beowulf have an Inglorious Youth?," 129–43. See also Richard North's essay in this volume.

which this volume was born, demonstrate. Far from being in a position of struggling for anything useful to say about Anglo-Saxon childhood, the scholarship in this book shows that there is almost no aspect of Anglo-Saxon textual or material culture research that cannot, and indeed should not, be carried out without a profound awareness of the importance of thinking, in an incisive and questioning way, about what childhood meant in Anglo-Saxon England.

2 Naming Children in Anglo-Saxon England: Ethnic Identity and Cultural Change

LEONARD NEIDORF

A central question in studies of medieval childhood has been whether the emotional investment of parents in children during the Middle Ages was commensurate with that of earlier and later epochs. Some scholars have argued for general continuity, contending that parental concern for children is a human universal, which is evolutionarily conditioned and evident in many medieval sources.[1] Other scholars have maintained that the material conditions of medieval life would have created notions of childhood and attitudes towards children utterly unlike those that obtain in the modern world.[2] It has been believed, for example, that the high rate of infant mortality in the pre-modern world would have inspired a certain degree of callousness or indifference towards infants. In the famous words of Philippe Ariès: "People could not allow themselves to become too attached to something that was regarded as a probable loss."[3] Medievalists throughout the past half-century, such as Barbara A. Hanawalt and Nicholas Orme, have disputed Ariès's thesis of discontinuity on many

---

1 See the conspectus of views presented in Sally Crawford, *Childhood in Anglo-Saxon England*, 1–13. A particularly forceful proponent of the continuity hypothesis is Linda Pollock, *Forgotten Children: Parent/Child Relations from 1500–1900*; see also Mary Martin McLaughlin, "Survivors and Surrogates: Children and Parents from the Ninth to the Thirteenth Centuries," 101–82.

2 See Philippe Ariès, *Centuries of Childhood: A Social History of Family Life*; Edward Shorter, *The Making of the Modern Family*; Lawrence Stone, *The Family, Sex and Marriage in England 1500–1800*; and Lloyd de Mause, "The Evolution of Parent-Child Relationships as a Factor in History," 1–71.

3 Ariès, *Centuries of Childhood*, 37.

grounds and have called attention to literary and pictorial sources indicative of continuity.[4] This paper aims to contribute a new dimension to the study of parental investment in children by analysing Anglo-Saxon name-giving behaviour.

The argument of this paper is that certain manifestations of diachronic change in the Anglo-Saxon onomasticon can be interpreted as the consequences of some of the same sociolinguistic motivations that govern name-giving in the modern world. Studies of modern naming data indicate that many factors inform the selection of names, but one of the clearest factors is that of instrumental value. As Stanley Lieberson and Eleanor O. Bell observed:

> The naming activity is ultimately a social process, and the resulting pattern of name usage reflects the combined influence of the imagery associated with each name, the notions parents have about the future characteristics of their children, estimates of the response of others to the name, the awareness and knowledge of names through the mass media and other sources, parents' beliefs about what are appropriate children's names for persons of their status, and institutionalized norms and pressures.[5]

Parents aim to give their children names that will not inconvenience them: they select names that are conducive to prosperity and a positive reception in the world, which effectively articulate gender and class distinctions.[6] It is well known, for example, that a masculine name will often cease to be given to male children once that name has begun to be given regularly to

---

4 Barbara A. Hanawalt, "Medievalists and the Study of Childhood," 440–60; Nicholas Orme, *Medieval Children*. See also Albrecht Classen, "Philippe Ariès and the Consequences," 1–65.

5 Stanley Lieberson and Eleanor O. Bell, "Children's First Names: An Empirical Study of Social Taste," 511–54, at 514.

6 On names and gender, see Carole Hough, "Towards an Explanation of Phonetic Differentiation in Masculine and Feminine Personal Names," 1–11; and Richard D. Alford, *Naming and Identity: A Cross-Cultural Study of Personal Naming Practices*, 65–8. On ethnic and socio-economic implications in name-giving, see Lieberson and Bell, "Children's First Names"; L. Allen, V. Brown, L. Dickinson, and K.C. Pratt, "The Relation of First Name Preferences to their Frequency in the Culture," 279–93; and Susan Cotts Watkins and Andrew S. London, "Personal Names and Cultural Change: A Study of the Naming Patterns of Italians and Jews in the United States in 1910," 169–209.

female children.[7] Men are now rarely named Whitney, Stacey, or Lindsay, though such names were once relatively common among men. By avoiding problematic names of this sort, modern parents perform their first act of kindness for their children. The desire to perpetuate ethnic or familial traditions is subordinated to the desire to provide the child with a socially acceptable name. This paper argues that the same sociolinguistic considerations informed the selection of names during the Anglo-Saxon period. To explain changes to the Old English onomasticon that took effect between the seventh and tenth centuries, it is necessary to posit that parental concern for the well-being of their children was an operative factor, then as now. Some names ceased to be given, while others soared in popularity, because parents avoided inconvenient names and sought advantageous ones. The criterion of social acceptability, it will be argued, cannot be underestimated.

Onomastic scholars have long recognized that the English name-stock changed in manifold ways during the Anglo-Saxon period: the names attested in Bede's *Historia ecclesiastica gentis Anglorum*, for example, differ markedly from the names attested in the tenth-century annals of the *Anglo-Saxon Chronicle*. The name-stock in Bede's history reflects the conservation of a wider variety of elements from the Proto-Germanic name-stock, whereas tenth-century texts show that the formation of a small canon of dithematic names – Ælfred, Eadgar, Godric, Wulfstan, etc. – had driven many others out of use.[8] This paper focuses on two aspects of diachronic change: it first assesses the use of ethnonyms in personal names and then explores the use of names from Germanic heroic legend. In both cases, the corpus of recorded Old English names exhibits a similar pattern: exogenous ethnonyms and continental Germanic heroes appear in name-giving predominantly from the seventh and eighth centuries; they occur on a relatively infrequent basis thereafter. I argue that these names and name-elements gradually fell out of use because they had

7 See Stanley Lieberson, Susan Dumais, and Shyon Baumann, "The Instability of Androgynous Names: The Symbolic Maintenance of Gender Boundaries," 1249–87; and Herbert Barry III and Aylene S. Harper, "Feminization of Unisex Names from 1960 to 1990," 228–38.

8 See Frank M. Stenton, "Personal Names in Place Names," 165–89, at 176–7; Mats Redin, *Studies on Uncompounded Personal Names in Old English*, 184–9; Cecily Clark, "English Personal Names ca. 650–1300," 31–60, at 34; Clark, "Onomastics," 452–89, at 461; and John Insley, "Pre-Conquest Personal Names," 367–96, at 381.

become disadvantageous. Parents sought conventional and socially acceptable names for their children. As an English national identity spread and solidified during the ninth and tenth centuries, a canon of stereotypically English names took shape.[9] These names and their constitutive elements came to be preferred over the names that reflected the various continental Germanic identities that had flourished in the earlier Anglo-Saxon period.

Before the evidence is examined, a word concerning the principles of Anglo-Saxon name-giving is necessary. Because our sources contain no direct articulations of these principles, scholars must deduce the customs and motivations informing name-giving practices from the corpus of extant names. Of course, this necessity does not debilitate onomastic research, since the attempts of native speakers to formulate the principles governing aspects of language use are often erroneous or misleading. Just as speakers of a language are not entirely conscious of the reasons for their usage preferences, parents are not entirely conscious of the reasons why some names are appealing, while others seem implausible or repugnant. The psychology of these parents has never been accessible, but the empirical effects of their decisions can be studied, and some understanding of their motivations can be achieved through the formulation of hypotheses that explain observable patterns in the data. Thus, when Helmut Gneuss writes that "[i]t was a principle of name-giving that the names of close relatives should alliterate or even that a child's name should include one element of its father's (or sometimes mother's) name,"[10] he is referring to a principle

9 On the efforts of West Saxon kings to promote a unified English identity during the ninth and tenth centuries, see Sarah Foot, "The Making of the *Angelcynn*: English Identity before the Norman Conquest," 25–49; and Michael Wood, "The Making of King Aethelstan's Empire: An English Charlemagne?," 250–72. See also Nicholas Brooks, "English Identity from Bede to the Millennium," 33–51; Alfred P. Smyth, "The Emergence of English Identity: 700–1000," 24–52; and Patrick Wormald, "*Engla Lond*: The Making of an Allegiance," 1–24. The use of the term "national" in premodern contexts is defended in Anthony D. Smith, "The Myth of the 'Modern Nation' and the Myths of Nations," 1–25.

10 Helmut Gneuss, "The Old English Language," 19–49, at 47. For the evidence in support of Gneuss's claim, see Henry Bosley Woolf, *The Old Germanic Principles of Name-Giving*; sporadic discussion of reconstructed principles of name-giving also appears in Fran Colman, *The Grammar of Names in Anglo-Saxon England: The Linguistics and Culture of the Old English Onomasticon*, though this work (contrary to its title) is primarily concerned with the linguistic description and classification of the names of Anglo-Saxon moneyers.

that is conjectured from the evidence, not taken from some Anglo-Saxon parent's testimonial. Its conjectural status does not affect its validity, however, since the evidence overwhelmingly supports the existence of such a principle, regardless of whether Anglo-Saxons parents were consciously aware of it. In this vein, the present study seeks to identify motivations for diachronic change, with respect to exogenous ethnonyms and heroic-legendary names that may not have been consciously apprehended, but which nevertheless exerted a force upon naming behaviour and left a dent in the written record.

Table 2.1, printed below, provides some data pertaining to the use of ethnonyms in personal names, culled from the Prosopography of Anglo-Saxon England (PASE)[11] and from my own analysis of the *Northumbrian Liber Vitae*,[12] a rich source for name-giving that has not yet been incorporated into the PASE database. As can be seen, the name-elements that signal identification with ethnic groups that do not loom large in Anglo-Saxon history – *Swæf*, *Wendel*, *Wern*, and *Pect* – are found predominantly in personal names from the seventh and eighth centuries, with limited attestation thereafter. Presumably, the use of these elements in the early onomasticon reflects the transient social currency of various ethnic identities in the early period. Archaeological studies have confirmed that the Germanic migrations to the British Isles, which spanned the fifth and sixth centuries, included individuals from many peoples besides the Angles and the Saxons.[13] It is possible that Swabians, Vandals, and Werns who participated in the migrations preserved memory of their places of origin and used personal names to assert a continental Germanic identity. The relatively high incidence of the *Pect* name-element, meanwhile, is a probable sign of Pictish pride cultivated among individuals with indigenous connections.[14] Notably, while these four name-elements decline in popularity

11 To search the PASE database, visit http://www.pase.ac.uk (last accessed 30 July 2017).

12 David Rollason and Lynda Rollason, eds., *The Durham Liber Vitae*. On the distinction between the archaic Northumbrian core of the *Durham Liber Vitae* and the remainder of the book, see David N. Dumville, "The Northumbrian Liber Vitae," 109–82.

13 See, for example, John Hines, *The Scandinavian Character of Anglian England*; and Hines, "The Becoming of the English: Identity, Material Culture, and Language in Early Anglo-Saxon England," 49–59; also relevant is Sam Newton, *The Origins of "Beowulf" and the Pre-Viking Kingdom of East Anglia*.

14 The most straightforward explanation for the presence of the *Pect* ethnonym in early English name-giving is that individuals who considered themselves Pictish, after assimilating into Anglo-Saxon society, created dithematic names that combined the name of

Table 2.1 Incidence of Ethnonyms in Personal Names

Swæf (= Swabian)[15]	6 Names in PASE [7th c.: 4, 8th c.: 1, 9th c.: 1]
Wendel (= Vandal)[16]	1 Name in *NLV* [7th–8th c.] 1 Name in PASE [Wendelbeorht, moneyer, fl. 840–8]
Wern (= Wern, Lat. Varini)	10 Names in *NLV* [7th–8th c.], including 3 women [Werngyð, 2 Wernðryð] 5 Names in PASE [8th c.: 1, 9th c.: 3, 10th c.: 1, all Wernbeorht]
Pect (= Pict)	13 Names in *NLV* [7th–8th c.] 8 Names in PASE [7th c.: 2, 8th c.: 4, 9th c.: 2]
Seax (= Saxon)	22 Names in PASE [7th c.: 4, 10th c.: 9, 11th c.: 9], including 2 women [2 Seaxburg]
Dene (= Dane)	2 Names in *NLV* [7th–8th c.] 20 Names in PASE [8th c.: 4, 9th c.: 9, 10th c.: 3, 11th c.: 4]

as the centuries of the Anglo-Saxon period progress, the same fate does not befall the *Seax* and *Dene* name-elements, both of which are well attested in names from the seventh to the eleventh century. The disparity is not surprising: people were proud to assert a Saxon or Danish identity throughout the Anglo-Saxon period, since identification with these groups continued to confer social advantages, but the time to be a Swabian, a Vandal, a Wern, or a Pict came to an end relatively early, for reasons to be explained below.[17]

their ethnic group with elements from the Anglo-Saxon onomasticon (thus generating names such as *Pecthelm*). It is possible, however, that this ethnonym entered the English onomasticon for different reasons: for example, it might have been adopted as a symbol of victory, much as Publius Cornelius Scipio acquired the agnomen *Africanus* after the Second Punic War.

15 The ancient and medieval peoples who labelled themselves Swabians (*Suevi*, *Suebi*, *Swæfe*) should not be conflated ethnically or geographically with modern groups bearing this name. On the pre-modern usage of this ethnonym, see Alexander Riese, "Die Sueben," 331–46.

16 Old English *Wendel* probably refers not to the East Germanic Vandals, but to a homonymous North Germanic people situated in Jutland. See John Insley and David Rollason with P. McClure, "English Dithematic Names," at 156; and Rudolf Müller, *Untersuchungen über die Namen des nordhumbrischen Liber Vitae*, 103.

17 On the fluid, non-biological, and instrumental nature of early medieval ethnicities, see Patrick Geary, "Ethnic Identity as a Situational Construct in the Early Middle Ages," 15–26; and Walther Pohl, "Ethnic Names and Identities in the British Isles," 7–40.

The presence of various ethnonyms in early personal names reminds us that the formation of a national English or Anglo-Saxon identity was not inevitable. The Germanic migrants living in the British Isles during the sixth, seventh, and eighth centuries appear to have applied many different ethnonyms to themselves. The Angle and Saxon ethnonyms eventually came to subsume the others, but it seems that some Germanic inhabitants of the British Isles had once considered referring to themselves as the Anglo-Swabians rather than the Anglo-Saxons. The personal names containing the *Swæf* name-element occur in some notably high places: we have Swæberht and Swæfheard, seventh-century kings of Kent; Swæfred, a seventh-century king of the East Saxons; and the rather interesting Suebdæg, a mythical ancestor of the Northumbrian kings recorded in the Anglian genealogies.[18] Recognizing the aristocratic currency of the Swabian name-element during the seventh and eighth centuries explains a peculiar feature of the poem *Widsith*.[19] After mentioning the Swabians in the catalogue of kings – "Witta weold Swæfum" (Witta ruled the Swabians, line 22a) – the poet twice establishes a connection between the Angles and the Swabians. First, for reasons that are now obscure, the Swabians are presented as the allies of the Angles in the poet's brief account of Offa, the legendary ruler of Angeln:

Offa weold Ongle, Alewih Denum;
se wæs þara manna modgast ealra,
no hwæþre he ofer Offan eorlscype fremede,
ac Offa geslog ærest monna,
cnihtwesende, cynerica mæst.
Nænig efeneald him eorlscipe maran
on orette. Ane sweorde
merce gemærde wið Myrgingum
bi Fifeldore; heoldon forð siþþan
Engle ond Swæfe, swa hit Offa geslog. (lines 35–44)

[Offa ruled Angeln, Alewih the Danes; he was the boldest of all those men, yet he never performed more valiant deeds than Offa, for as a boy Offa

18 See David N. Dumville, "The Anglian Collection of Royal Genealogies and Regnal Lists," 23–50, at 30–7.

19 Passages from *Widsith* and other Old English poems are cited by line number from their editions in ASPR.

achieved, earliest of men, the greatest kingdom. No man equal to him in age performed more valiant deeds on the battlefield. With a single sword he established the boundary against the Myrgings at the Eider River; the Angles and the Swabians have since occupied the land, as Offa obtained it.]

The connection between the "Engle ond Swæfe" is then reinforced in the section of the poem where the wandering *scop* lists the peoples he has visited:

Mid Gefþum ic wæs ond mid Winedum   ond mid Gefflegum.
Mid Englum ic wæs ond mid Swæfum   ond mid Ænenum.
Mid Seaxum ic wæs ond Sycgum   ond mid Sweordwerum.   (lines 59–61)

[I was with the Gepids and Wends and the Gefflegs. I was with the Angles and the Swabians and the Ænenas. I was with the Saxons and the Sycgas and the Suardones.]

The poet's decision to link the Angles and the Swabians by twice placing their names into a single verse indicates that he recognized a certain affinity between the two groups. That the ordering of the names in the poem is not random is apparent from lines where extant sources elucidate the poet's logic, such as "mid Sweom ond mid Geatum ond mid Suþdenum" (with Swedes and with Geats and with South-Danes, line 58), which contains the three groups that figure most prominently in the legendry informing *Beowulf*. For the *Widsith*-poet, who probably composed during the seventh or eighth century,[20] the ethnic group naturally paired with the dominant Angles was the Swabians, not the Saxons.[21] His perspective clarifies the motivations of the seventh-century dynasties in which the Swabian name-element was used.

20 There are compelling linguistic reasons to regard *Widsith* as one of the earliest Old English poems: see Leonard Neidorf, "The Dating of *Widsið* and the Study of Germanic Antiquity," 165–83; Neidorf, "Lexical Evidence for the Relative Chronology of Old English Poetry," 7–48; Dennis Cronan, "Poetic Words, Conservatism, and the Dating of Old English Poetry," 23–50; and Bellenden R. Hutcheson, *Old English Poetic Metre*, 32. For a methodological discussion of the evidence bearing on the dating of *Widsith*, see Neidorf, "On the Epistemology of Old English Scholarship," 631–46.

21 Because "Swæfe" and "Seaxe" are metrically equivalent, there are no formal constraints determining the poet's verse construction here. In fact, the verse "Engle ond Seaxe" is attested twice in the later poetry: once in *The Battle of Brunanburh* (line 70a) and once in *The Menologium* (line 185b).

Closer to the migration period, it meant something to be a Swabian, a Vandal, a Wern, a Frisian, a Wulfing, and so forth. Pre-national texts such as *Beowulf*, *Widsith*, and the Anglian genealogies testify to the interest that these various peoples held in England before continental Germanic identities were discarded and an English national identity was aggressively promoted.[22] In *Beowulf*, the poet notes of Wulfgar, an official at Hroðgar's court: "þæt wæs Wendla leod" (he was a man of the Vandals, line 348b). Two allusions to the Wernas occur in *Widsith*: in the catalogue of kings, we are told that "Billing [weold] Wernum" (Billing ruled the Wernas, line 25b); and the travelling poet later claims "mid Wen[d]lum ic wæs ond mid Wærnum" (I was among the Vandals and the Wernas, line 59a). The Anglian royal genealogies bear further witness to the social currency of identification with these peoples: in addition to Suebdæg's presence in the Northumbrian genealogy, Witta, the legendary ruler of the Swabians (according to *Widsith*, line 22a), appears in the Kentish genealogy.[23] There are no comparable indications of social currency in the much fuller documentation of cultural and political endeavours from the later Anglo-Saxon period. The changing name-stock is but one sign of the processes of assimilation and ethnogenesis that took effect during the ninth and tenth centuries. Parents ceased to use exogenous ethnonyms when naming their

22 Recent philological research has suggested that *Beowulf* was probably composed between 685 and 725: see Robert D. Fulk, *A History of Old English Meter*, 381–92; Michael Lapidge, "The Archetype of *Beowulf*," 5–41; Cronan, "Poetic Words"; and Leonard Neidorf and Rafael J. Pascual, "The Language of *Beowulf* and the Conditioning of Kaluza's Law," 657–73. This conclusion is supported on various grounds in the essays compiled in *The Dating of "Beowulf": A Reassessment*, ed. Leonard Neidorf. On the chronological significance of the Anglian collection of royal genealogies, see Dumville, "The Anglian Collection," 45–50; and Leonard Neidorf, "Germanic Legend, Scribal Errors, and Cultural Change," 37–57, at 49–53. Philological research has not persuaded all observers of the relative antiquity of *Beowulf*, though few new arguments for late composition have materialized in recent years. An outstanding exception to this trend is Helen Damico's *"Beowulf" and the Grendel-kin: Politics and Poetry in Eleventh-Century England*. Damico argues that *Beowulf* was composed ca. 1040, several decades after palaeographers date the production of its extant manuscript; for a critique of her argument and a review of the history of the dating controversy, seeNeidorf, "Philology, Allegory, and the Dating of *Beowulf*," 97–115.

23 Because Witta is listed as the father of Hengest in the Kentish genealogy, Kemp Malone regards Hengest as a Swabian as well, with some interesting consequences for the interpretation of the Hengest legendry. See *The Literary History of Hamlet*, 20–1.

children presumably because these elements were no longer effective in providing children with advantages or distinctions. For parents eager to assimilate and embrace an English identity, the ethnic connotations of a name probably led to its avoidance and obsolescence. The same sociolinguistic considerations are operative in modern name-giving: "the assimilating groups will tend to give up those first names which are distinctive to their group, i.e. those first names which are either unique to their language and/or those which are simply more common to their group."[24] Names that broadcast the ethnicity of their bearers are often discarded in immigrant communities where assimilation is prioritized and no instrumental value attends the preservation of a distinct ethnic identity.[25]

What is to be made, then, of the appearance of Scandinavian names and name-elements (such as *þor* and *ketil*) in English documentation from the ninth and tenth centuries, after the arrival of the Vikings and the establishment of the Danelaw?[26] To a large extent, the significance of these names in the present context depends on prosopography. That is to say, if the bearers of these names were born in Scandinavia or descended from Scandinavian parents living in the Danelaw, then there is nothing peculiar about this development, and it poses no difficulties to the hypothesis that name-giving behaviour was influenced by instrumentalist considerations connected to the spread of English nationalism. Cecily Clark favours this interpretation of Scandinavian names attested in records from the Anglo-Saxon period, concluding from their concentration in Danelaw areas that "any family that used a succession of purely or even predominantly Scandinavian names may, without too much danger, be presumed likely to be of actual part-Viking descent."[27] The ongoing currency of Scandinavian

24 Stanley Lieberson, "What's in a name? ... Some Sociolinguistic Possibilities," 77–88, at 81.

25 For example, in their study of name-giving among Italian and Jewish immigrants in the United States, Watkins and London observed that "second-generation Italian males drop Salvatore, Pasquale, Giovanni, and Domenico, and second-generation Jewish males drop Isaac, Meyer, and Israel." See "Personal Names and Cultural Change," 180; see also Ernest Maass, "Integration and Name Changing among Jewish Refugees from Central Europe in the United States," 129–71.

26 For a comprehensive treatment of these names, see Erik Björkman, *Nordische Personennamen in England in alt- und frühmittel-englischer Zeit: ein Beitrag zur englischen Namenkunde*.

27 Clark, "English Personal Names," 37.

names in the Danelaw, with the lack of onomastic assimilation that this implies, illustrates the connection between name-giving and social prestige. In these areas, advantages presumably accrued to individuals marked as Scandinavian, since this distinction connected them to the wealthiest and most powerful families in the region. Under these circumstances, it would not be surprising if the prestige value of Scandinavian names led some native Anglo-Saxon families living in the Danelaw to adopt them. Certainly, the prestige associated with the names of the Norman conquerors led their naming conventions to be widely imitated throughout England in subsequent centuries.[28] The changes in English name-giving wrought by conquest and invasion support the argument of this paper insofar as they encourage the interpretation of diachronic change in the onomasticon in terms of instrumentalist considerations. Yet the later spread of Scandinavian and continental Germanic names in England also requires the present argument to be qualified in chronological and perhaps topographical terms. The development of an English national identity over the course of the ninth and tenth centuries affected the stock of etymologically Anglo-Saxon names used in England during those centuries, and this paper seeks only to explain patterns within this corpus of linguistically and chronologically restricted data. The first of these patterns, the decline in names containing exogenous ethnonyms, seems best explained as a consequence of their declining social value at a time when assimilation was pursued and identification with the *Angelcynn* conferred advantages.

Similar sociolinguistic considerations might be responsible for the decline in the use of names from Germanic heroic legend during the later Anglo-Saxon period. In 1912, H.M. Chadwick noted that the names of legendary heroes were frequently borne during the seventh and eighth centuries, but were rarely given during the ninth and tenth centuries.[29] About a decade ago, Patrick Wormald reaffirmed and strengthened Chadwick's conclusions with evidence drawn from the Prosopography of Anglo-Saxon England database.[30] My recent study of heroic-legendary names attested in the *Northumbrian Liber Vitae* identified some new pieces of evidence

28 Clark, "English Personal Names," 40.
29 H. Munro Chadwick, *The Heroic Age*, 44–6, 64–6.
30 Patrick Wormald, "*Beowulf*: The Redating Reassessed," 71–81, 98–105.

Table 2.2 Incidence of Names from Germanic Legend in the *Northumbrian Liber Vitae*

Ælfwine: 3	*Froda: 1	*Offa: 9
*Ætla: 1	Garwulf: 1	Sigeferð: 2
Æðelmund: 10	*Hama: 2	Sigemund: 2
Alewih: 2	Heardred: 11	*Þeodric: 4
Beaduca: 4	*Helpric: 6	*Wada: 3
*Beowulf: 1	Herebeald: 8	*Wærmund: 3
*Diori: 3	*Heremod: 1	*Widia: 1
Eadgils: 1	Hereric: 1	*Widsið: 1
Eanmund: 8	Hildeburg: 1	*Wiglaf: 1
Eadwine: 21	Hildegyð: 2	Wihtgils: 1
*Folcwald: 1	*Hroðulf: 3	*Witta: 1
Folcwine: 2	Hunfrið: 4	Wulfgar: 1
Friðuric: 1	Hygelac: 4	*Wyrmhere: 1
Friðwulf: 4	*Ingeld: 16	

in support of Chadwick's and Wormald's chronological argument.[31] As Table 2.2, printed above, makes clear, the use of names from Germanic legend in the early Anglo-Saxon period was pervasive.

This table offers a complete list of heroic-legendary names in the *Northumbrian Liber Vitae*, the original core of the *Durham Liber Vitae*, which commemorates and records the names of more than two thousand individuals (Lynda Rollason reckons the figure to be 2,819 names in total) born during the seventh and eighth centuries, making it by far the richest source for early Anglo-Saxon name-giving.[32] Many of the heroic-legendary names included in this table will not be found in sources from the ninth and tenth centuries, as Chadwick and Wormald observed. The

31 Leonard Neidorf, "Beowulf before *Beowulf*: Anglo-Saxon Anthroponymy and Heroic Legend," 553–73. Another recent and important contribution to this line of research is Tom Shippey, "Names in *Beowulf* and Anglo-Saxon England," 58–78.

32 Prosopographical indications of the text's chronological scope are discussed in Elizabeth Briggs, "Nothing but Names: The Original Core of the Durham *Liber Vitae*," 63–85. On the number of names in the collection, see Lynda Rollason, "History and Codicology," 1:5–42, at 7.

emergent canon of stereotypically English names excluded the foreign-sounding names of continental Germanic heroes.

A sceptical scholar might ask: how do we know that the names of continental Germanic heroes would have sounded foreign to Anglo-Saxon ears? By focusing on the finite corpus of onomastic data preserved in the *Northumbrian Liber Vitae*, this question can be answered on a statistical basis. Many of the heroic-legendary names contained elements that were foreign to or unproductive in the Old English onomasticon. To take one clear example: the name Ætla – that is, Attila the Hun – derives from the diminutive form of the Gothic word *atta*; the name Widia is also of Gothic derivation.[33] Dithematic names such as Ingeld, Beowulf, Theodric, Widsið, Hroðulf, and Wyrmhere all contain an element that was not productive on English soil. Monothematic names such as Breca, Froda, Hama, Offa, Wada, and Witta all derive from elements that were never individually productive in English name-giving. Consequently, these monothematic names cannot plausibly be construed as hypocoristic forms of common dithematic names, but must instead represent full names given at birth. Table 2.3, printed below, provides some figures to facilitate apprehension of the distinction between productive and unproductive name elements.

In the *Northumbrian Liber Vitae*, productive name-elements such as *beorht*, *æðel*, *ræd*, and *wine* appear in hundreds of personal names, because these elements were regularly used to generate new names in Anglo-Saxon England from the earliest period to the eleventh century. By contrast, many of the elements found in heroic-legendary names occur exclusively in these fossilized formations. Name-elements such as *frod*, *beow*, *geld*, *sið*, and *þeod* might continue to be used on the continent, but they were demonstrably unproductive in English name-giving. In Table 2.2, printed above, an asterisk was placed beside all of the heroic-legendary names that contain a foreign or unproductive name-element. As can be seen, roughly half of the names have merited an asterisk.

The presence of foreign or unproductive elements in heroic-legendary names is significant for several reasons. First, it confirms that in the early Anglo-Saxon period, there must have been a recognized custom of naming children after legendary heroes. Instead of generating a name from productive elements, some Anglo-Saxon parents deliberately chose a name

33 See Moritz Schönfeld, *Wörterbuch der altgermanischen Personen- und Völkernamen*, 263 and 275.

Table 2.3 Incidence of Productive vs. Unproductive Elements in the *Northumbrian Liber Vitae*[34]

Beorht: 543	Frod: 1 (Froda x1)
Ead: 256	Beow: 1 (Biuuulf x1)
Frið: 245	Deor: 3 (Diori x3)
Ræd: 214	Wid: 1 (Widsið x1)
Wulf: 462	Sið: 1 (Widsið x1)
Mund: 111	In: 17 (Ingeld x16)
Cyne: 112	Geld: 17 (Ingeld x16)
Æðel: 92	Hroð: 8 (Hroðulf x3)
Helm: 130	Wyrm: 1 (Wyrmhere x1)
Wine: 307	Þeod: 4 (Þeodric x4)

encountered in heroic-legendary poetry. Names such as Ætla or Ingeld could not have been accidentally generated through the combination of elements that circulated in England. Men bearing these names probably knew that their parents selected for them a distinctive name associated with a prominent migration-era hero. At the same time, the fact that heroic-legendary names were etymologically and phonologically distinct must have facilitated their systematic disappearance from the Anglo-Saxon name-stock. If parents wanted to avoid names belonging to this group, it would not have been difficult to avoid them, due to their distinctiveness. It is important to remember that we are dealing here not with certain names arbitrarily falling out of fashion, but with the systematic avoidance of a group of names. These names were unusual and they carried certain connotations. There are several probable reasons why Anglo-Saxon parents avoided giving these names to their children during the ninth, tenth, and eleventh centuries.

34 The *Northumbrian Liber Vitae* is used for these incidence figures because I had already undertaken an etymological study of its names and tabulated the incidence of their constituent elements. A similar project could profitably be undertaken for the names in PASE, though the requisite labour goes far beyond what is necessary for the present study. Were the data from PASE incorporated into these figures for productive and unproductive name-elements, I am sure it would make little difference. The exceptionally productive elements in the *Northumbrian Liber Vitae* remained productive throughout the Anglo-Saxon period, whereas the unproductive elements remained confined to peculiarities.

One straightforward reason for such avoidance is the desire to assimilate and adopt conventional, ethnically unmarked names. Positing that an impulse towards conformity and assimilation was operative during the Anglo-Saxon period would explain why so many men were named Godric, Wulfstan, Ælfred, and Eadward in the tenth and eleventh centuries. It should come as no surprise to find changes in the name-stock during the centuries that witnessed what Sarah Foot has called "the making of the *Angelcynn*." Alfred and his descendants actively promoted an English identity that positioned the English as a people ethnically distinct from their Scandinavian and continental Germanic cousins.[35] The pan-Germanic ethnic perspective articulated in texts such as *Widsith* and the Anglian genealogies was no longer in fashion. Families seeking to assert their Englishness, their belonging to the *Angelcynn*, naturally gravitated towards names with strongly English connotations. The names and name-elements characteristic of the West Saxon dynasty, for example, soared in popularity during the tenth century.[36] By the same token, names from Germanic heroic legend, like the exogenous ethnonyms discussed above, fell out of use because these names failed to confer commensurate advantages or distinctions on their bearers.

The names of continental Germanic heroes might also have lost social currency when the legends from which they derived were forgotten. Sources such as the Franks Casket, the *Liber monstrorum*, the *Vita Sancti Guthlaci*, and the *Northumbrian Liber Vitae* indicate that legends of migration-era heroes circulated in England as early as the seventh century.[37] Considering the early date of the transmission of Germanic legend to England, it is not unlikely that new enthusiasms should eventually supplant old ones: that tales of Goths, Huns, and Heaðobards, which were recited during the seventh and eighth centuries, might be forgotten during the ninth and tenth centuries. It is worth noting that in the extant manuscript of *Beowulf*, copied out around the year 1000, many of the

35 As Foot demonstrates, the West Saxon kings strove to promote a "vision of one people united through a shared history, common faith, and opposition to the Danes under a single rulership." See "The Making of the *Angelcynn*," 45.

36 See Stenton, "Personal Names," 177.

37 The chronological significance of these texts is discussed in Neidorf, "Germanic Legend," which surveys the evidence for the transmission and circulation of Germanic legend in England.

names of continental Germanic heroes and peoples are corrupted in ways that suggest that the scribes had never heard them before.[38] Presumably, new national heroes like Alfred and Æthelstan displaced the petty kings of the migration era in the popular imagination. Changes in popular culture might therefore be reflected in the changing name-stock. Then as now, celebrity is an unstable phenomenon: names rise and fall in popularity depending on who is admired and who is loathed at a particular moment.

Much work remains to be done on the changing nature of the Anglo-Saxon onomasticon. Patrick Wormald, for example, noted that the element *gūð* (battle) occurs predominantly in early Anglo-Saxon names, whereas the element *gōd* (good) occurs predominantly in late Anglo-Saxon names.[39] Such regularities in the onomastic data provide valuable insight into changes in culture, religion, and ideology that were taking place among the populace. This paper has focused on two aspects of diachronic change in its effort to explain the declining incidence of exogenous ethnonyms and heroic-legendary names. Most of the data in this study has necessarily been drawn from the male name-stock, though it is worth noting that the female name-stock has also yielded several forms relevant to the criteria under scrutiny (i.e., Werngyð, Wernðryð, Seaxburg, Hildeburg, and Hildegyð). In both cases of diachronic change, the evidence offers a tantalizing suggestion that Anglo-Saxon parents were emotionally invested in the success of their infants. The changes in the name-stock appear to have arisen because parents sought to avoid giving their children disadvantageous names. When selecting a name for their child, parents prioritized the desire for their child to flourish over the desire to perpetuate ethnic or familial traditions. Sociolinguistic considerations that inform name-giving in the modern world can be seen to have been operative during the Anglo-Saxon period as well. In short, the onomastic evidence lends support to the hypothesis of continuity between medieval and modern conceptions of childhood.[40]

38 See Leonard Neidorf, "Scribal Errors of Proper Names in the *Beowulf* Manuscript," 249–69.

39 Wormald, "The Redating Reassessed," 78.

40 I thank Susan Irvine and Winfried Rudolf for their perceptive comments on this paper. I also thank R.D. Fulk, Joseph Harris, and Rafael J. Pascual for reading this paper in draft and improving it in various ways. I'm also grateful to Carole Hough for a correspondence in which she helpfully discussed some points of onomastics with me.

3 Anglo-Saxon Preaching on Children

WINFRIED RUDOLF

Anglo-Saxon England around the year 1000, inhabited by probably fewer than two million people,[1] was a society in which a person could witness someone die on a daily basis.[2] This omnipresence of death, the leveller asking neither for social status nor age, could be felt not least through widespread infant mortality.[3] Since the AD 980s, the country had again been troubled by Viking raids and had to ensure that its Christian population would grow despite ongoing warfare and the danger of regional relapse into pagan practices. Those newly born into this society could therefore hope for special protection by the church, while their mostly illiterate parents were strongly reminded by the clergy to observe Christian morals and raise their children in this spirit. Homilies in the Old English vernacular, whose surviving manuscript versions date from the late ninth to the late twelfth century, touch on a variety of sensitive issues regarding children,

1 Demographic figures suggested for the period vary. For a summary of opinions see Olga Timofeeva, "Anglo-Latin Bilingualism before 1066: Prospects and Limitations," 1–36, at 13–14. She rehearses the notable arguments by Josiah C. Russell, *British Medieval Population*, 54; Frederic W. Maitland, *Domesday Book and Beyond*, 437; John Hatcher, *Plague, Population and the English Economy 1348–1530*, 68; and Edward Miller and John Hatcher, *Medieval England: Rural Society and Economic Change 1086–1348*, 28–9.

2 An anonymous homily in Oxford, Bodleian Library, MS Hatton 115 reproaches its audience: "La hwæt, we us huru þinga ne ondrædaþ þæt we dæghwæmlice geseoþ beforan urum eahum ure nehstan sweltan" (Behold, we are not in the least terrified, given that daily we see our fellow man die before our eyes); see Donald G. Scragg, ed., *The Vercelli Homilies and Related Texts*, no. IX, MS: L, 159–83.

3 Sally Crawford, "Children, Death, and the Afterlife in Anglo-Saxon England," 340.

including pregnancy and contraception, baptism and breastfeeding, infanticide and abandonment, education and disobedience. They can hence be considered as key texts concerning the demographic, socio-economic, religious, and military stability of late Anglo-Saxon England. Although these addresses to lay audiences assemble a number of age-old commonplaces and superstitions about children, largely due to their drawing on Latin sources, they still offer independent Anglo-Saxon notions of the status of children to the attentive student. In more than a few aspects catechetical homilies and their contemporary revisions reflect the zeitgeist more accurately than most other surviving Old English texts. Even so, we must keep in mind that a preacher's address only presents us with a limited and somewhat distant perspective on child-parent relations, which is of course problematic. A dedicated homilist will feel obliged to admonish his audience and bring up painful subjects, therefore many pastoral references to children necessarily occur in connection with criticism of parental behaviour. Bearing in mind this bias of a problematic child-parent relation that homilies inevitably shape, we can still find intriguing traces of the actual situation of Anglo-Saxon children when we read between the lines. This information, as hidden as the Anglo-Saxon child itself, invites some interpretation, even if it may often resist ultimate conclusions.[4] Passages of child-parent regulations in Old English catechetical homilies are therefore of primary interest to this paper.

Anglo-Saxon clerics preaching on children were teachers in a twofold sense: on the one hand, they had to impart the ideals and methods of proper nurturing and educating to mostly illiterate parents; on the other, they would then have to guarantee that parents whose children were excluded from the privilege of monastic or other education would raise their children accordingly.[5] Homilies therefore not only address actual problems concerning the survival, well-being, and education of the Anglo-Saxon child, but they also use children as powerful rhetorical tools to remind adults of their own responsibilities, both as teachers and as good Christians. This didactic mode of homiletic discourse often makes it difficult to spot the

4 On the silence of children in Old English literature see Mathew Kuefler, "'A Wryed Existence': Attitudes Towards Children in Anglo-Saxon England," 823.

5 This privileged role of the priest is made particularly manifest in Gregory the Great's *Cura Pastoralis*, a work considered to be essential for the educational reform by the Alfredian circle and therefore translated into the Old English vernacular. See Henry Sweet, ed., *King Alfred's West-Saxon Version of Gregory's Pastoral Care*, 1, chs. I–II.

emotional aspects of childcare and family life among the political and economic interests of the church in the growth and moral control of the Christian population. In view of the influential work by Philippe Ariès, Lloyd deMause, and Edward Shorter, all of whom have characterised medieval childhood as an experience dominated by parental aloofness,[6] it is legitimate to ask if the late Anglo-Saxon church sought to improve the lives of children and in which ways Old English homilies could at all appeal to the parental instincts if such emotional distance was indeed the sentiment of the day. The paper will test this claim of aloofness, analysing pre- and postnatal regulations, including baptism and sponsorship, conscious and unintentional infanticide, as well as the forgotten pagan ritual of drawing children through the earth, arguing for the existence of various forms of tough love in Anglo-Saxon England.

Conception and Pregnancy

The Anglo-Saxon church reserved itself the right to control the protection of new human lives, yet not from the cradle, but from conception. Even as secular legislation demanded *wergild* for the unborn,[7] so recipes and charms preserved in the monastic context promised to help a woman conceive or avoid miscarriage,[8] while prognostics gave clear dietary instructions to expectant mothers.[9] The latter would, for instance, recommend abstinence from nuts and acorn, from unripe fruit, or any meat of a male animal from the fourth or fifth month of pregnancy onwards in order to avoid the child becoming stupid ("disig"), humpbacked ("hoforode"), or hydrocephalous ("healede").[10] Such superstitions were supplemented with practical advice, as in the popular homily titled *De infantibus non baptizandis*, where the issue of potential miscarriage is addressed as follows:

6 Philippe Ariès, *Centuries of Childhood*; Lloyd deMause, ed., *The History of Childhood*; Edward Shorter, *The Making of the Modern Family*.

7 Felix Liebermann, ed., *Die Gesetze der Angelsachsen*, 1: *Alfred* 9.

8 Thomas O. Cockayne, ed., *Leechdoms, Wortcunning and Starcraft of Early England*, 3:67 and 69. See also Sally Crawford, *Childhood in Anglo-Saxon England*, 59.

9 The Canterbury manuscript containing this text is London, British Library, MS Cotton Tiberius A.iii. For the localisation see especially Helmut Gneuss, "Origin and Provenance of Anglo-Saxon Manuscripts: The Case of Cotton Tiberius A.III," 13–48.

10 For the text see László S. Chardonnens, *Anglo-Saxon Prognostics 900–1100: Study and Texts*, 244, no. 3.2/1, lines 13–18. For the varying translations of *healede* see ibid., 242.

Warnige eac seo modor þonne heo mid cilde gæð þæt heo mid nanre higeleaste hit ne amyrre. ne mid nanum hefe ne mid nanum plegan. oððe mid rade. oððe mid ænigum ungerade. forþan ðe hit sceal eft of deaðe arisan on domes dæg gif hit ær cucu wæs innan þære meder. ⁊ hæfð þonne helle wite. gif hit hæðen acwylð. (MS Hatton 115, fol. 60r)[11]

[Let the pregnant mother also take heed that she does not destroy her child through any thoughtlessness, neither through any heavy lifting, nor any playing, neither through riding on horseback nor any foolishness, because the child must rise from death on Doomsday if it had been alive before inside the mother and it will then have the torture of hell if it dies a heathen.][12]

Prenatal or postpartum anxiety of losing a child or risking a potential disability is a common worldwide phenomenon.[13] Triggering and intensifying this fear could enhance the elocutionary force of a homilist's rhetoric considerably, especially when his warnings pictured a gloomy outlook on the lives and afterlives not only of the lost child but also its irresponsible parents. Napier homily XLV, uniquely preserved in CCCC MS 419, is a particularly ruthless piece with regard to such emotional manipulation.[14] Here the preaching voice first threatens the audience with the theft of family property and abduction of women and children by heathens if the tithe were not brought forth regularly. In the tradition of the so-called Sunday Letter homilies,[15] the text then continues to command the observance of Sunday as a holy day, whose violation – and this included any sexual

11 Three versions of this homily survive, all preserved in manuscripts connected with Worcester (Cambridge, Corpus Christi College [henceforth CCCC], MS 178, pp. 139–40; Oxford, Bodleian Library, MS Hatton 115, fols. 59v–60r and MS Hatton 116, pp. 379–80). The low degree of textual variation suggests that all three stand very close to each other in transmission. The only printed edition to date is Arthur S. Napier, "Ein altenglisches Leben des heiligen Chad," 154–5, but it is too obscure in word division, so that a direct transcript from Hatton 115 with my own layout is given here. For the idea of resurrected children blaming their careless parents see below. Pope suggests Ælfric as author of the piece; see John C. Pope, ed., *Homilies of Ælfric: A Supplementary Collection*, 1:56 and 69.

12 All translations, unless otherwise indicated, are my own.

13 Marni L. Jacob and Eric A. Storch, "Postpartum Anxiety Disorders," 63–8.

14 Arthur S. Napier, ed., *Wulfstan – Sammlung der ihm zugeschriebenen Homilien nebst Untersuchungen über ihre Echtheit*, 231, lines 14–17; henceforth referred to as "Napier" followed by homily number, page and line.

15 Clare A. Lees, "The 'Sunday Letter' and the 'Sunday Lists,'" 129–51.

intercourse carried out on that day[16] – would lead to the conception of disabled children and sickness of their parents:

> Gif ge ne healdað þone halgan sunnandæg, ðonne beoð on eowrum husum acennede cild, þe ne geseoð ne ne gehyrað ne ne gað, and ge forweorðað.[17]
>
> [If you do not keep the Holy Sunday, then in your houses there will be born children who neither see nor hear nor are able to walk. And you will become sick.]

Equally straightforward in its warning, another anonymous homily extends this prohibition of Sunday-sex to the nights before feast days, combining it with a condemnation of cursing:

> And þa cildra þe beoð begiten on sunnan niht and on þam halgan freolsnihtum hi sceolan beon geborene butan eagon and butan fotum and butan handon and eacswilce dumbe, for þam þe ge ne heoldon mid clænnesse þa halgan niht and ne wiðtugan mid eowre tungan to cursiende.[18]
>
> [And the children begotten in the night of Sunday and in the nights before festivals must be born without eyes and without feet and without hands, and also mute, because you did not keep the holy nights in purity and did not refrain from cursing with your tongues.]

All these passages capitalise rhetorically on the fears and superstitions of parents-to-be by raising the sensitive topics of miscarriage, infant mortality, and congenital disability. Yet through their warnings, these examples also seek to explore the causes of such misfortunes, identifying them as consequences of either careless or sinful behaviour. Undoubtedly, the causes given in the aforementioned homilies had the potential to incite a congregation to the public shaming of unfortunate parents, but they also reveal the fascinating interaction of two dimensions – the medical and the spiritual. While the medical knowledge of Anglo-Saxon monasticism shows a fusion with folklore traditions, as is evident in the hybrid

16 Napier XLV, 228:29–31.

17 Napier XLV, 231:20–2.

18 Robert Priebsch, "The Chief Sources of Some Anglo-Saxon Homilies," 129–47, lines 89–93.

instructions of many an Anglo-Saxon charm,[19] the church would intertwine both areas of knowledge with religious doctrine, exploiting the spiritual awe of congregations in order to authorise a particular Christian way of pre- and postnatal care and to put it into practice. This is a central concern of the regulations concerning the baptising of the newborn.

Baptismal Regulations and Sponsorship

De infantibus non baptizandis, as we have already seen, is an important preaching text on the precautions that should be taken both before and after birth in order to prevent infants from dying unbaptised. It survives in three manuscripts,[20] in all of which it occurs in close proximity to other homiletic instructions *ad populum*.[21] All surviving versions open with a direct *we-eow* address that urges parents to baptise their child as soon as possible, lest it end up in hell in case of an untimely death:

> WE BIDDAÐ EOW MEN ⁊ BEODAÐ ON GODES naman þ*æt* ge wislicor ⁊ wærlicor dón embe eower hǽþenan cild þonne ge oððis dydon. þ*æt* swa feala sawla ne losian swa swa her doð betweox eow on godes naman. þ*æt* ge eowre cild læton fullian swa hraðe swa hi acennede beoð. forþan ðe þu nast his líf gewis oð merigen. ⁊ þu dest þinum cilde mycelne hearm gif þu him þurh þine gymeleaste heofonan rices myrhðe benæmst. ⁊ hit besengst on helle grund mid eallu*m* deoflum á on ecnysse; Ðu miht þine gymeleaste wið god gebetan. ac þam cilde ne cymð næfre nan bot. forþan ðe nan hæðen man ne mót næfre into heofonan rice becuman. (Hatton 115, fol. 59v)

> [We ask you, people, and command you in God's name that you act more wisely and more carefully about your unbaptised children than you have hitherto done, so that not as many souls are lost as there are right now among you, in God's name: that you have your children baptised as quickly as they

19 See for example the charms *For a Sudden Stitch* or *For Delayed Birth*; *The Anglo-Saxon Minor Poems*, ASPR 6:122–4.

20 See above, note 11.

21 Notable among them are especially the Ælfrician homily *De auguriis* (ed. Pope, *Homilies of Ælfric*, no. XXIX, 2:786–98), an address titled *De sanguine* (also known as *Letter to Brother Edward*; for an edition see Mary Clayton, "An Edition of Ælfric's Letter to Brother Edward," 280–3), and a short piece titled *De cogitatione* (ed. Napier, "Ein altenglisches Leben," 155).

are born, because you cannot be certain of its (the child's)[22] life the next morning. And you do great harm to your child if you deprive it of the bliss of the kingdom of heaven through your negligence and cause it to sink to the bottom of hell, with all devils, forever in eternity. You can repent your carelessness before God, but the child will never receive help, because no heathen can ever enter the heavenly kingdom.]

Ubiquitous infant mortality must have prompted this warning to keep the interval between birth and baptism as short as possible. However, administering the first sacrament to the Anglo-Saxon newborn was a sensitive issue because it involved economic interests, both of the child's parents and of the church. One important aspect on the parents' side was the preference for rich and influential sponsors who would act as god- or co-parents.[23] This did not only guarantee future support for the child, but it could also create new or tighten already existing bonds between families. The Anglo-Saxon church was not in favour of this widespread practice of sponsorship, as the *Vita Sancti Rumwoldi* confirms, in which little Rumwold, able to speak at a premature age and imitating the humility of Christ, vehemently rejects aristocratic sponsors.[24] In the same way, *De infantibus non baptizandis* rejects the socio-economic dimension of god- or co-parenthood in connection with baptism:

Nu cweð sum man *þæt* he wẏle cepan him holdra freonda mid his cilde. ⁊ abit ðæs hwilon to lange. forþan ðe us segð *þæt* halige godspell *þæt* godes grama wunað ofer þone hæðenan ⁊ betere byð þam hæþenan cilde. *þæt* hit nime an ælmesman þonne hit næbbe ða ecan myrhðe. ⁊ hæbbe ða ecan wítu. (Hatton 115, 59v–60r)

[Now a man will say that he wishes to gain himself good friends for his child and waits for too long a time. Therefore the holy gospel tells us that God's wrath dwells with the heathen. And it is better for the child that a beggar

22 The preacher switches from the plural to the singular in the sub-clause here, increasing the immediacy of address. This interesting feature of oral discourse might reveal this text to be an original composition in Old English, not necessarily depending on a direct Latin source.

23 On this issue see especially Joseph H. Lynch, *Christianizing Kinship: Ritual Sponsorship in Anglo-Saxon England*, 46–150.

24 Rosalind C. Love, ed., *Three Eleventh-Century Anglo-Latin Saints' Lives*, 98–101. See also Joyce Hill's contribution to this volume.

(as a sponsor) take it than that it not have the eternal joy and have eternal punishments.]

The spiritual benefits that a quick baptism promised to the child may have been less tangible than the financial profit that certain members of the clergy expected from the immediate calling of a baptiser. There is plenty of evidence suggesting that many Anglo-Saxon priests expected illegal payment before administering the sacraments. Ælfric, in his *Letter to Wulfsige*, would hardly have had any reason to prohibit such corrupt practice, had it not been the matter of the day.[25] Looking back at mid-eleventh-century Worcestershire, William of Malmesbury's *Vita Wulfstani* paints a perhaps slightly too colourful, yet nonetheless matching picture:

> For by that time bribery had made its appearance from the shades of Hell, with the result that priests would not give even this sacrament (baptism) to infants unless parents greased their palms. Wulfstan took pity on the poverty of the parents, and in thought and deed chastised the greed of the priests; and he gave the poor baptism of his free will. People flocked to him from town and country alike, particularly those who were not prepared(?) to use cash to buy their children's baptism. The custom passed from the poor to the rich, so that few in the district thought one of their offspring properly baptized if Wulfstan had not officiated.[26]

Anglo-Saxon bishops would threaten priests with dismissal from their ranks if they did not officiate promptly, even if parents were unable to pay, as we learn from the widely disseminated address *To folce*, known as Napier homily XXIV, where we read:

> And ic bidde ⁊ beode. þæt ælc cild sy binnan seofan nihtum gefullad; Gif hit þonne dead weorðe butan fulluhte. ⁊ hit on preoste gelang sy. þonne þolige he

25 Bernhard Fehr, ed., *Die Hirtenbriefe Ælfrics*, no. 17, 72.

26 William of Malmesbury, *Saints' Lives*, 32–5: "Iam enim uenalitas ex infernalibus umbris emerserat, ut nec illud gratias presbiteri preberent infantibus sacramentum, si non infarcirent parentes marsupium. Horum igitur Wlstanus miseratus inopiam, illorum animo et facto pertundens auaritiam, in baptizandis pauperibus ultroneae dignationis impendebat offitium. Currebatur ad eum ex urbibus et agris, ab illis precipue quorum non intererat dare nummum ut soboli suae mercarentur lauacrum. Transfusa est a tenuiori fortuna in diuites consuctudo, ut nemo fere illius regionis iure baptizatum aliquem ex suis putaret quem Wlstanus non baptizasset."

his hádes. ⁊ deadbete georne. Gif hit þonne þurh maga gemeleaste gewyrðe. þonne þolige se þe hit on gelang sy. ælcere eardwununge. ⁊ wræcnige of earde. oððon on earde. swiðe deope gebette. swa biscop him tæce. (CCCC 419, 248–9)[27]

[And I ask and command that each child be baptised within seven days. If it then dies without baptism owing to the priest, then he should forfeit his office and repent zealously. If it dies through the carelessness of the parents (or kinsmen), then the person responsible should give up his home and be an exile from home or repent on his home soil as deeply as the bishop teaches him to.]

Apart from divesting priests of their ordination – a sacrament for a sacrament so to speak – and the relatively short deadline of only one week[28] within which baptism had to be administered, this version from CCCC 419 also proclaims rigorous punishment for those parents guilty of careless infanticide. Exile from one's own home soil or, instead, extensive public penance was a considerable prize to pay, possibly too severe a compensation to convince some parents of confessing their sin. It is therefore a telling fact that all other surviving versions of Napier homily XXIV relax the baptismal deadline for priests to thirty days, and replace the punishment of exile for parents with the significant formulation "þonne wite se þe hit on gelang sy gif he his silfes recce. þæt he swyðe deope gebette swa biscop him tæcce" (then know he who is responsible – if he confess it himself – that he repent as deeply as the bishop teaches him to).[29] We may take this as a broad hint that the omnipresent infant mortality, as much as the parental worries surrounding it, provoked a spectrum of preaching on punishments, reaching from the idealistic to the pragmatic, the latter perhaps being necessary in order to create a mutually profitable compromise between parents and priests (i.e., if the baptiser was not paid, the confessor certainly would be). Arguably, the stricter versions may stand closer to the ideal of the original regulation.[30]

27 A manuscript transcription is preferred here for the sake of subsequent highlighting of important textual variations with parallel versions.

28 This strict prescription also occurs in Wulfstan's *Canons of Edgar* on which more below (see 62–3).

29 See also Napier homily LVIII, 300:16–26.

30 CCCC 419 may be considered the earliest manuscript version of homily Napier XXIV.

Infanticide

The basic precondition for administering the sacrament of baptism was the living newborn, which is why the avoidance of infant death remained a primary concern of catechetical preaching. One of the causes of unintentional infanticide is prominently tackled by the final part of *De infantibus non baptizandis*, namely, the tragic suffocation of the child after inappropriate breastfeeding:

> Nu is eft oðer þincg þe dysige wif doð lecgað heora cild betwux him. ⁊ oflicgað hit þonne hi on slæpe beoð forþan ðe se slæpenda mann nat hwæt he deð. ⁊ we secgað þæt seo modor gif heo to ðam unwær byð. mid hyre breoste mæg þ*æt* cild acwellan. gif heo hit læt sucan ⁊ wyrð þonne on slæpe. þonne ofligð þ*æt* breost þæs cildes fnæst. oððæt hit byð forsmorod· forþan ðe hit ne cann. ne ne mæg. hit aweg dón. þonne byð heo hyre agenes cildes bana. (Hatton 115, fol. 60r)

> [There is another thing that foolish women do: they put their children between (beside?)[31] them and lie on it in their sleep, because the sleeping person knows not what he does. And we say that the mother, if she is further unaware, may kill the child with her breast if she lets it suck and then falls asleep. Then the breast hinders the child's breathing until it is smothered, because it does not know (how) nor is it able to push it away. Then she becomes the killer of her own child.]

This admonition of a male preaching voice addressing female members of an audience can be taken as a case in point for the meeting of spiritual knowledge with the practical concerns of mothers lying in.[32] Although a direct source for this homily has not been discovered (yet), its background is probably the famous episode in 1 Kings 3:17–28, the judgment of King Solomon settling a quarrel of two women, one of whom had smothered a child in her sleep. The dangers of inappropriate breastfeeding or other accidental smothering during co-sleeping that the text discusses

31 *DOE*, s.v. *betweox*, sense A.14 "glossing *iuxta*."

32 An exception may have been the Anglo-Saxon élite during the Christian period, which used wet nurses (see Crawford, *Childhood in Anglo-Saxon England*, 70).

are, however, as current today as they were then.[33] Anglo-Saxon penitentials prescribe three years of fasting for the confessing parent, the intensity of it depending on whether the mother or father had been drunk during the deed.[34]

By calling careless mothers "bana" (killer), a word that also glosses Latin *homicida* (murderer) in Anglo-Saxon manuscripts, the homily implicitly adds them to the group of "bearnmyrðan"(child-murderers), a term that may be gender neutral, but repeatedly occurs in doublets with female agents such as "wiccan" (witches) or "myltestran" (prostitutes) in Wulfstan's lists of evildoers.[35] Such collocations in his catalogues could be accidental, or typically inspired by sound and style rather than contents, but it is likely in this case that they hint at extant practices of abortion and abandonment of illegitimate and therefore unwanted children by helpless mothers.[36] The practice was considered a serious crime by the church, prompting preachers to remind their congregations of the raising of the dead on Judgment Day, when, as Napier homily XXIX warns, "þær swutelað ælc cild, hwa hit formyrðrode" (each child will reveal who murdered it).[37] Bazire-Cross homily 4 makes no mistake about a special infernal place of punishment prepared for child-murderesses and adulteresses, filled with hellhounds ("mid hellehundum afylled").[38] More explicit about extant practices of infanticide is Ælfric in his homily *De auguriis,* where he states with abhorrence:

> Sume hi acwellað heora cild ær ðam þe hi acennede beon, oððe æfter acennednysse þæt hi cuðe ne beon, ne heora manfulla forligr ameldod ne

33 See the comment on recent debates in Scott D. Krugman, "Parent-Infant Bedsharing Is Not Recommended," 386–7.

34 Roger Fowler, "A Late Old English Handbook for the Use of a Confessor," 25; Josef Raith, ed., *Die altenglische Version des Halitgar'schen Bussbuches*, 69–70, art. 2.

35 Dorothy Bethurum, ed., *The Homilies of Wulfstan*, XIII, line 95 and XX (EI), line 162.

36 On reasons for and practices of abandonment see Crawford, *Childhood in Anglo-Saxon England*, 63–7, and John Boswell, *The Kindness of Strangers: The Abandonment of Children in Western Europe from Late Antiquity to the Renaissance*, 208–16. A notable hagiographical example is the Old English *Life of St. Margaret* in CCCC, MS 303, which implies that the saint is cast out as an infant because she is a girl. The act itself is not criticised in the text. See Mary Clayton and Hugh Magennis, eds. and trans., *The Old English Lives of St Margaret*, 153 and 173n.5.

37 Napier XXIX, 137:27–8.

38 Joyce Bazire and James E. Cross, eds., *Eleven Old English Rogationtide Homilies*, no. 4, lines 61–4.

wurðe; ac heora yfel is egeslic, and endeleaslic morð. Þær losað þæt cild laðlice hæðen, and seo arleasa modor, butan heo hit æfre gebete.[39]

[Some (women) kill their children before they are born, or after birth, so that they may not be discovered, nor their wicked adultery be betrayed; but their wickedness is awful, and everlasting their perdition. Then the child perishes, a loathsome heathen, and the wicked mother, unless she ever do penance for it.]

In order to force women to repent, Ælfric threatens those who refuse motherhood with excommunication, a punishment even stronger than the exile resulting from accidental infanticide that we have discussed above. In both cases, however, concealing the sin is identified as a key issue, while the varying punishments suggest a distinction between accidental and intentional infanticide whenever parents confessed. How common either form of infanticide was and how often parents openly admitted to the (accidental) murder of their children is still a matter of controversy. John Boswell touches on the question of child abandonment (and subsequent death) explaining that, despite opposing accounts in Tacitus's *Germania* and later Christian writings, the custom may have been acceptable among the Germanic tribes, resisting the vigorous condemnation by the Christian missionaries.[40] Remarkably, Boniface's attack on the practice of infanticide in a letter to Æthelbald of Mercia, written ca. AD 747, is directed at the secular as well as the monastic milieu:

And it should be noted that another terrible wrong is implicit in that one [fornication], namely, homicide. For when these harlots, whether in the world or in convents, bear in sinfulness their ill-conceived offspring, they also for the most part kill them, not filling the churches of Christ with adopted children, but rather filling tombs with their bodies and hell with their pitiful souls.[41]

39 Walter W. Skeat, ed. and trans., *Ælfric's Lives of Saints*, no. XVII, 1:364–82, lines 151–6.

40 Boswell, *The Kindness of Strangers*, 209–14. See also Crawford, *Childhood in Anglo-Saxon England*, 63–4.

41 Boswell, *The Kindness of Strangers*, p. 210. For an edition of the letter see Arthur W. Haddan and William Stubbs, eds., *Councils and Ecclesiastical Documents Relating to Great Britain and Ireland*, 3:354: "Et notandum, quod in illo scelere aliud inmane flagitium subterlatet, id est homicidium. Quia, dum illæ meretrices, sive monasteriales sive sæculares, male conceptas soboles in peccatis genuerint, et sepe maxima ex parte occidunt non inplentes Christi ecclesias filiis adoptivis, sed tumulos corporibus et inferos miseris animabus satiantes."

This criticism, which might even include nuns themselves and not just women taking shelter among them, could indeed suggest the survival of a persistent practice in Anglo-Saxon England, even after the widespread conversion to Christianity. Yet even within Christian parameters the issue of child abandonment brings to the fore a fundamental conflict inherent in this new belief: an illegitimate child would contradict the Christian ideal of female chastity and marital fidelity, and it could be exactly the fear of condemnation by the church, apart from the probable loss of social and familial protection, that would have caused women to abandon their children rather than rearing them into a new generation of believers. Whether it was established pagan custom, shame of illicit unions, patriarchal bias against female offspring, or postpartum depression that caused a continuation of infanticide practices in Anglo-Saxon England, in any case the women's fear of punishment and exclusion from society crystallises as a major problem in these examples.[42] This fear seems to have dominated women's behaviour, and it testifies to a lack of female power within late Anglo-Saxon society as much as to a lack of trust this society had in them.

Drawing Children through the Earth

Among his various condemnations of contemporary pagan superstitions and practices, Ælfric criticises a mysterious ritual in his homily *De auguriis*, namely, the custom of mothers drawing their children through the earth at crossroads:

> Eac sume gewitlease wif farað to wega gelætum and teoð heora cild þurh ða eorðan, and swa deofle betæcað hi sylfe and heora bearn.[43]
>
> [Likewise some unscrupulous women go to crossroads and draw their children through the earth, and thus commit themselves and their children to the devil.]

The *Fontes Anglo-Saxonici Database* notes that this reference, together with its analogue in the penitential of Pseudo-Ecgbert, may be "perhaps

42 The myth underlying the enigmatic poem *Wulf and Eadwacer* could possibly preserve a fitting literary response to this sentiment. See *The Exeter Book*, ASPR 3:179–80.

43 Skeat, *Ælfric's Lives of Saints*, no.XVII, lines 148–50. Also cf. Raith, *Die altenglische Version des Halitgar'schen Bussbuches*, 4.16.

the only evidence of current practices" of this kind.[44] There are, however, a number of further mentions of this custom to be found in Old English texts,[45] one other instance being Assmann homily XI:

> And næfre nan man ne geþristlæce ænigne deofles bigencg to donne, ne on wiglunge, ne on wiccedome, ne on ænegum idelum anginne. And þæt nan man ne sece to nanre wellan, ne to nanum stane, ne to nanum treowe, ne nan man his cild þurh þa eorðan ne teo, forðam se ðe þæt deð, he betæcð þæt cild eallum deoflum and seo moder forð mid.[46]
>
> [And let no one dare to perform any devil-worship, neither by sorcery, nor witchcraft, nor by any idle undertaking. And let no one seek out any spring-well, nor any stone, nor any tree, nor anyone drag his child through the earth, because whoever does that commits to all the devils, and the mother as well.]

The beginning of this passage, as well as the homily at large, shows textual correspondence with a Latin homily titled *Item alia in die initii* contained in Cambridge, Pembroke College Library, MS 25.[47] Nevertheless, in this only complete surviving Anglo-Saxon copy of the Latin Homiliary of Saint-Père de Chartres specific details on pagan animistic worship are missing.[48] The evidence supports Malcolm Godden's conjecture that these Old

---

44 Malcolm Godden, "The Sources of Ælfric Lives 17 (On Auguries) (Cameron C.B.1.3.18)," *Fontes Anglo-Saxonici: World Wide Web Register*, http://fontes.english.ox.ac.uk/, accessed July 2015.

45 Apart from further instances mentioned below there is for example the unedited piece Oxford, Bodleian Library, MS Hatton 115, fol. 65; Neil R. Ker, *A Catalogue of Manuscripts Containing Anglo-Saxon*, no. 332, art. 18; *DOE* (Short Title: HomM 2): "Þa wifmen þe berað hyra cild to wegelætum and teoð þurh þa eorþan ne begytað hi næfre godes miltsa butan hi geswicon and hit æfre beton forþon witodlice hi ofriað hi sylfe deoflon and hyra bearn þe þis doð"; *DOE* transcript; see also Crawford, *Childhood in Anglo-Saxon England*, 89–90 and 182nn.55–9.

46 Bruno Assmann, ed., *Angelsächsische Homilien und Heiligenleben*, no. XI, 143, lines 123–7. The homily survives in two MSS.

47 On the parallels see James E. Cross, *Cambridge Pembroke College MS 25: A Carolingian Sermonary used by Anglo-Saxon Preachers*, 209–18.

48 This manuscript may represent a reimported version of the homiliary, carried to Bury St Edmunds (Rebecca Rushforth, "Cambridge, Pembroke College 25: The Manuscript and its Historical Context," 19, http://www.stoa.org/Pembroke25/Website-tv/essays/Rushforth.pdf), but there is English manuscript evidence of around AD 1000 for this text in Canterbury, Cathedral Library and Archives, MS Add. 127/12. See Helmut Gneuss, *Handlist of Anglo-Saxon Manuscripts*, no. 210, dated s. xi$^{in.}$. This fragment

English vernacular texts, perhaps mutually serving each other as sources, are "remarking on a contemporary practice," while we may add, on account of this self-contained variant in comparison with the Latin source, that this practice was possibly a more specifically English problem around the turn of the first millennium.[49]

Despite the frequency of reference to the earth ritual, both the origins and full significance of the custom remain difficult to determine. Ælfric, in *De auguriis*, refers to mothers drawing children through the earth right before he turns to the topic of infanticide, as discussed above. At first sight, this seems to suggest a connection with child-murder, a pagan burial rite, or a practice succeeding abortion. However, it is more likely that Ælfric is simply enumerating various deeds of new mothers here, moving from pagan worship to infanticide, using such juxtaposition for rhetorical effect in order to demonise the custom. Sally Crawford states that the practice "may be more of an initiation or dedication ceremony," and this can be further supported by the adjacent references to the animistic worship of spring-wells, trees, and stones in all of the surviving texts.[50] While infanticide is by no means always part of the agenda, in *De auguriis*, as much as in all the other accounts, elements of natural religion are mentioned each time in the immediate context of the earth ritual.

More tellingly even, in Wulfstan's *Canons of Edgar*, the condemnation of drawing children through the earth succeeds the prescription of urgent baptism after birth:

> 15. And riht is þæt preosta gehwylc fulluhtes and scriftes tyðige sona swa man gyrne, and æghwær on his scriftscyre beode þæt ælc cild sy gefullod binnon vii nihtum and þæt ænig man to lange unbiscopad ne wyrðe.
> 16. And riht is þæt preosta gehwylc cristendom geornlice lære and ælcne hæþendom mid ealle adwæsce, and forbeode wyllweorðunga, and licwigelunga, and hwata, and galdra, and treowwurðunga, and stanwurðunga, and

---

is, however, dated to s. x$^{3/3}$ by Richard Gameson, *The Earliest Books of Canterbury Cathedral: Manuscripts and Fragments to c. 1200*, 79–83. The Pembroke homily simply reads at this point: "Nec ullam diabolicam culturam facere presumatis; sed quando ad aecclesiam conueniatis. cum timore et silentio et summa reuerentia. intrate in domum dei." (Nor should you presume to perform any diabolical worship practice, but instead if you gather in the church, quiet, shy, and in awe, you are entering the house of God; Cross, *Pembroke College*, 214, lines 74–5; my translation).

49 Godden, "The Sources of Ælfric Lives 17 (On Auguries)."

50 Crawford, *Childhood in Anglo-Saxon England*, 90.

ðone deofles cræft þe man dryhð þær man þa cild þurh þa eorðan tihð, and ða gemearr þe man drihð on geares niht on mislicum wigelungum and on friðsplottum and on ellenum, and on manegum mislicum gedwimerum þe men on dreogað fela þæs þe hi ne sceoldan.[51]

[15. And it is right that each priest should grant baptism and confession as soon as one desires, and command everywhere in his parish that each child be baptised within seven days and that no man remain unconfirmed too long. 16. And it is right that each priest teach the Christian faith eagerly and extinguish all heathendom with all means, and forbid well-worship, and necromancy, auguries and divinations, and tree-worship and stone-worship, and the devil's craft that one performs where people draw children through the earth, and the fraud that people perform on New Year's Eve with various auguries and in sanctuaries and on elder-trees, and with many apparitions on which people perform many things that they should not.]

References to infanticide are missing from the *Canons*; instead, the next paragraph admonishes parents to teach their child the Creed and Pater Noster.[52] This context in particular may hold a further clue for a pagan initiation rite concurring with baptism, possibly one of comparable significance in strengthening, healing, and protecting infants at an early age.

The existence of a strong pagan belief in the healing powers of nature further surfaces in Ælfric's criticism of women who "nellað understandan hu stuntlice hi doð, oððe hu se deada stan oððe þæt dumbe treow him mæge gehelpan, oððe hæle forgifan" (do not want to understand how foolishly they act, nor how the dead stone nor the mute tree may ever help or heal them).[53] His tone of disappointment in this statement suggests a practice deeply rooted in Anglo-Saxon cultural memory that could not so easily be extinguished.[54] Ælfric's disapproval of pagan worship and the

51 Roger Fowler, ed., *Wulfstan's Canons of Edgar*, 5.

52 Ibid., 6.

53 Skeat, *Ælfric's Lives of Saints*, no. XVII, lines 132–4.

54 Similar references to animistic worship survive in later medieval hagiographic literature, such as Stephen of Burbon's *De superstiсione*, in which he addresses the cult of St Guinefort, the dog-saint. The saint is invoked to justify the healing of children in sacred groves by means of sacred trees (Jean-Claude Schmitt, *The Holy Greyhound: Guinefort, Healer of Children since the Thirteenth Century*, 71–2). See further Patricia Healy Wasyliw, *Martyrdom, Murder, and Magic: Child Saints and Their Cults in Medieval Europe*, 87.

evident relapses into such practices among the Anglo-Saxons were also aired by him in his homily *De falsis diis*, a text later revised by Wulfstan and originally drawn from Martin of Braga's tract *De correctione rusticorum*.[55] Both Ælfric and Wulfstan identify crossroads as important places of pagan worship where offerings and divinations were made because Germanic people would assume the presence of gods there (in this case Thor).[56] Supernatural agents, such as gods or demons, were held responsible for sicknesses and could apparently be driven out most effectively in such locations.

The other key element of the ritual, the earth contact of newborn children, was studied by Albrecht Dieterich as early as in 1905. He traced the widespread cult of the mother-earth across Europe and beyond,[57] finding its best known textual materialisation from Anglo-Saxon England to survive in the Old English *Æcerbot*-charm's powerful formulas "Erce, erce, erce, eorðan modor" and "Hal wes þu, folde, fira modor!" (Hail, earth, mother of men!).[58] Among the possible functions of the earth ritual across the globe, Dieterich discusses the strengthening of the newborn against sickness and the reconfirmation of the mother's fertility, suggesting also a connection with some related customs of the father subsequently picking up the child from the soil. According to Dieterich, the different roles of mother (laying down the child) and father (picking up) in this ritual originally symbolised the relation between earth and heaven, matter and spirit, with the father's act later becoming a binding symbol of the acceptance of the infant.[59] Dieterich's evidence comes from ancient Greece, medieval Scandinavia, and various parts of medieval and Renaissance Germany, but as rich and varied as it is, its patchiness does not allow for more substantial conclusions on the precise origins and functions of the Anglo-Saxon custom.[60] The limited evidence from our texts renders it difficult to ascertain

55 Pope, *Homilies of Ælfric*, no. XXI, 667–724, lines 136–8, and Napier XVIII, 107:2–6.

56 Hanns Bächtold-Stäubli, Eduard Hoffmann-Krayer et al., eds., *Handwörterbuch des deutschen Aberglaubens*, s.v. *Kreuzweg*, 5:516. Burchard of Worms expresses a contemporary criticism of pagan rituals celebrated at crossroads in his *Decreta*; see Burchard of Worms, *Opera omnia*, PL 150:960–1.

57 Albrecht Dieterich, *Mutter Erde: Ein Versuch über Volksreligion*, 6–19.

58 *The Anglo-Saxon Minor Poems*, ASPR 6, 117–18, lines 51 and 69. The definition and translation of *erce* remains controversial (see ibid., 208).

59 Dieterich, *Mutter Erde*, 8–9.

60 Richard North is equally neutral on the origins of Anglo-Saxon earth worship, but notes some intriguing connections between *Æcerbot* and the Old Norse *Skírnismál*; see Richard North, *Heathen Gods in Old English Literature*, 246–55.

which exact hopes Anglo-Saxon women pinned on this practice or to what extent the custom was potentially connected or mixed up with child abandonment in the case of illegitimate birth. Even so, the tenacity of this ritual of possible remedy and protection, evident in multiple textual manifestations, may still grant an insight into the cultural reality of its time. It seems to reflect pure maternal care, which would even transgress the boundaries of Christian doctrine in order to protect an infant from any sickness or harm. This transgression may have been favoured especially by those parents who (mis)understood baptism as a death sacrament that primarily assured the peaceful rest of their children having died prematurely.[61]

Disobedience

Baptism required that godparents would confess the Christian belief instead of the infant too young to speak for itself ("Þeah þæt cild to þam iung sy, þæt hit sprecan ne mæge").[62] They were asked, in accordance with their name, to raise their charges as children of God ("þonne beoð hi rihtlice, swa swa hi genamode beoð, godfæderas, gif hi gode heora godbearn gestrynað").[63] As a first step, this included the teaching of the Pater Noster and the Creed, but must surely have extended to the Ten Commandments, as is suggested by Ælfric's admonition in his third pastoral letter to Wulfstan. In this text, Ælfric supplements the Fourth Commandment, "Arwyrða þinne fæder and eac þinre meder" (Honour your father and your mother also), with the warning "Se ðe wyrgeð fæder oððe modor, se is deaðes scyldig" (He who curses father or mother is guilty of causing death).[64] For Ælfric this commandment further had to be understood in a spiritual sense as well, extending to the obedience to God the Father and the church as spiritual mother.[65] Respect for both types of parents then becomes central in an

61 On this problem see Crawford, "Children, Death, and the Afterlife," 353.

62 Napier LVIII, 301:10–11.

63 Napier LVIII, 301:3–5.

64 Fehr, *Hirtenbriefe*, no. 129, 196–7.

65 Ibid., no. 130, 198–9: "Æfter gastlicum andgite God is ure fæder and his halige gelaðuncg, þæt is geleaffull folc, ure gastlice modor, on ðære we beoð accennede on þam haligan fulluhte, Gode to bearnum, and we forþig sceolan God, urne fæder, and his gastlice bride, þa haligan cyrican, simble wurðian." (After the spiritual sense God is our father and his holy congregation, that is the faithful people, our spiritual mother in which we are born in the holy baptism, as children of God. And therefore we must always worship God our Father and his spiritual bride, the Holy Church.)

example about a cursing child that Ælfric employs in his sermon on the Greater Litany in the second part of his *Catholic Homilies*:

> Eft is awriten on oðre stowe. Arwurða ðinne fæder. and eac ðine moder. and se ðe fæder oððe modor. manlice wyrigð. he sceal deaðe sweltan. … Be sumum cilde we rædað þe wæs receleaslice afedd; Hit wolde wyrian. wælhreawlice drihten. and se fæder ne rohte. his receleasnysse; Þa æt nextan comon cwelmbære deoflu. swutellice gesewene. on sweartum hiwe. into ðam cilde. and hit sona hrymde; Fæder min. fæder min. me nimað þas deoflu. and behydde his heafod. on his fæder bosme. and wyrigde drihten. and swa gewat sona. mid þam sweartum deoflum. forscyldgod to helle; Ða cild ðe beoð syferlice afedde. and wið unðeawum eallunge gestyrede. hi geðeoð gode.[66]

> [Elsewhere it was written: "Honour your father and your mother also. And he who curses father or mother in an evil way must suffer death …" We read about a child that was carelessly reared. It would cruelly curse the Lord and the father cared not for its recklessness. Then entered deadly demons, clearly visible and of black complexion, into the child and it soon cried: "My father, my father, these devils are grabbing me," and hid its head in the bosom of its father, and cursed the Lord, and so instantly departed with these black devils, condemned to hell. Those children who are prudently reared and thoroughly guided against vices, thrive to the good.]

Ælfric is drawing on Book 4, chapter 19 of the Old English translation of Gregory's *Dialogi* for this example.[67] Its popularity among eleventh- and twelfth-century preachers is evident not only in the reuse of Ælfric's version of it in the modified context of Bazire-Cross homily 7,[68] but also from Worcester preacher Coleman's selective bookmarking of the story in an Old English version of Gregory's work.[69] Being one of only few instances in Anglo-Saxon homiletic literature in which a child is speaking directly, its imploring *geminatio* "Min fæder, min fæder…" (no less than Goethe's "Mein Vater, mein Vater…" in *Erlkönig*) becomes a particularly

66 Malcolm Godden, ed., *Ælfric's Catholic Homilies*, no. XIX, 186, lines 204–10.

67 Hans Hecht, ed., *Bischofs Waerferth von Worcester Übersetzung der Dialoge Gregors des Grossen*, 288–90. Noted also by James E. Cross, "Source and Analysis of Some Ælfrician Passages, 447. See also Bazire and Cross, *Rogationtide Homilies*, 92.

68 Bazire and Cross, *Rogationtide Homilies*, no. 7, 95–9, lines 175–83.

69 See London, British Library, MS Cotton Otho C.i, part 2, fol. 113v/29 and further David F. Johnson and Winfried Rudolf, "More Notes by Coleman," 120.

touching appeal to Anglo-Saxon parents, urging them to mind a stricter education to counter the recalcitrance of children. The example turns blasphemy – spiritual violence with words – into the equivalent of a reckless physical deed that can cause the ruin of young people and even lead to their death. For Gregory, this example served to illustrate that the Heavenly Jerusalem was not primarily inhabited by children, at least not by those who were able to speak ("nis hit na to gelyfanne, þæt ealle þa geongan men, þe sprecan magon, moton gan to ðam heofonlican ricum" [It should not be believed that all the youths who can speak may be allowed into the heavenly kingdom]).[70] Yet the homilies deliberately shift the Gregorian focus, directing it to the responsibility of parents, thus disapproving of the too indulgent education that brought about the child's weakmindedness and promoting vigorous correction ("swiðlicere steorre") of children as a precondition of good behaviour ("godum ðeawum") and wisdom.[71] Through the child's blasphemy and subsequent punishment the story also rehearses the Augustinian concept of equivalence between sins in word and in deed, thus focusing on language as the first immediate reflection of thought and desire that needs to be formed and fostered under strict moral guidance.[72] This idea strongly corresponds with Ælfric's incessant arguing for the diligent training of the intellectual faculties vested by God in every human being.[73] Children, although as yet lacking the physical power to perform a murderous deed, should abstain from its spiritual equivalent – blasphemous language.

At the surface, this example appears to blame childish disobedience, but its ultimate criticism of overly lenient parents exonerates children to a certain extent and portrays their innocent minds as fertile fields that adults have the responsibility of cultivating with care and discipline. In an allegorical sense, the story admonishes every Christian, as a spiritual child of God, to obey the teachings of the church, no matter how demanding they may be. However, Ælfric's ideal of monastic education according to his own rigorous standards of Latinity and spiritual depth remained out of reach for most Anglo-Saxon children. It is no surprise then that the vernacular homilies addressed to lay audiences, for lack of pedagogical alternatives, have little more to offer than prescriptions of harsh physical

70 Hecht, *Dialoge*, p. 288, lines 23–5.

71 Godden, *Catholic Homilies. Second Series*, no. XIX, 186, lines 195–6.

72 Augustine, *Contra Faustum Manichaeum*, PL 42:417–18.

73 See for example Pope, *Homilies of Ælfric*, no. XVI, 2:547–59, lines 49–52.

chastisement of children along the lines of the well-known Old Testament rhetoric: "Styr ðinum cilde. and sleh hit mid gyrde. and ðu swa alyst. his sawle fram deaðe; Se ðe sparað his gyrde. he hatað his cild" (Correct your child and strike it with the rod and you so shall redeem its soul from death. He who spares the rod, hates his child).[74] The homiletic episode of the spoilt child thus involuntarily reveals a fundamental contradiction within these medieval ideals of Christianity: the child, though stained by original sin, is perceived as innocent at a young age, with its innocence often being proclaimed as a spiritual ideal to adults. Yet the survival of a child, while growing up, depends on social interaction, whose success depends on pious language, adequate behaviour, and experience in general. Education is therefore identified as essential to the moral stability of Christians, not least since Augustine's influential *Confessiones*, a work that evidently influenced the œuvre of notable Anglo-Saxon teachers such as Alcuin, Bede, and Byrhtferth.[75] The Anglo-Saxon church's very restricted admission to higher education, however, meant that many children, no less than the majority of adults, remained in a state of intellectual infancy. Social peace therefore remained dependent on the success of homiletic instruction of the laity, while this instruction offered parents only little support other than promoting the didactics of corporeal punishment.

Conclusion

Old English homilies show a sporadic concern for the survival and well-being of Anglo-Saxon children and command their strict Christian education. In doing so they seek to stabilise late Anglo-Saxon society politically and ideologically. Children also serve as a rhetorical device to manipulate

---

74 Godden, *Catholic Homilies. Second Series*, 186, lines 192–4. See also Prov. 13:24.

75 See Augustine, *Confessiones*, PL 32:670. Teresa Webber doubts that Augustine's work exerted significant influence on medieval thought prior to its recovery by Petrarch; see her "The Diffusion of Augustine's Confessions in England during the Eleventh and Twelfth Centuries." Yet her argument with regard to Anglo-Saxon England is primarily based on the surviving manuscript evidence of the work itself, disregarding the ample quotations by earlier Anglo-Saxon authors. There are a number of Latin works that can be traced in the works of Anglo-Saxon authors, although no direct manuscript copy may survive today. See for example the *Libri miraculorum* by Gregory of Tours (Winfried Rudolf, "The Source and Textual Identity of 'Homily' Napier XXXI – Ælfric and the *Munuccild* of Saint-Maurice d'Agaune," 607–22). See also the introduction to this volume.

the audiences of preaching addresses to improve childcare and education, as well as their own moral behaviour. Anglo-Saxon homilists are willing to threaten parents by predicting harm or an unfortunate fate to them and their (future) children, urging them to yearn for the sacraments of baptism and repentance. This rhetorical strategy would hardly have been successful had families chiefly been interested in practical needs and economic necessity, as proposed by Ariès. Rather, it seems, these pastoral texts propose a middle ground of authoritative education by promising punishment both to those who spoil and those who mistreat their offspring. Ariès's idea of emotional detachment[76] may, at first glance, find some support in the references made to (careless) infanticide and child abandonment, but it remains difficult to ascertain how frequently such cases ultimately occurred (in fact, they still occur in purportedly child-loving Western societies today). Besides, the warning of accidental infanticide through inappropriate breastfeeding seeks to correct a problem caused by ignorance, while the fact itself is proof of a desired and close physical contact between mother and child. The customary preference for wealthy godparents indicates Anglo-Saxon parents' economic awareness, yet this behaviour – although risky for the spiritual welfare of the newborn in the next world – equally expresses the parental desire of creating a long-term benefit for the child born into a world of evidently sharp social differences. A similar health risk might have been involved in the pagan initiation rite of drawing children through the earth, which may possibly be a prime example of how a harsh ritual could combine with a firm belief in its ultimate benefit for the child.

In view of this evidence it seems too simple to declare sentiments of parental love to be suppressed by an emotional detachment caused by economic necessity, as held by Ariès.[77] Old English homilies ultimately seem to refute this assertion: a) because they confirm how a number of historical sources, such as many of those consulted by Ariès, make the problems rather than the joys of childhood the subject of their discussion; and b) because between the lines the homiletic sources present us with caring, yet largely uneducated, parents, who may even have distrusted the church

76 This detachment ultimately remains a vague and relative concept in Ariès's theory; what is clear, though, is its undeniable dependence on some modern twentieth-century notion of *attachment*.

77 Ariès, *Centuries of Childhood*, 162. See also John Clarke, "The Origins of Childhood: In the Beginning ...," 6.

authorities whenever these authorities tried to interfere with long-established customs of childcare. Instead, summarising the evidence discussed here, it seems that fear of social ostracism, more than economic hardship, forced especially Anglo-Saxon women into acting harshly or even cruelly towards their children in order to protect their personal honour and status. This does not automatically entail, nor does it prove, a lack of emotional bonding; rather, such behaviour could have its cause in Anglo-Saxon parents' despair about their hopeless situation in view of the social, political, and ecclesiastical powers.

Ariès's claim is still useful in reminding us of potential distortions that the modern Western concept of the child-centred family can impose on our perception of the emotional spectrum expressed in Anglo-Saxon sources, yet we should also admit that parent-child relations, at any historical period, have always allowed for expressions of tough love.[78] In my view, many of the sentiments we find expressed in Anglo-Saxon homilies can be interpreted in this sense. This form of love can combine expressions of emotional care with a severe treatment of children in certain situations, both of which parents may have considered as beneficial for the development of preferred character traits in children that would potentially guarantee their survival and success in life. Old English homilies also indicate that parents would go to extremes whenever the welfare of their offspring was in jeopardy and would do so in spite of constraints of religious doctrine and at the earliest stages of their children's lives. This fact, perhaps more than anything, shows the parental instincts to be intact, while, at the same time, it may hint at persistent superstitions surrounding the sacrament of baptism. The Anglo-Saxon church, supporting, and ultimately profiting from, the hegemony of the aristocracy, had no obvious interest in a profound increase of the educational opportunities of children, nor a unified agenda for improving the social conditions for this future workforce. Its only achievement can be seen in a spiritual redefinition of the value of a child's life, whose welfare is declared to be dependent on the grace of God and the piety and repentance of its parents, while the education of these parents had to remain limited and under pastoral control.

78 The term "tough love" was first used in 1968 (see William Millekin and Char Meredith, *Tough Love*) and expresses a sentiment about child-rearing, almost contemporary to Ariès's sentiment of *detachment*.

4 Tender Beginnings in the Exeter Book *Riddles*

SHU-HAN LUO

It was hard being a child in Anglo-Saxon England, or so it is said. Poverty and the harshness of life posed practical constraints on the attention of parents. For those fortunate enough to survive the fragile early years, severe disciplining still attended both domestic and formal education. As the preamble to adulthood, childhood was often defined in its shadow – vulnerable, irrational, and incomplete. Well before the age of child labour laws, play blended into industry from a young age.[1] This is not to say that children were not loved: they were cared for by their parents, protected by law, and recognised for qualities that grown-ups sometimes admired.[2] Nevertheless, "The ultimate goal of childhood," note centuries of authorities, "was to grow to a *better* state," to put away childish things and become "a fully functional adult."[3] Our picture of childhood in the Anglo-Saxon period remains largely Dickensian: a stage of life not particularly

1 On infant mortality and accounts of child slavery in Anglo-Saxon England, see Sally Crawford, *Childhood in Anglo-Saxon England*, 75–7, 173–4.

2 For example, Asser wrote about the child's aptitude for learning in his *Life of Alfred*, while Bede, echoing St Columban, wrote that the child does not persist in anger, does not bear a grudge, does not delight in the sight of a beautiful woman, does not say one thing and intend another ("non perseverat in iracundia, non laesus meminit, non videns pulchram mulierem delectatur, non aliud cogitat, aliud loquitur"). For Asser, see William H. Stevenson, ed., *Asser's Life of King Alfred*, 21; Bede, *In Marci evangelium expositio*, PL 92:230–1. See also Mathew Kuefler, "'A Wryed Existence': Attitudes towards Children in Anglo-Saxon England," 823–43.

3 Crawford, *Childhood in Anglo-Saxon England*, 174. Emphasis mine. Augustine would have agreed, having famously declared, "Quis autem non exhorreat et mori eligat, si ei proponatur aut mors perpetienda aut rursus infantia?" (Who would not shiver with dread and choose to die, if he were offered the choice of death or a second infancy?).

enjoyable and never sentimentalised. And yet, in the Exeter Book *Riddles*, we encounter moments where poets speak fondly about the early stages of life, and describe it lovingly and nostalgically as a better, yearned-for past. These riddles seem to see childhood differently, through rose-coloured glasses at once imaginative and perceptive.

The broader dialogue that this study engages began with Philippe Ariès's controversial statement in 1960, arguing that "in medieval society the idea of childhood did not exist" – childhood "passed quickly and ... was just as quickly forgotten."[4] In the years since, scholars have responded with new evidence and sensitivity towards the treatment of children across the medieval period, looking to works of art, wills, law codes, and leechbooks, among other sources.[5] It is no longer tenable to assert that the Anglo-Saxons lacked a sense of childhood,[6] although the precise nature of that sense remains elusive and challenging to interpret. A particular difficulty of the subject lies in its limited and usually mediated evidence, for children leave few traces of their own in written and archaeological records.[7]

Augustine, *City of God*, ed. and trans. Green, XXI.xiv. James A. Schultz similarly reports views of children as "deficient" in Middle High German literature – "that which is worth striving for or writing about is adulthood." *The Knowledge of Childhood in the German Middle Ages, 1100–1350*, 246–51.

4 Philippe Ariès, *L'enfant et la vie familiale sous l'Ancien Régime*; Robert Baldick, trans., *Centuries of Childhood*, 128 and 134. Subsequent citations of Ariès are from Baldick's text.

5 Ilene Forsyth, for example, offered an early corrective to the prevalent opinion that medieval artists lacked both accuracy and interest in portraying children, while Mary Martin McLaughlin and Barbara Hanawalt demonstrated how laconic sources can nevertheless reveal important themes and concerns of childhood. See Forsyth, "Children in Early Medieval Art: Ninth through Twelfth Centuries," 31–70; McLaughlin, "Survivors and Surrogates: Children and Parents from the Ninth to Thirteenth Centuries," 101–81; and Hanawalt, *The Ties That Bound*, 171–204. Shulamith Shahar's *Childhood in the Middle Ages* considers a wide array of documentary sources from medieval Europe, while Sally Crawford's seminal studies focus on Anglo-Saxon children, setting a broad range of textual sources in dialogue with archaeological evidence. See Crawford, *Childhood in Anglo-Saxon England*; and "When Do Anglo-Saxon Children Count?," 17–24.

6 For a catalogue of vocabulary items relating to childhood – including *cildhad* (childhood) and *childsung* (childishness) – see Crawford, *Childhood in Anglo-Saxon England*, 44–6.

7 Crawford writes of Anglo-Saxon England, "children have a marginal place in the documentary sources ... largely because the literature, like the furnished burial ritual, was designed by adults for adult audiences." Crawford, *Childhood in Anglo-Saxon England*, 46. Nicholas Orme similarly reports the scant focus on childhood in (auto-) biographies until the mid-sixteenth century in *Medieval Children*, 340–1.

Among learned writers attitudes were also complex and ambivalent: the child embodied the Christian ideal of spiritual purity, but children's propensity for mischief was deemed evidence of moral weakness and sin.[8] Moreover, while writings about unbaptised infants and child saints, Latin-learning schoolboys and a young verse-loving king attest to a range of social preoccupations about childhood, we hear little about what childhood felt like in its everyday proceedings, or looked like in the mind's eye after growing up. Attempting to recover affect from the writings that survive, we lament that our sources "do not give much indication that they treated their children very well."[9] The Anglo-Saxon childhood, as lived experience and personal memory, appears to us marginalised, and hardly the stuff of dreams.

Yet if childhood were indeed marginal in life and in thought, then what could have moved riddle-poets to paint these scenes in gentle brush-strokes, frequently shaping them in the immediate personal voice, rather than in the third-person sketched at arm's length?[10] Old English riddles

8 The influence of Christian thought on Anglo-Saxon attitudes towards children is as central as it is complex. For an overview, see Janet Nelson, "Parents, Children, and the Church in the Earlier Middle Ages," 81–114; Shahar, *Childhood in the Middle Ages*, 16–20; and Kuefler, "'A Wryed Existence,'" 824. Further discussion of the child in scripture may be found in Judith M. Gundry-Volf, "The Least and the Greatest: Children in the New Testament," 29–60. For Anglo-Saxon accounts of children's mischief, see, for example, Bede on the child Cuthbert, and Guthlac's biographer Felix describing what the precocious young Guthlac distinctly was not. Bertram Colgrave, ed., *Two Lives of Saint Cuthbert*, 154–9; Colgrave, ed., *Felix's Life of Saint Guthlac*, 79. See also the discussion of Guthlac's *vita* by Joyce Hill in this volume.

9 Kuefler, "'Wryed Existence,'" 823.

10 Though both first- and third-person riddles are common in the Exeter collection, the majority of riddles that hark back to a time of growing up are narrated in the first person, such as *Riddles* 9 ("cuckoo"), 10 ("barnacle goose"), 72 ("bull calf"), 73 ("spear"), and 88 ("inkhorn"). It is also those narrated in the first-person voice that carry the most detail and emotion about children and childhood, including not only the cuckoo, bull calf, and inkhorn, but also the parental laments of the porcupine (*Riddle* 15) and the spear (*Riddle* 20). *Riddles* 13 ("ten hatchlings") and 37 ("bellows"), described by a marvelling observer, as well as 53 ("battering ram"), stand as the third-person counterpoints.

have gained attention in recent years in the context of vernacular education and literature for children.[11] The stories that they tell, however, still hold a largely untapped dimension for exploring the Anglo-Saxon idea of childhood, for their verses are rich with creatures ever changing, growing up and growing old.

The notion of *childhood* in the riddles requires clarification. Indeed, the riddle-poets do not describe human children, and no *cild* – the direct ancestor of the modern word *child* – appears in the collection.[12] Their subjects instead are birds and beasts, books and keys, among other members of nature and the man-made world. Yet the language of families arises from the riddle-poets' categorising impulse, which understands formal similarities as kin and transformation as a kind of life.[13] Children and childhoods emerge when speakers talk about their offspring – their *bearn*, *eafora*, *sunu* and *dohtor* – and when they relate personal biographies that hark back to beginnings, to youth and growing up.[14] In this essay, my consideration of childhood encompasses all the early years of birth and growth in life's plot-lines from *augmentum* to *decrementum*. I do not press distinctions between infancy and later parts of childhood or adolescence, in part because absolute ages are seldom clear in the riddles, but also because these

11 Seth Lerer, *Children's Literature: A Reader's History from Aesop to Harry Potter*, 61–6; Lerer, *Literacy and Power in Anglo-Saxon Literature*, 97–125. Winfried Rudolf examines the riddles' richness as vernacular reading exercises in "Riddling and Reading: Iconicity and Logogriphs in Exeter Book *Riddles* 23 and 45," 499–525. On the relationship between the explicitly pedagogical Anglo-Latin riddle tradition and that of the vernacular, see Andy Orchard, "Enigma Variations: The Anglo-Saxon Riddle Tradition," 1:284–304; and Dieter Bitterli, *Say What I Am Called: The Old English Riddles of the Exeter Book and the Anglo-Latin Riddle Tradition*.

12 Elsewhere, the word *cild* refers mainly to human children and the Christ child. Writing in the fourteenth century, John Trevisa could say that "fisshe loveth here childerne," but in Old English, the word *cild* seems more to have distinguished the human from the animal kind, than to blend and blur them as riddle-poets are wont to do. See Michael C. Seymour et al., eds., *On the Properties of Things: John Trevisa's Translation of Bartholomaeus Anglicus De proprietatibus rerum*, 1:678. See also *DOE* s.v. *cild*, *MED* s.v. *child*, sense 8a, and *OED* s.v. *child*, sense II.9b. Cf. *DOE* s.v. *bearn*, sense IE: "the young of animals and birds."

13 The sense that the "universe is in a continual process of gestation, birth and growth" is one that the vernacular riddles share with the Anglo-Latin; see Michael Lapidge and James L. Rosier, trans., *Aldhelm: The Poetic Works*, 64–5.

14 These are the riddle-poets' primary vocabulary for children, and additionally the heroic variation "geoguþcnosl."

divisions are inherently blurred as riddle-poets actively trace the metamorphoses of their subjects.[15]

"Riddle-children" are the offspring of imagination, but imagination does not stand wholly apart from life. This study begins by tracking the ingredients and textures of the riddles' childhood moments – what emblems did the mind associate with childhood, what sentiments or worries? In the riddles' hallmark fascination with reproduction, the subject of part two, fantastical offspring show poets investing inanimate objects with life and life-giving powers, and additionally something like parental emotions. Finally, as a personal past seen through the prism of a later time, riddle-childhoods teach us something about growing up. They trace stories of utility emerging from passivity and dependence, often showing appreciation for how things become mature members of society, but not forgetting the sheltered tenderness traded in exchange. Though still but glimpses, they reveal reflections richer and softer than previously thought possible on the earliest stage of life, a stage as elusive in textual records as it is fleeting in reality.

Tender Beginnings

If a prairie can be made in "One clover, and a bee. / And reverie,"[16] what essential motifs can conjure the landscape of childhood? Some riddles portray their subjects in a snapshot of hearth and home, while others unfold little biographies that move from a past *then* to an ultimate *now*. In both, themes of growth and care are richest in the childhood scenes. The cuckoo, for example, has fond recollections of its foster-mother, described as one who provided it with covering, food, and protection:

Þa mec an ongon
welhold mege, wedum þeccan,
heold ond freoþode, hleosceorpe wrah
...

15 Childhood also naturally lacks distinct boundaries, as Orme notes, even though writers from antiquity to modern times have sought to name and define each of its stages. Orme, *Medieval Children*, 3. Terminological ambiguities are also discussed by Andreas Lemke in this volume.

16 Emily Dickinson, "To Make a Prairie," 3:1521.

Mec seo friþe mæg fedde siþþan,
oþþæt ic aweox, widdor meahte
siþas asettan. (*Riddle* 9, lines 3b–11a)[17]

[Then a kindly kinswoman began to cover me with clothes; she cherished and protected me, and wrapped me in a protective gown ... The protectress then fed me, until I grew up and could set out on farther journeys.]

Such intimations of shelter, nourishment, and safety cluster at beginnings. The battering ram (*Riddle* 53) and wooden spear (*Riddle* 73), once growing trees, recall being fed by earth and clouds. "Ic on wonge aweox," says the spear, "wunode þær mec feddon / hruse ond heofonwolcn" (I grew up on a plain, dwelled where the earth and cloud fed me, *Riddle* 73, lines 1–2). Both bull-calf riddles (*Riddles* 38 and 72) delight in suckling, a "geoguðmyrþe" (joy of youth, *Riddle* 38, line 2). The young are also frequently envisioned as being covered, a notion repeatedly linked to a sense of security. The cuckoo recalls being swaddled in a "hleosceorpe," the shelter-garment of its foster-mother's robe; the inkhorn remembers a covering of protective trees:

ful oft unc holt wrugon,
wudubeama helm wonnum nihtum,
scildon wið scurum (*Riddle* 88, lines 12b–14a)

[very often the forest, the protection of trees, covered the two of us in dark nights, shielded us against storms.]

The barnacle goose was incubated in the sea's embrace (*Riddle* 10),[18] just as the oyster was enveloped in waves that both protected and nourished it:

17 Poems from the Exeter Book cited according to *The Exeter Book*, ASPR 3. Translations from Old English are mine unless otherwise noted.

18 This may be seen as consistent with, and perhaps an extension of, Rudolf's interpretation of covering as incubation in the cuckoo and barnacle goose riddles. "Riddling and Reading," 513–14.

Sæ mec fedde, sundhelm þeahte
ond mec yþa wrugon (*Riddle* 77, lines 1–2a)

[The sea fed me, watery covers concealed me, and waves enveloped me.][19]

Historians remind us that an appreciation of childhood depends on understanding children as being physically and emotionally different from adults – an appreciation that some had deemed the early Middle Ages to lack.[20] These constellated themes map tendencies rather than rules, but their gravitation towards the early stages of life nevertheless tint childhood-like moments as subtly different from later maturity, as a time of dependence and need for shelter and care.

Siblings, also, frequently and particularly populate the childhood stage.[21] The hatchling chicks (*Riddle* 13), the porcupine pups (*Riddle* 15), and the little cuckoo (*Riddle* 9) all grow up in the company of brothers and sisters. Formal resemblance within categories of things can also translate as sibling relations, like peas in a pod alike, in size and shape. For the inkhorn that recalls growing up atop the head of a stag, its beloved twin brother is none other than the stag's matching antler. More peculiar is the bull calf of *Riddle* 72, which, not unlike an imaginative child, speaks joyfully of make-believe companions: it recalls a sister ("sweostor") that fed it and four dear brothers ("feor ... swæse broþor") whom it could tug on for drinks – an unusual turn of phrase referring to the mother cow and her four udders. Such "puzzling play,"[22] as one scholar remarked, may become more intelligible when read alongside other childhood scenes. Even as the language of siblinghood in these moments operates metaphorically, the literal image of affectionate brothers and sisters warms an early memory

19 I follow here Williamson, Mackie, and Grein in emphasising the sense of protection in *sundhelm*. Grein translates *maris galea*, a "sea-helmet," cited in Craig Williamson, ed., *The Old English Riddles of the Exeter Book*, 356. See also William S. Mackie, ed., *The Exeter Book: Part II: Poems IX–XXXII*, 214–15.

20 Ariès, *Centuries of Childhood*, 128.

21 *Riddles* 9, 13, 15, 72, and 88. Crawford notes that the "cordial relationships between brothers and sisters are a particular feature of Anglo-Saxon documentary sources. The sources never draw any particular attention to this family link, perhaps because it seemed unremarkable, and often an underlying close bond between brother-and-sister pairings only emerges by chance," in Sally Crawford, *Daily Life in Anglo-Saxon England*, 68; Crawford, *Childhood in Anglo-Saxon England*, 120–1.

22 Bitterli, *Say What I Am Called*, 33.

with the presence of companions. Metaphors of child and family are not merely convenient ciphers, but suggest an imaginative understanding of the world informed by human life itself.

The vocabulary for family members in the riddles is tender: they refer to one another as "swæs" (one's very own, one's dear). Yet amid this sweetness, riddle-poets also confront the darker shadows that loom in childhood, the sibling rivalry within and the harsh world beyond the walls of home. The aforementioned cuckoo, for example is incubated "ungesibbum" (*Riddle* 9, line 8) – not only "in the company of unrelated ones," but potentially also "in hostility,"[23] foreboding strife among its foster-siblings.[24] The young cuckoo's happy childhood offers an alternate scenario to common assumptions about the loveless lives of fosterlings, but also implies a woeful fate for its fellow nestlings.[25] Such arrangements can be advantageous to the foster-child even to the disadvantage of one's biological offspring, an anxiety familiar to us in Wealhtheow's words to Hrothgar.[26] We hear more ambivalence towards siblinghood in *Riddle* 88,

---

23 The former is the usual translation, but consider "ungesibbe wæron" in the Old English *Bede*, which translates the Latin *discordabant*. For the Latin, see Bertram Colgrave and Roger A.B. Mynors, eds. and trans., *Bede's Ecclesiastical History of the English People*, 230; for the Old English, see Thomas Miller, ed., *The Old English Version of Bede's Ecclesiastical History of the English People*, 1:166.

24 This riddle offers unusually the cuckoo chick's perspective, unattested in any of the riddles' identified sources or analogues. Medieval encyclopaedias and bestiaries relate this parasitic behaviour as a third-person observation, whereas in the pseudo-Symphosian version, the story is told briskly by the cuckoo mother. Sources and analogues surveyed in Williamson, *Old English Riddles*, 159–61; Dieter Bitterli, "The Survival of the Dead Cuckoo," 95–114, esp. 98–102. My discussion focuses on the sentiments and concerns attributed to this child voice, though like many other riddles, *Riddle* 9 also lends itself to interpretations of social commentary and spiritual allegory. Jennifer Neville explores these facets in "Fostering the Cuckoo: Exeter Book Riddle 9," 431–46.

25 Addressing such assumptions, McLaughlin, Hanawalt, and Crawford bring to light a range of fostering situations, and interactions both good and bad within them. McLaughlin focuses on early high medieval Europe, Hanawalt on England specifically across the Middle Ages, and Crawford on Anglo-Saxon England, with specific reference to this riddle. See McLaughlin, "Survivors and Surrogates," 104–5, 111 ff.; Hanawalt, *Ties That Bound*, 245–56; Crawford, *Childhood in Anglo-Saxon England*, 122–38. See also Susan Irvine's essay in this volume.

26 Wealhtheow's words betray anxiety over the fate of her sons against potential pretenders to Hrothgar's throne – ostensibly cousin Hrothulf, but possibly also Beowulf. See *Beowulf*, lines 1180–7, and also Richard North's analysis of her speech in his essay in this volume. Citations of *Beowulf* are from Robert D. Fulk, Robert E. Bjork, and John D. Niles, eds., *Klaeber's "Beowulf."*

considered more closely in the third part of this paper. The inkhorn's story is woven of both the best and the worst of brotherhood: one horn misses its twin dearly, both having been exiled by their younger brothers, the newly grown antlers.[27]

The historical narrative of childhood is inflected by the looming presence of danger, both because children are especially vulnerable, and because loss teaches us something about love. *Riddle* 15 frames a story of parenthood, one that speaks to parents' perennial worry of threats to the safety of their children. The protagonist of the riddle is a heroic figure, a mother porcupine determined to protect her offspring against a hostile world:[28]

> Me bið gyrn witod,
> gif mec onhæle an onfindeð
> wælgrim wiga, þær ic wic buge,
> bold mid bearnum, ond ic bide þær
> mid geoguðcnosle, hwonne gæst cume
> to durum minum, him biþ deað witod.
> Forþon ic sceal of eðle eaforan mine
> forhtmod fergan, fleame nergan,
> gif he me æfterweard ealles weorþeð;
> ...
> Eaþe ic mæg freora feorh genergan,
> gif ic mægburge mot mine gelædan
> on degolne weg þurh dune þyrel
> swæse ond gesibbe; ic me siþþan ne þearf
> wælhwelpes wig wiht onsittan.
> Gif se niðsceaþa nearwe stige
> me on swaþe seceþ, ne tosæleþ him
> on þam gegnpaþe guþgemotes (*Riddle* 15, lines 6b–26)

27 Bitterli, *Say What I Am Called*, 154.

28 The cue for the speaker's female sex is the feminine ending to the adjective "onhæle" (secret, hidden, line 7). As to the precise identity of the speaker, a range of burrowing species has been proposed, including a porcupine, vixen, hedgehog, and badger, among others. For an overview of arguments to date, see Dieter Bitterli, "Exeter Book Riddle 15: Some Points for the Porcupine," 461–87. Both grammatical gender and proposed solutions are also addressed in Williamson, *Old English Riddles*, 173–6.

> [I am doomed to grief if a certain bloodthirsty warrior finds me hidden where I dwell, my home with my children. If I wait there with my young offspring until the guest should come to my doors, then they are doomed to death. Therefore I, frightened, must carry my children away from our home, save them by flight, if he comes after me in close pursuit ... I can easily save the life of my freeborn children, if I can lead my family, those near and dear to me, on a secret path through a burrow. Then I need not fear at all the slaughter-hound's attack. If the hateful foe seeks me on the narrow trail, he will not want for a hostile encounter on the opposing path.]

The courageous mother roams the plains carrying spear-like spikes, her "beaduweapen," promising a fierce attack on any threat or foe. She is valiantly dressed in heroic diction, and her young are "geoguðcnosle," her little inexperienced warriors who depend on her, their brave leader.[29] For Ariès and his followers, a pre-modern world of imminent dangers and high child mortality rates would inevitably hinder close emotional bonds between parents and their offspring. This influential line of reasoning asserted that "people could not allow themselves to become too attached to something that was regarded as a probable loss."[30] But we see Anglo-Saxon poets framing love and loss in a different relationship. It is upon a panorama of life's dangers in *The Fortunes of Man* that its poet sets, prominently if precariously, a loving vignette of doting parents.[31] Father and mother cradle and guide their child ("fergað swa ond feþað," line 7) and dress it in colourful clothes ("mid bleom gyrweð," line 3), despite knowing anticipation of the hazardous unpredictability of fate. In *Solomon and Saturn II*, the sage Solomon echoes this unrelenting anxiety of parenthood, foregrounding the helplessness of mothers mourning "oft and gelome" (frequently and often, line 198) for the young that they cannot fully protect.[32] It is not only that parents continued to love despite the vulnerability of the young: if indeed daily affairs in the medieval world afforded "little room or incentive ... for the spontaneous expression of tenderness

---

29 I accept here Nelson's suggestion that this *hapax legomenon* may gesture towards the heroic binary "duguþ ond geoguþ" (old and young retainers) and resonate with the riddle's rich display of heroic diction. Marie Nelson, "Old English Riddle No. 15: The 'Badger': An Early Example of Mock Heroic," 447–50, at 449.

30 Ariès, *Centuries of Childhood*, 38.

31 This is at the centre of Stacy Klein's essay in this volume.

32 Daniel Anlezark, ed. and trans., *The Old English Dialogues of Solomon and Saturn*, 88.

and affection,"[33] threats of loss tended to bring love into particularly intense focus. In Barbara Hanawalt's sensitive reading of later-medieval coroner's reports, for example, the characteristically unsentimental documents yield up poignant and telling details of parental devotion in the face of a child's death.[34] We should note, looking back to the porcupine's monologue, that the mother's heroism is indivisible from her fear for the safety of her offspring: she is "forhtmod" (frightened), but promises fierce resistance should the foe threaten her young. Fear for her children's safety is the motivation of her heroism. The attendant fragility of childhood is not necessarily a deterrent of maternal love as some have feared, but rather occasions the most necessary displays of maternal strength.

The Family Tree

The child, as emblem of life's continuation, plays an important part in the family tree. Characteristically, riddle-poets revel where these branches are most tangled and family relations most riddling. In the puzzle of Lot's family, mathematical disorder mirrors incestuous disaster: "one man ... and his two wives, his two sons, and his two daughters, dear sisters, and their two sons, noble firstborns" (*Riddle* 46, lines 1–4) must awkwardly amount to a party of five.[35] On the subject of procreation, it is paradoxically the inanimate things that have the most to say, as an object's perceived life-generating capacity itself becomes the central animating theme.[36] While the mother-daughter and father-son motifs derive from inherited tropes, riddle-poets often dramatised and embellished in making old conceits their own. The fantastical *Riddle* 33, for example, presents an

33 Noting this tendency, McLaughlin cautions that the reticence of formal works on tender interactions within the family does not mean that such emotions did not exist. "Survivors and Surrogates," 127.

34 Hanawalt, *Ties That Bound*, 184–7.

35 Archer Taylor traces variations and analogues in "Riddles Dealing with Family Relationships," 25–37.

36 The riddles' fascination with eggs can also be seen in this light, for the hatching of birds was understood as life emerging from death, a transformation from something inanimate into something inspirited and alive that paralleled the growth of the human fetus. Likewise, when Isidore sought to explain fetal development, he looked to birds' eggs as an illustrative analogue. *Etymologiae*, XI.i.143, see Stephen A. Barney, W.J. Lewis, J.A. Beach, and Oliver Berghof, trans., *The Etymologies of Isidore of Seville*, 240.

iceberg as a fierce warrior and proud mother approaching the waterfront.[37] It codes the water cycle as a mother-daughter paradox – one that aptly captures the fluidity inherent in the idea of the child, for daughters may one day become mothers, and mothers are always themselves daughters:

Wiht cwom æfter wege   wrætlicu liþan,
...
sægde searocræftig   ymb hyre sylfre gesceaft:
"Is min modor   mægða cynnes
þæs deorestan,   þæt is dohtor min
eacen up liden,   swa þæt is ældum cuþ,
firum on folce,   þæt seo on foldan sceal
on ealra londa gehwam   lissum stondan."   (*Riddle* 33, lines 1–13)

[A wondrous creature came sailing along the wave ... The artful one spoke about her own nature: "My mother, who comes from the most excellent of all womenkind, is my daughter when grown great. Likewise, it is known to folk among mankind that in every land, she shall stand graciously on earth."]

The apparent impossibility of the proposition lies in "modor" and "dohtor" being seemingly one and the same. Semantically speaking, they are, for both the source and product of water can be located to the simple solution "ice." But the paradox simultaneously alludes to a broader framework that figures the circle of life. As the seasons move through temperatures and time, water, as daughter, will "upaleodan" (grow up), and become "eacen": "increased in size" as it freezes into ice, but also "pregnant," now a mother herself, ready to perpetuate the cycle further. Excellence ("deore") and grace ("liss") run in this family: the "gesceaft" the mother declaims is her "creation," the process of her coming into being, as well as the "nature" and "destiny" of her ongoing lineage. She looks ahead to her

37 An interesting parallel to such imagery is the modern expression of an iceberg "calving" (from Old English *cealfian*) – describing the detachment of a mass of ice from the main glacier as a birth-like event – which dates from the nineteenth century. See *OED*, s.v. *calve*, sense 3. I am grateful to Traugott Lawler for this observation. For discussions of the heroic imagery at the beginning and medieval analogues of the water/ice trope, see Williamson, *Old English Riddles*, 237–42; Patrick J. Murphy, *Unriddling the Exeter Riddles*, 9–13.

daughter growing up, to her bodying forth with grace the qualities of earlier generations.

Unlike mothers who busy about their children, fathers in this animated realm do little in the way of childcare. Historians report that Anglo-Saxon parents were likely both involved in the rearing of offspring, though a particular ritual significance was invested in the role of the father while mothers were the main caretakers.[38] As tokens of imagination, fathers and mothers in the riddles echo this division of labour as well, for fathers figure primarily in riddles wrapped in patrilineal glory and paradoxes of procreation. One example is the bellows of *Riddle* 37, a close neighbour of the iceberg, which plays on a similar trope of "generation as procreation." Yet its technique is also different, rendering more explicitly a celebration of virility, and fusing, as Patrick Murphy writes, the "traditional conceit of paradoxical offspring to the charged images of ... swollen innuendo."[39]

> Ne swylteð he symle,   þonne syllan sceal
> innað þam oþrum,   ac him eft cymeð
> bot in bosme,   blæd biþ aræred;
> he sunu wyrceð,   bið him sylfa fæder.   (*Riddle* 37, lines 5–8)

> [He never dies when he has to give what is inside to the other, but a remedy returns to his bosom, glory is raised up. He creates a son; he is his own father.]

The "innað" given away and the "bot" received likely refer to the bellows' expense and return of air;[40] likewise, "blæd" can denote the breaths of air that inspirit and restore the humble instrument to its fullness.[41] The riddle may be seen to straddle the suggestive and the sublime, as the legacy of one immortal father-son pair echoes another across the pages of the Exeter Book: just as the bellows will not die when sustained by cycles of air, so the phoenix lives immortally through cycles of decline and self-restoration – "bið him self gehwæðer / sunu and swæs fæder" (he is to

38 Crawford, *Childhood in Anglo-Saxon England*, 117–19; and Hanawalt, *Ties That Bound*, 172–3, 184–6.

39 Murphy, *Unriddling*, 219.

40 Williamson, *Old English Riddles*, 254; Murphy, *Unriddling*, 218.

41 *DOE* s.v. *blǣd* and *blēd*, *blǣd*.

himself both son and dear father, *The Phoenix*, lines 373b–74a).[42] The other sense of "blæd" as "glory" further dramatises the homely scene with triumphal colours – "glory is raised up," just as Hrothgar declares upon Beowulf's return from the mere, "blæd is aræred" (*Beowulf*, line 1703b). Yet while delighting in play upon inexhaustible libido, the riddle also offers a simple statement about the father-son bond. The metaphoric "blæd" that issues from the father engenders the child – "blæd" now in the sense of "fruit, that which is produced" – which is in turn received into the father's bosom as "bot" (reparation, remedy, relief). The child is a source of comfort, is glory renewed.

In *Riddle* 20, the child as the promise of self-perpetuation is cast in stark negative relief as a sword laments a conflict between career and family: it boasts of its prowess as a warrior, but mourns bitterly the family that its way of life precludes.[43] The subject laments its inability to father a son – unlike that *other* sword, with its joys in the marriage bed and promise of offspring:

Ic me wenan ne þearf
þæt me bearn wræce on bonan feore,
gif me gromra hwylc guþe genægeð;
ne weorþeð sio mægburg gemicledu
eaforan minum þe ic æfter woc,
nymþe ic hlafordleas hweorfan mote
from þam healdende þe me hringas geaf.
Me bið forð witod, gif ic frean hyre,
guþe fremme, swa ic gien dyde
minum þeodne on þonc, þæt ic þolian sceal
bearngestreona. Ic wiþ bryde ne mot

42 The phoenix, rising from its own ashes and thus to itself both son and father, symbolised Christ in animal lore. James E. Cross, "The Conception of the Old English *Phoenix*," 129–52, esp. 135; Frans N.M. Diekstra, "The Physiologus, the Bestiaries and Medieval Animal Lore," 142–55, at 143.

43 Bitterli gives the answer of *Riddle* 20 as, potentially, "falcon," but makes no mention of the more commonly accepted solution "sword" (or "weapon"). See Bitterli, *Say What I Am Called*, 19, 128–9, and 165. For an overview and analysis of proposed solutions, see Williamson, *Old English Riddles*, 193; Murphy, *Unriddling*, 207–9.

hæmed habban, ac me þæs hyhtplegan
geno wyrneð, se mec geara on
bende legde; forþon ic brucan sceal
on hagostealde hæleþa gestreona. (*Riddle* 20, lines 17b–31)

[I have no need to expect that a son will avenge me on the life of my slayer, if an enemy assails me in battle, nor will the tribe from which I sprang be increased by children of mine, unless I can turn away, lordless, from the guardian who gave me rings. I am doomed, if I obey my lord and wage war, just as I still did at my lord's pleasure, to be without the treasure of offspring. I cannot have marriage-bed pleasures with a bride, but he who had laid bonds on me ever denies me that joyous play. Therefore I must enjoy the treasures of warriors as a bachelor.]

The riddle turns on the polysemy of the word *wæpn,* in the sense of both "sword" and "membrum virile,"[44] with the object's barrenness both necessitated by its inanimate nature, and ironised for its phallic symbolism. As Craig Williamson perceptively notes, the symbolism itself is inherently paradoxical, for while sexual connotations of the sword may suggest procreation and life, the sword's true duty as a warrior's companion in war is to serve as an instrument of death.[45] These layered conflicts between fatherhood and professional duty, between life-giving and death-giving, lie at the heart of the sword's pathos. If this riddle's irony plays on the dual referents of *wæpn*, its poignancy lives in the double sense of *gestreon.* The *bearngestreona* after which the speaker longs, a *hapax legomenon* usually translated as "offspring" or "the begetting of children," must be read against the compensation for the warrior's barren servitude. The child is longed for, akin to precious riches.[46] The father bewails a life rich with all treasures but one – replete in "hæleþa gestreona," the treasures of heroes, but fated ever to lack "bearngestreona," the treasure of fathering a child.

44 See BT, s.v. *wæpen*, senses I and II, where sense I is "weapon," with many examples in which "weapon" refers to a sword.

45 Williamson, *Old English Riddles*, 193–9, esp. 195.

46 This implicit comparison is felicitously preserved in Williamson's rendering of "bearngestreona" as "child-treasure." Craig Williamson, *A Feast of Creatures: Anglo-Saxon Riddle Songs*, 78.

Growing Up

Eventually, children grow up and leave home, and riddle-poets show us that transition, too. If the earliest moments of life's plot lines are associated with the home and family, the turning point is often marked by a journey.[47] For some, it is free-spirited travel; for others, it is reluctant departure and exile.

Things that change and develop over time in the riddles tend to move towards something like a career, a new stage in life heralded by a process of transformation. Crafted by tools and by a shaping hand, the reed previously enveloped by playful waves on the shore welcomed, to its own surprise, a poet-like future in the mead-hall:

Lyt ic wende
þæt ic ær oþþe sið æfre sceolde
ofer meodubence muðleas sprecan,
wordum wrixlan. (*Riddle* 60, lines 7b–10a)

[Little did I expect that, early or late, I would ever speak, mouthless, over the mead-bench, mix words.]

A cow or a goat becomes a Bible, its story one of martyrdom and subsequent glorification.[48] It speaks proudly of its work as an educator to help "bearn wera" (the children of men) become "heortum þy hwætran ond þy hygebliþran, / ferþe þy frodran" (bolder of heart and more blessed of mind, wiser in spirit, *Riddle* 26, lines 20–1). Birds fulfil their natures soaring in the sky, while an animal horn, splendidly decked with "golde and sylfore / woum wirbogum" (gold and silver coiled wires, *Riddle* 14, lines 2–3), enters into aristocratic company.[49] The riddles are silent as to the age when such transformations happen, but the pattern itself suggests a way of conceptualising stages of life. Childhood and its dependent, sheltered world end, in this schema, when a marked period of change and transformation takes over.

47 For example, *Riddles* 9, 10, 60, 72, 73, and 88.
48 Bitterli, *Say What I Am Called*, 188–90.
49 See Bitterli, in *Say What I Am Called*, 166; Williamson, *Old English Riddles*, 170.

Growing up can take many guises in the riddles, its paths not always painless or encouraging. In *Riddle* 38, an onlooker describes a happy, suckling calf, while another voice explicates its grim future: living, the cow will labour in the fields; dead, it will bind men ("bindeð," line 7) by giving its hide for leather. This arc from carefreeness to hardship also structures *Riddles* 53 and 73, in which trees are rent from home, painfully readied for battle as battling ram and spear. Their life stories, like that of the young calf, begin in rosiness, until the fateful *oþþæt* comes,[50] uprooting them from shelter and shaping them forcefully into useful members of society.

Another bull calf, in *Riddle* 72, relates in no uncertain terms the physical and psychological stress of growing up. It looks back upon a time when it was "lytel" (little), when it had siblings, food aplenty, and joy:

Ic wæs lytel[51]
...
sweostor min,
fedde mec [...]   oft ic feower teah
swæse broþor,   þara onsundran gehwylc
dægtidum me   drincan sealde
þurh þyrel þearle.   Ic þæh on lust,
oþþæt ic wæs yldra   ond þæt an forlet
sweartum hyrde,   siþade widdor,
mearcpaþas Walas træd,   moras pæðde,
bunden under beame,   beag hæfde on healse,
wean on laste   weorc þrowade,
earfoða dæl.   Oft mec isern scod
sare on sidan;   ic swigade,
næfre meldade   monna ængum
gif me ordstæpe   egle wæron.   (*Riddle* 72, lines 1–18)[52]

50 Cf. *Riddle* 53, line 4b and *Riddle* 73, line 2b, where the bitter turns are set against initial nurturing and growth at home (*Riddle* 73, line 5b), in happiness (*Riddle* 53, line 2b). The *Beowulf*-poet also deploys, to dramatic effect, the conjunction *oþþæt* to herald major turning-points in the plot. See, for example, *Beowulf*, lines 100b and 2280b.

51 Manuscript damaged; three lines abbreviated.

52 Line 12a "mearcpaþas Walas træd" is metrically overburdened and poses difficulty for translation. See Williamson, *Old English Riddles*, 344; also, Bernard J. Muir, ed., *The Exeter Anthology of Old English Poetry*, 2:667.

> [I was little ... my sister fed me ... and I often pulled at four dear brothers, each of whom, throughout the day, gave me drinks through a small hole. I indulged in happiness, until I was older and gave it up for a dark herdsman. I journeyed farther: I trod the Welsh border-paths, and paced the moors, bound under a beam. On my neck I had a ring; I endured labour on my path of misery, a great deal of hardship. Often the iron pricked me sorely on my side. I was silent, and never complained to any man, even if the goads were painful to me.]

For the calf, the turn from joy to sorrow is explicitly associated with growing up, a change structured around a journey and two temporal anchors, "I was little... [and] indulged in happiness, until I was older, and ... journeyed farther." Anne Klinck observes an affinity between riddles and elegies in their shared emphasis on a speaker's personal identity, but argues also their essential difference in "the elegy's preoccupation with psychology, as opposed to the riddle's with physical being."[53] This distinction, if broadly accurate, begins to blur when it is precisely the physical conditions and change therein that evoke a network of emotions.[54] The calf's story, related with stoicism but palatable sadness, exhibits many symptoms of elegy:[55] set in the past tense and in the first-person voice, the speaker reckons present sorrows while reflecting nostalgically upon a golden-aged before. The exile from home – the iconic turn of the elegiac mode – echoes the journey at the end of childhood, while the elegiac speaker's typical submersion in hostile surroundings is painfully present in the labour and goads to be endured.

Growing up often entails solitude and separation from family, the converse of finding siblings clustering in childhood scenes. This separation becomes the centre of the inkhorn's lament in *Riddle* 88, when it is taken from home and forced "to join the monastic orders of the scriptorium."[56] Even as the lonely speaker bemoans the usurpation of its younger siblings, it speaks lovingly of its twin brother:

53 Anne Klinck, ed., *The Old English Elegies: A Critical Edition and Genre Study*, 228.

54 On the attraction to subjective experiences and mental states as characteristic of traditional Old English verse generally, see Britt Mize, *Traditional Subjectivities: The Old English Poetics of Mentality*, 12.

55 Bitterli, *Say What I Am Called*, 34.

56 Ibid., 166.

Ic weox þær ic s[…][57]
…
Ful oft unc holt wrugon,
wudubeama helm wonnum nihtum,
scildon wið scurum; unc gescop meotud.
Nu unc mæran twam magas uncre
sculon æfter cuman, eard oðþringan
gingran broþor. Eom ic gumcynnes
anga ofer eorþan; is min agen bæc
wonn ond wundorlic. Ic on wuda stonde
bordes on ende. Nis min broþor her,
ac ic sceal broþorleas bordes on ende
staþol weardian, stondan fæste;
ne wat hwær min broþor on wera æhtum
eorþan sceata eardian sceal,
se me ær be healfe heah eardade.
Wit wæron gesome sæcce to fremmanne;
næfre uncer awþer his ellen cyðde,
swa wit þære beadwe begen ne onþungan.
Nu mec unsceafta innan slitað,
wyrdaþ mec be wombe; ic gewendan ne mæg. (*Riddle* 88, lines 1–30)

[I grew where I [stood] … Often, the woods concealed the two of us, the covering of trees sheltered us in dark nights and shielded us from showers. The Lord created us both. Now we, a glorious pair, must be succeeded by our kinsmen; our younger brothers shall seize our place. I am alone on earth among the race of men; my back is dark and wondrous. I stand on wood, at the end of a table. My brother is not here, but I, brotherless, have to guard this place, and stand fast at the end of the table. I do not know where, in the regions of the earth, my brother shall dwell amid man's possessions, he who used to live high by my side. The two of us were engaged in battle together; neither of us would display his valour unless we both succeeded in the battle. Now monsters tear at me within, injure me in my stomach. I cannot escape.]

57 MS damaged; ten lines abbreviated.

Here, as with the bull calf's lament, the Old English riddle bears little similarity to its decidedly more succinct Latin counterpart.[58] As Bitterli traces beautifully, the Old English riddle oscillates between past and present: it dramatises the reversal of fate from dual to singular pronouns, from the past *staþol* of a childhood home to the new *staþol* of present duty; from being protected within the woods, to being tormented on the wood of the scribal desk.[59] Chiastic repetition further recalls the twin company fondly remembered:

Ic on wuda stonde
bordes on ende. Nis min *broþor* her,
ac ic sceal *broþorleas* **bordes on ende**
staþol weardian,

Like the shadow of an absent twin, these structural doublets accompany the riddle's richness in sound, where crossed alliteration and assonance enhance the lyrical resonance of the lament:

Ne wat hwær min broþor on wera æhtum
eorþan **sc***ea*ta *ea*rdian **sc***ea*l,
se me ær be **he***a*lfe **he***a*h *ea*rdade.[60]

It has been argued that the riddles portray man and nature in dialectical opposition, that the violent transformations that objects undergo exemplify "human triumphs" over the natural world.[61] Yet to read the inkhorn or the bull calf's laments in this light misses their particular beauty, and stresses only antagonism where the poetry is also powerfully shaped by

58 Eusebius, *Riddle* 30, "De atramentorio." For Eusebius's text and comparison, see Williamson, *Old English Riddles*, 380–1. Williamson addresses analogues of the bull calf in Aldhelm and Eusebius, ibid., 255 and 342–3.

59 Bitterli, *Say What I Am Called*, 154–5. On the interpretation of *staþol*, a word used particularly frequently in the riddles, see Eric Stanley, "*Staþol*: A Firm Foundation for Imagery," 319–32.

60 Bold marks alliteration, italics assonance.

61 Jennifer Neville, *Representations of the Natural World in Old English Poetry*, 110–15. Neville's discussion focuses on the Bible, reed pen, and inkhorn riddles. In contrast, Bitterli's juxtaposition of the fates of the inkhorns and drinking horns – the former woeful, the latter prosperous – speaks to the artistic range and imaginativeness with which riddle-poets portrayed man's multifaceted relationship with nature. Bitterli, *Say What I Am Called*, 151–69.

empathy. It is true that things of nature become displaced and shaped to be useful for society, but so, too, are the children of man. The human voice that animates the speaking "I" wells with concerns about dangers, pain, lost siblings, and loneliness – concerns that suggest a sympathetic connection to members of nature even as man inevitably takes from nature. The human metaphors are not divisive but inclusive, and explore the processes of growing, changing, and maturing as experiences that govern man and nature analogously.

Bitterli remarks the uniqueness of the inkhorn's story, unparalleled in the *Physiologus* or other writings on the stag. "So consistent is the metaphorical disguise," he writes, "that the whole could indeed be taken as an account of human loss and displacement."[62] If the cogency of this "disguise" has no precedent in encyclopaedic descriptions of animal life, a parallel may be found in observations of human life. The imagination here resonates with the wisdom of *Maxims I,* also in the Exeter Book:

> Earm biþ se þe sceal ana lifgan
> ...
> betre him wære þæt he broþor ahte, begen hi anes monnes,
> eorles eaforan wæran, gif hi sceoldan eofor onginnan
> oþþe begen beran; biþ þæt sliþhende deor.
> ...
> Hy twegen sceolon tæfle ymbsittan, þenden him hyra torn toglide,
> forgietan þara geocran gesceafta, habban him gomen on borde.
> (*Maxims I*, lines 172–82)

> [Wretched is he who must live alone. ... It would be better for him that he have a brother, and that they both be of the same man, both sons of a nobleman, in case they have to fight a boar or bear together, for that is a beast with savage paws ... The two of them shall sit around the game-table as their grief slips away from them; they shall forget harsh fate and find joy at the table.]

Both these passages describe brotherhood built on mutual protection and emotional companionship, and the grief that comes when such bonds are lost. In the light of the *Maxims*' wisdom, we may recognise another layer

62 Bitterli, *Say What I Am Called*, 155.

of pathos in the inkhorn's loneliness at the edge of the table, "bordes on ende" – in both its grief, and the impossibility of its relief, while it is stationed there alone "on borde," the very place where the cheering companionship of brothers ought to relieve sorrow. Regardless of whether these echoes reflect direct allusion or independent utterances, they remind us of the link between imagination and insight, connected in an outlook on world and on life. The wisdom of riddles – the *ræd* (counsel) in a *rædels* (riddle)[63] – often lies in its delivery of one truth in the guise of another. More than a sentimental fantasy, the inkhorn's lament echoes the distilled wisdom of siblinghood.

The children we encounter in the riddles are as varied as the collection itself, each with its own story, its own puns and points to make. The elegiac riddles in particular highlight the workings of memory, and draw attention to the persisting resonance of childhood for adulthood: neither can be studied in isolation. Backward glances often find a vision of the past that is inevitably inflected by the present; such is the Boethian sentiment that present sorrows make the past glow brighter. Surely, the riddles' juxtapositions of youth and experience, leisure and labour, participate in the sheer riddling delight in opposites, in the drama of sudden reversal. But their fond reminiscences also show that childhood has a place in elegy – that, despite ups and downs, it was a time of life that many could have held dear. The elegiac riddles offer some of the fondest depictions of growing up, but elegies proper in the Exeter Book hardly speak of childhood at all, just as portrayals of childhood are rare and fleeting in the manuscript as a whole. In contrast, the Exeter Book *Riddles,* with their handful of imaginations of the earliest stage of life, seem to provide a sweet spot where such stories are possible, or even appropriate.

"The past," it is lamented, "is peopled in the minds of most academics by a 'norm' consisting of adult males, which marginalises and makes invisible both women and children."[64] Archaeological research has shown how frequently the traces of Anglo-Saxon children slip by undetected in the historical jumble of large adult bones.[65] So too in textual history, the

63 BT, s.v. *rædels*, senses I–IV, "counsel; speech; conjecture, imagination, interpretation; enigma, riddle." On the similarly rich semantic range of the related verb *rædan*, see Rudolf, "Riddling and Reading," 503.

64 Sally Crawford and Carenza Lewis, "Childhood Studies and the Society for the Study of Childhood in the Past," 5–16, at 10.

65 See Sally Crawford's essay in this volume.

footprints of children are smaller and more elusive than their grown-up counterparts, and they will continue to hide until we change the way we seek. This study has focused mainly on those riddles in which a sense of childhood is marked by the riddle's vocabulary and narrative structure, but more child-sized shadows may be spotted in the landscape, once our minds become sensitised to the gentle suggestions of their presence.

Like the study of texts, our assumptions about their readers have long been governed by a norm of adults, but recent scholarship calls our attention to a potential audience of children, and the lessons they might have gleaned of literacy and of faith.[66] In this light, the riddles' textured details invite more careful consideration of how child-characters in the riddling landscape might have spoken, both intellectually and affectively, to potential young readers looking in. If, as St Guthlac's biographer remarks, children were wont to imitate the calls of birds, how engaging the literal image of *Riddle* 57's alphabet-chirping flock might have been for young readers-of-words:[67] "Þeos lyft byreþ lytle wihte" (This breeze bears little creatures, *Riddle* 57, line 1), ushered through halls and hills in a feminine embrace. How knowingly might the lament of the bull calf, taken from home at a young age to a life "bunden under beame" (bound under the wood) have spoken to young oblates living *sub iugo*, bound by the monastic yoke. Things of nature are shaped in ways that evoke the process of growing up into society – "an education in the arts of everyday existence,"[68] not unlike the professional dialogues of Ælfric's *Colloquy.* After all, as Nicholas Howe observes, humans have long burdened animals "to teach us how to behave like human beings."[69] Even if we cannot know with certainty whether the Exeter Book *Riddles* were made for, or used in, the Anglo-Saxon classroom, the collection as a whole sketches a broad arc of transformations, drawing lessons of growth and decline conceivably pertinent to young and old alike. The recurring retrospective voice also reminds us that the colours of childhood can stay with those who have outgrown it, and inform perceptions on the rhythms of the world.

Children can be vulnerable and childhood can be harsh, a fact the porcupine mother knows all too well. But another thing that we learn from

66 See footnote 12.

67 Colgrave, *Felix's Life of Saint Guthlac*, 79. For a compelling reading of *Riddle* 57 as letters of the alphabet, see Murphy, *Unriddling*, 79–107.

68 Lerer, *Children's Literature*, 63.

69 Nicholas Howe, "Fabling Beasts: Traces in Memory," 641–59, at 643.

these imaginations is that outgrowing childhood, and the life thereafter, also entailed its own share of heavy burdens. Observing later literary representations of children, Adrienne Gavin writes,

> Childhood sometimes reflects a desire to return to a world without responsibility, of freedom and unsullied imagination where magic lies behind the coal scuttle or within the nursery walls. At other times it represents a stage thankfully escaped from.[70]

The riddles, significantly, do not show us much of the latter.[71] What emerges from the mosaic of narratives is a steady association of the earliest age of life with tenderness – with a joy that is tested, and sometimes lost, when the time comes to leave home and enter a world of responsibilities. While the early medieval child might not have enjoyed a pampered, extended childhood, and while there lurked dangers, difficulties, and painful reminders of children's weakness and ignorance, the riddles suggest that, at least for some, memories of childhood occupied a soft spot in Anglo-Saxon hearts. It may be "swiðe tedre and swiðe hreosende"[72] (very frail and very fleeting), but sometimes the dearer for it.[73]

70 Adrienne Gavin, ed., *The Child in British Literature: Literary Constructions of Childhood, Medieval to Contemporary*, 2.

71 Kuefler's example from *The Wife's Lament* might also support this pattern of a gentler childhood in contrast to later sorrow, although he interprets it to suggest the contrary. He reads the speaker's woes as encompassing childhood, though the hardship "syþþan ic up weox" more readily means "since (or after) I grew up." "'Wryed Existence,'" 830.

72 Malcolm Godden and Susan Irvine, eds., *The Old English Boethius*, 1:262 (B Text, ch. 11, lines 72–3).

73 I am grateful to the editors of this collection, and to Roberta Frank, Traugott Lawler, Ting-yao Luo, Ya-huei Lin, and the two anonymous readers at UTP, for their wealth of insights and suggestions that have improved this essay. Opinions expressed are my own, as are any errors that remain. My interest in how the riddles imagine childhood and arcs of life is shared by a recent study by Harriet Soper, "Reading the Exeter Book Riddles as Life-Writing," 1–25, which was published when this collection was already in press.

5 Parenting and Childhood in *The Fortunes of Men*

STACY S. KLEIN

One of the saddest images of parenting in Anglo-Saxon literature is found in the opening of the ninety-eight-line wisdom poem preserved in the late tenth-century Exeter Book and known variously as *The Fortunes of Men*, *The Fates of Men*, and *The Fates of Mortals*. After a moving account of a father and mother wholly devoted to the care and early development of their young son, the poet matter-of-factly describes the child's future as a mystery that lies beyond the boundaries of human understanding and that can be known by God alone:

> Ful oft þæt gegongeð, mid godes meahtum,
> þætte wer ond wif in woruld cennað
> bearn mid gebyrdum ond mid bleom gyrwað,
> tennaþ ond tætaþ, oþþæt seo tid cymeð,
> gegæð gearrimum, þæt þa geongan leomu,
> liffæstan leoþu, geloden weorþað.
> Fergað swa ond feþað fæder ond modor,
> giefað ond gierwaþ. God ana wat
> hwæt him weaxendum winter bringað! (*The Fortunes of Men*, lines 1–9)[1]

> [Very often it happens by God's might that a man and woman bring a child into the world by birth, clothe him in bright colours, tend and teach him, until the time comes, with the passing of years, that the young limbs, the

1 Quotations of all Old English poems according to ASPR. For *The Fortunes of Men*, see *The Exeter Book*, ASPR 3:154–6. Unless otherwise noted, all translations are my own.

members endowed with life, become mature. Thus father and mother carry and lead (or possibly "feed") him, give him gifts and provide for him. God alone knows what the winters will bring to the growing child.]

The Anglo-Saxon convention of reckoning time in terms of winters rather than years invoked in the concluding "God ana wat" (God alone knows) maxim realizes its more literal valence here, presaging a bleak future in store for the growing boy that is further concretized by the verses that follow, which consist largely of a "*sum* catalogue" detailing a variety of forces that might cut short a person's life: "Sumne sceal hungor ahiþan, sumne sceal hreoh fordrifan" (one shall be devoured by hunger; another swept away by storm, line 15). The list is long and includes not only the ravages of nature, such as famine and tempestuous weather, wild animals, disease, physical and mental infirmity, and falling from a tree, but also social threats such as unchecked battle, intemperate drinking, mead-hall excesses, suicide, death at the gallows or on the pyre, and exile.

The emotional weight of *Fortunes*' opening has not gone unnoticed. Nicholas Howe refers to the parenting scene as a "tender, almost brooding description of a father and mother,"[2] while Hugh Magennis characterises the poet's subsequent account of maternal sorrow as "some of the most affective lines in Old English poetry."[3] Indeed, so poignant is the description of parental care in these initial lines of gnomic verse and so painful the images of human mortality that follow, that Sally Crawford, eminent archaeologist and arguably the leading expert on the history and material culture of Anglo-Saxon childhood, is led to view *Fortunes* as textual evidence that Anglo-Saxon "parents [as opposed to, say, hired nurses or other family members] held the prime responsibility for nurturing their children, and that this was perceived as being ordinarily a duty of love and affection."[4] Crawford's interpretation of these early lines of *Fortunes* as evidence for an Anglo-Saxon family structure in which "children were, normally, valued, loved and wanted by both their parents"[5] is best understood as part of a first wave of historical childhood studies, which focused on identifying children in pre-modern texts in order to redress a widespread misconception about medieval childhood, namely, that high rates

2 Nicholas Howe, *The Old English Catalogue Poems*, 116.
3 Hugh Magennis, *Images of Community in Old English Poetry*, 110.
4 Sally Crawford, *Daily Life in Anglo-Saxon England*, 66–7.
5 Crawford, *Daily Life*, 67.

of infant mortality, along with iconography and portraiture depicting medieval children as "miniature adults," were signs that society lacked what Philippe Ariès has called "le sentiment de l'enfance."[6]

Yet literature rarely bears such a direct relationship to society. This is particularly true in the case of wisdom poetry and gnomic verse, whose formal leanings towards both the catalogue and the list may create an illusion of descriptive comprehensiveness and cultural inventory that masks a broader (and arguably more insidious) didactic project: to shape social practices and human interactions by presenting them, quite simply, as matters of common sense. Scholarly understandings of wisdom literature have been transformed over the past half century: from considering these writings as embarrassingly crude, moralistic compilations of clichéd material, to regarding them as highly self-conscious and carefully crafted aesthetic productions that were employed by Anglo-Saxon authors to address difficult questions of faith, philosophy, and daily living.[7] My essay

---

6 Ariès's phrase, "le sentiment de l'enfance," is best known in the context of his infamous claim that "Dans la société médiévale, ... le sentiment de l'enfance n'existait pas" ("In medieval society ... the idea of childhood did not exist"): *L'enfant et la vie familiale sous l'Ancien Régime*, 134; the English translation is from Philippe Ariès, *Centuries of Childhood: A Social History of Family Life*, trans. Robert Baldick, 128. The fact that the English term "sentiment" is closely associated with emotional attachments and affective life contributed to the widespread misconstrual of Ariès's research as suggesting that medieval people were emotionally distant from their children. We have now come to understand that Ariès's claim was less about parental care or emotional investment in children during the Middle Ages than about the lack of an awareness of childhood as a particular phase distinct from adult life. For a good synopsis of the issues at hand, see Daniel T. Kline, review of Albrecht Classen, ed., *Childhood in the Middle Ages and the Renaissance*. Kline makes the important point that although the paradigms established and popularised by Ariès have been largely overturned by medieval historians working, in some cases, nearly three decades ago, these findings have been slower to take hold in literary studies.

7 The term "wisdom literature" was first coined in the late nineteenth century as a rubric for designating a group of Old Testament writings considered to contain wisdom, including Job, Proverbs, Ben Sirach (Ecclesiastes), Song of Songs, Wisdom of Solomon, a few psalms (typically 1, 37, 127, 128), and Ecclesiasticus. Anglo-Saxon wisdom literature is best understood less as a discrete genre than as a number of genres and discourses that interact with one another and also with related genres (e.g., maxims, gnomes, riddles, charms, elegies), or even simply as a heuristic label for a rather vague assemblage of Old English poems that share an interest in cataloguing knowledge, defining human wisdom in relation to that of the divine, and enshrining common sense. For an excellent introduction to the complexities of the genre, see Elaine Tuttle Hansen, *The Solomon Complex: Reading Wisdom in Old English Poetry*.

builds on these new lines of enquiry by examining the *Fortunes*-poet's use of images of parental anxiety and of the child under siege neither as heart-rending symbols of the ever-present perils of earthly life nor as realistic portrayals of Anglo-Saxon child-rearing, but rather as complex vehicles for exploring the broader issues of human vulnerability and of how one might go about pursuing a productive life within an essentially hostile social world. The *Fortunes*-poet's depictions of children as fragile entities at the mercy of the world's harshness point to a classically Boethian view of life as subject to the vagaries of fortune, with one's destiny in the hands of a capricious ruler, content to dole out suffering and misfortune or, on occasion, skills and prosperity, as the infamous wheel might decree. Yet as the numerous linguistic refrains and repetitive formal structures in *Fortunes* join forces with the poem's thematic emphasis on the relentless rhythms of human development and predictable patterns of parental care, both catalogue poetry and the nuclear family emerge as potentially viable structural principles for organising human experience and finding meaning within a seemingly random and chaotic social world. The repeated juxtaposition of images of nuclear parenting and individual nurturing with more communally based forms of social and cultural "making," such as hawk-taming, goldsmithing, and poetic performance, works to suggest further that in spite of the mutability of earthly life, it is nevertheless the duty of every man to strive to shape his own destiny, a destiny defined less as a strictly personal self-fashioning than as a commitment to pursuing one's divinely ordained craft, with the ultimate goal of shaping people, animals, and things prepared to take up productive roles within society. When read in this manner, representations of childhood and parenting in *Fortunes* shed valuable light on the poem's formal design in relation to its broader Christian message: although human understanding is contingent and context-driven, if we can manage to organise our observations and interpretations correctly, the world around us is rightly understood as a sign of the orderly design of a powerful, albeit deeply concerned, deity, and human labour as a central aspect of that design.

Literary Patterns and Formal Structures for Organising Human Experience

Representations of parenting and childhood in *The Fortunes of Men* are highly formulaic in many respects. As Paul Cavill notes, the "God ana wat" maxim (or some variant thereof) in *Fortunes*, lines 8b–9, is found in at least half a dozen other Old English poems.[8] In several of these instances, formulaic statements regarding God's omniscience centre on the wonders of birth, as in *The Phoenix*, which repeatedly contrasts God's foreknowledge of the bird's sex with mankind's more limited vision:

God ana wat,
cyning ælmihtig, hu his gecynde bið,
wifhades þe weres; þæt ne wat ænig
monna cynnes, butan meotod ana,
hu þa wisan sind wundorlice,
fæger fyrngesceap, ymb þæs fugles gebyrd. (*The Phoenix*, lines 355b–60)

[God alone knows, the almighty king, what its sex may be, whether male or female. No one of all the race of man knows that, except the Creator alone, what the wondrous ways, the fair decree of old, may be regarding the birth of the bird.][9]

So too in *Psalm 50* (a loose Old English verse translation of and commentary on the *Miserere*), similar claims are made for God's exclusive knowledge of the mysteries of birth:

Đu ðæt ana wast,
mæhtig dryhten, hu me modor gebær
in scame and in sceldum. (*Psalm 50*, lines 61b–63a)[10]

[You alone know, mighty Lord, how my mother bore me in disgrace and guilt.]

The sheer number and variety of extant Anglo-Saxon prognostics, in which different kinds of signs (e.g., weather conditions, dramatic natural events) were believed capable of predicting the sex, personality traits, health, and future occupation of an unborn child, or of portending the date and manner of one's own death (or that of one's child) indicate that

8 Paul Cavill, *Maxims in Old English Poetry*, 53–4.
9 *The Exeter Book*, ASPR 3:94–113.
10 *The Anglo-Saxon Minor Poems*, ASPR 6:88–94.

forecasting matters relating to birth and death was of great interest during the early Middle Ages, much as it is today.[11] The collocation of parenting with the "God ana wat" formula in *Fortunes* effectively reminds readers that knowledge of birth and death was reserved as God's alone, underscoring the poem's central religious teaching about the limitations of human understanding, the prescience of God, and mankind's inability to control (or even to foresee) his own destiny.

Yet *Fortunes* does not begin with a lofty theological statement about the limitations of human knowledge but with a homely image of birth, child-rearing, and family life. As Howe explains: "the poet does not subordinate the interest of human life to his doctrine, but rather recognises that the didactic value of his work lies in his ability to illustrate and embody his theology throughout the catalogue."[12] Many of the activities recorded in *Fortunes*, such as hawking, warfare, swordplay and other kinds of gaming, mead-hall festivities, and service to one's warlord, were strongly associated with heroic culture, comitatus structures, lay (as opposed to monastic) life, and with the conspicuous consumption and ceremonial practices that played a central role within the upper tiers of Anglo-Saxon society. By opening *Fortunes* with an anonymous, non-class-specific image of childhood and parenting, a kind of "every-family" image focused on two parents' efforts to meet the basic physical needs of their child, the poem and its teachings are rendered accessible to a broad range of readers, including those of lower social status. The most conventional aspects of human experience, or what Stanley Greenfield has called "the human ritual of begetting, birth, and rearing offspring," are invested with mystery and wonder,[13] while the repetitive cycles and predictable rhythms of childcare and early human development, captured in the efforts of both mother and father as they "tennaþ ond tætaþ ... [f]ergað swa ond feþað ... giefað ond gierwaþ" (tend and teach ... carry and lead ... give gifts and provide, lines 4a–7a), mimic the regularity and order inherent in catalogue poetry itself.

Anglo-Saxon wisdom poetry and gnomic verse have long been noted for their investment in order and structure. Poetic devices such as comparison

11 For an insightful introduction to Anglo-Saxon prognostics, as well as a superb edition and translation of the many different kinds of prognostics found in London, British Library, MS Cotton Tiberius A.iii, see Roy M. Liuzza, ed., *Anglo-Saxon Prognostics*.

12 Howe, *Old English Catalogue Poems*, 116.

13 Stanley B. Greenfield and Daniel G. Calder, *A New Critical History of Old English Literature*, 263; cited in Howe, *Old English Catalogue Poems*, 117.

and contrast, similarity and opposition, duality of thinking (e.g., right versus wrong, good versus evil), a reliance on lists and numbering, and binary forms such as cause and effect and logical pairings (e.g., bow and arrow, song and singer) all figure prominently in a genre often identified as "inherently structural" in nature.[14] Representations of parents and children play an important role in wisdom literature's quest to find order and structure in the world, and particularly in the practical realities of daily living. Scholars of biblical wisdom literature have identified the family as the initial locus for Israel's sapiential activity and suggested that the vast majority of biblical proverbs were probably transmitted in a household setting, as opposed to that of a temple or royal court.[15] The popular Near Eastern wisdom genre of "parental instruction," in which a father's advice to his son serves as a framing device for conveying ethical and practical guidance on righteous living, finds expression in Old Irish and Old English texts as well, most notably in the Old English *Precepts* and in Hrothgar's "sermon" in *Beowulf* (lines 1700–84).[16] In such texts, parent-child relations are rightly interpreted not as mimetic descriptions of actual human experience but as complex literary devices for ordering it. The narrative frame of father-as-teacher and son-as-pupil mobilises the voice of paternal authority and the fiction of child obedience to create an idealised audience for the reception of wisdom, to the point where Old English poems such as *Precepts* may be thought to "recognize and celebrate the act of parental instruction as it epitomizes the human capacity to structure reality."[17]

Although *Fortunes* does not feature parents as fictional voices of authority, or even as developed literary personae, it nevertheless relies on familial imagery to impose order and structure on human experience. The

14 The phrase is originally found in Nigel F. Barley's discussion of *Maxims II*: "Structure in the Cotton Gnomes," 244–9, at 245. It is also cited by Hansen, *The Solomon Complex*, 48, with reference to *Precepts*.

15 James L. Crenshaw, *Old Testament Wisdom: An Introduction*, 51–2. The issue is complicated, however, and is usefully explored in Ronald E. Clements, "Wisdom and Old Testament Theology," 269–86, especially 273, 281. Also useful on wisdom's transition from a cult- to a family-centred enterprise in the post-exilic period is Dave Bland, "The Formation of Character in the Book of Proverbs," 221–37.

16 Hansen provides a useful overview of the analogies between ancient Near Eastern and Old English wisdom literature in chapter one of *The Solomon Complex*, 12–40; the second chapter of this book focuses specifically on the genre of "parental instruction," 41–67.

17 Hansen, *The Solomon Complex*, 48.

parenting scene introduces a series of oppositions that are felt throughout the poem: between God's prescience and the limitations of human vision; between the certainty of parental love and the unpredictability of human fortune; between the convivial warmth of the family and the loneliness of life on the heath; between the comforts of the social world and the harshness of the natural landscape; and between being fed by one's parents and becoming food for the wolf or raven. Indeed, *Fortunes* is itself structured as two opposing catalogues (of bad and good fortunes) united by the recurrent image of a child. The child featured at the start of the first catalogue is devoured in its youth by a wolf; while the second child, who appears at the poem's midpoint, when the list of good fortunes commences, endures great hardship in its youth but ultimately finds joy and prosperity in old age. The lives of the two children epitomise the different kinds of fortune to which humans are subject, while repetition of the phrase "mid godes meahtum" (through God's might, lines 1 and 58) leaves little doubt that the fates of both children lie in the hands of a single, higher power.

The prevalence of binary oppositions in *Fortunes* has contributed to the critical consensus that the poem is motivated by a desire not only to structure reality but also to simplify it, by presenting a world of stable difference in which ethical and epistemological choices are clear-cut. Indeed, T.A. Shippey suggests that, unlike *Precepts*, *Fortunes* has no need to bring in a fictional voice of authority as the poem's overriding message – God is powerful and men are weak – "seems so irresistibly obvious that authority is not needed," and further, that this message expresses a sentiment that is common to Old English didactic poetry.[18]

One does not have to look far to find poems that support Shippey's point regarding the formulaic and highly conservative nature of Old English wisdom poetry. Immediately following *Fortunes* (fols. 87r–88v) in Exeter Cathedral Library, MS 3501 is *Maxims I* (fols. 88v–92v), a textbook example of Anglo-Saxon wisdom poetry that contains a passage on parenting strikingly similar to that found in *Fortunes*:

Tu beoð gemæccan;
sceal wif ond wer   in woruld cennan
bearn mid gebyrdum.   Beam sceal on eorðan
leafum liþan,   leomu gnornian.

18 T.A. Shippey, *Poems of Wisdom and Learning in Old English*, 11–12, with quotation at 10.

Fus sceal feran, fæge sweltan
ond dogra gehwam ymb gedal sacan
middangeardes. Meotud ana wat
hwær se cwealm cymeþ, þe heonan of cyþþe gewiteþ.
Umbor yceð, þa æradl nimeð;
þy weorþeð on foldan swa fela fira cynnes,
ne sy þæs magutimbres gemet ofer eorþan,
gif hi ne wanige se þas woruld teode. (*Maxims I*, lines 23b–34)[19]

[Two are mates; a man and a woman shall bring forth a child into the world by birth. A tree must lose its leaves on earth, lament its branches. The ready one shall depart, the doomed man shall die, and every day fight at parting from the world. The Lord alone knows where death comes which departs hence from this land. (He) increases children, whom (or possibly "when") early illness takes (them). Thus there come to be so many of the race of man on earth. There would not be a limit of progeny (literally "child/son timber") if he who established the world did not decrease them.]

In addition to the obvious lexical parallels between the parenting passages in *Fortunes* and *Maxims I*, both passages emphasise God's prescience, particularly with respect to his power to know and respond to the deaths of children. In both poems, too, the loss of a child occasions emotions so severe as to surpass the parents' ability to handle them. In *Fortunes*, loss of a child leads to an immediate splintering of the parental unit as the idyllic image of a husband and wife united in the care of their young son gives way to the stock poetic trope of the isolated *geomuru ides* (sorrowful woman) mourning her son's death. In *Maxims I*, human sorrow is also displaced, but here it is projected on to the natural world (i.e., the tree), a coping strategy that tends to emerge in Old English poetry when the strictures of Anglo-Saxon stoicism are confronted by affective demands too powerful to be suppressed, such as in *Wulf and Eadwacer* and *The Wife's Lament*, in which the female speakers' tears and sense of entrapment are symbolised, respectively, through *renig weder* and thick, restrictive hedges.

The parallels between *Maxims I* and *Fortunes* are perhaps most apparent in their authors' shared fascination with dualisms, and, similarly, in their

19 *The Exeter Book*, ASPR 3:157–63.

efforts to use poetic devices rooted in binary thinking as a potential means of satisfying one of the most fundamental of all human drives, namely, the desire to organise one's life. The opening claim in *Maxims I* that "Tu beoð gemæccan" (two are mates, line 23) and subsequent statement (appearing almost verbatim in *Fortunes*) that "sceal wif ond wer in woruld cennan/ bearn mid gebyrdum" (a man and woman shall bring forth a child into the world by birth, lines 24–25a) points to the emphasis in both poems on rightful pairings, or on things that belong together (e.g., counsel with wisdom, gold on a man's sword, man and woman), and, more generally, to the dualistic thinking so characteristic of wisdom poetry, in which behaviour is either right or wrong, fortune good or bad.

In spite of *Fortunes*' reliance on formal poetic devices designed to reduce and to simplify the complexities of human experience, the clear-cut dualities proffered by the narrator cannot be sustained. The poet's opening fantasy of the parental unit as a microcosm of the social world and, by extension, as a temporary bulwark against the ravages of the natural world, crumbles quickly in the face of a series of tragic fates whose causes cannot be tethered to either world with any certainty.[20] As *Fortunes* proceeds, some of the poem's most essential binaries begin to unravel. The seemingly elemental pairing of *wer* and *wif* is shown to be little match for the powers of Fortune – after his child dies, the husband simply disappears from the poem – while even the binary of good versus bad fortune that structures the poem's two halves proves difficult to sustain. Ultimately readers learn that there are not two but rather three possible fates for the child: a youth marked by death at the jaws of a wolf; a hardship-filled youth that eventually cedes to joy and prosperity in the wake of old age; and finally, a youth graced by good fortune from the start.

The issue is not simply that the binary oppositions and dualistic thinking so prevalent in *Fortunes* are easily revealed as interdependent, interrelated terms or even merely as inadequate systems for capturing the complexities of language or human thought. Rather, the poem's strict

20 Lindy Brady makes the compelling case that the contrast in *Fortunes* between the alleged safety of the social world and the presumed dangers of an unforgiving natural landscape is an illusion meant to conceal the human agency and deeds of man that may well lie at the core of these grim fates: "Death and the Landscape of *The Fortunes of Men*," 325–36. Thomas D. Hill focuses more on the issue of vengeance and on the problems posed by deaths that cannot be attributed fully either to natural or to cultural forces: "Hæthcyn, Herebeald, and Archery's Laws: *Beowulf* and the *Leges Henrici Primi*," 210–21.

adherence to binaries such as nature and culture, followed up by images that blur any clear sense of boundaries between the two, points to a driving force that lies at the heart of *Fortunes* and of wisdom poetry more generally: the quest to find reliable categories and structural arrangements that might allow one to stand apart from and to exert order and control over the world, or, conversely, to identify an underlying order already in place and hence to find ways to, as Morton Bloomfield puts it, "associate humanity with the fundamental rhythms of nature," and see the universe and man's relation to nature as part of a single, comprehensible whole.[21] It is thus that one finds in *Fortunes* strict binaries and harsh oppositions, such as human versus animal, nature versus culture, or parental love versus environmental threat, juxtaposed with images that blur the boundaries between these seemingly opposed phenomena. The child's human limbs, for example, are compared to the branches of a tree (*leomu*), a term perhaps invoking the idea of genealogical lineage and the family "tree" as in the *Maxims I*-poet's reference to *magutimber* (child timber);[22] the rearing of a child is echoed later on in *Fortunes* by the taming of a hawk, an animal itself symbolising the fine line between the wild and the tamed; and in between these beneficent images of the socialisation of a human being and a bird is the curious tale of a man who hovers uneasily between these two orders of life. Perhaps believing himself capable of flying, or perhaps taking part in some sort of ritual hanging, the man jumps out of a tall tree but upon finding himself "fiþerleas" (featherless, *Fortunes*, line 22), is unable to fly; his body, bereft of its soul, then falls to the ground.[23]

21 Morton W. Bloomfield, "Understanding Old English Poetry," 5–25, with quotation at 17.

22 Carolyne Larrington, *A Store of Common Sense: Gnomic Theme and Style in Old Icelandic and Old English Wisdom Poetry*, 161–73, offers a useful discussion of wisdom's poetry complex relationship to the natural world. Larrington also calls attention to the comparison between human and tree in both *Fortunes* and in *Maxims I* as well as in the Old Norse *Sonatorrek*; see 140, 169–70, and 177.

23 Precisely what is happening in this enigmatic scene (lines 21–6), as well as its possible relationship to the tree-climbing image found in *Christ II*, lines 678b–679a, has occasioned much debate. The hanged man-as-bird figure has been interpreted as referring to a variety of different activities, including house-building, Christ's ascending the cross, watching for enemies, gathering falcons, and a shamanistic initiation associated with Odinic ritual. For a good overview, see Neil D. Isaacs, "Up a Tree: To See *The Fates of Men*," 363–75. Also useful on these lines is Karen Swenson, "Death Appropriated in 'The Fates of Men,'" 123–39.

The *Fortunes*-poet's efforts to identify literary structures that might aid in organising human experience into meaningful categories that reveal an orderly and just design resonate with formal experimentation found in numerous other texts from this period. As Peter Clemoes has argued, literary patterns and rhythmical structures in the late Anglo-Saxon prose texts of Ælfric and Wulfstan were meant to "extract from language ... the regular, patterned relationships which they and their contemporaries believed were ubiquitous in a divinely created universe, and ... the apprehensible manifestation of ideal truth."[24] The same point has been made about Old English wisdom poetry, in which "meaning is constructed out of accumulated observation and experience, from what is repeatedly seen ... and what frequently happens," as evident, for example, in the formal refrains of *swa* and *sceal* that reverberate throughout *Fortunes* or in the consistent appearance of gnomic verbs in the simple present tense.[25] These regular and unchanging forms belie *Fortunes*' overarching message about the uncertainties of human existence, suggesting instead the poet's ability to impose order on a chaotic world or perhaps simply to reveal the providential order that was there all along.[26]

When considered as discrete events, the fates depicted in *Fortunes* appear random and nonsensical. When read in their broader formal and thematic contexts, however, these events emerge as part of a coherent narrative that points to a single origin and purposeful order beneath the apparent diversity of human experience.[27] Many scholars have demonstrated the richness and vitality of the catalogue as an accumulative, open-ended structure for preserving cultural tradition and constructing ethical norms;[28] yet few have taken note of how centrally images of children and family life figure in this enterprise. Whether it be the fact that *Fortunes* opens with the birth of a child, suggesting poetry's capacity for starting at the beginning of things

24 Peter Clemoes, *Rhythm and Cosmic Order in Old English Christian Literature*, 24.

25 See Hansen, *The Solomon Complex*, 95–7, with quotation at 95.

26 Whether wisdom literature is driven by an attempt to impose order on human life or by the belief that an inherent order already exists in the created world and is simply waiting to be revealed is a major point of contention among scholars. See Roland E. Murphy, *The Tree of Life: An Exploration of Biblical Wisdom Literature*, who engages both positions: 115–18, and 126.

27 See Hansen, *The Solomon Complex*, 96.

28 For important discussions of Anglo-Saxon catalogue poetry, see Howe, *Old English Catalogue Poems*; and also Hansen, *The Solomon Complex*.

and proceeding in a logical fashion;[29] or the fact that the poem moves from an image of childhood tragedy to that of youthful bliss, thus illustrating the process of conversion and journey of the human soul to God;[30] or the formulaic refrains about parental impotence and maternal sorrow that reverberate throughout Old English wisdom writings, signalling the poet's ability to produce regular, unchanging verse across a more comprehensive textual corpus; or simply the recurrent appearance of a child at the beginning, middle, and end of *Fortunes* that functions as an unspoken structural promise that God will provide new children to replace the ones taken in early illness – a kind of formal articulation of the *Maxims I*-poet's overt statement that "Umbor yceð, þa æradl nimeð" (He increases children, whom [or possibly "when"] early illness takes [them], line 31) – images of parenting and childhood play a crucial role in the *Fortunes*-poet's efforts to reveal an underlying meaning and deliberate order in an apparently senseless world. The sheer variety of God's providential, and often painful, design makes the task a difficult one. Yet as the repetitive rhythms of childcare, ongoing nature of parental concern, and predictable stages of human development echo the orderliness of the catalogue form itself, representations of parenting and childhood bolster the *Fortunes*-poet's efforts to assure readers that life is infused with meaning and structure and that poetry, like human life cycles, will follow a predictable course, at least for a little while.

Raising Children, Rearing Hawks, and Other Crafts of "Making"

The *Fortunes*-poet greatly emphasises the labour of child-rearing. Many other Old English texts highlight the difficulty of parenting; most memorable in this regard is Ælfric's *Colloquy*, in which the Merchant explains that both his labour and his profit motives are driven by the need to feed

29 Howe remarks that "the poet understood that he must satisfy his audience's desire to learn of stories from the beginning," *Old English Catalogue Poems*, 117.

30 For more on the poet's use of literary patterns to invoke ideas of conversion, see Howe, *Old English Catalogue Poems*, 116.

31 "Ac ic wille heora cypen her luflicor þonne gebicge þær, þæt sum gestreon me ic begyte, þanon ic me afede ⁊ min wif ⁊ minne sunu" (But I will sell them here for more than I bought them there so that I may acquire for myself some profit by which I might feed myself and my wife and my son): George N. Garmonsway, ed., *Ælfric's Colloquy*, 34. Interestingly, the Latin has the plural "filios," yet the Old English "sunu" is singular, suggesting that the Anglo-Saxon writer may have intended to underscore the difficulty of providing for even a single child.

his wife and child.[31] However, *Fortunes* is unusual in its efforts to characterise the labour of parenting less as a burden than as a worthy and highly regarded enterprise. Unlike other poems in the Exeter Book, such as the "Lot riddle," in which parenting serves as the substrate for sly jokes and illicit humour,[32] or prose texts such as Wulfstan's sermons, in which familial love is shamelessly exploited to incite male warriors to defend children, wives, and "motherland,"[33] (or, indeed, in its absence, mobilised as a sign of the world gone awry),[34] parenting in *Fortunes* is depicted as an activity that requires great skill – a kind of craft or art. As several scholars have noted, the poem's opening image of parenting is echoed at the close of the poem by an elaborate description of a young man's taming of a hawk:[35]

Sum sceal wildne fugel   wloncne atemian,
heafoc on honda,   oþþæt seo heoroswealwe
wynsum weorþeð;   deþ he wyrplas on,
fedeþ swa on feterum   fiþrum dealne,
lepeþ lyftswiftne   lytlum gieflum,
oþþæt se wælisca   wædum ond dædum
his ætgiefan   eaðmod weorþeð
ond to hagostealdes   honda gelæred.   (*The Fortunes of Men*, lines 85–92)

---

32 *Riddle* 46, in *The Exeter Book*, ASPR 3:205.

33 "⁊ oft tyne oððe twelfe, ælc æfter oþrum, scendað to bysmore þæs þegenes cwenan, ⁊ hwilum his dohtor oððe nydmagan, þær he on ... locað, þe læt hine sylfne rancne ⁊ ricne ⁊ genoh godne ær þæt gewurde" (And often ten or twelve, each after the other, shamefully insult the wife of a nobleman, and sometimes his daughter or near kinswoman there where he looks on, who considered himself important and powerful and brave enough before that happened): Dorothy Whitelock, ed., *Sermo Lupi ad Anglos*, 59–60.

34 "Ne bearh nu foroft gesib gesibban þe ma þe fremdan, ne fæder his bearne, ne hwilum bearn his agenum fæder, ne broþer oðrum; ... Eac we witan georne hwær seo yrmð geweard þæt fæder gesealde bearn wið weorþe, ⁊ bearn his modor, ⁊ broþor sealde oþerne fremdum to gewealde; ⁊ eal þæt syndon micle ⁊ egeslice dæda, understande se þe wille" (Now very often a kinsman will not protect a kinsman more than he would a stranger, nor a father his son, nor sometimes a son his own father, nor one brother the other; ... Also we know well where the crime has happened that a father sold his son for a price, and a son his mother, and one brother gave another into the power of foreigners; and all those are great and dreadful deeds. Understand that, he who will): Whitelock, *Sermo Lupi ad Anglos*, 55, 58. It is also worth noting that Wulfstan uses images of child enslavement (lines 46–7) and infanticide (line 170) as further evidence of England's deplorable state during the early eleventh century.

35 Michael D.C. Drout, "*The Fortunes of Men* 4a: Reasons for Adopting a Very Old Emendation," 184–7.

[One shall tame the arrogant wild fowl, the hawk on the hand, until the battle-swallow becomes gentle; he puts jesses (i.e., leather straps with foot-rings) on it, feeds the proud one, with its wings still in fetters, weakens the air-swift one with little morsels until the foreign one (i.e., the bird) becomes humble in weeds (i.e., plumage) and deeds to his provider and trained at the hand of the young man.]

Hawking and falconry were highly regarded pastimes during the early Middle Ages, practised most often by young men of elite social status,[36] and the poet's comparison between raising a child and rearing a hawk suggests, first, that child-rearing requires significant care and skill, comparable to that necessary in the art of falconry; and second, that the skills acquired in sports undertaken by adolescent men of social privilege, such as hawking, may serve as a basis for parenting later on in life.

Yet the *Fortunes*-poet's comparison between raising a child and rearing a hawk is also marked by a darker sensibility. In both cases, socialisation is conveyed through images of clothing or adornment – be it the brightly coloured garments in which the parents clothe their child or the hawk's proud plumage, which must ultimately be brought low so that it may become humble in "wædum ond dædum" (weeds and deeds, line 90) and subservient to its provider. This emphasis on clothing and adornment reminds us that both child-rearing and hawking were strongly associated with secular life and with worldly values such as materialism and pride – an association that is further suggested by the poet's claim that the socialisation of young, untamed beings (whether child or hawk) may be done through strictly physical processes, such as the provision or withholding of food, or through the care or control of limbs, be it the tending of the child's legs as he learns to walk or the hobbling of the bird's legs with jesses. Both hawks and children symbolised social status and earthly wealth, as indicated by the narrator's characterisation of gift-giving as a crucial component of child-rearing, as well as by his underscoring of the hawk's voracious appetite though his assertion that the bird might be tamed by feeding it with only "lytlum gieflum" (little morsels, line 89). The Fowler in Ælfric's *Colloquy* corroborates the association between hawks and consumption in his claim that hawks were big eaters, quite

36 Note that in *The Battle of Maldon* (line 9) the hawk owner is referred to as a *cniht*, a term that typically suggests youth and social status; see *Anglo-Saxon Minor Poems*, ASPR 6:7–16.

literally,[37] while Mercian and West Saxon charters from the eighth and ninth centuries point to a more metaphorical link between hawks and excessive consumption, suggesting that taxes on the royal hawks were high and at times a real strain on landlords, who were required to support the king's entire hunting retinue, including not only his servants, horses, and hounds, but also his hawks.[38]

The hawk's association with materialism, consumption, and human excess made it a ready symbol for the tenuousness of socialisation itself, and for the fine line between the wild and the tamed, a tension that is nicely captured in the *Maxims II*-poet's claim that "Hafuc sceal on glofe / wilde gewunian" (The hawk, a wild creature, shall dwell on a glove, lines 17b–18a),[39] the glove's associations with nobility and civilised life contrasting sharply with the wildness of the bird. Hawks, unlike, say, wolves or boars, were situated at the border of the natural and social worlds and were able to move between these two realms with ease, as indicated by the remarks of the Fowler in Ælfric's *Colloquy*, who claims to release his tamed hawks back into the wild every spring on account of his ability to catch and tame new ones with little trouble; or by the *Maldon*-poet's reference to Offa's kinsman, who releases his beloved hawk into the woods before the battle (lines 5–10), an act that points not only to the hawk's liminal status at the threshold of nature and culture, but also to the young man's own liminal status on the brink of adult masculinity as signified through his new-found willingness to relinquish personal attachments for the greater good.[40]

While the *Fortunes*-poet exhibits a high regard for the skill required in both raising a child and rearing a hawk, the association of both activities with worldliness, consumption, and carnality lent a deep ambivalence to his discussion. This ambivalence may be traced in part to the fact that *Fortunes*, like almost all Old English poetry, was likely to have been

37 "Forþam ic nelle fedan hig on sumera, forþamþe hig þearle etaþ" (I do not wish to feed them over the summer because they eat ravenously): Garmonsway, *Ælfric's Colloquy*, 32.

38 The taxes for royal hawking must have been significant, for in 855 King Burgred of Mercia granted a privilege to Bishop Ealhhun of Worcester, releasing the monastery at Blockley from the feeding and maintenance of all hawks and falcons in the land of the Mercians (as well as from several other obligations) in exchange for three hundred silver shillings. For this point, as well as for a host of other information on hawking in Anglo-Saxon England, I am indebted to C. James Bond's excellent entry, "Hawking and Wildfowling," 236.

39 *Anglo-Saxon Minor Poems*, ASPR 6:55–7.

40 *Anglo-Saxon Minor Poems*, ASPR 6:7–16.

composed (or at least copied) by monastic writers, whose fraught relationships with biological parents and families have often been noted by medieval historians.[41] Precisely how monasticism, and Christianity more generally, shaped cultural attitudes towards childhood and parenting is a complex question. However, it may suffice as a place of departure to point on the one hand to biblical idealisations of childhood purity and innocence as gateways to heaven (Matt. 18:2–3); and on the other, to the long-standing belief that children were signs of carnality and desire, vehicles for the transmission of sin, and unwelcome competition for the "true spiritual family" to be found in Christian community.[42] Heightened caution is especially necessary when interpreting the literary output of the late tenth-century Benedictine reforms, the very period during which *Fortunes* was copied and circulating. Reformers at this time championed clerical celibacy, urging married priests to abandon their wives and children on the grounds that devotion to one's spiritual flock was incompatible with the demands of family life,[43] or as Augustine succinctly put it: "the coming of Christ is not served ... by the ... begetting of children."[44]

Such sentiments are felt throughout *Fortunes.* Although *Fortunes* treats parenting seriously, the poem nevertheless drives home a fairly typical monastic message about the transitory nature of earthly life and the misery occasioned by putting stock in worldly attachments. Parent-child bonds, no matter how painstakingly cultivated, are shown in the end to be fragile and fleeting entities subject to the vicissitudes of fortune, a force

41 See Janet L. Nelson, "Parents, Children, and the Church in the Earlier Middle Ages (Presidential Address)," 81–114. Nelson makes the useful point that parents exerted much force on churchmen, as well as the other way around; see 82.

42 On the coming of Christianity as a powerful factor contributing to the devaluation of motherhood, see Clarissa W. Atkinson's valuable study, *The Oldest Vocation: Christian Motherhood in the Middle Ages*. Like Atkinson, Gillian Clark takes a rather dark view of Christianity's impact on social attitudes toward childhood but is similarly provocative and helpful: "The Fathers and the Children," 1–27.

43 As Pauline Stafford has argued, the biological family, conceived in sin and supported with earthly wealth and labour, was viewed by reformers as the ultimate symbol of carnality and of one's attachment to earthly wealth and prosperity. For a rich discussion of these issues, see Stafford, "Queens, Nunneries and Reforming Churchmen: Gender, Religious Status and Reform in Tenth- and Eleventh-Century England," 3–35.

44 Augustine's statement appears in his treatise *Holy Virginity*, which constitutes part of his answer to the Jovinianist controversy: *Treatises on Marriage and Other Subjects*, 159; quoted in David Herlihy, *Medieval Households*, 24–5, in a survey that contains much useful information on medieval parenting.

so strong that it is depicted as capable of destroying not only the bond between parent and child but also that between father and mother. As the poet details the various horrors that lie in store for the growing child, the charming image of two parents united in the care and raising of their son is replaced by the stock image of a lone mother lamenting her son's death:

> Sumum þæt gegongeð   on geoguðfeore
> ...
>   Sceal hine wulf etan,
> har hæðstapa;   hinsið þonne
> modor bimurneð.
> ...
> Sumne on bæle sceal   brond aswencan,
> ...
>   reoteð meowle,
> seo hyre bearn gesihð   brondas þeccan.
> (*The Fortunes of Men*, lines 10, 12b–14a, 43, 46b–7)

[To one of them it happens in his youth that ... a wolf, a hoary heath-stepper, shall eat him. Then the mother mourns his passing ... Flames will torment another in the fire ... The woman weeps who sees the flames cover her child.]

The *Fortunes*-poet's emphasis on the isolated female mourner is consistent with tropes of gendered labour in Old English poetry, in which mourning is typically coded as women's work and the strictures of masculine stoicism tend to prohibit overt displays of male grief. The collocation of maternal mourning, human powerlessness, and divine caprice is found in numerous Old English poems, such as in *Solomon and Saturn*, whose treatment of motherhood closely echoes that of *Fortunes*. As Solomon states:

> "Modor ne rædeð,   ðonne heo magan cenneð,
> hu him weorðe geond worold   widsið sceapen.
> Oft heo to bealwe   bearn afedeð,
> seolfre to sorge,   siððan dreogeð
> his earfoðu   orlegstunde.
> Heo ðæs afran sceall   oft and gelome
> grimme greotan,   ðonne he geong færeð,
> hafað wilde mod,   werige heortan,
> sefan sorgfullne,

...
Forðan nah seo modor geweald, ðonne heo magan cenneð,
bearnes blædes, ac sceall on gebyrd faran
an æfter anum; ðæt is eald gesceaft." (*Solomon and Saturn*, lines 373–87)[45]

["When she bears a son, a mother cannot direct how the wide journey through the world may be shaped for him. Often she nurtures her child to harm, to her own sorrow, later endures his torment at the fated hour. Often and frequently she must greet the fierce one grimly, when he is faring about as a young man, has a wild mind, a weary heart, a sorrowful spirit ... Therefore, a mother does not have control, when she bears a son, over her child's glory but one must go after the other in birth. That is the ancient decree."]

If mother-child separation in these texts symbolises an unknown, unpredictable world beyond the boundaries of human control, the opposite is also true, that is, the image of mother and child united often serves in Anglo-Saxon literature to reflect a perfectly ordered society, in which the future is knowable, predictable, and under man's control, such as in Bede's account of the reign of King Edwin as a time of "so great a peace in Britain, ... that ... a woman with a new-born child could walk throughout the island from sea to sea and take no harm."[46] Yet *Fortunes*' emphasis on mother-child separation and on maternal mourning transcends the standard feminisation of mourning in Anglo-Saxon poetry and urges a more sustained questioning of the role of emotion in wisdom literature. As many biblical scholars have noted, wisdom texts do not work to discourage negative emotions such as displeasure, pain, fear, or dispassion towards God but instead provide opportunities for using one's faith to express these emotions productively: chiefly by rationalising and presenting them as human reactions to life that must be expressed and endured. Maternal mourning in Anglo-Saxon wisdom poetry is not indicative of female passivity or of women's helplessness when confronted with forces beyond her control. For much as the female mourners in heroic poetry perform important cultural work, giving dignity and meaning both to the lives lost in heroic warfare as well as to the wars themselves, so too, the female mourners in Anglo-Saxon wisdom literature serve a crucial social

45 *Anglo-Saxon Minor Poems*, ASPR 6:31–48.
46 Bertram Colgrave and Roger A.B. Mynors, eds. and trans., *Bede's Ecclesiastical History of the English People*, ii.16, 193.

function, by rationalising the seemingly senseless deaths of their children and modelling acceptance of the divine forces that have taken them away.

The female mourner who appears so consistently in Old English poetry has no obvious male counterpart. Indeed, masculine emotion has always presented a problem in Anglo-Saxon literature, in which stoicism and control of one's tongue are crucial components of heroic masculinity, a point that is clearly illustrated in the *Fortunes*-poet's brief account of the "self-slayer," whose inability to control his emotions and check his tongue leads ultimately to his own death. The fate of the self-slayer, like so many of the fates catalogued in *Fortunes*, including death by falling out of a tree, death by starvation or excessive drinking, death by hanging from a gallows, or being eaten by a wolf, are, as Thomas Hill notes, "modes of death which cannot be avenged for one reason or another."[47] Hill's point provides a useful gloss on the abrupt absence and departure of the father after *Fortunes*'s opening lines. Deprived of his customary paternal role of avenging his son's death, and prohibited from mourning by its excessive associations with femininity, the father in *Fortunes* simply fades to the background and is, in a sense, forced out of the poem.

Although *Fortunes* does not comment openly on the emotions and social consequences occasioned by the separation of father and child, there are numerous other depictions of "masculine parenting" in this text, namely, images of men who, like the adolescent hawk tamer, are invested with the power of shaping young and untamed beings or of moulding raw and unformed natural substances. The latter half of *Fortunes* consists of a catalogue of divinely ordained crafts and of figures such as the goldsmith, who is lauded for his skill in shaping and adorning metal for the great king; or the *scop* who is shown composing music at his warlord's feet. Numerous scholars have noted *Fortunes*' obsessive interest in death, as well as the poet's somewhat peculiar concern with cataloguing people whose fate it is not only to die but to be consumed, both literally and figuratively.[48] As

47 Hill, "Hæthcyn, Herebeald, and Archery's Laws," 214.

48 Victoria Thompson, *Dying and Death in Later Anglo-Saxon England*; and Stefan Jurasinski, "Caring for the Dead in *The Fortunes of Men*," 343–63. See also the forthcoming essay by Jill Hamilton Clements, "Sudden Death in Early Medieval England and the Anglo-Saxon *Fortunes of Men*." Clements reads *Fortunes* as deeply concerned with death but as nevertheless urging readers to take an active role in this life by using one's time on earth to prepare for sudden death. I am grateful to Jill for sharing her essay with me prior to publication and for a stimulating exchange of ideas on *Fortunes*.

Stefan Jurasinski puts it: "this is a poem that delights not simply in depicting death, but in seeing the living body as potential food either for animals or for destructive natural forces."[49] Yet so insistent is the poem's emphasis on mortality, destruction, and consumption that it may obscure the very real emphasis on production and human labour, and on the various kinds of crafts that comprise the social world. This is not to argue that *Fortunes* privileges production as opposed to destruction; rather, both undertakings point to the poet's deep interest in materiality, or in the making and unmaking of "things" – be they children, sporting hawks, or poems – as well as the social contexts in which this work occurs. By following the poem's opening description of parenting with images of medieval craftsmen or artisans, such as the falconer, the goldsmith, or the *scop* making music for his warlord, the implication is that parenting is to be understood as yet another kind of secular craft, one that like goldsmithing entails the shaping, hardening, or moulding of unformed material; or that like hawking, entails the taming of a wild being so that it might contribute to the social world.

Fortunes' emphasis on human craft is consistent with its centrality in wisdom literature, both biblical and medieval. For biblical scholars, craft is associated with the practical or technical skill of an artisan (Exod. 31:1–6; 35:30–5; 36:8), and is one of the many different forms that wisdom may take, along with the art of government (1 Kings 3:12, 28), simple cleverness (2 Sam. 14:2), the practical skill of coping with life (Prov. 1:5; 20–2), the pursuit of proper ethical conduct (Prov. 2:2–11), and the Torah or Law (Eccles. 24:32–3).[50] For Anglo-Saxonists, however, *cræft* is perhaps best understood less as a discrete strand of wisdom, than as a "complex of skills and virtues that both help one in this life and make this life a path to the next."[51] Nicole Guenther Discenza has traced the intimate connection between physical, mental, and moral *cræftas* in the works of Alfred, most notably in the *Boethius*,[52] while Peter Clemoes argues that Alfred's use of *cræft* as a means of "synthesizing ... spiritual, moral, and material elements ... in a God-devoted wisdom" is also found in the Old English poetry that

49 Jurasinski, "Caring for the Dead," 347.

50 Roland E. Murphy, "Wisdom," 1135–6, with the different forms of wisdom outlined on 1135. I have changed the numbering of biblical chapter and verses slightly in order to reflect that given in the Vulgate.

51 Nicole Guenther Discenza, *The King's English: Strategies of Translation in the Old English* Boethius, 119.

52 Discenza, *The King's English*, 105–22.

inspired Alfred.[53] For both Discenza and Clemoes, the journey to God in the *Boethius* "becomes inseparable from the pursuit of *cræft*";[54] and the multivalence of the term, which unites notions of earthly skill and labour with more abstract intellectual and spiritual pursuits, furthers the connection between human artisanship and divine creation.

If the concept of *cræft* in Anglo-Saxon texts adumbrates the heady idea that human labour offers the possibility of mimicking divine creation, and hence of bridging the gap between this world and the next, this same concept is also, paradoxically, premised on notions of subjection and on highly conservative notions of social order. Representations of human artisanship and craft in Old English writings are often driven by a desire to concretise existing social hierarchies, an idea famously exemplified in Ælfric's *Colloquy*, when the counsellor admonishes his young charges to "beo þæt þu eart" (Be that which you are).[55] *Fortunes* is no exception. All of the crafts and occupations depicted in the poem highlight the link between socialisation and servitude. In a mere ninety-eight lines, the *Fortunes* narrator effectively constructs a portrait of a kind of great chain of being, a strict hierarchical structure beginning with God and extending out to encompass all matter, natural substances, animals, and human beings of different ages and social stations. *Fortunes* suggests that to become socialised is synonymous with accepting, and even embracing, subjection and allowing the self to be moulded by the hands of one's superior; be it the gold that takes shape in the expert hand of the goldsmith, the hawk that becomes subservient to the hands of his young master, the poet who composes songs at the feet of his warlord, and especially the child, who is even positioned syntactically as subservient to his parents – they figure consistently as the subject of the sentence (lines 2–3 and 7–8) – and as the object of their direction and care.[56] The poem ultimately conveys a very conservative message: namely, that natural matter will be dominated by artisans; animals dominated by humans; children dominated by their

53 Peter Clemoes, "King Alfred's Debt to Vernacular Poetry: The Evidence of *ellen* and *cræft*," 213–38, with quotation at 232; discussed further in Discenza, *The King's English*, 110–11.

54 Discenza, *The King's English*, 114.

55 Garmonsway, *Ælfric's Colloquy*, 42.

56 This final point about the ways in which the syntax of *Fortunes*, lines 2–3 and 7–8, positions the child as an object of parental care is made by Howe, *Old English Catalogue Poems*, 117.

parents; and parents (along with everyone and everything) subject to the vagaries of Fate and the might of God. We are all, in effect, like the hawk, bound in its tresses, and "hobbled by circumstance."[57]

In spite of this very conservative message equating socialisation with servitude, *Fortunes* does offer some room for agency, much as in, say, Wordsworth's "Nuns Fret Not at Their Convent's Narrow Rooms," or Lovelace's claim in "To Althea, from Prison": "Stone walls do not a prison make, / Nor iron bars a cage."[58] To be sure, parents and children in *Fortunes*, along with poets, are all depicted as subject to fate and God's might, an overarching portrait of life that has led many scholars to view *Fortunes* as endorsing a passive outlook on earthly life; as Shippey wrote, "the whole poem invites the paraphrase: 'These are the fortunes of men. There is nothing to be done about them'."[59] Yet the narrator suggests that in spite of death's grim certainty, and the brief life of subjection allotted prior to one's demise, there is nevertheless great joy and fulfilment to be found in pursuing one's divinely ordained craft on earth, a claim that is perhaps unsurprising in light of the fact that to pursue a craft is to mimic the generative acts of God himself as master craftsman. Whether one has been destined to shape gold, compose poems, tame hawks, or rear children, *Fortunes* celebrates human labour and the shaping of unformed matter so that it may be put to productive use within society, be it the lump of gold, hardened and presented to the king as decorative object; the wayward hawk who is tamed for human sport; or the child who is raised by its parents in preparation for entering the social world. In contrast to so much Old English literature, which takes death as an overarching theme for the purposes of driving home the well-worn message, so relentlessly promulgated by medieval clerics, namely, that life is short, meaningless, and to be viewed merely as a prelude to a greater life

57 The phrase is Robert DiNapoli's in his essay "Close to the Edge: *The Fortunes of Men* and the Limits of Wisdom Literature," 127–47, at 146.

58 For a groundbreaking account of the ways in which agency in later Anglo-Saxon England was made possible through obedience, responsibility and service to others, see Katherine O'Brien O'Keeffe, *Stealing Obedience: Narratives of Agency and Identity in Later Anglo-Saxon England.*

59 Shippey, *Poems of Wisdom and Learning*, 11. Jill Hamilton Clements's forthcoming essay "Sudden Death" offers a provocative rebuttal to this line of thinking. Clements argues that *Fortunes* dramatises the very real prospect of sudden death and hence urges readers to prepare actively for one's death in this life.

yet to come, *Fortunes* honours human production, craft, and all of the effort and labour that go into shaping the social world. Foremost in these enterprises is the rearing of children and the importance of both men and women in this enterprise.

The parenting passage in the opening of *Fortunes* is brief. Yet it is also powerful, so powerful that R.D. Fulk and Christopher Cain comment that "one cannot help feeling that the pathos of the parents' sad misfortune was the inspiration for the [entire] poem."[60] Whether or not this was the case, the passage sheds new light on wisdom literature, a notoriously fraught category, whose lack of a central structuring principle has led biblical scholars and Anglo-Saxonists to view the genre, respectively, as a kind of "errant child" or "orphan in the biblical household,"[61] and as an inadequate rubric for addressing the complexities of Old English poetry.[62] Where the category of wisdom literature does aid our understanding of poems such as *Fortunes*, however, is in alerting us to the centrality of parenting and family life in a textual tradition rooted in the practical shaping of moral character and in the ethical training of the individual on earth. Parenting is in many respects a unique kind of labour, and one that parts ways with the various other crafts and occupations depicted in *Fortunes*.[63] In comparison with crafts such as hawk-taming, parenting is depicted as a form of labour that may be ongoing and intensive but that, unlike hawking, can never be mastered. In the same way, parenting exhibits clear differences from goldsmithing and poetic performance: while shaping gold for one's king and composing poetry for one's warlord may be understood as crafts that are lucrative and mutually beneficial to both artisan and patron, parenting is depicted as a form of labour that is non-reciprocal. More strikingly,

60 Robert D. Fulk and Christopher M. Cain, *A History of Old English Literature*, 176.

61 Ronald E. Clements, for example, contends that "whether canon, saving history or covenant is taken as the central structuring concept for Old Testament theology, wisdom is forced to appear at the periphery rather than at the centre": "Wisdom and Old Testament Theology," in *Wisdom in Ancient Israel*, 270. The characterisations of wisdom literature as an "errant child" and as an "orphan in the biblical household" are given, respectively, by Roland E. Murphy, "Wisdom Literature and Biblical Theology," 4; and James L. Crenshaw, "Prolegomena," 1.

62 See DiNapoli, "Close to the Edge," 127–47.

63 Interestingly, parenting does not appear in the Exeter Book's *The Gifts of Men*.

it brings neither material gain nor affective rewards, but only death and sorrow. Nevertheless, parenting in *Fortunes* entails a special kind of sorrow, one that insists not only on the depth of feeling that one individual might extend towards another, but also on the inherent meaning of human bonds, regardless of how fleeting their existence, how laborious their maintenance, or how painful their outcome. In this respect, parenting in *Fortunes* offers the possibility of a kind of "dialogue with divinity." It is a craft that seeks to emulate both God's creative potency as well as his supreme love, and in doing so to make sense of the seemingly incoherent workings of Fate through the only routes available to us: human experience, labour, and care for the other.

6 Children and the Conversion of the Anglo-Saxons in Bede's *Historia ecclesiastica gentis Anglorum*[1]

ANDREAS LEMKE

The *Historia ecclesiastica gentis Anglorum* (*HE*) by the Northumbrian scholar Bede, who completed it ca. AD 731, is well known as one of the most influential specimens of Anglo-Latin scholarship during the European Middle Ages.[2] It is the grand narrative of the *gentis Anglorum* and their church, embedded in the larger framework of salvation history. In his work Bede combines historiography and hagiography in a way that specifically encourages exegetical readings. At the same time, the didactic principle of the work stands out: the *HE* is a gallery of exempla, good and bad, as the author himself relates in his preface.[3] It contains the stories of various prominent religious figures such as Pope Gregory the Great, Augustine of Canterbury, Cuthbert, Hild of Whitby, and Theodore of Canterbury, and a great number of Anglo-Saxon kings such as Oswald of Northumbria and Æthelberht of Kent. Although the *HE* can be regarded as one of the best-studied texts of the Anglo-Saxon period, little attention has been paid to what Bede has to say about children and childhood in this work. In this essay I seek to argue that the Northumbrian monk

1 I have discussed some of the basic ideas of this essay in my "*Puer* and *pueritia* in Bede's *Historia ecclesiastica gentis Anglorum*." I wish to thank Brepols Publishers for their kind permission to include material originally published in that article.

2 See Joshua Westgard, "Bede in the Carolingian Age and Beyond," in *The Cambridge Companion to Bede*, 201–15; George H. Brown, *A Companion to Bede*, 117–34. Westgard lists 164 copies of the *HE* that were copied from the eighth to the fifteenth century throughout Europe ("Carolingian Age," 210, table 1).

3 Bertram Colgrave and Roger A.B. Mynors, eds. and trans., *Bede's Ecclesiastical History of the English People*, 3. All subsequent references cite this edition by book, chapter, and page.

provides us with ample evidence that children, the often invisible and unheard members of society, were of great importance to him, and a key element in his story of the conversion and subsequent establishment of the early English Church.

Bede's interest in children seems to have been integral to his self-perception as a monastic instructor. On Bede's role as a teacher at Jarrow, Calvin Kendall remarks: "Bede loved the innocence of children, praised their readiness to learn, and regarded them as capable of wisdom, which hints that he may have enjoyed teaching the very young as well as the advanced students."[4] This positive attitude, which arguably concerns primarily male oblates, is already evident in his *De temporum ratione* (ca. AD 703). In chapter 35 of that work he notes with regard to the four elements, seasons, and humours that of the humours blood was most active in children (*infantibus*), and describes its effects as follows: "Item sanguis eos in quibus maxime pollet facit hilares, laetos, misericordes, multum ridentes et loquentes" ([B]lood makes those in whom its potency is greatest, cheerful, joyous, tender-hearted, much given to laughter and speech).[5] Bede holds a consistently positive attitude towards children, which is far from ubiquitous in medieval literature.[6] Even though accounts of children are not numerous within the *HE*,[7] they provide key passages for Bede's narration of the Christianisation of England.

In this essay I will analyse four episodes in the *HE* that are seminal with regard to the conversion of the Anglo-Saxons and the manifestation of God's power working among them: Pope Gregory and the Anglian slave boys, the birth of Eanflæd, daughter to King Edwin of Northumbria, a miraculous account from the monastery of Selsey, and, finally, the baptism and death of two young princes of the Isle of Wight. In each case I will analyse Bede's account with regard to the child characters, paying special attention to his terminology. It is therefore necessary first to give a brief outline of the interpretative tools, namely, Isidore of Seville's

4 Calvin B. Kendall, "Bede and Education," in DeGregorio, *Cambridge Companion*, 99–112, at 105.

5 Bede, *De temporum ratione. Bedae opera didascalica*, pars 2, ed. Jones, 392; trans. Faith Wallis, *Bede: The Reckoning of Time*, 101. Although Bede uses *infans* instead of *puer* it appears that his terminology encompassed all children before the period of adolescence as his division in chapter 35 is *infans, adulescens, transgressor, senex*.

6 See Shulamith Shahar, *Childhood in the Middle Ages*, 9–20.

7 Accounts of children can be found in 21 of the 138 chapters.

Etymologiae, passages from the Gospels, and Bede's commentaries on those passages wherever they may throw light on Bede's attitude towards children and childhood.[8]

Terminology

Associating the Latin term *puer* with a precise age range is difficult, if not impossible, because it is used inconsistently by medieval authors, referring both to children and to youths.[9] We therefore have to look for alternative ways of interpretation. Among those sources that may have defined Bede's notion of the term *puer*, Isidore of Seville's *Etymologiae* seems an apposite starting point. Isidore distinguishes between seven ages in his chapter entitled *De aetatibus hominum*: *infantia*, *pueritia*, *adolescentia*, *iuventus*, *gravitas*, *senectus*, and *senium*. Here, *pueritia* is "etymologically" defined as an age that is "pura et nec dum ad generandum apta, tendens usque ad quartum decimum annum" (pure and not yet apt for procreating, running until the fourteenth year).[10] In this reading, *puer* specifically denotes a certain form of purity prior to the awakening of the carnal desires of *adolescentia*. Isidore adds a definition based on the human phenotype, when he claims that a boy (*puer*) is so called from his purity (*puritas*):

> quia purus est, et necdum lanuginem floremque genarum habens. Hi sunt ephebi, id est a Phoebo dicit, necdum [pronati] viri, adolescentuli lenes.
>
> [Because he is pure and still retains, without the hint of a beard, the bloom of the cheeks. They are ephebes (ephebus), so called after Phoebus, gentle youths, not yet (grown) men].[11]

He further relates that the word *puer* is applied in three ways: a) with reference to birth in general, b) to indicate age, and c) "pro obsequio et fidei

---

8 Bede, *In Lvcae evangelium expositio. In Marci evangelium expositio. Bedae opera exegetica* 3, ed. Hurst.

9 On the fuzziness of terminology applied by medieval authors, see Edward James, "Childhood and Youth in the Early Middle Ages," 11–24. See Sally Crawford, *Childhood in Anglo-Saxon England*, 33–56, for a survey of the different stages of childhood and youth as evident from Anglo-Saxon documentary and literary sources.

10 Isidore, *Etymologiae* XI.ii.3, ed. Lindsay, 1: n.p.; Stephen A. Barney, W.J. Lewis, J.A. Beach, and Oliver Berghof, trans., *The Etymologies of Isidore of Seville*, 241.

11 Isidore, *Etymologiae*, XI.ii.10, 1: n.p.; trans. Barney et al., *Etymologies*, 241.

puritate, ut Dominus ad prophetam (Jer. 2:7): 'Puer meus es tu, noli timere,' dum iam Ieremias longe pueritiae excessisset annos" (In reference to obedience and purity of faith, as in the words of the Lord to the prophet (Jer. 1:7): "You are my child, do not be afraid," spoken when Jeremiah had already left behind the years of childhood a long time before).[12] This third interpretation of Isidore's is of particular interest. Here, no specific age is associated with the term, but rather – on a metaphorical level – it is extended to the spiritual attitude of a true believer. The relation between Jeremiah and God the father is built on the prophet's pure faith in him.

This metaphorical usage of *puer* is also retained in the Gospel of Luke. Being the only one of the synoptic gospels that relates stories of Jesus's childhood, it refers to Christ solely as *puer* when not using a demonstrative pronoun. When Jesus is presented to Symeon in the temple (Luke 2:22–40), for example, the Gospel relates:

> [E]t cum inducerent puerum Iesum parentes eius ut facerent secundum consuetudinem legis pro eo et ipse accepit eum in ulnas suas et benedixit Deum.
>
> [And when his parents brought in the child Jesus, to do for him according the custom of the law, he also took him into his arms, and blessed God.][13]

In this instance *puer* probably does not refer to the exact age of the child, at least not when we take into account that *puer* would commonly denote a person of the age of seven to fourteen years, as we have seen with Isidore. The passage begins: "et postquam impleti sunt dies purgationis eius secundum legem Moysi tulerunt illum in Hierusalem ut sisterent eum Domino" (And after the days of her purification, according to the law of Moses, were accomplished, they carried him to Jerusalem, to present him to the Lord).[14] According to the precepts of the Old Law, this would have happened thirty-three days after the birth of the child.[15] By that age, however, the boy Jesus would still have been identified as an infant (*infans*). It is therefore possible that *puer* specifically refers to Jesus's uncommon

12 Isidore, *Etymologiae*, XI.ii.11, 1: n.p.; trans. Barney et al., *Etymologies*, 241.

13 Luke 2:27–8. All Latin quotations from the Bible are taken from Robert Weber, ed., *Biblia sacra iuxta latinam Vulgatam versionem*, and all translations taken from Richard Challoner, ed., *The Holy Bible Translated from the Latin Vulgate*.

14 Luke 2:22.

15 Luke 12:1–4.

maturity and the special grace of God vested in him. This is underscored by the conclusion to this passage, which states that after Joseph and Mary had returned to Nazareth, "puer autem crescebat et confortabatur plenus sapientia et gratia Dei erat in illo" (the child grew, and waxed strong, full of wisdom; and the grace of God was in him).[16]

A caveat is necessary here in relation to the analysis of *puer*: it is evident not only that the Isidorian terminology is used inconsistently during the Middle Ages, but also that the Vulgate translation may by no means apply terms like *infans*, *puer*, or *vir* with a technical, age-bound consistency. What does seem clear is that in the case of Jesus the term *puer* takes on a metaphorical meaning, reflecting the grace of God that Jesus is bestowed with. This, in turn, might have worked as a blueprint for medieval writers who applied it to children more generally.

Apart from the story of Christ, there is ample evidence in the Gospels that children are blessed with purity of faith and granted special grace. In Mark 9:36 Jesus tells his audience:

> "[Q]uisquis unum ex huiusmodi pueris receperit in nomine meo me recipit. Et quicumque me susceperit non me suscipit sed eum qui me misit."[17]
>
> ["Whosoever shall receive one such child as this in my name, receiveth me. And whosoever shall receive me, receiveth not me, but him that sent me."]

He then famously rebukes his disciples in Mark 10:14–15:

> "[S]inite parvulos venire ad me et ne prohibueritis eos talium est enim regnum Dei, amen dico vobis, quisque non receperit regnum Dei velut parvulus non intrabit in illud."[18]
>
> ["Suffer the little children to come unto me, and forbid them not; for of such is the kingdom of God. Amen I say to you, whosoever shall not receive the kingdom of God as a little child, shall not enter into it."]

Despite terminological inconsistencies (*pueris* vs. *parvulos*), these references exalt the apparent naive and eager readiness of children to believe,

---

16 Luke 2:40.

17 Mark 9:36.

18 Mark 10:14–15.

seemingly going hand in hand with notions of incorruption and moral purity, while silently assuming the inevitable corruption of grown-ups. Medieval writers frequently draw on this conception of children's ability to access "a higher truth" and of their being blessed with divine favour.[19] This perspective is reinforced in Bede's own commentary on the two passages from Mark. On the first passage (Mark 9:36) he notes:

> Quod enim ait, *Quisquis unum ex huiusmodi pueris receperit in nomine meo me recipit*, uel simpliciter pauperes Christi ab his qui uelint esse maiores pro eius ostendit honore recipiendos uel certe malitia paruulos ipsos esse suadet ut instar aetatis paruulae simplicitatem sine arrogantia caritatem sine inuidia deuotionem sine iracundia conseruent. Quod autem complectitur puerum significat humiles suo dignos esse complexu ac dilectione talesque cum impleuerint quod praecepit.

> [By saying "whoever receives one of these children in my name receives me" he simply shows that the poor of Christ are to be received by those who wish to be greater in return for his honour, or he truly urges with cunning that they be children so that in the manner of those of young age they observe simplicity without arrogance, charity without envy, and devotion without anger. His embrace of the boy signifies that the humble and those who fulfil his commands are worthy of his embrace and his love.][20]

Bede's exegesis here suggests that belief in Christ must be unconditional and that it should not be undermined by vices, a danger associated with adulthood. Moreover, Bede's interpretation presupposes a categorical switch from children to adults, who have to remain as uncorrupted and naive in their belief as children in order to be worthy of God's grace. Bede further elaborates on that point in his commentary on the second passage (Mark 10:14–15), where he emphasises that children are worthy recipients of divine grace, because, unlike adults, they do not question the word of God, but are true believers devoid of any doubts:

> Aliter. Regnum Dei, id est doctrinam euangelii, sicut paruulus accipere iubemur quia quo modo paruulus in discendo non contradicit doctoribus neque

19 Shahar, *Childhood*, 17.
20 Bede, *In Marcum*, 551, my translation.

rationes et uerba componit aduersum eos resistens sed fideliter suscipit quod docetur et cum metu obtemperat et quiescit ita et nos in oboediendo simpliciter et sine ulla retractatione uerbis domini facere debemus.

[We are also told to accept the heavenly kingdom, that is the doctrine of the gospel, as a small child would accept it because just as a small child when it is learning does not contradict its teachers nor does it in resistance against them fashion verbal arguments but faithfully accepts what it is taught and silently obeys in fearful reverence, so we, too, must act in simple obedience and without any reservation to the words of God.][21]

Whereas children's simple readiness to believe seems to be at the heart of the first commentary, Bede's exegesis of the second passage stresses unconditional obedience to the doctrine and unquestioning belief in order to obtain God's grace – qualities, it may seem, which Bede could still see in children, yet not in grown men.

Jesus taught his followers to consider themselves as children of God as stated in Matt. 18:3–5:

[E]t dixit amen dico vobis, nisi conversi fueritis et efficiamini sicut parvuli non intrabitis in regnum caelorum quicumque ergo humiliaverit se sicut parvulus iste hic est maior in regno caelorum et qui susceperit unum parvulum talem in nomine meo me suscipit.[22]

[And said, "Amen I say to you: unless you be converted, and become as little children, you shall not enter into the kingdom of heaven. Whosoever therefore shall humble himself as this little child, he is the greater in the kingdom of heaven. And he that shall receive one such little child in my name, receiveth me."]

These lines again imply that the pure and true belief of children is a prerequisite for entering the heavenly kingdom, wrapped in a warning that adults have to assume children's attitudes in order not to jeopardise their own place in heaven.

All these examples show that the term *puer* – in addition to its reference to an exact age – encourages a metaphorical reading with reference

21 Ibid., 559, my translation.
22 Matt. 18:3–5.

to spiritual purity, special grace, and the status of children as role models to be emulated by grown-ups in order to become children of God. I will now turn to some key passages of the *HE* and assess them in the light of this interpretative approach.

Pope Gregory and the Anglian Slave Boys

Bede tells us in *HE* II.1 how Gregory, not yet pope, was inspired to instigate the conversion of the Anglo-Saxons. It may be useful here to rehearse the well-known episode in full:

> Nec silentio praetereunda opinio, quae de beato Gregorio traditione maiorum ad nos usque perlata est, qua uidelicet ex causa admonitus tam sedulam erga salutem nostrae gentis curam gesserit. Dicunt quia die quadam, cum aduenientibus nuper mercatoribus multa uenalia in forum fuissent conlata, multi ad emendum confluxissent, et ipsum Gregorium inter alios aduenisse, ac uidisse inter alia pueros uenales positos candidi corporis ac uenusti uultus, capillorum quoque forma egregia. Quos cum aspiceret, interrogauit, ut aiunt, de qua regione uel terra essent adlati; dictumque est quia de Britannia insula, cuius incolae talis essent aspectus. Rursus interrogauit utrum idem insulani Christiani, an paganis adhuc erroribus essent inplicati. Dictum est quod essent pagani. At ille, intimo ex corde longa trahens suspiria, "Heu, pro dolor!" inquit, "quod tam lucidi uultus homines tenebrarum auctor possidet, tantaque gratia frontispicii mentem ab interna gratia uacuam gestat!" Rursus ergo interrogauit, quod esset uocabulum gentis illius. Responsum est quod Angli uocarentur. At ille: "Bene" inquit; "nam et angelicam habent faciem, et tales angelorum in caelis debent esse coheredes. Quod habet nomen ipsa prouincia, de qua isti sunt adlati?" Responsum est quia Deiri uocarentur idem prouinciales. At ille "Bene" inquit "Deiri, de ira eruti et ad misericordiam Christi uocati. Rex prouinciae illius quomodo appellatur?" Responsum est quod Aelle diceretur. At ille adludens ad nomen ait: "Alleluia, laudem Dei Creatoris illis in partibus opportet cantari."
>
> [We must not fail to relate the story about St Gregory which has come down to us as a tradition of our forefathers. It explains the reasons why he showed such earnest solicitude for the salvation of our race. It is said that one day, soon after some merchants had arrived in Rome, a quantity of merchandise was exposed for sale in the marketplace. Crowds came to buy and Gregory too amongst them. As well as other merchandise he saw some boys put up for sale, with fair complexions, handsome faces, and lovely hair. On seeing them

> he asked, so it is said, from what region or land they had been brought. He was told that they came from the island of Britain, whose inhabitants were like that in appearance. He asked again whether those islanders were Christians or still entangled in the errors of heathenism. He was told that they were heathen. Then with a deep-drawn sigh he said: "Alas that the author of darkness should have men so bright of face in his grip, and that minds devoid of inward grace should bear so graceful an outward form." Again he asked for the name of the race. He was told that they were called Angli. "Good," he said, "they have the face of angels and such men should be fellow-heirs of the angels in heaven." He asked: "What is the name of the kingdom from which they have been brought?" He was told that the men of the kingdom were called *Deiri*. "Deiri," he replied, "*De ira*! good! snatched from the wrath of Christ and called to his mercy. And what is the name of the king of the land?" He was told that it was Ælle; and playing on that name, he said: "Alleluja! the praise of God the creator must be sung in those parts."][23]

Several aspects of this passage deserve to be highlighted. First, Bede refers to the Anglian youths as *pueros venales* (boys for sale, slave boys). The exact age of the boys is not disclosed, but in view of the classical division between *infantia*, *pueritia*, *adolescentia*, and *iuventus*, we may perhaps take them to have been between seven and fourteen years old.[24] It is worth noting, however, that Bede uses the term *puer* elsewhere to describe a boy not more than three years old.[25] Therefore it seems more appropriate to assume a wider connotation for Bede's usage of *puer*, extending beyond meanings merely connected with age. Taking into account Isidore's interpretation of *puer* outlined above, Bede's use of *pueros* in the case of the Anglian boys may also connote an inherent uncorrupt and naive readiness to adopt the pure faith in God, untainted by doubt or false (unorthodox) interpretation. In this specific case, however, we can also read Bede's metaphorical terminology as an essential part of the Christian promise to the English, because the boys are explicitly depicted as heathens ("essent pagani"). In the wider context of the *HE* as master narrative of the Christianisation of the Anglo-Saxons, Bede is therefore outlining some crucial terms of its implementation here: as the children have not yet been confronted with the Christian belief and its – from Bede's point of view

23 *HE* II.1, 132–5.

24 See Shahar, *Childhood*, 21–31.

25 *HE* IV.8.

– unorthodox strands, they are therefore entitled to accept the pure orthodox faith directly from Rome. This image of the "meek heathen" is indeed remarkable, and it shows the Anglo-Saxons as especially deserving of the divine grace.

Second, the purity of the slave boys is mirrored in their outward appearance, which Bede describes emphatically: they have fair complexion, handsome faces, and lovely hair.[26] As Stephen Harris notes, Bede here applies the well-known Christian topos that acknowledges outward beauty as a sign of inner grace,[27] and that these boys have (potential) inner grace is confirmed by Gregory's response after he is told that the English are still heathen.[28] This image of the English youths is then further ornamented by Gregory's famous pun on their *gens*, namely, *angelicum* and *angelorum*, both pointing to the tribe of the Angles. Their angelic appearance, evident sign of their purity, singles them out as worthy recipients of heavenly grace, despite their ignorance of the Christian faith. Thus the story of the Anglian *pueros* in the Roman market square becomes the starting point for the Christianisation of the English. They appear to be predestined to receive the divine grace, granted through the mission that their outward beauty prompted. Gregory, as a Father of the church, is staged here as the first teacher of a tribe of school starters in Christian education.

A third aspect is that the application of the term *pueros* appears to denote an evident contrast to adolescents or full-grown adults. Referring to Isidore's definition again, their naiveté and purity makes them more ready recipients of the faith than their elders. Moral purity of children – in the sense that their morality has not yet been tested – can be considered a commonplace in the works of medieval writers such as St Augustine of Hippo, St Columbanus, or Asser. Mathew Kuefler has shown that the exact terminology (e.g., *infans*, *puer*, *parvulus*) with regard to their actual age can differ within these sources.[29] This exacerbates the difficulties in distinguishing between very young children (*infantes*) or youths (*pueri*). Kuefler refers to Columbanus, who rejoiced in teaching young oblates as he regarded children to be better monks than adults. Columbanus gives

26 *HE* II.1 (as cited above).

27 Stephen Harris, *Race and Ethnicity in Anglo-Saxon Literature*, 47–51.

28 *HE* II.1, 133: "Alas that the author of darkness should have men so bright of face in his grip, and that minds devoid of inward grace should bear so graceful an outward form."

29 See Mathew S. Kuefler, "'A Wryed Existence': Attitudes toward Children in Anglo-Saxon England," 823–34, at 824–5.

four reasons: the child does not persist in anger, does not bear a grudge, does not take delight in the beauty of women, and expresses what it truly believes. The Welsh monk Asser, biographer of the West Saxon King Alfred (AD 871–99), remarked in his *Vita Ælfredi* (ch. 93) that children were sometimes the only voluntary candidates for monastic orders, since they were not yet corrupted by the materialistic pursuits of adults:

> [N]ullum de sua propria gente nobilem ac liberum hominem, nisi infantes, qui nihil boni eligere nec mali respuere pro teneritudine invalidae aetatis adhuc possunt, qui monasticam voluntarie subire vitam, habebat; nimirum quia per multa retroacta annorum curricula monasticae vitae desiderium ab illa tota gente, nec non et a multis aliis gentibus, funditus desierat, quamuis plurima adhuc monasteria in illa regione constructa permaneant, nullo tamen regulam illius vitae ordinabiliter tenente, nescio quare, aut pro alienigenarum infestationibus, qui saepissime terra marique hostiliter irrumpunt, aut etiam pro nimia illius gentis in omni genere divitiarum abundantia, propter quam multo magis id genus despectae monasticae vitae fieri existimo.[30]

> [He [Alfred] had no noble or freeborn man of his own race who would of his own accord undertake the monastic life, except for children, who could not as yet choose good or reject evil because of the tenderness of their infant years – not surprisingly, since for many years past the desire for the monastic life had been totally lacking in that entire race (and in a good many other peoples as well!), even though quite a number of monasteries which had been built in that area still remain but do not maintain the rule of monastic life in any consistent way. I am not sure why: either it is because of the depredations of foreign enemies whose attacks by land and sea are very frequent and savage, or else because of the people's enormous abundance of riches of every kind, as a result of which (I suspect) this kind of monastic life came all the more into disrespect.][31]

Asser employs the term *infans*, not *puer*, which leaves us to wonder whether he actually meant children under the age of seven. Up to the twelfth century, oblates were usually admitted to monastic education at the age of five or six, sometimes earlier. Children trained for secular church

---

30 William H. Stevenson, ed., *Asser's Life of King Alfred together with the Annals of Saint Neots Erroneously Ascribed to Asser*, 80–1.

31 Simon Keynes and Michael Lapidge, eds., *Alfred the Great*, 103.

service usually started schooling at reading or song school at the age of seven.[32] Regardless of the terminology, the notion of innocent and pious children compared to their adolescent and adult counterparts, is evident in Asser's work.

Taking this into consideration, one may argue that Bede's account of the Anglian slave boys prefigures the salvation of the English, because the boys' representation as innocent children holds a promise for the future conversion of the Anglo-Saxon kingdoms. In other words, if the Anglian boys are ready, eager, and pure enough to receive the faith, then so are the English in general. In this clever parallelism, the story identifies the status of the English as the elect children of God, whose representative on earth is Pope Gregory. The use of *pueri* is crucial in this context as writers of early Christianity often refer to a male of any age who had received baptism as *puer*.[33] In this context it is worth noting that St Augustine of Hippo, who had a lasting influence on the negative image of children in medieval writings, claims that although an infant is born in sin and motivated by its drives, it would become more innocent than its elders through the act of baptism. The same holds true for children past the age of *infantia*.[34] Thus, the use of *puer* in this episode serves to encapsulate the Anglian boys' uncorrupted purity, and also heralds their future conversion through baptism. In this they become a metonym for the subsequent Christianisation of the English as a people.

The Birth of Eanflæd

My second example is the birth of Eanflæd, daughter of king Edwin of Northumbria. After the initial conversion of Kent through Augustine of Canterbury's preaching, the faith spreads north through one of his disciples – Paulinus. He is sent to the court of Edwin of Northumbria to instruct the king in the mysteries of the Christian faith. Edwin admits the possibility of accepting the Christian faith if it should prove better than his old (pagan) belief, but is reluctant to convert immediately. In the course of events Edwin escapes an attempt on his life on Easter Day, while two of his followers are killed:

32 Shahar, *Childhood*, 187–91.
33 James, "Childhood and Youth," 16.
34 Shahar, *Childhood*, 16.

Eadem autem nocte sacrosancta dominici paschae pepererat regina filiam regi, cui nomen Eanfled; cumque idem rex praesente Paulino episcopo gratias ageret diis suis pro nata sibi filia, econtra episcopus gratias coepeit agere Domino Christo, regique astruere, quod ipse precibus suis apud illum obtinuerit, ut regina sospes et absque dolore graui sobolem procrearet. Cuius uerbis delectatus rex promisit se abrenuntiatis idolis Christo seruiturum, si uitam sibi et uictoriam donaret pugnanti aduersus regem, a quo homicida ille, qui eum uulnerauerat, missus est; et in pignus promissionis implendae, eandem filiam suam Christo consecrandam Paulino episcopo adsignauit, quae baptizata est die sancto Pentecostes prima de gente Nordanhymbrorum cum XI aliis de familia eius.

[On the same night, the holy night of Easter Day, the queen had borne the king a daughter named Eanflæd. The king, in the presence of Bishop Paulinus, gave thanks to his gods for the birth of his daughter; but the bishop, on the other hand, began to thank the Lord Christ and to tell the king that it was in answer to his prayers to God that the queen had been safely delivered of a child, and without great pain. The king was delighted with his words, and promised that if God would grant him life, and victory over the king who had sent the assassin who wounded him, he would renounce his idols and serve Christ; and as a pledge that he would keep his word, he gave his infant daughter to Bishop Paulinus to be consecrated to Christ. She was baptised on the holy day of Pentecost, the first of the Northumbrian race to be baptised, together with eleven others of his household.][35]

In what can be regarded as strong Easter symbolism of death and resurrection, as Sharon Rowley has pointed out, the two deaths are followed by the birth of Edwin's daughter Eanflæd.[36] Although Edwin overcomes his enemy, King Cwichhelm of Wessex, he himself still remains undecided which religion he should follow and does not yet convert, while Eanflæd, by contrast, becomes the first Northumbrian to be baptised, along with eleven others of the royal household. Bede foregrounds the royal child as God-given recipient of the new faith, while the fact that her baptism takes place on Pentecost marks a promise of future conversion, as on Pentecost the disciples of Christ received the Holy Spirit and the Great Commission.

35 *HE* II.9, 164–7.

36 Sharon M. Rowley, "Bede in Later Anglo-Saxon England," 216–28, at 223.

Accordingly, the baptism of Eanflæd and the eleven household members even numerically foreshadows the spread of the Christian faith in England. King Edwin's sustained doubts provide a marked contrast to the swift adoption of the new faith by the younger generation, as Edwin's daughter heralds the inevitable Christian future of Northumbria, whereas her father deliberates for two years before he turns humbly to the new religion. Bede shows here that conversion, even within the same family, can take more or less time, the important point being that it eventually takes place. After his eventual conversion in AD 627, Edwin and his successors as kings of Northumbria become figureheads of the Christianisation of England and gain unprecedented political power as overlords over the heptarchy. This Northumbrian story of military and political success, however, begins with the birth and baptism of the child Eanflæd, whom Bede presents as the seed of this achievement.

The Selsey Miracle

The conversion of the English kingdoms comes full circle with the Christianisation of the South Saxons and the Isle of Wight, as will be shown in my third and fourth examples. Bede, having received the account from his close friend, Acca of Hexham, tells his readers a story about a little boy (*puerulus*) who lived among the brethren in the monastery of Selsey.[37] Neither his age nor his name is mentioned. He might have been a very young oblate, to judge by the diminutive Bede uses here. It is said that he was "nuper uocatus ad fidem"[38] (recently called to the faith) and "puer multum simplicis ac mansueti animi, sinceraque deuotione sacramenta fidei quae susceperat seruans"[39] (a boy of simple and gentle disposition, with faithful devotion observing the sacraments of the faith which he had received).[40] This description again builds on the "etymological" sense of *puer* outlined above. The boy is presented as uncorrupted and gentle, a behaviour that serves to reflect his newly converted status. Given that he had received more than one sacrament, which would include at least penance, if not the Holy Communion, may make him older than seven, but

37 *HE* IV.14, 376–81.
38 Ibid., 376.
39 Ibid.
40 Ibid., 377.

not necessarily much older than nine years. He is infected by a pestilence that has struck all Sussex and the monastery, with the other brethren being sick.[41] While the boy is lying in bed, the apostles Peter and Paul appear "diuina dispositione"[42] (by divine dispensation) in a vision and tell the boy:

> Noli timere, fili, mortem, pro qua sollicitus es; nos enim te hodierna die ad caelestia sumus regna perducturi ... sed omnes qui alicubi de uestris hac aegritudine laborant, resurrecturi a languore, pristina sunt sospitate recuperandi – praeter te solum, qui hodierna es die liberandus a morte et ad uisionem Domini Christi, cui fideliter seruisti, perducendus in caelum.
>
> [Son, do not let the fear of death trouble you, for we are going to take you today to the heavenly kingdom ... But all those people who are now suffering from the sickness shall be raised up from their sickbeds and restored to their former health – all except you alone, for you will today be freed from death and taken to heaven to behold the lord Christ whom you have faithfully served.][43]

While the boy subsequently dies, all other brethren recover from their sickness. The passage thus constructs a motif of redemption: the boy saves the other members of the monastery through his death, reflecting Christ's sacrifice for mankind. Through this comparison the story gives consolation by assigning meaning to what seems an unnecessary loss, but it also metaphorically juxtaposes adult sin with infant innocence and so inspires devotion and examination of one's conscience.

The didactic dimension of the story of the boy at Selsey becomes unmistakable when Bede explains that many who heard it were encouraged to pray for divine mercy in times of adversity. The priest to whom the boy told his vision of the apostles does not, however, believe him at first, but asks further questions. Only after the boy can give a detailed description of the apostles does the priest finally believe him. Does this mean that the word of children counted for less? It seems rather that Bede wishes to

41 The story seems to fit the characteristics of the common *oblatus mortuus* motif; see Winfried Rudolf, "The Source and Textual Identity of 'Homily' Napier XXXI – Ælfric and the *Munuccild* of Saint-Maurice d'Agaune," 607–22.

42 *HE* IV.14, 376.

43 Ibid., 376 and 379.

emphasise that the trustful purity of the boy made no further authorisation necessary as he was clearly speaking the truth. Nonetheless, that the priest does not immediately believe him emphasises a moral distance and distinction between adult and child, showing that distrust is to be associated with adulthood. The boy's ability to recognise the apostles not only confirms his willingness to embrace the Christian doctrine as a faithful and diligent pupil, but also verifies the quality of his teachers. The educational value of this passage would have been immense when we consider Bede's role as instructor of the oblates at Jarrow. His pupils may have felt invited to imitate the boy of Selsey, who enters the heavenly kingdom due to his piety and diligence, his example inspiring a religious zeal that would promise salvation to any monastic beginner.

Although the account focuses on the death of the *puerulus*, the purpose of the complete episode is to celebrate the sanctity of the Northumbrian king Oswald. The apostles tell the boy that the miracle is a result of the intercession of the Northumbrian saint, first martyr among the English, who was slain in battle on the same day. The chapter ends with Bede's comment that many – adults and children alike – were strengthened by this miracle leading to the beginnings of a cult of Oswald.[44] Oswald's martyrdom faintly reverberates in the boy's sacrificial death, which thus also serves as a reminder of the saint's consolidation of the faith of the English. Here, as in other examples of the *HE*, Bede has created an internal typology for his work in which the miracle performed on the boy and his community at Selsey becomes a rhetorical tool that conveys the sense of a deeper, divine plan of salvation.

This rhetorical use of children is a well-known topos in Christian writing. Outside the genre of hagiography we find a famous example in John 4:43–54, a story about Jesus healing the son of a royal officer at Capernaum. Jesus chides the bystanders: "Nisi signa et prodigia videritis non creditis"[45] (Unless you see signs and wonders, you believe not). The official and his whole household convert only after his son is healed. Bede draws on this topos as a way of approaching mission and conversion, the inculcation of Christian norms, and the need to invigorate the faith among the English. He deliberately selects the *puerulus* as a role model for others, since the boy embodies qualities that were apparently lacking in his adult brethren.

44 For the invigoration of a saint's holiness through children, see Shahar, *Childhood*, 17.
45 John 4:48.

The Two Young Princes of the Isle of Wight

The exalted role of children is also evident in the conversion of the last of the English kingdoms, namely, the Isle of Wight.[46] After the West Saxon king Caedwalla's conquest of the island, two young princes, brothers of the defeated king Arwald, flee the island. They are betrayed and sentenced to death by Caedwalla, who is described as having not yet converted in spirit ("quamuis necdum regeneratus ... in Christo"), although he agrees to share conquered land with bishop Wilfrid. After an appeal by Cynberht, abbot of Redbridge, the two royal prisoners are instructed in the mysteries of the Christian faith shortly before their execution. Bede writes that they "gladly submitted to temporal death through which they were assured that they would pass to the eternal life of the soul" ("[m]oxque illi instante carnifice mortem laeti subiere temporalem, per quam se ad uitam animae perpetuam non dubitant esse transituros").[47] He further recounts that the princes were "among the first fruits of the island who believed and were saved" ("in primitatis eorum, qui de eadem insula credendo saluati sunt") and "specially crowned with God's grace" ("speciali sunt Dei gratia coronati").[48] It is not exactly clear again how old these boys were, but the use of *puer* may suggest an age between seven and fourteen.

The central aspect here is that the princes are portrayed as willing believers, who, despite their imprisonment and inevitable death, show neither obstinacy nor doubt, but appear to be receptive to the Christian faith, which they readily embrace. Their description as "speciali Dei gratia coronati" mirrors Bede's high opinion of them, as he presents them almost as royal martyrs, who, in an allegorical reading of the passage, assume their crowns in an act of divine dispensation. Through this coronation image Bede also reminds his audience that they were potential heirs to a worldly kingdom, but are now receiving a new and much more rewarding heritage. The way that Bede closely entangles a question of political succession with the final steps of the conversion of England is intriguing. It leads to an almost paradoxical situation: while the children are portrayed as pious prisoners by Bede, he never openly doubts the necessity of their execution and instead presents the still pagan Caedwalla as a ruler who generously grants Cynberht's request to convert the princes. The children's ardent

---

46 *HE* IV.16, 382–5.
47 Ibid., 382–3.
48 Ibid.

faith makes them appear indifferent towards temporal death as much as towards a secular kingdom, because they joyfully accept the promise of life in the kingdom of heaven. This marks a stark contrast to the victorious, but not yet Christian, king Caedwalla, whose conversion Bede recounts shortly thereafter. The conversion of the defeated princes could even be seen as a foreshadowing of that of the West Saxon king, who is at least ready to allow their baptism. The heavenly reward for the princes also serves as an appeasement of the political sympathisers with Arwald's family because it outshines this family's extinction by the ruthless Caedwalla, who becomes the new ruler of the Isle of Wight.

Bede seems to struggle hard here to create a harmonious endpoint of the territorial conversion of the English. For the people of the Isle of Wight the young princes surpass the victorious Caedwalla through their early baptism, which is the promise of a new generation of the willing faithful, but at the same time calls for political and ecclesiastical protection of faithful rulers. Caedwalla, in turn, serves as a reminder that the unity of worldly power and Christian faith requires the ruler to convert not just formally but also in spirit. Bede may suggest here that, despite the conquest of the Isle of Wight, the conversion of the English is still far from being finished.

As I have shown, children appear in key episodes of Bede's narrative of the Christianisation of the *gens Anglorum*. They are depicted as uncorrupted and willing believers from the start, setting an example for adults and symbolising a promise of future conversion and salvation. The conversion of the English kingdoms begins with the *pueros venales* in the Roman market square and is completed by the conversion and subsequent execution of the two princes of the Isle of Wight. Apart from the four episodes discussed here there are several other cases where Bede refers to children and adolescents, which could not be addressed in this essay. Children feature prominently in the context of miracle stories in which the power of the saints and therefore the power of God can be grasped by Bede's readers. However, children hardly ever appear as agents themselves, but often rather seem to function only as a rhetorical tool. This may be underscored by the fact that Bede – with one exception – does not mention their names.[49] In his work children seem less important to him as individuals: rather they serve as general role models for the ideals of purity and ardent faith. At the same time their receiving of saintly grace

49 *HE* IV.8, 358–9. The boy's name is given as "Æsica."

testifies to their special status as pure and uncorrupted Christians, who do not need to see in order to believe, who simply believe in the mysteries of the faith with all their heart and are therefore adequately rewarded. Bede thus constructs the general ideal of a child-like faithful, which he sets as a prerequisite for the proper acceptance of the new faith, no matter how old the person.

In the key episodes of the Christianisation of England in the *HE*, children inspire exegetical readings in dialogue with the gospels. We find the topic of the elect children of God confirmed by the Anglian slave boys in Rome, whose angelical purity makes them deserving of Christianity; children also stand for the promise of the piety of future generations and the spreading of the belief, as illustrated in the story of Eanflæd; children appear as diligent pupils of the faith, and this faith may offer consolation for their premature loss, as in the Selsey miracle; and finally, the exchange of worldly for heavenly kingship, as well as the possibility of immediate salvation after conversion, is exemplified by the two princes of the Isle of Wight. In their incorruption and piety, children not only serve as role models in contrast to grown-ups but also symbolically represent through their baptism the (re-)birth of every new convert as a child of God. Accompanying Bede's apparently genuine interest in children as pure and ready believers of the Christian faith is his tendency to use them simultaneously as a rhetorical tool. Bede, as an orthodox teacher of the Christian church whose *HE* was designed to portray the story of the infancy of the Anglo-Saxon Church as a struggle for the spread of orthodox Christianity, thus manipulates his readership, be it oblates in the Northumbrian monasteries or the magnates of Ceolfrith's court. They are asked to become true believers in the pure and orthodox teachings of the Roman Catholic Church, to refrain from questioning or interpreting the precepts of the faith, but to embrace it like ingenuous children in order to obtain the heavenly kingdom. Bearing in mind Bede's didactic focus, it seems appropriate to extend Kendall's claim mentioned at the beginning of this essay by arguing that Bede not only loved to educate children, but also through his account of children in the *HE* tried to educate his readers in general in order to make them worthier children of God.[50]

50 I would like to thank Prof. Winfried Rudolf, Prof. Gernot Wieland, Dr Dirk Schultze, and Sascha Bargmann, MA, for their helpful comments and feedback. All remaining errors or shortcomings are of course my own.

7 Childhood in the Lives of Anglo-Saxon Saints

JOYCE HILL

Childhood figures in several of the lives of Anglo-Saxon saints, but scenes of children having fun are rare. The life of Cuthbert, in its various textual forms, is a notable exception:

> Dum ergo puer esset annorum octo, omnes coaetaneos in agilitate et petulantia superans, ita ut sepe postquam fessis menbris requiescebant alii, ille adhuc in loco ioci quasi in stadio triumphans aliquem secum ludificantem expectaret. Tunc congregati sunt quadam die multi iuuenes in campi planicie, inter quos ille inuentus est, ioci uarietatem, et scurilitatem agere ceperunt. Alii namque stantes nudi uersis capitibus contra naturam deorsum ad terram, et expansis cruribus erecti pedes ad coelos sursum prominebant. Alii sic, alii uero sic fecerunt.[1]
>
> [When he was a boy of eight years, he surpassed all of his age in agility and high spirits, so that often, after the others had gone to rest their weary limbs, he, standing triumphantly in the playground, as though he were in the arena, would still wait for someone to play with him. At that time many youths were gathered together one day on a piece of level ground and he too was found among them. They began thereupon to indulge in a variety of games and tricks; some of them stood naked, with their heads turned down unnaturally towards the ground, their legs stretched out and their feet lifted up and pointing skywards; and some did one thing and some another.]

1 Bertram Colgrave, ed., *Two Lives of Saint Cuthbert*, 64. The translation is that of Colgrave, 65.

This description of boys at play is from the life of St Cuthbert written by an anonymous monk of Lindisfarne sometime between AD 699 and 705, not so very long after Cuthbert's death in AD 687.[2]

The anonymous *vita* follows this with another typical boyhood scene: the young Cuthbert has a swollen knee, which makes it painful to walk, although it does heal, among other things by the application of some kind of hot poultice made from wheat flour cooked with milk.[3] Single-knee trouble of this kind among physically active boys, especially those who, like Cuthbert, are triumphant about their prowess – and thus most likely to show off – is usually caused by the trauma of a fall or landing awkwardly. Rest and the application of poultices to stimulate the blood supply and provide soothing comfort for the pain are still among the treatments used, with complete healing often taking some months.

What subsequently happens in the first scene, the handstand episode, is that a child of three appears among the boys and chastises Cuthbert for indulging in foolish play. Cuthbert takes no notice, and so the child bursts into tears, seeming to be inconsolable. When asked what is the matter, the child cries out: "O sancte episcope et presbiter Cuðberhte, hec tibi et tuo gradui contraria nature propter agilitatem non conueniunt"[4] (O holy Bishop and priest Cuthbert, these unnatural tricks done to show off your agility are not befitting to you or your high office). Cuthbert, aged eight, does not understand this, but he comforts the child and returns home, bearing these prophetic words in mind.

In the second episode, as the lame Cuthbert sits outside in the warmth of the sun, a man of noble appearance, dressed in white and riding on a magnificently adorned horse, arrives on the scene and asks Cuthbert if he will minister to him as a guest. Cuthbert says that he would have been willing to do so, but that his lameness prevents him. The traveller examines the knee, which Cuthbert explains has not been attended to by a doctor, and recommends the poultice. He then rides on his way. Cuthbert's knee is better within a few days.

We see here two highly plausible childhood scenes – one of boys enjoying physical play and another of a member of the group sitting alone as he suffers from a knee injury – being used in the hagiography as the bases for Cuthbert's initial encounters with the divine, the purpose being to mark him out as destined for higher things and gifted with God's favour. The

2 On the evidence within the text for this dating, see Colgrave, *Two Lives*, 13.

3 Ibid., 66–8.

4 Ibid., 64. The translation is that of Colgrave, 65.

first scene provides a prophecy of his future status and a foreshadowing of his ascetic withdrawal from the attractions of daily life, an asceticism which was *the* defining characteristic of his sanctity. At this point in his life, as a foreshadowing scene, it is dramatised as withdrawal from the frivolous activities of young boys, in which he had previously taken rather self-satisfied pleasure. In the second scene, the visitation of the angel – for that is how the figure is identified in the hagiographer's interpretation of the episode – shows that Cuthbert will always be given divine help.

The episodes are so critical in the presentation of Cuthbert as a saint that they are also told by Bede and Ælfric. Bede's prose version offers more elaborate moralising and slightly more vivid dramatisation: in the games episode running, jumping, and wrestling are included in the boys' activities, and Cuthbert actually boasts that he beats those who are his equals and even some who are older;[5] while in the scene with the swollen knee the affliction appears to be more grave in itself, by implication doctors have been consulted since we are told that none can help, and the boy's condition is in a deteriorating state when the rider appears.[6] The effect of these enhancements to the human dimension is to strengthen the hagiographic impact of both episodes, emphasising the virtue of Cuthbert's renunciation of childhood pleasures, his bearing of the burden of suffering, and the miraculous nature of the divine healing. Ælfric, in his homily for the Feast of the Deposition of St Cuthbert in the Second Series of *Catholic Homilies* (homily X), combines details from Bede's verse and prose *vitae*,[7] but by comparison with Bede, his Cuthbert narrative has very limited historical contextualisation and biographical interest. Rather, Ælfric's efforts are directed firmly towards presenting Cuthbert as a universal saint since it is in this way that his status can be further enhanced. It is all the more revealing, then, that this construct begins with the two childhood scenes that we have been discussing. Their representation of the renunciation of worldly delights at a young age and their demonstration of the early favour of God are essentials in this narrative pattern; they could not be left out, even though Ælfric's text, taken as a whole, is essentially a sequence of miracles by Cuthbert, with little biographical connection or causality.

5 Ibid., 154–8.

6 Ibid., 158–60.

7 Malcolm Godden, ed., *Ælfric's Catholic Homilies: The Second Series*, 81–91. Ælfric's sources, as he declares at the outset, are Bede's prose and verse *vitae*. The way in which he draws upon them is analysed in detail in Malcolm Godden, *Ælfric's Catholic Homilies: Introduction, Commentary and Glossary*, 412–29.

The use of the saint's childhood to mark him out as chosen by God is of course a commonplace of hagiography; what is exceptional with Cuthbert is the amount of dramatic realisation regarding the circumstantial detail. The saintly childhood may more commonly be defined by a sharper focus on what the saint does not do, coupled with an almost impossibly idealised statement of his virtues, which in turn implies that the opposite is the norm, so providing the hagiographer with an opportunity to be censorious about everyday behaviour, which he is thus able to suggest is both frivolous and indulgent. Felix's account of Guthlac's childhood behaviour is one of the more extreme examples:

> XII. Igitur transcensis infantiae suae temporibus, cum fari pueriliter temtabat, nullius molestiae parentibus nutricibusve seu coaetaneis parvulorum coetibus fuit. Non puerorum lascivias, non garrula matronarum deliramenta, non vanas vulgi fabulas, non ruricolarum bardigiosos vagitus, non falsidicas parasitorum fribulas, non variorum volucrum diversos crocitus, ut adsolet illa aetas, imitabatur.
> XIII. sed eximia sagacitate pollens, hilari facie, sincera mente, mansueto animo, simplici vultu,
> XIV. in pietate parentibus, in oboedientia senioribus, in dilectione conlactaneis, neminem seducens, neminem increpans, neminem scandalizans, nulli malum pro malo reddens, aequanimis utebatur.[8]

> [XII. And as the time of his infancy passed and he tried to speak in his childish way, he was never troublesome to his parents or nurses or to the bands of children of his own age. He did not imitate the impudence of the children nor the nonsensical chatter of the matrons, nor the empty tales of the common people, nor the foolish shouts of the rustics, nor the lying triflings of flatterers, nor the different cries of the various kinds of birds[9] as children of that age are wont to do;

8 Bertram Colgrave, ed., *Felix's Life of Saint Guthlac*, 78. The translation is that of Colgrave, 79.

9 Colgrave's translation implies that it was customary for boys to imitate the singing of birds, but this apparently attractive detail sits oddly within the censorious statements about human behaviour. It could, of course, be seen as a small example of general frivolity. But the Latin "crocitus" is not a general word for the song of birds; it is, rather, a word denoting the harsh cry or croak of ravens. The implications of Colgrave's translation may thus be misleading, though it is difficult to determine precisely what point Felix was seeking to make here by his rather particular choice of words.

XIII. but possessing remarkable wisdom, he showed a cheerful face, a pure mind, a gentle spirit, a frank countenance;
XIV. he was dutiful to his parents, obedient to his elders, affectionate to his foster-brothers and sisters, leading none astray, chiding none, causing none to stumble, recompensing no man evil for evil, always even-tempered.]

Wilfrid is described in a similar platitudinous way, but more simply:

> parentibus oboediens, omnibus carus, pulcher aspectu, bonae indolis, mitis, modestus, stabilis, nihil inane more puerorum cupiens.[10]

> [obedient to his parents and beloved of all men, fair in appearance, of good parts, gentle, modest, and firm, with none of the vain desires that are customary in boyhood.]

And again at the beginning of adolescence, when he was about to embark on serious study, Stephen of Ripon tells us that he was "decorus aspectu et acutissimi ingenii"[11] (comely in appearance and exceedingly sharp of wit), a student who fulfilled all that was required of him in the monastery, where he was loved by the older monks as a son, by his equals as a brother, because, with a loving heart, he lived the monastic life with humility and obedience.

One may well wonder whether this is the character of the Wilfrid we come to know later. But the point is that, in order to establish him from the outset as a saintly figure, Stephen has to present him in the mould of other universal saints, although admittedly another factor to be borne in mind, in this as in all the Anglo-Saxon saints' lives, is that the childhood scenes may be predominantly motif-driven because of relative lack of information. It is certainly the case that the nearer Stephen comes in time to the Wilfrid he knew personally, the closer his account moves towards biography, notwithstanding the biases created by his strongly partisan

10 Bertram Colgrave, ed., *The Life of Bishop Wilfrid by Eddius Stephanus*, 4. The translation is that of Colgrave, 5. Since Kirby demonstrated that this work had been wrongly attributed to Eddius Stephanus, the author is now customarily identified as Stephen of Ripon: David P. Kirby, "Bede, Eddius Stephanus and the 'Life of Wilfrid,'" 101–14.

11 Colgrave, *The Life of Bishop Wilfrid*, 6. The translation is that of Colgrave, 7.

agenda.[12] Even so, it says something about the value of childhood within the hagiographic paradigm that someone like Stephen, who knows so much about Wilfrid's adult life, nevertheless responds to the pressure of narrative expectation in dealing with his earlier years.

In addition, for those whose sanctity is predicated on their position within the institutional church, as bishops or as scholars, there has also to be a demonstration of their outstanding aptitude for Christian learning, often manifested in the saint's rapid mastery of the psalter. Wilfrid is a case in point[13] and so, according to Byrhtferth's account, is Ecgwine, Bishop of Worcester AD 693–717.[14] By contrast, because their sanctity is differently defined, it is a detail that is not present in the boyhood of Guthlac,[15] nor in that of Cuthbert since, despite his late and reluctant agreement to be consecrated bishop, his hagiographical narratives are mainly concerned to trace his progress, as Kirby summarises it, "from youthful virtue, through the rigours of monastic and anchoretic discipline, to total self-denial and contemplative ecstasy."[16]

Of course, just because a detail functions as part of a standard motif, it does not mean that it was untrue in a particular instance. Wilfrid clearly was very able and was doubtless very good at his studies. It is, after all, common enough for someone who rises high in a profession that requires a mastery of literacy and skill in languages to have been a good, even an exceptionally good, student, and this fundamental, given an educational context defined by book learning, as was the case for saintly clerical leaders and scholars, does not change over time. Furthermore, we know from the anonymous *Life of Ceolfrith* that when plague struck down the new community at Jarrow, in AD 685/6, there was a young member of the

12 Stephen's agenda in writing a defensive apologia for Wilfrid is explored by Alan Thacker, "Wilfrid, His Cult and His Biographer," 1–16.

13 Colgrave, *The Life of Bishop Wilfrid*, 6 (ch. 2). In fact so exceptional does Stephen want Wilfrid to seem that he makes the point that he also learnt several other books by heart at this time.

14 Michael Lapidge, ed. and trans., *Byrhtferth of Ramsey: The Lives of St Oswald and St Ecgwine*, 220.

15 The education that Guthlac received in his father's hall, as appropriate for a young man of high status, evidently revolved around the deeds of heroes and ancestors, which then spurred him on to lead a band of warriors: see Colgrave, *Felix's Life of Saint Guthlac*, 78, 80.

16 David P. Kirby, "The Genesis of a Cult: Cuthbert of Farne and Ecclesiastical Politics in Northumbria in the Late Seventh and Early Eighth Centuries," 383–97, at 389.

community, a "puerulus," who was capable of maintaining the daily liturgy with Abbot Ceolfrith.[17] It has commonly been assumed, although with no real justification, that this was Bede, who, if he had been born ca. AD 673, would have been about twelve at the time.[18] Ecgwine is said to have learnt the psalter after beginning sacred learning at the age of seven. In Wilfrid's case, by contrast, this feat is attributed, perhaps more realistically, to his period of study at Lindisfarne, when he was at least fourteen, since we are told that this was his age when he left home, first to go to court, and from there to Lindisfarne with the support of Queen Eanflæd.

What Wilfrid does share with Guthlac, however, are birth portents. In Guthlac's case, a human hand in gold-red splendour reached down from the clouds and made a sign on the door, just as his mother was in labour.[19] In Wilfrid's case, at the moment of his birth some men standing outside saw the house apparently on fire, although miraculously the fire did not actually burn anything, rather like Moses's Burning Bush, as Stephen of Ripon notes.[20] Two of the key texts that justify all such birth portents are included in this narrative: Rom. 8:29–30, to the effect that the child in question was already foreknown, called, justified, and glorified by God; and the words from Jer. 1:5, "Priusquam te formarem in utero, novi te; et antequam exires de vulva sanctificavi te; prophetamque gentibus dedi te" (Before I formed thee in the belly I knew thee; and before thou camest forth out of the womb I sanctified thee, and I ordained thee a prophet unto the nations).

In these early lives of Anglo-Saxon saints, then, even without looking beyond the periods of boyhood and adolescence, we can clearly see that the overriding determiner is the need to achieve what Donald Bullough has usefully called "literary canonisation"[21] – a fashioning of the story in such a way that it fits the new native saint into the pattern of hagiographic universality. Yet, even so, there are occasional details that reflect

17 Christopher Grocock and Ian N. Wood, eds., *Abbots of Wearmouth and Jarrow*, 92, and 92n.70, for the use of "puerulus," which may be a diminutive, rather than indicative of few years: thus "lad," as Grocock and Wood translate it (93), although in any event it denotes someone who is still quite young.

18 See the discussion by Ian Wood, *The Most Holy Abbot Ceolfrid*, 16, and 34n.207.

19 Colgrave, *Felix's Life of Saint Guthlac*, 74–6.

20 Colgrave, *The Life of Bishop Wilfrid*, 4. In quoting Jeremiah here, I follow Stephen of Ripon's text and Colgrave's translation.

21 Donald A. Bullough, "The Missions to the English and the Picts and Their Heritage (to *c.* 800)," 1.80–98, at 94.

the culture of the day and result in interesting differences between the individual saints. Cuthbert, we subsequently learn, had a foster-mother, Coenswith, for whom he clearly had considerable affection: he evidently called her "mother" and visited her in later life,[22] while Guthlac, though seemingly not fostered himself, was brought up among foster-brothers and foster-sisters in his father's household.[23] Bede, we know, was separated from his kinsmen at the age of seven, when he was given over to Benedict Biscop and subsequently Ceolfrith to be educated, presumably as an oblate,[24] a practice still known in tenth-century England, as we see from a passing comment in Byrhtferth's *Life of Oswald*;[25] a more unfortunate circumstance was the death of a parent, as with Wilfrid, whose decision to leave home at the age of fourteen was in part influenced by his having a harsh and cruel stepmother.[26] Separation from parents, through various cultural practices and through death, must have been an experience of many children; and we should also not forget the evidence that saints' miracles provide of the illness and death of children, which everyone would have confronted from their earliest years.

What these Anglo-Saxon saints also have in common is their relatively high social status. Cuthbert is fostered, as we have noted, takes up arms for a time (mentioned only in the anonymous *vita*, not by Bede or Ælfric),[27] and later moves with social ease among the nobility and royalty of Northumbria, notwithstanding his personal asceticism; Felix makes it clear that Guthlac's father is very well-to-do;[28] and Wilfrid is quintessentially aristocratic, ministering to nobles in his father's house, and as an adolescent of fourteen having the social standing that allows him to go to the royal court, where he is presented to the queen by the very nobles to whom he had ministered as a boy.[29] Such circumstances have a functional value within the saint's life in pointing to their natural authority status and the

---

22 Colgrave, *Two Lives*, 88–90 (anonymous *vita*), 200–2 (Bede's prose *vita*).

23 Colgrave, *Felix's Life of Saint Guthlac*, 78.

24 Bertram Colgrave and Roger A.B. Mynors, eds. and trans., *Bede's Ecclesiastical History of the English People*, 566.

25 Lapidge, *Byrhtferth of Ramsey: The Lives of St Oswald and St Ecgwine*, 68. The comment is not a detail about Oswald's life, but about the composition of a particular community.

26 Colgrave, *The Life of Bishop Wilfrid*, 6.

27 Colgrave, *Two Lives*, 72.

28 Colgrave, *Felix's Life of Saint Guthlac*, 72, 74.

29 Colgrave, *The Life of Bishop Wilfrid*, 4, 6.

virtue of their self-denial in committing to life as a religious. Furthermore, they demonstrate how the new saints of Anglo-Saxon England align with the saints of the universal church, many of whom reveal their heroic commitment to God by turning away from the attractive and successful lives that they are offered through their relatively well-to-do social standing. But such details should not be seen as merely literary motifs: they may also reflect social reality, where freedom to pursue a life dedicated to God and to engage in study at an early age was a privilege available only to those who could be spared for it, as Alfred notes in the Preface to the *Cura pastoralis*.[30] In any case, the founding of monasteries and churches took time, wealth, and social influence, so that the early saints who shaped the Anglo-Saxon church needed to have the necessary social capital, with all that this will have meant for their experience of childhood.

The same is true of the leaders of the Benedictine Reform, whose literary canonisation includes clear signals that they were of high social status, through their parents in the case of Æthelwold and Dunstan, and through his uncle Archbishop Oda of York in the case of Oswald, although the fact that he had an archbishop for an uncle suggests that his parents were of relatively high status also. Even so, there are signs that the pressure of narrative expectation is at work since it is likely, as Nicholas Brooks has argued, that the nobility of Dunstan's parents was somewhat exaggerated in B's hagiography.[31] If that was the case, it only serves to reinforce the point that, in hagiographical terms, the nobler a man's birth, the higher his material expectations and the greater his sacrifice in following the monastic life. More particularly, within the context of the Reform, which was fundamentally about institutional organisation, power, and control, requiring royal and aristocratic support, it was important that the process of literary canonisation should present the leaders unequivocally as men of standing equal to anyone else in the realm. Indeed, as Rollason has noted, those who, through their writings, asserted the saintly credentials of the Reform's leaders had to engineer something of a shift in the idea of what

30 Henry Sweet, ed., *King Alfred's West Saxon Version of Gregory's Pastoral Care*, 6 (Cotton MSS), 7 (Hatton MS).

31 Nicholas Brooks, "The Career of St Dunstan," in *St Dunstan: His Life, Times and Cult*, 1–23, at 5–11. B's hagiography is the earliest of the accounts of Dunstan's life, written by someone who knew him at the beginning of his career, before he became archbishop. However, we do not know who the author was: in the manuscript he simply identifies himself by the first letter of his name.

a saint was.[32] He argues that they had to emphasise asceticism, authority, and close association with the king, although given their mode of life, their power, and their use of royal and aristocratic connections in furthering the Reform, we need to redefine asceticism in this context as a renunciation of the mode of life that a high-status worldly career would have provided, rather than asceticism as practised by Cuthbert in his periods of withdrawal and prayer.

Presentations of childhood were thus an essential element in the narrative paradigm of the reformer saint. For Dunstan and Æthelwold, their entitlement to claim religious authority is initially established through birth portents. In Dunstan's case, when his pregnant mother is attending Candlemas, all the candles are suddenly extinguished, apart from hers. Interestingly, this episode is not in B's narrative, written in the AD 990s, but is in the Lections for the Deposition of Dunstan, written by Adelard of Ghent between AD 1006 and 1012.[33] The inclusion of the birth portent here perhaps reflects the need to confirm that Dunstan was indeed chosen by God, and that by implication the Reform was God's work, given that in these years the movement had lost some of its momentum and certain of its secular supporters found themselves in a difficult position.[34] For Æthelwold, there are already two birth portents in Wulfstan of Winchester's *vita*, and both are retained by Ælfric, even though he drastically reduces and simplifies Wulfstan's rhetorical presentation.[35] These are dreams by Æthelwold's mother when pregnant as she sits outside her house in Winchester. Byrhtferth gives us nothing comparable for Oswald. But one can easily see how the portents function within the lives of Æthelwold and Dunstan to establish their divine authority, and further confirmation of divine favour is provided for them through miracles in their childhood: Dunstan is cured of a severe fever;[36] and the presence of Æthelwold on the lap of his nurse (as in Wulfstan) or his mother (as in Ælfric) is clearly the reason why the woman's piety is rewarded in finding herself, with the baby still on her lap,

32 David Rollason, *Saints and Relics in Anglo-Saxon England*, 169–74.

33 Michael Winterbottom and Michael Lapidge, eds. and trans., *The Early Lives of St Dunstan*, 114. On the dating of Adelard's text, see cxxv.

34 Barbara Yorke, "Aethelmaer, the Foundation of the Abbey at Cerne and the Politics of the Tenth Century," 15–25, at 19–20.

35 Michael Lapidge and Michael Winterbottom, eds., *Wulfstan of Winchester: The Life of St Æthelwold*, 4–6 (Wulfstan's *Vita*), 71 (Ælfric's *Vita*, where chapters 2 and 3 of Wulfstan's *Vita* are condensed into one chapter).

36 Winterbottom and Lapidge, *The Early Lives of St Dunstan*, 14–16.

suddenly transported to the church, when exceptionally bad weather had thwarted her intention to venture out for the feast-day celebration.[37]

As sanctified leaders of the church, they naturally share the common essential of being extraordinarily good children, precocious in their maturity, wholeheartedly committed to God, and displaying considerable aptitude for their studies. Even if some of these characteristics reflected reality in a given case – albeit with retrospective and agenda-driven exaggeration – it is commonly presented in the familiar summary terms, so that within its literary context it makes its rhetorical impact as an expected motif. Oswald, while still a boy, "cepit summo saluatori propensius seruire"[38] (began willingly to serve the High Saviour). He then

> sacris litteris eo precipiente est traditus. Qui, transacto pueritie sue temporis spacio, miro pollebat ingenio, quia erat preuentus egregie spiritus sancti dono. Sitiebant ipsius penetralia cordis largiter haurire semper doctrinam sacre eruditionis, quam conditor clementius contulit in pectore beati tyronis – quem "presciuit et predestinauit" ante sue natiuitatis tempora preesse ecclesie filiis.[39]

> [was handed over to the study of sacred letters at Oda's request. After he had passed through the age of childhood, Oswald blossomed with astonishing intelligence, because he was marked out excellently by the gift of the Holy Spirit. The recesses of his mind were continually thirsting to drink in abundance the instruction of divine learning, which the Creator mercifully implanted in the heart of His beloved recruit – whom "He had foreseen and predestined" to be the foremost among the sons of the Church even before the time of his birth.]

In the partial quotation of Rom. 8:29, which we noted in Stephen of Ripon's *Vita Wilfridi*, we also see here a nod to the powerful expectation that the saint should be identified by God before birth, even though Byrhtferth records no portents for Oswald. For Æthelwold, Wulfstan has a whole chapter (ch. 6) headed "qvod stvdiose et diligenter in ipsa pveritia sacris

37 Lapidge and Winterbottom, *Wulfstan of Winchester: The Life of St Æthelwold*, 8 (Wulfstan's *Vita*) and 72 (Ælfric's *Vita*).

38 Lapidge, *Byrhtferth of Ramsey: The Lives of St Oswald and St Ecgwine*, 32. The translation is that of Lapidge, 33.

39 Ibid., 32–4. The translation is that of Lapidge, 33–5.

litterarvm stvdiis animvm dederit"[40] (How even as a child he devoted himself studiously and industriously to studying holy literature). This chapter emphasises how gifted he was, blessed with a quick and sharp mind and a retentive memory, and how "Studebat etiam teneros pueritiae annos morum honestate et uirtutum maturitate uincere"[41] (he was keen to overcome his tender boyhood years by good conduct and maturity in virtue), always devoting himself to the service of God. The details of aptitude for Christian learning and the overcoming of boyhood frivolity, functioning as a motif to demonstrate Æthelwold's potential for asceticism and authority, were so important in defining the saint that they became the first of twelve *lectiones* in the thirteenth-century Ely breviary in Cambridge University Library, MS Ii.4.20, where the text is lifted directly from Wulfstan's chapter 6.[42] Dunstan likewise benefited from early studies. In his boyhood,

> religiosi iam dicti pueri Dunstani parentes sacris eum litterarum otiis curiose contulerunt. Cui confestim Dominus tantam in his largitatis suae conferre dignatus est gratiam ut coetaneos quosque precelleret et suorum tempora studiorum facili cursu transilisset.[43]

> [his devout parents took care to give the boy Dunstan the leisure to devote to holy scripture. At once the Lord was pleased so to bless him with the grace of His largesse in these studies that he came to excel all his peers, easily racing through his student days.]

In adolescence,

> quantum fuerat crescendo sublimior, tanto erat acuitatis ingenio locupletior, quantumque roticulis annorum maturior, tanto Dei dilectione feruentior, et quantum in diuinis laudibus assuetior, tanto perseueranti animo instantior.[44]

---

40 Lapidge and Winterbottom, *Wulfstan of Winchester: The Life of St Æthelwold*, 8. The translation is that of Lapidge and Winterbottom, 9.

41 Ibid., 10. The translation is that of Lapidge and Winterbottom, 11.

42 Ibid., cxxxi. The occasion for these twelve readings is not specified, but they were probably put together for the Feast of Æthelwold's Deposition, celebrated on 1 August.

43 Winterbottom and Lapidge, *The Early Lives of St Dunstan*, 14. The translation is that of Winterbottom and Lapidge, 15.

44 Ibid., 16. The translation is that of Winterbottom and Lapidge, 17.

[the taller he grew, the richer he became in sharpness of intellect; the riper he became, as the years rolled by, the more ardent was he in his love of God; the more he grew accustomed to praising God, the more earnest and assiduous his mind became.]

But trouble was to come. When he persisted in study and good works, certain young men at court and his own kinsmen became increasingly hostile, finally waylaying him, binding his hands and feet, and trampling him down in some muddy marshland.[45] Dunstan survived and was of course vindicated, the episode serving as the first in a sequence of expulsions and returns that, as Brooks has observed, are such a distinctive characteristic of his life.[46] Again, the point is that the pattern is set in his younger years.

The stages of growing up in these saints' lives are carefully identified by the language used: *infans/infantia*, *puer/pueritia*, and *adolescens/adolescentia*, broadly reflecting the stages of development set out by Isidore in his *Etymologiae.*[47] For Isidore, *infantia* is the first seven years of life and is characterised by the child not being able to talk, endearingly accounted for by the fact that it does not have its full complement of teeth and so has less ability to articulate. *Pueritia* lasts until the age of fourteen, although Isidore notes that the term *puer* may be also used in a more general sense. *Adolescentia* lasts from fourteen to twenty-eight, the period when, as he notes, men can already procreate. In Isidore's terminology *iuvenis/iuventus* is the prime of life, lasting from twenty-eight to fifty, although in the Anglo-Saxon saints' lives under discussion, it sometimes seems to be used in a more general sense for "youth"/ "young person," with *vir* being used for the mature man. We recognise consistency in the allocation of activities: the ability to study, which depends on capacity for words and speech, being regularly ascribed to *pueritia*, and the decision to leave home voluntarily and to lead an independent life being made in *adolescentia*. Descriptions of the saint's precocious character occur in the *pueritia* phase, but there may also be a further definition as the stage of *adolescentia* is embarked upon, as with Wilfrid, for example, and Dunstan.[48] The infant is generally a passive figure, the object of portents when still

45 Ibid., 20–4.
46 Brooks, "The Career of St Dunstan," 11.
47 Isidore, *Etymologiae*, XI.ii, "De aetatibus hominum," ed. Lindsay, 1: n.p.
48 See above, 143 and 150–1, for Wilfrid and Dunstan respectively.

in the womb,[49] a babe on the lap in the Æthelwoldian miracle,[50] a child laudably baptised by pious parents at eight days old, as Guthlac was – a time frame that was not always possible in Anglo-Saxon England, but technically correct and thus the period to be specified in saints' lives, if it is specified at all.[51] Bede is looked after by his family until he is seven;[52] Wilfrid, having brought a young boy back to life, demands that the parents send the boy to him when he reaches seven years old;[53] Cuthbert has his first encounter with the divine at the age of eight, which Bede in his prose *vita*, independently of the anonymous *vita*, notes "post infantiam puericiae primus est"[54] (is the end of infancy and the beginning of boyhood); Wilfrid, we are told, leaves home at fourteen;[55] Dunstan toys with the idea of getting married when in his adolescence;[56] and it is in his adolescence that Cuthbert is seen moving around the area on his own, watching the sheep on the Lammermuir Hills when he sees the soul of Aidan rising to heaven, taking shelter in a wayside hut when travelling on horseback and being miraculously fed and, in a miracle added by Bede, rescuing by prayer at Tynemouth the monks who were being swept out to sea by a storm that had caught their rafts laden with wood that they were bringing downstream to the monastery.[57]

The female saints of Anglo-Saxon England were fashioned according to a different set of social expectations since they were hardly able to live in

49 See above, 145 (Guthlac and Wilfrid), and 148 (Æthelwold and Dunstan).

50 See above, 148–9.

51 Colgrave, *Felix's Life of Saint Guthlac*, 76, and the editor's note on ecclesiastical tradition, 177. It is instructive that in his First Latin Pastoral Letter for Wulfstan, Ælfric specifies how soon the baby should be baptised, but that in his vernacular adaptation, carried out at Wulfstan's request, and also in Wulfstan's further modifications to Ælfric's Old English text, the standard specification is replaced with the instruction that children should be baptised as soon as possible (see also Winfried Rudolf's discussion of this problem in this volume, 55–7]. This must be seen as a pragmatic accommodation to the realities of Anglo-Saxon life, even in the early eleventh century. See Bernhard Fehr, ed., *Die Hirtenbriefe Ælfrics in altenglischer und lateinischer Fassung*, 53 (Latin letter §163) compared with 130–1 (Old English letter §177, Wulfstan's own modification being MS D); and also Joyce Hill, "Authorial Adaptation: Ælfric, Wulfstan and the Pastoral Letters," 63–76, especially 68.

52 See above, 146.

53 Colgrave, *The Life of Bishop Wilfrid*, 38.

54 Colgrave, *Two Lives*, 154.

55 See above, 145.

56 Winterbottom and Lapidge, *The Early Lives of St Dunstan*, 24–8.

57 Colgrave, *Two Lives*, 68–70 (anonymous *vita*), 160–70 (Bede's prose *vita*).

isolation, wrestling with devils, in the manner of Guthlac, nor were they able to become bishops and archbishops, in the manner of many of the prominent male saints of the period. Monasticism offered some opportunities for prominence and influence, with Hild of Whitby and Æthelthryth of Ely being the two most distinguished examples. But in both their cases, although we are made conscious of their wisdom, the foundation of their virtue is their dedication in virginity, and in neither case are there childhood narratives. Of course, virginity and celibacy are essential features of most Anglo-Saxon male saints also, with B making a particular point of it in Dunstan's *Vita* when he takes time to discuss Dunstan's youthful interest in women and the possibility of marriage.[58] But with the saintly male monks, solitaries, priests, and bishops, this is only one of many shaping forces, and not necessarily the one that is particularly accented. Æthelthryth's virginity, by contrast, is celebrated as being held to through a series of marriages, and as Deshman has pointed out, it is this status as a virgin bride of Christ that gives her such standing among the Benedictine Reformers.[59] In common with the male saints, she and Hild are of high social rank, from which, as with the men, comes much of their authority, not to mention their freedom to withdraw from the world and build up their monastic communities. But in secular life such women are expected to marry appropriately, at the behest of their families, and to bear children, so that the virgin life, despite being highly prized within the church, is countercultural in social terms.[60]

For the Anglo-Saxons the predominant model of the virgin saint was that of the virgin martyr, as exemplified particularly by Agnes (21 January), Agatha (5 February), and Lucy (13 December). All three are very well represented in Anglo-Saxon Calendars,[61] and all are significant for the Benedictine Reform tradition, with its emphasis on virginity and chastity: they occur in the Cotton-Corpus Legendary,[62] and Ælfric writes on all

58 Winterbottom and Lapidge, *The Early Lives of St Dunstan*, 24–8.

59 Robert Deshman, *The Benedictional of Æthelwold*, 121–4, and in chapters 5 and 6, where he discusses the Reform's monastic and royal programmes.

60 The Anglo-Saxons did, however, have many royal saints, male as well as female, although childhood does not necessarily figure in their narratives: see Susan J. Ridyard, *The Royal Saints of Anglo-Saxon England*.

61 Rebecca Rushforth, *Saints in English Kalendars before A.D. 1100*.

62 Peter Jackson and Michael Lapidge, "The Contents of the Cotton-Corpus Legendary," 131–46.

three.[63] They meet their supreme test at an early age: Agnes at twelve or thirteen, Agatha at fifteen, and Lucy at twenty-one. But apart from the fact that their narratives show that their age and social status put them under the control of others, which was equally the case for such females in Anglo-Saxon England, the focus is on their resolve in their commitment to God, tested and demonstrated through their determined dedication to virginity at the climactic moment. Thus, although they are youthful martyrs, their hagiographies have a very particular focus and do not deal with the trajectory of their lives, with the result that they tell us nothing about their experiences in childhood beyond the crucial test.

Even though historical circumstances meant that the female saints of Anglo-Saxon England were not martyrs, the influence of this model can nevertheless be seen in their narratives.[64] One recurrent feature is the near-absence of childhood, apart from references to it as the time when the commitment to the Christian life is already apparent, as with the universal saints. Æthelthryth, for example, dedicates herself to virginity as the expression of her commitment to God, "ab ipsis infantie rudimentis"[65] (from the earliest beginning of her childhood). But this isolated reference to her early years functions merely to confirm that her resolution, to which she holds through her successive socially determined marriages, was integral to her very being. Eormenhild, likewise, briefly described as a sweet-natured infant, commits herself to virginity from girlhood,[66] although in her case, since she is married for dynastic reasons and gives birth, there is much manoeuvring on the part of Goscelin in order not to betray the underlying commitment to the virgin-model, at least as a rhetorical construct. Again, however, as with Æthelthryth, there is little more in this narrative format than a passing reference to her childhood, which serves as a time marker to confirm the depth of her commitment. The only other childhood detail is that she was educated in her letters and the Christian life by her parents.[67] Eormenhild in turn educates her own daughter Werburga

63 Walter W. Skeat, ed., *Ælfric's Lives of Saints*, I, 170–86 (Agnes), 194–208 (Agatha), 210–18 (Lucy).

64 Stephanie Hollis, *Anglo-Saxon Women and the Church: Sharing a Common Fate*, particularly 71–2; and Rosalind C. Love, ed. and trans., *Goscelin of Saint-Bertin: The Hagiography of the Female Saints of Ely*, cvi–cxiii.

65 Love, *Goscelin of Saint-Bertin: The Hagiography of the Female Saints of Ely*, 100. The translation is that of Love, 101.

66 Ibid., 12.

67 Ibid., 14.

in a life of devotion to Christ.[68] In common with her mother, Werburga is described in her own *vita* as being beautiful – surely to be understood as a motif signalling the spiritual beauty within – and she too is committed to virginity from her earliest years.[69] Sexburga's *vita* follows a similar pattern of renouncing cultural norms in childhood, although in this case it is described in slightly more detail:

> In annis itaque puellaribus cum in sericis et purpura deaurata incederet, rudes animi fluenta euuangelica perbiberunt, uirtutesque fulciebantur uirtutibus et uitiorum Caribdim ipsa sine uitio persequebatur. Non lasciua, non garrula, sed sobria et modesta thalamorum secretis intererat paternorum. Non est egressa cum Dina ut uideret filias aliene regionis neque eam ui uiolator castitatis oppressit. Non iuuenibus cincinnatis arridebat, nec applaudebat procis forma delicatis.[70]

> [So it was that in the years of her girlhood while she went about in silken garments and gold-edged purple, her young mind drank deeply of the running waters of the gospels, and virtues were sustained by virtues, and she passed through the Charibdis of the vices herself without vice. Not lustful, or prattling, but sober and modest, she entered into the secrets of the inner rooms of the Fathers. She did not go out like Dinah to see the daughters of foreign regions nor did the violator of chastity oppress her with force. She did not smile at youths with curly locks nor show her approval of suitors comely in form.]

She does not, in the end, withdraw from the world, but lives a royal life in marriage, giving birth as her social condition requires. Nevertheless, in maintaining these themes of renunciation, control and dedication throughout the *vita*, Goscelin manages to convey a sense of her sanctity resting on spiritually virginal purity in the midst of an aristocratic life that satisfied the social norms. Edburga, on the other hand, in what for the female saints is a rare dramatic childhood scene, chooses monasticism over the royal life at three years old. Her *vita* describes how, presented with objects of the richest royal finery on the one hand, and a nun's veil, chalice, patten, and psalter

68 Ibid., 34.
69 Ibid., 32–4.
70 Ibid., 138–40. The translation is that of Love, 139–41.

on the other, she at once chooses the ecclesiastical group.[71] She subsequently enters a religious community in her childhood, where she demonstrates her holiness in reading alone and undertaking humble tasks. It is perhaps indicative of social expectations that, in the description of the childhood test, it is her father who is credited with assembling the secular objects and her mother who is said to have laid out the religious items. This harmonises with the detail that it is the mother who educates Werburga in the Christian life. By contrast, concern with the social norm of dynastic marriage and childbearing might be seen as a preoccupation of the royal father.

What is distinctive about these female *vitae* is thus the focus on a single dominant virtue as the recurrent saintly characteristic (even in the face of the complicating historical realities of marriage and motherhood), and a narrative structure that does not systematically trace progress through various aspects of childhood and adolescence into a diversity of saintly roles in maturity. Of course, the female saints move from childhood to adulthood, but childhood and a still developing adolescence are far smaller elements in the narrative pattern than is the case with men, and there is no clear sense of structured progression through the conventional sequence of ages as defined by Isidore and noted above as a feature in the male *vitae*.[72] Indeed, Isidore's interpretations of the various words for women (*puella*, *mulier*, *virgo*, *virago*, *femina*, *vetula*) are for the most part presented in terms of how they embody their lesser position relative to men and in relation to their sexual desire;[73] apart from *puella* and *vetula*, these words are not related to age or progression through life, and even *puella* and *vetula* are not age specific in the sense of being defined by years. Isidore's numerically defined sequence of ages is thus to be seen as relating essentially to the trajectory of men's lives rather than women's. It is a distinction that further helps us understand why the treatment of childhood and adolescence in the lives of female Anglo-Saxon saints is so perfunctory compared with that of the men: male and female lives are conceptualised quite differently, with a consequent difference in the hagiographic treatment of the saints' earlier stages of life.

A final category needing to be examined is that of the child-saint. Among the universal saints adopted by the English we can count Agatha and Agnes in this category, given their ages when martyred, and to them

71 Ridyard, *The Royal Saints of Anglo-Saxon England*, 265.
72 See above, 151.
73 Isidore, *Etymologiae*, XI.ii, 1: n.p.

we can add St Pancras (12 May), whose legend relates that he was martyred at the age of fourteen. His cult was well established in Rome by the time of the Augustinian mission to England, and Augustine dedicated a church to him in Canterbury. Bede records that Pope Vitalian sent relics of St Pancras to King Oswig of Northumbria,[74] and he is commemorated in Anglo-Saxon martyrologies[75] and in all but one of the surviving Anglo-Saxon Calendars.[76] He is also included in the Cotton-Corpus Legendary.[77] But with St Pancras, as with Saints Agatha and Agnes, the ultimate sacrifice for the faith at a young age is what the hagiography is about, not their childhood as such: their stories serve as emotively charged inspiration for faithful resolution.

In England it is only from the eleventh century that we have any developed hagiographies of Anglo-Saxon child-saints, and even then they are rare, although the saints in question were already recognised in Anglo-Saxon Calendars from before this date. Kenelm, commemorated on 17 July, is particularly well represented, being included in seventeen of the twenty-seven calendars tabulated by Rushforth, with one possible additional instance where there is now an erasure.[78] Other liturgical evidence suggests that his cult was indeed widespread.[79] Rumwold is less frequently recorded: there are entries in five calendars for 3 November, and one for 2 November.[80] But there are complications with this evidence since his inclusion in two of these (Oxford, Bodleian Library, MS Hatton 113 and Cambridge, Corpus Christi College, MS 9) are later eleventh-century additions, possibly in the same hand, and dating from the time of the *Vita Rumwoldi*.[81] On the one hand, then, the Calendar entries for this saint seem to reflect a resurgence of interest around the time of the hagiography's composition, possibly responding to the same set of circumstances that brought the Latin text into existence; on the other, the entries in Salisbury Cathedral Library, MS 150, London, British Library, MS Cotton

74 Colgrave and Mynors, *Bede's Ecclesiastical History*, 320.

75 Christine Rauer, ed. and trans., *The Old English Martyrology: Edition, Translation and Commentary*, 260, for the textual traditions.

76 Rushforth, *Saints in English Kalendars before A.D. 1100*.

77 Jackson and Lapidge, "The Contents of the Cotton-Corpus Legendary," 137.

78 Rushforth, *Saints in English Kalendars before A.D. 1100*.

79 Rosalind C. Love, ed. and trans., *Three Eleventh-Century Anglo-Latin Saints' Lives*, cxiii–cxvii.

80 Rushforth, *Saints in English Kalendars before A.D. 1100*.

81 Love, *Three Eleventh-Century Anglo-Latin Saints' Lives*, cxli.

Nero A.ii, and London, British Library, MS Additional 37517 (for 2 November) point to the existence of his cult in some form, perhaps with limited dissemination, before the end of the tenth century.

Rumwold, supposedly the grandson of the pagan king Penda of Mercia (died AD 655), is the most extreme kind of child-saint, and so his life, such as it is, reveals nothing about childhood.[82] According to his hagiography, he cries out "Christianus sum, christianus sum, christianus sum" (I am a Christian, I am a Christian, I am a Christian)[83] as soon as he is born, he is baptised, delivers a sermon, explains what is to happen to his body, and dies three days later. Not surprisingly, he does not appear in the historical record. But there is a distinctive Anglo-Saxon tradition of murdered royal princes, whose deaths were open to being interpreted as martyrdom where this served factional interest.[84] The names might thus be preserved over the years, along with some narrative traditions and pious associations of place, as, for example, was the case for Ealhmund of Northumbria, Æthelræd and Æthelberht of Kent, Wigstan, Wulflæd and Rufinus of Mercia, and Æthelberht of Hereford (perhaps already a king when killed), although they are often shadowy figures of varying degrees of historical validity. Their ages at death are not always clear, but many are remembered as being boys or young men. If nothing else, their deaths remind us of the vulnerability of young claimants to the throne.

Kenelm (Cynehelm), the supposed son and heir of Coenwulf of Mercia, is a member of this group of murdered royal saints, but he is distinguished by being quite precisely described as a child of seven, killed soon after he succeeded his father in AD 821. There is much about his rather colourful hagiography that is problematic: the *Anglo-Saxon Chronicle* says that Coenwulf was directly succeeded by his brother Ceolwulf; there was a Cynehelm, perhaps Coenwulf's son, who, as *dux* and *princeps*, witnessed Coenwulf's charters in the period from AD 803 to 811, but there is no trace of him after this, presumably because he died; even if he had lived, he would not, therefore, have been seven years old in AD 821 when Coenwulf died; while the wicked sister of the hagiography, who engineers Kenelm's death and then rules for a time, was historically the abbess of

82 Ibid., 92–114, with facing translation. For discussion of his parentage, see clxii–clxiv.

83 Ibid., 98 (Latin), 99 (translation).

84 David W. Rollason, "The Cults of Murdered Royal Saints in Anglo-Saxon England," 1–22.

Minster-in-Thanet.[85] A possible factor in the development of the idea that Kenelm was a child martyr is the likelihood that the historical Cynehelm was originally buried at Winchcombe in a church dedicated to St Pancras, before being translated in the tenth century,[86] and that by association this led in time to a belief that he, like St Pancras, must have been martyred when he was a child. But this is, of course, simply conjecture: we do not know how the Kenelm story developed before its written forms in the eleventh century.[87]

According to the eleventh-century hagiographical narrative, Kenelm succeeds Coenwulf at the age of seven, only to have his older sister Cwoenthryth plot against him. The boy, typically described as "euo paruulum sed animo ac pietate magnificum"[88] (little in years, yet eminent in mind and holiness), has a vision which foreshadows that he will have an untimely death. His tutor Æscberht, heavily bribed by the wicked sister to kill the child, lures him into the forest on a hunting trip and there, in a secluded spot, Æscberht digs a grave. The boy, realising what is to happen, asserts that he will lie in a more distant place, but to mark this spot he plants his staff in the ground, where an ash-tree immediately grows up. This, the hagiographer asserts, is visible to the present day. The evil tutor then drags him off to a deep valley in the Clent Hills, where Kenelm bravely urges him to act quickly. He sings the *Te Deum* as he dies and falls down dead when he reaches the verse "Te martyrum candidatus laudat exercitus" (The white-robed army of martyrs praise you),[89] somehow managing to catch his head at the same time. The tutor buries him there. Cwoenthrith, now in control of the kingdom, forbids anyone to look for the body, but miraculously a dove transports to Rome a piece of white parchment inscribed with gold letters, and deposits it on the altar when Pope Leo is saying Mass. This reveals where Kenelm's body is to be found. It is duly

85 See Love, *Three Eleventh-Century Anglo-Latin Saints' Lives*, lxxxix–xc, for discussion of the historical evidence.

86 The evidence for a church dedicated to St Pancras and the possibility that Cynehelm was originally buried there is discussed by S.R. Bassett, "A Probable Mercian Royal Mausoleum at Winchcombe, Gloucestershire," 82–100.

87 There are two recensions of the Life of Kenelm: see Love, *Three Eleventh-Century Anglo-Latin Saints' Lives*, xc. Love edits the longer *Vita et miracula*, 50–88, with facing translation, and it is on this that I draw here.

88 Love, *Three Eleventh-Century Anglo-Latin Saints' Lives*, 54. The translation is that of Love, 55.

89 Ibid., 60, my own translation.

recovered and taken to Winchcombe in the province of Gloucester where, after a dispute en route with men from the province of Worcester, who had some claim because the site of Kenelm's martyrdom was in their territory, it is laid beside his father in the royal mausoleum.[90] Miracles ensue.

In common with those of the other murdered royal saints, Kenelm's hagiography, and Rumwold's likewise, were written just after the Norman Conquest. We know that the Normans queried the validity of some Anglo-Saxon cults – Lanfranc's questioning of Anselm as to whether Ælfheah could properly be venerated as a martyr is the most famous case in point – and it seems some of their doubts might have been directed at cults that depended on oral tradition.[91] That would go some way towards accounting for the timely production of pious Latin narratives at this late date, laced with suitable motifs and biblical allusions. But it is a notable feature of these *vitae* that they are much concerned with particularities of locale.[92] It thus makes good sense to see them as propagandist works, accommodating the fact that several places had come to be associated with the veneration of the saint, as was certainly the case with Rumwold and Kenelm, and in particular consolidating the claim of a particular place to be the custodian of relics that were not only holy, but also royal. This was Buckingham for Rumwold and Winchcombe for Kenelm. As child-saints these two are characterised by the essential motif of childhood precocity. But such late narratives, of decidedly shadowy figures, are wholly different in concept and purpose from those of earlier Anglo-Saxon saints' narratives discussed above.[93]

---

90 The detail that Cynehelm's body lay by that of his father reflects the circumstances at the time of the Latin narrative's composition, by which time it had been translated from its initial burial place in the church of St Pancras: see Bassett, "A Probable Mercian Royal Mausoleum," 90.

91 Susan J. Ridyard, "*Condigna Veneratio*: Post-Conquest Attitudes to the Saints of the Anglo-Saxons," 179–206. The exchange between Lanfranc and Anselm is discussed 200–1. See Richard W. Southern, ed., *The Life of St Anselm Archbishop of Canterbury by Eadmer*, 50–4.

92 Discussed by Love, *Three Eleventh-Century Anglo-Latin Saints' Lives*, clix–clxii, in relation to Rumwold, and cx–cxiii in relation to Kenelm.

93 These retrospective eleventh-century hagiographies are also to be distinguished from the many stories of child-saints that appeared from the twelfth century onwards, such as William of Norwich, Harold of Gloucester, Little St Hugh of Lincoln, and others, whose hagiographies propagate the anti-Semitic ritual murder libel. On the cult of William of Norwich and its place within the blood-libel tradition, see John M. McCulloch, "Jewish Ritual Murder: William of Norwich, Thomas of Monmouth, and the Early Dissemination of the Myth," 698–740.

The twelfth-century account of another early and shadowy Anglo-Saxon saint, the seventh-century bishop of London, St Erkenwald, likewise served a particular propagandist purpose, which the author addressed by devising a familiar stereotypical narrative. But it is instructive that childhood has to figure, even when (as for much else in his life) little was known: Erkenwald is "etate paruus sed mente maturus"[94] (young in years but mature in mind), and he puts away all transitory and worldly things, even as a small boy, a *puerulus*.

Pueritia and *adolescentia*, then, were essential and powerful tools in the hands of the hagiographer of Anglo-Saxon male saints. For female saints childhood and a distinctive adolescence are less prominent as clearly marked stages within the narrative, but reference to the early years, even when brief, is an established means of making it clear that their dedication to chaste purity is integral to their very being, whatever the social circumstances of their later life might bring about. Of course, the frequently formulaic treatment of the early phases of the saint's life tells us more about literary tradition and religious expectation than about historical reality. But even so, in the lives of some of the male Anglo-Saxon saints, written before the Norman Conquest often at no great chronological remove from the saints themselves, we can perhaps allow that there are occasional touches of humanity, and one or two rare glimpses of the contemporary conditions of boyhood and adolescence.

94 E. Gordon Whatley, ed., *The Saint of London: The Life and Miracles of St Erkenwald*, 86. The translation is that of Whatley, 87. The reasons why it might have been politic to revivify interest in St Erkenwald by producing a Latin *vita* in the twelfth century are discussed by Whatley, 59–66.

8 Alcuin's Educational Dispute: The Riddle of Teaching and the Teaching of Riddles

ANDY ORCHARD

For the Anglo-Saxons, especially those in the earlier period whose lives have left traces in the written record, childhood generally seems to have been a time of training for and transition towards adulthood, with a particular focus on the acquisition of knowledge and experience; those few references to childhood play that do survive are only emphasised through contrast.[1] The stern didactic focus of so many Anglo-Saxon texts aimed at the young may seem at first glance both disconcerting and somewhat joyless, but it is evident that some Anglo-Saxons, at least, took a rather more relaxed and even playful attitude towards educating the young, particularly as they approached adolescence. Such was certainly the case with regard to Alcuin (ca. AD 735–804), an Anglo-Saxon who, while most of his extant works were clearly written on the continent, nonetheless famously retained and exhibited many aspects of his native culture.[2]

---

1 There are several particularly relevant papers on more general attitudes to positive aspects of childhood (rather than the education of children) elsewhere in this volume; see, for example, several excellent playful examples in Joyce Hill, "Childhood in the Lives of Anglo-Saxon Saints"; Shu-han Luo, "Tender Beginnings in the Exeter Book *Riddles*," though her opening sentence, "It was hard being a child in Anglo-Saxon England," highlights the general rather negative impression; Winfried Rudolf, "Anglo-Saxon Preaching on Children," gives a further nuanced, if still overall somewhat sombre, view.

2 Alcuin is indeed mocked for retaining his insular fondness for beer and porridge by the rather more sophisticated Carolingian poet, Theodulf of Orléans, writing in AD 796 (Ernst Dümmler, ed., *Theodulfi carmina*, 437–581, *carmen 25*, lines 191–8 [488]):

> Et pater Albinus sedeat pia verba daturus,
> Sumpturusque cibos ore manuque libens.
> Aut si, Bacche, tui aut Cerealis pocla liquoris
> Porgere praecipiat, fors et utrumque volet,

Alcuin was one of the most prolific and erudite Anglo-Saxons whose name we know, a man who stepped out of the shadow of his Northumbrian model, Bede, and indeed out of Northumbria altogether, to make a massive mark on the international stage.[3] Alcuin composed a vast number of works in an astonishing variety of fields, including orthography, grammar, rhetoric, dialectic, astronomy, and mathematics, as well as biblical exegesis, theology, and saints' lives in both prose and verse. There are also more than 270 letters from the correspondence of Alcuin extant, as well as around 120 poems, the vast majority of them written to and for his students past and present, so offering a further set of perspectives.[4]

The thoughtful and wide-ranging scholar Luitpold Wallach wrote more than sixty years ago that "[Alcuin's] accomplishments as educator, statesman, administrator, poet, writer, and scholar were not paralleled by any of his gifted friends of the palace school fellowship, though the Goth Theodul[f] of Orléans may have been a better poet, the Lombard Paul the

---

Quo melius doceat, melius sua fistula cantet,
Si doctrinalis pectoris antra riget.
Este procul pultes, et lactis massa coacti,
Sed pigmentati sis prope mensa cibi.

[And let father Albinus [Alcuin] sit, about to sound forth pious words,
freely about to take food in hand and mouth.
Either, Bacchus, he is to demand fetched beakers of yours
or hoppy liquid [beer], or perhaps he wants both,
the better to teach, the better tune to lend his pipe,
if he moistens the caverns of his learned heart.
Begone, porridge and lumps of coagulated milk,
but approach, table of spiced food!]

See further Andy Orchard, "Wish You Were Here: Alcuin's Courtly Verse and the Boys Back Home," 21–43, at 35–7.

3 The bibliography on Alcuin and his oeuvre is vast; see, for example, Marie-Hélène Jullien and Françoise Perelman, *Clavis des auteurs latins du moyen âge (territoire français, 735-987). II. Alcuin*; Donald A. Bullough, *Alcuin: Achievement and Reputation.* Mary Garrison has written several articles with a direct bearing on the discussion that follows, notably "The Emergence of Carolingian Latin Literature and the Court of Charlemagne (780–814)," 111–40; "An Aspect of Alcuin: 'Tuus Albinus': Peevish Egotist or Parrhesiast?," 137–51; "The Library of Alcuin's York," 633–64; and "The Social World of Alcuin: Nicknames at York and at the Carolingian Court," 59–79; and "The English and the Irish at the Court of Charlemagne," 97–123.

4 The main standard editions of Alcuin's poems and letters remain Dümmler, ed., *Alcuini carmina*, 160–351; Dümmler, ed., *Alcuini epistolae*, 1–481.

Deacon a better historian, and the patriarch Paulinus of Aquileia a more original theologian."[5] It is striking that in celebrating Alcuin's impact across a wide range of fields and disciplines, Wallach speaks of him first as an educator, and that is surely how Alcuin considered himself. Moreover, Alcuin's own educational experience seems to have been greatly formative, to judge only from his effusive dedication to his own teacher, Ælberht, whose death left a huge gap in Alcuin's personal life, one that he seems to have attempted to fill through continually attempting to forge similarly close relations with his own young charges.[6]

Alcuin wrote several didactic dialogues,[7] of which the most elevated is probably the *Disputatio de rhetorica et virtutibus sapientissimi regis Karoli et Albini magistri* (Debate about rhetoric and the virtues between the most wise King Charlemagne and Alcuin the schoolmaster),[8] but others are explicitly aimed at the young, including the *Dialogus Franconis et Saxonis de octo partibus orationis* (Dialogue between a Frank and a Saxon on the eight parts of speech).[9] A further rather baffling and perplexing set of mathematical story-problems evidently aimed at the young, the so-called *Propositiones ad acuendos iuvenes* (Propositions for sharpening up youths),[10] has also with high probability, given its playful tone, been attributed to Alcuin,[11] whose propensity for such lively and challenging compositions was evidently well known enough around the Carolingian

5 Luitpold Wallach, *Alcuin and Charlemagne: Studies in Carolingian History and Literature*, 3.

6 See further Orchard, "Wish You Were Here," 24–7.

7 For an overview, see E. Ann Matter, "Alcuin's Question-and-Answer Texts," 645–56.

8 The standard edition is Wilbur S. Howell, ed. and trans., *The Rhetoric of Alcuin and Charlemagne*.

9 The standard edition is PL 101:854–902.

10 See further Menso Folkerts, *Die älteste mathematische Aufgabensammlung in lateinischer Sprache: Die Alcuin zugeschriebenen* Propositiones ad acuendos iuvenes*: Überlieferung, Inhalt, Kritische Edition*; John Hadley and David Singmaster, "Problems to Sharpen the Young: An Annotated Translation of *Propositiones ad acuendos iuvenes*, the Oldest Mathematical Problem Collection in Latin, Attributed to Alcuin of York," 102–26; Menso Folkerts, "Die Alkuin zugeschriebenen *Propositiones ad acuendos iuvenes*," 273–81; David Singmaster, "The History of Some of Alcuin's Propositions," 11–29; Harald Gropp, "*Propositio de lupo et capra et fasciculo cauli* – On the History of River-Crossing Problems," 2:31–41.

11 See further my "Enigma Variations: The Anglo-Saxon Riddle-Tradition," 1:284–304.

court to be satirised by Theodulf of Orléans, in his poetic account, composed in AD 796, of the key players:[12]

Sit praesto et Flaccus, nostrorum gloria vatum,
  Qui potis est lyrico multa boare pede.
Quique sophista potens est, quique poeta melodus,
  Quique potens sensu, quique potens opere est.
Et pia de sanctis scripturis dogmata promat,
  Et solvat numeri vincla favente ioco.
Et modo sit facilis, modo scrupea quaestio Flacci,
  Nunc mundanam artem, nunc rediens superam:
Solvere de multis rex ipse volentibus unus
  Sit bene qui possit solvere Flaccidica. (*Carmen 25*, lines 131–40)

[Let Flaccus [Alcuin] be at hand, the glory of our poets,
who can shout out many things in lyric metre;
who is a mighty intellect and a melodious poet,
who is mighty in sense and mighty in deed.
And let him expound holy teachings from the sacred scriptures
and let him loose the bonds of number with a helpful jest;
and sometimes let Flaccus's question be easy, sometimes hard,
now explaining a secular art, now a pious one:
and may the king himself, amongst many wishing to find a solution,
be the only one to solve the *Flaccidica*.]

But perhaps the most accomplished and entertaining of Alcuin's educational texts, and one aimed squarely at an individual and identifiable adolescent, is the so-called *Disputatio regalis et nobilissimi iuvenis Pippini cum Albino scholastico* (Debate between the royal and most noble youth Pippin and the scholar Alcuin), hereafter *DPA*, which will be the primary focus here.[13]

---

12 Dümmler, *Theodulfi carmina*, 486. See further my "Wish You Were Here," 37–9; Martha Bayless, "Alcuin's *Disputatio Pippini* and the Early Medieval Riddle Tradition," 157–78, at 162–4.

13 The standard edition remains Walther Suchier, ed., "Disputatio Pippini cum Albino," 134–46. The whole volume also contains several other relevant texts, as noted below, and is designated here DS.

There are, inconveniently, two possible contenders for the most noble Pippin in question, both sons of Charlemagne. The elder, who was Charlemagne's eldest son, known as Pippin the Hunchback, and was born around AD 769, seems to have fallen out of favour, and the younger, whose birth-name Karlomann was changed to Pippin at baptism, was born in AD 777. Martha Bayless has convincingly identified the likely recipient of *DPA* as the younger namesake and dated the text itself to the period AD 790 × 793, when Alcuin was back in England, and the younger Pippin would have been between thirteen and sixteen years old.[14] Such a conclusion fits well with the Preface to the *Dialogus Franconis et Saxonis de octo partibus orationis*, a dialogue between two other unnamed students of Alcuin, one a Frank and the other a Saxon, which reads as follows:

> Fuerunt in schola Albini magistri duo pueri, unus Franco, alter Saxo, qui nuperrime spineta grammaticae densitatis irruperunt. Quapropter placuit illis paucis litterulis scientiae regulas memoriae causa per interrogationes et responsiones excerpere. At prior illorum Franco dixit Saxoni: Eia, Saxo, me interrogante responde, quia tu majoris es aetatis. Ego XIV annorum; tu ut reor XV. Ad haec Saxo respondit: Faciam; ita tamen, ut si quid altius sit interrogandum, vel ex philosphica disciplina proferendum, liceat magistrum interrogare. Ad haec magister: Placet, filii, propositio vestra: et libens annuo vestrae sagacitati. Et primum dicite unde vestram convenientius disputationem esse arbitramini incipiendam? *Discipuli.* Unde, domine magister, nisi a littera?

> [There were two boys in the school of Master Albinus (Alcuin), one a Frank, and the other a Saxon, who very recently had entered the thickets of grammatical density. As a result of which it seemed a good idea to them to make selections of the rules of knowledge in a few notes through questions and answers, in order to memorise them. And of them the Frank spoke first: "Hey, Saxon, reply to my questions, since you are older in age. I'm fourteen, but I think you're fifteen." The Saxon replied: "I'll do that; but in such a way that if the question is about anything that is too deep, or should be drawn from the philosophical teachings, we should ask the master." The master replied: "I like your idea: and I happily assent to your wisdom. So first say where you reckon your discussion should more suitably begin?" Students: "Lord master, where else but at the letter?"]

14 Bayless, "Alcuin's *Disputatio Pippini*," 157–78.

Like the *DPA*, the *Dialogus Franconis et Saxonis* is a highly original and entertaining didactic text, far more engaging than its rather dry grammatical sources, notably the *Ars minor* of Donatus and the *Institutiones grammaticae* of Priscian. Quite apart from the dialogue form, this introductory passage from the *Dialogus Franconis et Saxonis* connects itself to the *DPA* in at least three other ways, notably the use of Alcuin's nickname, Albinus, the idea that the first element to be discussed should be the "letter" ("littera"), just as at *DPA* 1, and the concern about questioning that is "too deep" ("altius"), which matches Pippin's alleged concern about travelling "on high" ("altum") in the pivotal section on "curiosity" (*CURIOSITAS*) at *DPA* 60.

As a teaching tool, the *DPA* betrays its didactic origins not only by its form, sources, and analogues, but also by two explicit references to "boys," or perhaps better "schoolboys" ("pueri"), both in the riddling section of the text, at *DPA* 77 and 82. Details of the structure of the *DPA* have been somewhat masked in the standard edition,[15] the relationship of which to the edition and translation presented in Appendix 1 below, can be summarised in Table 8.1 (overleaf).

After the initial nod towards the traditional didactic grammatical opening, dealing with "letter" (*LITTERA*) and "word" (*VERBUM*), Alcuin is then led through a chain of association via "tongue" (*LINGUA*) and "air" (*AËR*) towards much more existential questions of "life" (*VITA*) and "death" (*MORS*), culminating in a complex and multifaceted discussion of "mankind" (*HOMO*), consisting of no fewer than nine question-and-answer interchanges, before the linking concept of "sleep" (*SOMNUS*), explained as "the semblance of death" ("mortis imago"), so presenting mankind as essentially surrounded by death; the following section on "the freedom of mankind" ("libertas hominis") returns to the anthropocentric theme, and is followed by a lengthy sequence of twenty-eight interchanges on many and various body parts (*DPA* 10–37). After the earthbound nature of the preceding, the next sections describe in turn aspects of the natural world, beginning with celestial bodies (*DPA* 38–43), moving through natural phenomena (*DPA* 44–54), and concluding with the seasons and the year (*DPA* 55–9). The final section (*DPA* 59), on "year" (*ANNUS*),

15 Given here as DS; see n. 13 above.

Table 8.1 Index of Topics, Solutions, and Concordance to *DPA* and DS

[those riddle-sections marked * are also edited and translated by Martha Bayless][16]

DPA 01	DS 01	*LITTERA* (letter)
DPA 02	DS 02–03	*VERBUM* (word)
DPA 03	DS 04	*LINGUA* (tongue)
DPA 04	DS 05	*AËR* (air)
DPA 05	DS 06	*VITA* (life)
DPA 06	DS 07	*MORS* (death)
DPA 07	DS 08–16	*HOMO* (mankind)
DPA 08	DS 17	*SOMNUS* (sleep)
DPA 09	DS 18	*INNOCENTIA* (innocence)
		Body Parts
DPA 10–37	DS 19–46	*CAPUT* (head); *CORPUS* (body); COMAE (hair); *BARBA* (beard); *CEREBRUM* (brain); *OCULI* (eyes); *NARES* (nostrils); *AURES* (ears); *FRONS* (face); OS (mouth); *DENTES* (teeth); LABIA (lips); *GULA* (throat); *MANUS* (hands); *DIGITI* (fingers); *PULMO* (lung); *COR* (heart); *IECUR* (liver); *FEL* (gall bladder); *SPLEN* (spleen); *STOMACHUS* (stomach); *VENTER* (belly); *OSSA* (bones); *COXAE* (hips); *CRURA* (shins); *PEDES* (feet); *SANGUIS* (blood); *VENAE* (veins)
		Celestial Bodies
DPA 38–43	DS 47–52	*CAELUM* (sky); *LUX* (light); *DIES* (day); *SOL* (sun); *LUNA* (moon); *STELLAE* (stars)
		Natural Phenomena
DPA 44–54	DS 53–63	*PLUVIA* (rain); *NEBULA* (cloud); *VENTUS* (wind); *TERRA* (earth); *MARE* (sea); *FLUMINA* (*rivers*); *AQUA* (water); *IGNIS* (fire); *FRIGUS* (cold); *GELU* (ice); *NIX* (snow)
		The Seasons
DPA 55–8	DS 64–7	*HIEMS* (winter); *VER* (spring); *AESTAS* (summer); *AUTUMNUS* (autumn)
DPA 59	DS 68–73	*ANNUS* (year)
DPA 60	DS 74–5	*CURIOSITAS* (curiosity)
DPA 61	DS 76	*NAVIS* (ship)

16 Bayless, "Alcuin's *Disputatio Pippini*," 174–7; a brief commentary follows on 177–8. All these aspects are explored more fully in Andy Orchard, ed. and trans., *The Anglo-Saxon Riddle Tradition*, and *The Anglo-Saxon Riddle Tradition: Notes and Commentary*.

Table 8.1 Index of Topics, Solutions, and Concordance to *DPA* and DS (*cont.*)

DPA 62	DS 77	*HARENA* (sand)
DPA 63	DS 78	*HERBA* (grass)
DPA 64	DS 79	*OLERA* (herbs)
DPA 65	DS 80	*FAMES* (hunger)
DPA 66	DS 81	*LUCRUM* (wealth)
DPA 67	DS 82	*SOMNUS* (sleep)
		Faith, Hope, and Charity
DPA 68–70	DS 83–5	*SPES* (hope); *AMICITIA* (friendship); FIDES (faith)
**DPA* 71	DS 86–9	*IMAGO IN AQUA* (reflection in water)
**DPA* 72	DS 90	*SOMNIUM* (dream)[a]
**DPA* 73	DS 91	*IGNIS* (fire)[b]
**DPA* 74	DS 92	*TINTINNABULA* (bells)
**DPA* 75	DS 93	*SILEX* (flint)
**DPA* 76	DS 94	*LEBES* (cauldron)
**DPA* 77	DS 95	*PEDICULI* (lice)
**DPA* 78	DS 96	*PULLUS IN OVO* (chick in egg)
**DPA* 79	DS 97	*ECHO* (echo)
**DPA* 80	DS 98	*FLUMEN ET PISCIS* (river and fish)
**DPA* 81	DS 99	*HOMO QUI SOMNIT* (a dreamer)
**DPA* 82	DS 100	*FLEXUS DIGITORUM* (finger-counting)
**DPA* 83	DS 101	*PULUILLUS* (pillow)
**DPA* 84	DS 102–3	*ADAM, ENOCH/ELIAS, LAZARUS*
**DPA* 85	DS 104	*SAGITTA* (arrow)
DPA 86	DS 105	*MILES* (soldier)
DPA 87	DS 106	*NIHIL* (nothing)
DPA 88	DS 108–10	*EPISTOLA* (letter)

a Perhaps a better solution would be *HOMO IN SOMNIO VISUS* (man seen in a dream).

b This somewhat quirky interpretation of *IGNIS* (fire) has most in common in terms of language with *DPA* 76 (*LEBES* [cauldron]), with which it seems to form a natural pair: compare the sequence "Vidi mortuos … vivum et in ira vivi … mortui" here with the sequence "Vidi mortuum … vivum et in risu mortui … vivus." This link is part of a wider set of connections involving fire and water. The whole sequence *DPA* 72–9 is also notable for the carefully patterned responses by Alcuin, who effectively just says "yes" eight times in answer to Pippin's questions, each time in a different way.

is, like the earlier nine-part section (*DPA* 7) on "mankind" (*HOMO*), subdivided into six.

There follows a pivotal chapter (*DPA* 60), on "curiosity" (*CURIOSITAS*), linked to the preceding sections on "year," which had concluded with a discussion of the twelve signs of the zodiac, and to the following one on "ship" (*DPA* 61) through the inherent ambiguity of the Latin word *altum*, which can mean both "high" (with regard to the constellations) and "deep" (with regard to the sea). The younger Pippin, in a lordly fashion, offers to make a ship ready for Alcuin, apparently overseas, so that he might return to him, and there follow a chain of nine associated sections (*DPA* 62–70), beginning with "sand" (*HARENA*) and concluding with three sections (*DPA* 68–80) on "hope" (*SPES*), "friendship" (*AMICITIA*), and "faith" (*FIDES*). These last self-evidently allude to the more familiar triad of "faith, hope, and charity," more properly "faith, hope, and love" (*spes, fides, caritas*), with "friendship" (*AMICITIA*) substituting for "love" (*caritas*). Such a substitution is all the more suggestive given Alcuin's well-documented appeals to friendship and the linguistically related more common concept of "love" (*amor*) that pervade his poems and letters, especially those addressed to his past and current students.[17] The second part of Alcuin's answer to Pippin's query "What is faith?" ("Quid est fides?"), "The certainty of something unknown and wonderful" ("Ignotae rei et mirandae certitudo"), leads, through the usual mechanism of the catchword, to Pippin's follow-up question, "What is a wonder?" ("Quid est mirum?"), so leading on to the most original part of the entire *DPA*, where Alcuin (paradoxically enough, employing a range of identifiable sources) introduces a range of questions enigmatically posed and allusively answered in the form of riddles (*DPA* 71–85). The last few challenges bring the whole dialogue to an abrupt conclusion: the final riddle proper, solved *SAGITTA* (arrow), is followed, naturally enough, by a definitional question on *MILES* (warrior), linked by the kind of verbal repletion seen earlier in the *DPA*, and sharing the same kenning-like tone. It may be that the natural association of warriors and death leads on to the suitably terminal consideration of *NIHIL* (nothing), the quasi-grammatical feel of which links back, suitably enough, to the very beginning of *DPA*, and allows

17 See further Orchard, "Wish You Were Here," 21–43.

Alcuin to bring the whole text back vividly to the immediate present, and, we understand, to consideration of the very *EPISTOLA* (letter) in which the *DPA* is inscribed.

The originality of the *DPA* can best be assessed by considering it against the two anonymous texts with which it can be most closely compared, namely, the earlier *Altercatio Hadriani Augusti et Epicteti philosophi* (Discussion between the Emperor Hadrian and Epictetus the philosopher [*AHE*]),[18] and the later *Disputatio Hadriani cum Secundo philosopho* (Debate between Hadrian and Secundus the philosopher [*DHS*]).[19] It has often been noted that in adapting the *AHE* in his *DPA*, Alcuin casts Pippin in the role of the imperial Hadrian, while himself adopting the hardly unflattering persona of the philosopher Epictetus.[20] But a fuller analysis reveals not only the imaginative and innovative ways in which Alcuin fleshed out this backbone, but also how he subverted its form, in part by combining its structure with a number of other sources. Alcuin alludes very directly to *AHE* in a letter to an unidentified student that has been dated AD 793 × 796, just after the suggested date of the composition of *DPA* (AD 790 × 793), as follows (*Epistola 88*):

> De epistola interrogasti, quid esset. Nam epi "super," stola "habitus" Grece dicitur. Unde Hadrianus imperator Epictetum philosophum inter alias inquisitiones interrogavit, quid esset cinctum? At ille videns eum epistolam manu tenentem respondit: "Quod manu tenes." Volens intellegere, quasi supercinctorium esset epistolae sigillum, quo a foris vestiatur cartula.[21]
>
> [You have asked what a letter (*epistola*) is. In Greek, *epi* means "over," and *stola* means "clothing." For that reason, the Emperor Hadrian asked the philosopher Epictetus, among other inquiries, what is "tied up"? And he, seeing [Hadrian] holding a letter in his hand, replied: "What you are holding in your hand," wishing to indicate that the seal of the letter was tied up, and by it the document was clothed outside.]

18 The standard edition is DS, 70–81, as in n. 13 above.
19 The standard edition is DS, 38–70, as in n. 13 above.
20 Bayless, "Alcuin's *Disputatio Pippini*," 165.
21 Dümmler, *Alcuini Epistolae*, 132–3 (no. 88).

It is noteworthy that a similar conceit is also employed by Alcuin in a poem to a bishop, again underlining the way in which Alcuin's educational and didactic impulses pervade his works across many genres.[22]

The precise relationship between the *DPA* and its main Latin source, the *AHE*, is mapped out in Table 8.2, and illustrated in detail in both Appendix 1 and Appendix 2 below, where the main parallels are indicated by single underlining; parallels adopted from the *DPA* in the later and obviously highly derivative *DHS* are indicated by the use of double underlining in Appendix 1.

It will be clear that some twenty sections of the *AHE* are echoed, often very closely, in sixteen of the *DPA*, but with some radical shifts in sequencing, most obviously in Alcuin's decision to echo the opening two sections of the *AHE* (on the "letter" [*epistola*]) in the closing section of his own work.[23] In some cases, *AHE* has provided little more than the suggestion of subject matter (e.g., in *DPA* 5–6, equating to *AHE* 21 and 23), while in others successive sections of *AHE* provide a backbone that Alcuin fleshes out considerably (e.g., *DPA* 7 is based on *AHE* 33–5); in every case, Alcuin expands the kenning-like descriptions, especially those formed of a combination of the nominative and genitive case. But, as the passages given in double underlining clearly show, it is precisely these expanded combinations that are echoed verbatim by the anonymous author of *DHS*, and it is precisely in such a string of associations that Alcuin's original didactic contribution is laid bare. In particular, *DHS*, while echoing closely *DPA* 1–43, 55–9, and 61–70, seems deliberately to have passed over the sections dealing with "natural phenomena" (*DPA* 44–54) and "riddles" (*DPA* 71–85), as well as the structural section on "curiosity" (*CURIOSITAS*: *DPA* 60) that marks the turning point of the entire debate.

22 Dümmler, *Alcuini carmina*, 248 (no. 29.2):

Nulla manus cartam discingat, ni tua, praesul;
Solue, pater sancte, et lege tu feliciter illam.
Succinctum soluat, cupiat qui abscondita scire,
Nulla tamen dextra, ni tua, sancte pater.

[Let no hand untie the missive, bishop, except yours;
unbind it, holy father, and read it happily,
let him unbind what is tied up, who wants to know hidden things,
but no right hand, holy father, except yours.]

23 Note that *AHE* 1–2, uniquely among the sections echoed by Alcuin, employs the same catenary structure (with the linking word here, appropriately enough, "letter" ["epistola ... epistola"] itself) that Alcuin was to use as one of the main structuring devices of the *DPA*, as discussed below, 176–7.

Table 8.2. Sources, Parallels, and Analogues

DPA 01–04		*DHS* 22–6
DPA 05	*AHE* 21	*DHS* 20
DPA 06	*AHE* 23	*DHS* 21
DPA 07	*AHE* 33–5	*DHS* 8
DPA 08	*AHE* 53	*DHS* 19
DPA 09	*AHE* 17	*DHS* 27
DPA 10–21		*DHS* 28–39
DPA 22		
DPA 23–30		*DHS* 40–7
DPA 31		
DPA 32		*DHS* 48
DPA 33		*DHS* 51
DPA 34		*DHS* 50
DPA 35		*DHS* 52–3
DPA 36–7		
DPA 38	*AHE* 42	*DHS* 9
DPA 39		*DHS* 54
DPA 40		
DPA 41–2	*AHE* 40–41	*DHS* 5–6
DPA 43–6		*DHS* 55–8
DPA 47	*AHE* 47	*DHS* 7
DPA 48	*AHE* 48	
DPA 49–50		*DHS* 59–60
DPA 51 –2		
DPA 53–7		*DHS* 61–5
DPA 58 –60		
DPA 61	*AHE* 49–50	
DPA 62–4		
DPA 65		*DHS* 66
DPA 66	*AHE* 11	*DHS* 67
DPA 67		*DHS* 68
DPA 68	*AHE* 14	*DHS* 69
DPA 69	*AHE* 12	*DHS* 70

Table 8.2. Sources, Parallels, and Analogues (*cont.*)

DPA 70		*DHS* 71		
DPA 71–4				
DPA 75			*SYM* 76/76a	
DPA 76				ps-*BED* 10
DPA 77			*SYM* 30	
DPA 78			*SYM* 14	
DPA 79			*SYM* 98	
DPA 80			*SYM* 12	
DPA 81			*SYM* 99	
DPA 82			*SYM* 96	
DPA 83				*ALD* 41
DPA 84–5				
DPA 86	*AHE* 66			
DPA 87				
DPA 88	*AHE* 1–2			

Table 8.1 makes it clear that *DPA* has a clear chain of association linking many of its themes in different ways, and an envelope-structure that appears to play on the twin meanings of *littera* as "letter of the alphabet" (*DPA* 1) and, more generally in the plural *litterae*, "epistle" (*DPA* 88 [*EPISTOLA* (letter)]). In following "letter" with "word" (*DPA* 2), Alcuin may gesture towards the first book of Isidore, *Etymologiae* ("De grammatica" [On grammar]),[24] but even if the succeeding interchanges skip around in subject matter, they are very securely linked by the linguistic device (and by the universal experience of parents and teachers across the ages), whereby a young questioner repeats the last word of the respondent, and continues the interrogation: such is certainly the case in *DPA* 2–8 and *DPA* 10–11.[25] The latter pair of interchanges can also be seen to begin a sequence dealing with body parts (*DPA* 10–37), many of them the

24 Isidore, *Etymologiae*, ed. Lindsay, and Stephen A. Barney, W.J. Lewis, J.A. Beach, and Oliver Berghof, trans., *The Etymologies of Isidore of Seville*. See too the important work of Mercedes Salvador-Bello, *Isidorean Perceptions of Order: The Exeter Book Riddles and Medieval Latin Enigmata*.

25 See further below, 176–7.

same and in the same order as those considered in Isidore, *Etymologiae* I.i ("De homine et partibus eius" [On human beings and their body parts]). There follows a further sequence (*DPA* 38–59) dealing with celestial and calendrical subjects, partly paralleled in Isidore, *Etymologiae* XIII ("De mundo et partibus" [The world and its parts]), and easily broken down into subsections, for example dealing with the four seasons (*DPA* 55–8), which leads naturally into the concluding discussion of the year (*DPA* 59). Once again, there follows a group of ten interchanges somewhat hard to fathom as a connected sequence (*DPA* 60–9), but with mini-sequences containing verbal and thematic associations of the kind already witnessed (*DPA* 61–2 are linked by the word "sand," *DPA* 62–3 by the word "earth," *DPA* 67–8 by the word "hope"; likewise, *DPA* 64–5 are linked by the concepts of food and hunger, and *DPA* 66–7 by those of tiredness and sleep; the final three interchanges in this sequence, *DPA* 68–70, deal with the familiar triad of faith, hope, and charity, given here as hope, friendship, and faith). The whole arrangement is introduced by the notion of "curiosity" (*CURIOSITAS*: *DPA* 60), and the connection with the previous sequence dealing with celestial themes is elegantly made through the ambiguity of the word *altum* (which can mean both "high" and "deep"): Pippin sparks off the sequence at *DPA* 60 by making the intellectual leap towards thinking of the deep itself, essentially asking the question "What is a boat?" The notion of *curiositas* (curiosity) seems again invoked in *DPA* 71, where Pippin asks "What is a wonder?" and is given a concrete example, beginning a further sequence of fifteen rather more conventionally framed riddles (*DPA* 71–85), where the role of questioner has been at this point reversed, and it is now the youthful Pippin who takes up the challenge of supplying answers, which he does in a playfully cryptic fashion that in general merely hints at the solution. The switching of the roles of questioner and respondent seems to gesture towards the didactic tradition, and turns on the linguistic coincidence that while the Latin letters *M* and *D* stand for "master" (*MAGISTER*) and "student" (*DISCIPULUS*), the equivalent Greek letters M and Δ stand by contrast for "student" (ΜΑΘΗΤΗΣ) and "master" (ΔΙΔΑΣΚΟΛΟΣ) instead. Likewise, in the Old Norse Eddic poem *Vafþrúðnismál*, the two protagonists, in this case the giant Vafþrúðnir and the god Óðinn, take turns in asking a series of questions: in stanzas 11–18, the giant asks the questions, and the god supplies the answers, while in stanzas 20–55, the roles are reversed.[26]

26 See Gustav Neckel, ed., *Edda: Die Lieder des Codex Regius nebst einigen verwandten Denkmälern*, 3–13.

It is notable that the whole central sequence of nine *aenigmata* at *DPA* 75–83 seems drawn from earlier models, of which seven are from the *aenigmata* of Symphosius (SYM),[27] and the other two from the *aenigmata* of Aldhelm (ALD) and the pseudo-Bede *Collectanea* (ps-BED) respectively: the *aenigmata* in question are SYM 76 and 76a (*SILEX* [flint]), ps-BED 10 (*LEBES* [cauldron]), SYM 30 (*PEDICULI* [lice]), SYM 14 (*PULLUS IN OVO* [embryo chick]), SYM 98 (*ECHO* [echo]), SYM 12 (*FLUMEN ET PISCIS* [river and fish]), SYM 99 (*SOMNIUM* [dream]), SYM 96 (*FLEXUS DIGITORUM* [finger-counting]), and ALD 41 (*PULUILLUS* [pillow]);[28] *DPA* 85 has the same solution as SYM 65 (*SAGITTA* [arrow]), but the whole treatment is quite different. In the case of *DPA*, there is also the clear precedent of the anonymous and undated (but undoubtedly earlier) *AHE*, to which Alcuin alludes directly in one of his letters, and which supplies close and often verbatim parallels for a significant number of the questions that make up the text, while by contrast the later *DHS* borrows, always verbatim, from *DPA*, notably from that part of the work which seems most original.

One of the most striking features of *DPA* is the use of echo-words as linking features to dictate its structure. There are no fewer than fourteen such connecting features, where the final word of one section reappears in the first sentence of the section immediately following, often in sequence, as follows, with the link-word given in English in inverted commas: 2–3 "tongue" ("lingua ... lingua"); 3–4 "breath" ("aëris ... aër"); 4–5 "life" ("vitae ... vita"); 5–6 "death" ("mortis ... mors"); 6–7 "mankind" ("hominis ... homo"); 7–8 "sleep" ("somno ... somnus"); 10–11 "body" ("corporis ... corpus"); 33–4 "columns" ("columnarum ... columnae"); 46–7 "earth" ("terrae ... terra"); 58–9 "year" ("anni ... annus"); 61–2 "sand" ("harenae ... harena"); 67–8 "hope" ("spes ... spes"); 70–1 "wonder(ful)" ("mirandae ... mirum"); 85–6 "warrior" ("militum ... miles"); note that in eleven of these fourteen examples, a noun in the genitive is followed by the same noun in the nominative. Such a chain-like or catenary structure is, it has recently been demonstrated, a common feature of enigmatic collections, where the implicit association of adjacent individual elements seems

27 See further Manuela Bergamin, ed. and trans., *Aenigmata Symposii: La fondazione dell'enigmistica come genere poetico*; and Timothy J. Leary, ed. and trans., *Symphosius, The "Aenigmata": An Introduction, Text, and Commentary*.

28 All these texts appear in the footnotes to the text and translation of *DPA* in Appendix 1 below.

a key part in what the compiler at least perceived as the solution, at least for those riddles where there is no agreed answer. Of the fifteen sections that make up the highly innovative and unusual "riddles" section of *DPA* (71–85), eight begin with or include the opening "I saw" (*Vidi*) formula,[29] which is also found not only in other Anglo-Latin *aenigmata* but also with great regularity as the opening formula in the Exeter Book (in the form "Ic (ge)seah") in the Old English reflexes of the specifically Anglo-Saxon riddle tradition.[30] Such a vernacular parallel is all the more interesting, given the overwhelming evidence that many of the texts that comprise the Anglo-Saxon riddle tradition had a clear pedagogical and didactic function, alongside their more obviously diverting and entertaining aspects,[31] as well as indications that in his Latin writings Alcuin occasionally imitated the forms of Old English verse.[32] In one of the earliest extended discussions of the *DPA*, Helga Reuschel considered several of the more poetic answers to basic questions as analogous to the kinds of kennings found in Old English verse,[33] but her analysis seems to have made little impact, albeit that what is most striking about Alcuin's work is how few of the kenning-like designations in fact derive from Latin, and how many that were later echoed in Latin can be traced directly to the *DPA*.

As an original riddler, Alcuin's credentials are rather thin, but fit well within what we know elsewhere of the Anglo-Latin riddle tradition.[34] Alcuin's most polished *aenigma* in verse is evidently to be solved *PECTEN* (comb), and the circumstances behind its composition, sent along with a letter of thanks to Archbishop Riculf of Mainz (died AD 813), are known with some precision;[35] like several other Anglo-Latin *aenigmata* and a large number of the Old English Exeter Book *Riddles*, Alcuin's concludes

29 *DPA* 71, 73, 75, 76, 78, 80, 82, and 85.

30 See further Orchard, "Enigma Variations," 289–94.

31 These aspects are explored more fully in Orchard, *The Anglo-Saxon Riddle Tradition: Notes and Commentary*. There is also detailed discussion in Salvador-Bello, *Isidorean Perceptions of Order*.

32 See further Andy Orchard, "Reconstructing 'The Ruin,'" 47–70.

33 Helga Reuschel, "Kenningar bei Alcuin. Zur 'Disputatio Pippini cum Albino,'" 143–55. In general, see too Paul Sorrell, "Oaks, Ships, Riddles and the Old English *Rune Poem*," 103–16.

34 Dieter Bitterli, "Alkuin von York und die angelsächsische Rätseldichtung," 4–20; Paul Sorrell, "Alcuin's 'Comb' Riddle," 311–18.

35 Dümmler, *Alcuini carmina*, 223 (no. 5). See further Sorrell, "Alcuin's 'Comb' Riddle," and Orchard, "Wish You Were Here," 21–43.

with a final challenge to the would-be solver.[36] Alcuin also composed a sequence of logogriphs (ALC 2–6),[37] riddles based on variations of spelling, that might easily be considered part of one long poem;[38] the sequence again ends (ALC 6–7) with a challenge. There are a further three verse *aenigmata* (ALC 7–9), all with the same solution, *FORNAX* (furnace).[39]

In all these texts, however, Alcuin fits squarely with what we know of other Anglo-Saxons equally securely situated within the characteristically Anglo-Saxon riddle tradition, composing, recasting, and juxtaposing the familiar and the outlandish. In that important and quintessentially Anglo-Saxon sense and context, then, Alcuin's *DPA*, as a sophisticated and original composition with its roots in the past and with its influence on later texts, and with its Anglo-Saxon inspiration and continental audience, represents a high point in his own education, and in his development as the beloved and effective teacher he so wished to be. The *DPA* certainly exhibits Alcuin as an insular author with international aspirations, and marks a sea change in his understating of an ancient pedagogical and didactic truth, namely, that in educating the young, posing the right questions can often be more important than supplying the right answers.

Appendix 1: The Text and Translation of *DPA*

[parallels with *AHE* and parallels with *DHS* are indicated by single and double underlining, respectively]

DISPUTATIO REGALIS ET NOBILISSIMI IUVENIS PIPPINI CUM ALBINO SCHOLASTICO

(The Debate between the Most Royal and Most Noble Youth Pippin and the Scholar Alcuin)

---

36 See further Orchard, "Enigma Variations," 286–9.

37 Dümmler, *Alcuini carmina*, 281–2 (no. 63.1–5).

38 The sequence of logogriphs runs as follows: *MALUM* ("evil"; "apple") → *MULAM* ("mule"); *VIRTUS* ("power") → *TUS* ("incense") → *VIR* ("man") → *VIRUS* ("venom"); *CANUS* ("white-haired man") → *ANUS* ("old woman") → *US* ("swine" (in Greek)); *MAGNUS* ("mighty") → *AGNUS* ("lamb") → *MANUS* ("hand") → *MAGUS* ("magician") → *MUS* ("mouse") → *ANUS* ("old woman"); *SIC ET NON* ("yes and no") → *MEUM ET TUUM* ("mine and yours") → *EGO ET TU* ("I and you") → *NOS ET VOS* ("we and you").

39 Dümmler, *Alcuini carmina*, 283 (no. 64.1–2).

DPA 1

Pippinus. Quid est littera? Albinus. Custos historiae.[40]

(Pippin. What is a letter? Alcuin. The keeper of story (or "history").)

DPA 2

P. Quid est verbum? A. Proditor animi. P. Quid generat verbum? A. Lingua.

(P. What is a word? A. The betrayer of the mind. P. What produces a word? A. The tongue.)

DPA 3

P. Quid est lingua? A. Flagellum aëris.

(P. What is the tongue? A. The beater of breath.)

DPA 4

P. Quid est aër? A. Custodia vitae.

(P. What is breath? A. The guardian of life.)

DPA 5

P. Quid est vita? A. Beatorum laetitia, miserorum maestitia, exspectatio mortis.

(P. What is life? A. The joy of the blessed, the sorrow of the wretched, the expectation of death.)

40 The word *historia* covers both "story" and "history"; both seem appropriate here.

DPA 6

P. Quid est mors? A. Inevitabilis eventus, incerta peregrinatio, lacrimae viventium, testamenti firmamentum, latro hominis.

(P. What is death? A. An inevitable outcome, an uncertain journey, the tears of the living, the foundation of a testament, the robber of mankind.)

DPA 7

P. Quid est homo? A. Mancipium mortis, transiens viator, loci hospes. P. Cui similis est homo? A. Pomo. P. Quomodo positus est homo? A. Ut lucerna in vento. P. Ubi est positus? A. Intra sex parietes. P. Quos? A. Supra, subtus; ante, retro; dextra laevaque. P. Quot habet socios? A. Quattuor. P. Quos? A. Calorem, frigus, siccitatem, humorem. P. Quot modis variabilis est? A. Sex. P. Quibus? A. Esurie et saturitate; requie et labore; vigiliis et somno.

(P. What is mankind? A. The slave of death, a traveller passing through, a guest in the house. P. What is mankind like? A. A fruit tree. P. How is mankind placed? A. Like a lantern in the wind. P. Placed where? A. Boxed in six ways. P. Which? A. Above, below; before, behind; right and left. P. How many partners has he or she? A. Four. P. Which? A. Heat, cold, dryness, moisture. P. Liable to change in how many ways? A. Six. P. Which? A. From hunger and from fullness, from rest and from labour, from wakefulness and from sleep.)

DPA 8

P. Quid est somnus? A. Mortis imago.

(P. What is sleep? A. The semblance of death.)

DPA 9

P. Quid est libertas hominis? A. Innocentia.

(P. What is the freedom of mankind? A. Absence of harm.)

DPA 10

P. Quid est caput? A. Culmen corporis.

(P. What is the head? A. The top of the body.)

DPA 11

P. Quid est corpus? A. Domicilium animae.

(P. What is the body? A. The dwelling of the soul.)

DPA 12

P. Quid sunt comae? A. Vestes capitis.

(P. What is hair? A. The clothing of the head.)

DPA 13

P. Quid est barba? A. Sexus discretio, honor aetatis.

(P. What is a beard? A. A difference of gender, a badge of age.)

DPA 14

P. Quid est cerebrum? A. Servator memoriae.

(P. What is the brain? A. The keeper of memory.)

DPA 15

P. Quid sunt oculi? A. Duces corporis, vasa luminis, animi indices.

(P. What are the eyes? A. The rulers of the body, a vessel of light, the indicators of the mind.)

DPA 16

P. Quid sunt nares? A. Adductio odorum.

(P. What are the nostrils? A. The conduit for smells.)

DPA 17

P. Quid sunt aures? A. Collatores sonorum.

(P. What are the ears? A. The collectors of sounds.)

DPA 18

P. Quid est frons? A. Imago animi.

(P. What is the face? A. The semblance of the mind.)

DPA 19

P. Quid est os? A. Nutritor corporis.

(P. What is the mouth? A. The feeder of the body.)

DPA 20

P. Quid sunt dentes? A. Molae morsorum.

(P. What are teeth? A. The millstones of morsels.)

DPA 21

P. Quid sunt labia? A. Valvae oris.

(P. What are the lips? A. The doorways of the mouth.)

DPA 22

P. Quid est gula? A. Devorator cibi.

(P. What is the throat? A. The swallower of food.)

DPA 23

P. Quid sunt manus? A. Operarii corporis.

(P. What are the hands? A. The workers of the body.)

DPA 24

P. Quid sunt digiti? A. Chordarum plectra.

(P. What are the fingers? A. The pluckers of strings.)

DPA 25

P. Quid est pulmo? A. Servator aëris.

(P. What is a lung? A. The keeper of breath.)

DPA 26

P. Quid est cor? A. Receptaculum vitae.

(P. What is the heart? A. The coffer of life.)

DPA 27

P. Quid est iecur? A. Custodia caloris.

(P. What is the liver? A. The guardian of heat.)

DPA 28

P. Quid est fel? A. Suscitatio iracundiae.

(P. What is the gall bladder? A. The arousal of rage.)

DPA 29

P. Quid est splenis? A. Risus et laetitiae capax.

(P. What is the spleen? A. What holds laughter and happiness.)

DPA 30

P. Quid est stomachus? A. Ciborum coctor.

(P. What is the stomach? A. The cook of food.)

DPA 31

P. Quid est venter? A. Custos fragilium.

(P. What is the belly? A. The keeper of crumbs.)

DPA 32

P. Quid sunt ossa? A. Fortitudo corporis.

(P. What are the bones? A. The strength of the body.)

DPA 33

P. Quid sunt coxae? A. Epistilia columnarum.

(P. What are the hips? A. The supports of the columns.)

DPA 34

P. Quid sunt crura? A. Columnae corporis.

(P. What are the legs? A. The columns of the body.)

DPA 35

P. Quid sunt pedes? A. Mobile fundamentum.

(P. What are the feet? A. A moving foundation.)

DPA 36

P. Quid est sanguis? A. Humor venarum, vitae alimentum.

(P. What is blood? A. What flows through the veins, the nourishment of life.)

DPA 37

P. Quid sunt venae? A. Fontes carnis.

(P. What are the veins? A. The fountains of the flesh.)

DPA 38

P. Quid est caelum? A. Sphera volubilis, culmen immensum.

(P. What is the sky? A. The revolving sphere, an immeasurable height.)

DPA 39

P. Quid est lux? A. Facies omnium rerum.

(P. What is light? A. The revelation of all things.)

DPA 40

P. Quid est dies? A. Incitamentum laboris.

(P. What is day? A. The spur to work.)

DPA 41

P. Quid est sol? A. Splendor orbis, coeli pulchritudo, naturae gratia, honor diei, horarum distributor.

(P. What is the sun? A. The glory of the world, the beauty of the sky, the grace of nature, the adornment of the day, the distributor of hours.)

DPA 42

P. Quid est luna? A. Oculus noctis, roris larga, praesaga tempestatum.

(P. What is the moon? A. The eye of night, full of dew, the prophetess of storms.)

DPA 43

P. Quid sunt stellae? A. Pictura culminis, nautarum gubernatores, noctis decor.

(P. What are the stars? A. A painting on high, the steerers of sailors, the ornament of night.)

DPA 44

P. Quid est pluvia? A. Conceptio terrae, frugum genitrix.

(P. What is the rain? A. The fertilizer of earth, the spawner of produce.)

DPA 45

P. Quid est nebula? A. Nox in die, labor oculorum.

(P. What is a cloud? A. Night in the daytime, work for the eyes.)

DPA 46

P. Quid est ventus? A. Aëris perturbatio, mobilitas aquarum, siccitas terrae.

(P. What is the wind? A. The disturbance of the air, the moving of the waters, the drying up of the earth.)

DPA 47

P. Quid est terra? A. Mater crescentium, nutrix viventium, cellarium vitae, devoratrix omnium.

(P. What is the earth? A. The mother of growing things, the nurturer of living things, the storehouse of life, the devourer of all.)

DPA 48

P. Quid est mare? A. Audaciae via, limes terrae, divisor regionum, hospitium fluviorum, fons imbrium, refugium in periculis, gratia in voluptatibus.

(P. What is the sea? A. The path of boldness, the edge of the earth, the divider of territories, the resting place of rivers, the source of showers, a haven in dangers, a blessing in delights.

DPA 49

P. Quid sunt flumina? A. Cursus indeficiens, refectio solis, irrigatio terrae.

(P. What are rivers? A. An unceasing motion, the stimulus of the sun, the watering of the earth.)

DPA 50

P. Quid est aqua? A. Subsidium vitae, ablutio sordium.

(P. What is water? A. The foundation of life, the cleanser of stains.)

DPA 51

P. Quid est ignis? A. Calor nimius, fotus nascentium, maturitas frugum.

(P. What is fire? A. An excessive heat, the warming of the newborn, the ripening of fruit.)

DPA 52

P. Quid est frigus? A. Febricitas membrorum.

(P. What is cold? A. A shuddering of the limbs.)

DPA 53[41]

P. Quid est gelu? A. Persecutor herbarum, perditor foliorum, vinculum terrae, fons aquarum.

(P. What is ice? A. The persecutor of plants, the destroyer of leaves, the binding of the earth, a source of waters.)

DPA 54

P. Quid est nix? A. Aqua sicca.

(P. What is snow? A. Dry water.)

DPA 55

P. Quid est hiems? A. Aestatis exsul.

(P. What is winter? A. An exile from summer.)

DPA 56

P. Quid est ver? A. Pictor terrae.

(P. What is spring? A. The painter of the earth.)

DPA 57

P. Quid est aestas? A. Revestio terrae, maturitio frugum.

(P. What is summer? A. The recovering of the earth, the ripening of fruit.)

DPA 58

P. Quid est autumnus? A. Horreum anni.

(P. What is autumn? A. The storehouse of the year.)

---

41 The variants *fons* (spring, stream) and *pons* (bridge) seem equally feasible: one links back to the customary "ice" riddles, and how ice both produces and is produced from water, the other to the notion of ice binding of the waves.

DPA 59[42]

P. Quid est annus? A. Quadriga mundi. P. Quis ducit eam? A. Nox et dies, frigus et calor. P. Quis est auriga eius? A. Sol et luna. P. Quot habent palatia? A. Duodecim. P. Qui sunt praetores palatiorum? A. Aries, Taurus, Gemini, Cancer, Leo, Virgo, Libra, Scorpius, Sagittarius, Capricornus, Aquarius, Pisces. P. Quot dies habitant in unoquoque palatio? A. Sol XXX dies et decem semis horas. Luna duos dies et octo horas, et bisse unius horae.

(P. What is the year? A. The chariot of the world. P. Who pulls it? A. Night and day, cold and heat. P. Who is its charioteer? A. Sun and moon. P. How many palaces does it have? A. Twelve. P. Who are the heads of the palaces? A. Aries, Taurus, Gemini, Cancer, Leo, Virgo, Libra, Scorpio, Sagittarius, Capricorn, Aquarius, Pisces. P. How many days do they stay in each palace? A. Sun for thirty days and ten half-hours. Moon for two days and eight hours and two-thirds of an hour.)

DPA 60

P. Magister, timeo altum ire. A. Quis te duxit in altum? P. Curiositas. A. Si times, descendamus; sequar quocunque ieris.

(P. Master, I am afraid to go on high. A. What has led you on high? P. Curiosity. A. If you are afraid, let us go down. I shall follow you wherever you go.)

DPA 61

P. Si scirem quid esset navis, praepararem tibi, ut venires ad me. A. Navis est domus erratica, ubilibet hospitium, viator sine vestigiis, vicinus harenae.

(P. If I knew what a ship was, I should have made one ready for you, so that you might come to me. A. A ship is a wandering home, a lodging anywhere, a traveller without traces, a neighbour to the sand.)

42 The twelve palaces of the year are evidently the astrological houses of the relevant signs; see further Isidore, *Etymologiae*, V.xxxvi.1 and III.lxxi.23–32, 1: n.p.

DPA 62

P. Quid est harena? A. Murus terrae.

(P. What is the sand? A. The wall of the earth.)

DPA 63

P. Quid est herba? A. Vestis terrae.

(P. What is grass? A. The clothing of the earth.)

DPA 64

P. Quid sunt holera? A. Amici medicorum, laus coquorum.

(P. What are herbs? A. The friends of doctors, the praise of cooks.)

DPA 65

P. Quid est, quod amara dulcia facit? A. Fames.

(P. What is it that makes bitter things sweet? A. Hunger.)

DPA 66

P. Quid est, quod hominem non lassum facit? A. Lucrum.

(P. What is it that does not make anyone tired? A. Money.)

DPA 67

P. Quid est vigilanti somnus? A. Spes.

(P. What is sleep to the wakeful? A. Hope.)

DPA 68

P. Quid est spes? A. Refrigerium laboris, dubius eventus.

(P. What is hope? A. A relief from labour, an uncertain outcome.)

DPA 69

P. Quid est amicitia? A. Aequalitas animorum.

(P. What is friendship? A. The equality of minds.)

DPA 70

P. Quid est fides? A. Ignotae rei et mirandae certitudo.

(P. What is faith? A. The certainty of something unknown and wonderful.)

DPA 71

P. Quid est mirum? A. Nuper vidi hominem stantem, molientem ambulantem, qui nunquam fuit. P. Quomodo potest esse? pande mihi. A. Imago est in aqua. P. Cur hoc non intellexi per me, dum toties vidi hunc ipsum hominem? A. Quia bonae indolis es iuvenis et naturalis ingenii, proponam tibi quaedam alia mira; tempta, si per teipsum possis conicere illa. P. Faciemus ita tamen, ut si secus quam est dicam, corrigas me.

(P. What is a wonder? A. I recently saw a man who was never there standing, moving, and walking. P. How can this happen? Tell me. A. It was a reflection in water. P. Why did I not understand this myself, even though I saw him so often? A. Since you are a young man of fine talent and natural wit, I shall describe to you some other wonders; see if you are able to interpret them yourself. P. Let us do that, so long as you put me straight if I make a mistake.)

DPA 72

A. Faciam, ut vis. Quidam ignotus mecum sine lingua et voce locutus est, qui nunquam ante fuit, nec postea erit; et quem non audiebam, nec novi. P. Somnium te forte fatigavit magister?

(A. I shall do as you wish. Someone I did not know spoke with me without tongue or voice, one who had never been, nor shall be again, and whom I was not used to hearing, and did not recognise. P. Perhaps a dream disturbed you, master?)

DPA 73

A. Etiam, fili. Audi et aliud: Vidi mortuos generare vivum, et in ira vivi consumpti sunt mortui. P. De fricatione arborum ignis natus est, consumens arbores.

(A. Quite right, son. Hear another: I saw dead things produce something living, and the dead were consumed by the breath of one living. P. Fire is produced from the rubbing of wood, and it devours wood.)

DPA 74

A. Verum est. Audivi mortuos multa loquentes. P. Numquam bene, nisi suspendantur in aëre.

(A. That's true. I heard some dead men speaking loud. P. Never a good thing, unless they are hanging in the air.)

DPA 75[43]

A. Vere. Vidi ignem inexstinctum pausare in aqua. P. Silicem in aqua significare vis reor.

(A. True. I saw fire that had not been put out sitting in water. P. You mean flint in water, I reckon.)

---

43 Compare **SYM 76** and **76a** [*SILEX* (flint)]:

> Semper inest intus, sed raro cernitur ignis;
> intus enim latitat, sed solos prodit ad ictus;
> nec lignis ut vivat eget, nec ut occidat undis.
>
> [Fire is always inside me, but it is rarely seen;
> for it lurks inside, but is brought out only in response to blows;
> nor does it need wood to live, nor water to die.]
>
> Virtus magna mihi duro mollitur ab igne,
> cessantique foco intus mihi virtus adhaeret;
> semper inest in me, sed raro cernitur ignis.
>
> [I have great power; it is softened by hard fire;
> but when the flames die down, my power remains inside.
> Fire is always inside me, but it is rarely seen.]

DPA 76[44]

A. Ut reris, sic est. Vidi mortuum sedentem super vivum, et in risu mortui moritur vivus. P. Hoc coqui nostri norunt.

(A. It is what you reckon. I saw a dead thing sitting on top of a living thing, and the living dies from the laughter of the dead thing. P. Our cooks know that one.)

DPA 77[45]

A. Norunt. Sed pone digitum super os, ne pueri hoc audiant quid sit. Fui in venatione cum aliis, in qua si quid cepimus, nihil nobiscum portavimus; et quod capere non potuimus, domum portavimus nobiscum. P. Rusticorum est haec venatio.

(A. They do. But put your finger to your lips, so that the boys don't hear this one. I was out hunting with others, and if we caught anything we carried nothing with us; what we carried home with us is what we couldn't catch. P. That's poor people's hunting.)

---

44 Compare **ps-BED 10** [*LEBES* (cauldron)]:

> Vidi mortuum super vivum sedentem, et ex risu mortui moriebatur vivus.
>
> [I saw a dead man sitting on a live man, and the live man was dying from the laughter of the dead man.]

See further Martha Bayless, "The *Collectanea* and Medieval Dialogues and Riddles," in *Collectanea Pseudo-Bedae*, 12–24.

45 Compare **SYM 30** [*PEDICULI* (lice)]:

> Est nova nostrarum cunctis captura ferarum:
> ut si quid capias, et tu tibi ferre recuses,
> et quod non capias, tecum tamen ipse reportes.
>
> [Everyone has a novel kind of hunt for our wild beasts:
> since whatever you capture you may refuse to carry home,
> and whatever you fail to capture, nonetheless you may bring back with you.]

DPA 78[46]

A. Est. Vidi quemdam natum, antequam esset conceptus. P. Vidisti, et forte manducasti.

(A. It is. I saw something born before it was conceived. P. You did, and perhaps you ate it.)

DPA 79[47]

A. Manducavi. Quis est, qui non est, et nomen habet et responsum dat sonanti? P. Biblos in silvis interroga.

(A. I did eat it. Who is it who does not exist, who has a name, and answers whoever calls? P. Ask the reeds in the forest.)

DPA 80[48]

A. Vidi hospitem currentem cum domo sua; et ille tacebat, et domus sonabat. P. Para mihi rete, et pandam tibi.

---

46 Compare **SYM 14** [*PULLUS IN OVO* (chick in egg)]:

> Mira tibi referam nostrae primordia vitae:
> nondum natus eram, nec eram genitricis in alvo;
> iam posito partu natum me nemo videbat.
>
> [I'll tell you the amazing beginnings of my life,
> when I was not yet born, nor did I exist inside my mother's womb;
> and so with my birth already taken care of, no one saw me born.]

47 Compare **SYM 98** [*ECHO* (echo)]:

> Virgo modesta nimis legem bene servo pudoris;
> ore procax non sum, nec sum temeraria linguae;
> ultro nolo loqui, sed do responsa loquenti.
>
> [As a modest maiden, I keep the rule of chastity well;
> I am not shameful in speech, nor rash in talk;
> I won't speak unprompted, but I reply when someone speaks.]

48 Compare **SYM 12** [*FLUMEN ET PISCIS* (river and fish)]:

> Est domus in terris, clara quae voce resultat;
> ipsa domus resonat, tacitus sed non sonat hospes.
> Ambo tamen currunt, hospes simul et domus una.

(A. I saw a host running with his house, and he was silent, while his house was rowdy. P. Give me a net, and I'll show you.)

DPA 81[49]

A. Quis est, qui videre non potest, nisi clausis oculis? P. Qui stertit, tibi ostendit illum.

(A. Who is it that you can't see except with closed eyes? P. That guy snoring shows you.)

DPA 82[50]

A. Vidi hominem octo in manu tenentem, et de octonis subito rapuit septem, et remanserunt sex. P. Pueri in scholi hoc sciunt.

(A. I saw a man with eight in his hand, and from eight he took seven, and six were left. P. The boys in school know this one.)

[There is a home on earth that calls out with a clear voice:
the house itself resounds, but its silent guest makes no sound.
Yet both flow together, the guest alongside the house.]

There is a further parallel at EXE 81 (*FISC OND EA* [fish and river]). See in this regard Dieter Bitterli, *Say What I Am Called: The Old English Riddles of the Exeter Book and the Anglo-Latin Riddle Tradition*, 13–14.

49 Compare **SYM 99** [*SOMNIUM* (dream)], especially the third line:

Sponte mea veniens, varias ostendo figuras;
fingo metus vanos nullo discrimine veri,
sed me nemo videt, nisi qui sua lumina claudit.

[Coming of my own accord, I display different forms.
I feign empty fears with no distinction of truth;
but no one sees me, unless he closes his eyes.]

50 Compare **SYM 96** [*FLEXUS DIGITORUM* (finger-counting)]:

Nunc mihi iam credas fieri quod posse negatur;
octo tenes manibus, sed me monstrante magistro,
sublatis septem reliqui tibi sex remanebunt.

[Now you can believe what can be denied:
you hold eight in your hands, but when I show you as a teacher:
when seven are taken away, you will still have six.]

DPA 83[51]

A. Quid est, cui, si caput abstuleris, altior surgit? P. Vade ad lectulum tuum et ibi invenies.

(A. What is it that gets taller when you take away the head? P. Go to your bed, and you'll find it there.)

For a further (and rather clearer) description, see Bede, *De temporum ratione. Bedae opera didascalica*, pars 2, ed. Jones, 269.

> Cum ergo dicis unum, minimum in laeva digitum inflectens, in medium palmae artum infiges. Cum dicis duo, secundum a minimo flexum, ibidem impones. Cum dicis tria, tertium similiter adflectes. Cum dicis quattuor, itidem minimum levabis. Cum dicis quinque, secundum a minimo similiter eriges. Cum dicis sex, tertium nihilominus elevabis, medio dumtaxat solo, qui medicus appellatur, in medium palmae fixo. Cum dicis septem, minimum solum, ceteris interim levatis, super palmae radicem pones. Iuxta quem cum dicis octo, medicum.
>
> [If you want to say "one," you should bend the little finger of your left hand, and place its tip on the palm; for "two," place down the ring finger next to it; for "three," the middle finger as well; for "four," you must again raise the little finger; for "five," the ring finger as well; for "six," you must extend the middle finger, and then the ring finger, which is also called the "doctor," is the only one left bent down on the palm; for "seven," extend all the fingers, and bend only the little finger along the wrist; for "eight," place the ring finger down next to it.]

51 Compare **ALD 41** [*PULUILLUS* (pillow)], which is broadly similar:

> Nolo fidem frangas, licet irrita dicta putentur,
> credula sed nostris pande praecordia verbis.
> Celsior ad superas possum turgescere nubes,
> si caput aufertur mihi toto corpore dempto;
> at vero capitis si pressus mole gravabor,
> ima petens iugiter minorari parte videbor.
>
> [Please do not disbelieve me, although what I say may seem worthless;
> rather, keep your heart open to my words.
> I can swell up rather high towards the clouds above;
> if the head were to be removed from me, I'd be bereft in my whole body too;
> but if I were pressed down with the weight of a head,
> sinking, I would seem to be made the same size smaller.]

DPA 84[52]

A. Tres fuere: unus numquam natus et semel mortuus; alter semel natus, nunquam mortuus; tertius semel natus et bis mortuus . P. Primus aequivocus terrae; secundus Domino meo; tertius homini pauperi. A. Dic tamen primas litteras nominum. P. I. V. XXX.

(A. Three they were: one never born and once dead; another once born, never dead; the third once born and twice dead. P. The first has the same name as the earth, the second as my God, the third as a pauper. A. Tell me the first letters of their names. P. I. V. XXX.)

DPA 85[53]

A. Vidi feminam volantem, rostrum habentem ferreum, et corpus ligneum et caudam pennatam, mortem portantem. P. Socia est militum.

(A. I saw a female flying, with an iron beak, a wooden body, and a feathery tail, carrying death. P. She is the friend of warriors.)

DPA 86

A. Quid est miles? P. Murus imperii, timor hostium, gloriosum servitium.

(A. What is a warrior? P. The protection of the realm, the terror of enemies, service with glory.)

DPA 87

A. Quid est quod est et non est? P. Nihil. A. Quomodo potest esse et non esse? P. Nomine est et re non est.

52 The numbers at the end of this *enigma* must be understood as equating to the Greek system, where numbers equate to letters, in these cases α (I), ε (V), and λ (XXX), which are indeed (whether understood in Greek or in Latin) the first letters of the solutions. The Hebrew meaning of Adam is indeed "earth," as was widely understood in the Latin Middle Ages; both Enoch and Elijah are identified as types of Christ.

53 See further Bitterli, *Say What I Am Called*, 110–13.

(A. What is it that is and is not? P. Nothing. A. How can it be and not be? P. It exists in name but not in fact.)

DPA 88

A. Quid est tacitus nuntius? P. Quem manu teneo. A. Quid tenes manu? P. Epistolam tuam, magister. A. Lege feliciter, fili.

(A. What is a silent messenger? P. What I'm holding in my hand. A. What are you holding in your hand? P. Your letter. A. Enjoy reading it, son.)

Appendix 2:

Parallels between *AHE* and *DPA*

AHE 1 [cf. *DPA* 88]

H. Quid erit nobis, si cinctum solvas, neque nudaberis ipse? Respice corpus, quod et doceri possis. E. Epistola est.

(H. What will happen to us, if you loosen the tie, but won't yourself be made naked? Examine the body, and you can also be enlightened. E. That is a letter.)

AHE 2 [cf. *DPA* 88]

H. Quid est epistola? E. Tacitus nuncius.

(H. What is a letter? E. A silent messenger.)

AHE 11 [cf. *DPA* 66]

H. Qua ratione homo lassus non fit? E. Lucrum faciendo.

(H. In what way does someone not become tired? E. Making money.)

AHE 12 [cf. *DPA* 69]

H. Quid est amicitia? E. Concordia.

(H. What is friendship? E. Agreement.)

AHE 14 [cf. *DPA* 68]

H. Quid est spes? E. Vigilanti somnus, spectanti dubius eventus.

(H. What is hope? E. Sleep to the wakeful, an uncertain outcome to the one looking on.)

AHE 17 [cf. *DPA* 9]

H. Quid est libertas? E. Innocentia.

(H. What is freedom? E. Absence of harm.)

AHE 21 [cf. *DPA* 5]

H. Quid est optima vita? E. Brevissima.

(H. What is the best life? E. The shortest.)

AHE 23 [cf. *DPA* 6]

H. Quid est mors? E. Perpetua securitas.

(H. What is death? E. Eternal freedom from care.)

AHE 33 [cf. *DPA* 7]

H. Quid est homo? E. Pomo similis: poma ut in arboribus pendent, sic sunt et corpora nostra: ut matura cadunt, aut si cito acerba ruunt.

(H. What is mankind? E. Like a fruit tree: just as apples hang in the trees, that is how our bodies are too: either they fall in due season, or bitterly they quickly collapse.)

AHE 34 [cf. *DPA* 7]

H. Quid est homo? E. Sicut lucerna in vento posita.

(H. What is mankind? E. Like a lantern placed in the wind.)

AHE 35 [cf. *DPA* 7]

H. Quid est homo? E. Loci hospes, legis imago, calamitatis fabula, mancipium mortis, vite mora; quo fortuna sepe suos ludos faciet.

(H. What is mankind? E. A guest in the house, a spectre of law, a tale of calamity, the slave of death, a pause of life; where luck will often play its games.)

AHE 40 [cf. *DPA* 41]

H. Quid est sol? E. Splendor orbis; qui tollit et ponit diem; per quem scire nobis cursum horarum datur.

(H. What is the sun? E. The glory of the world; what produces and situates the day; by which the sequence of hours is granted us.)

AHE 41 [cf. *DPA* 42]

H. Quid est luna? E. Dies adultor, noctis oculus, fax tenebrarum.

(H. What is the moon? E. The paramour of the day, the eye of night, the torch of darkness.)

AHE 42 [cf. *DPA* 38]

H. Quid est celum? E. Culmen immensum.

(H. What is the sky? E. An unmeasurable height.)

AHE 47 [cf. *DPA* 47]

H. Quid est terra? E. Cellarium vite.

(H. What is the earth? E. The storehouse of life.)

AHE 48 [cf. *DPA* 48]

H. Quid est mare? E. Iter incertum.

(H. What is the sea? E. An unsure path.)

AHE 49 [cf. *DPA* 61]

H. Quid est navis? E. Domus erratica.

(H. What is a ship? E. A wandering home.)

AHE 50 [cf. *DPA* 61]

H. Quid est navis? E. Ubilibet hospicium.

(H. What is a ship? E. A lodging anywhere.)

AHE 53 [cf. *DPA* 8]

H. Quid est somnus? E. Mortis imago.

(H. What is sleep? E. The semblance of death.)

AHE 66 [cf. *DPA* 86]

H. Quid est miles? E. Murus imperii, defensor patrie, gloriosa servitus, potestatis indicium.

(H. What is a warrior? E. The protection of the realm, defender of the homeland, glorious servitude, proof of power.)

9 Foster-Relationships in the Old English *Boethius*

SUSAN IRVINE

In one of a number of passages condemning the arbitrary brutality of the Roman emperor Nero,[1] the author of the Old English *Boethius* describes how Nero had his own foster-father Seneca put to death:

> Hwæt we witon þæt se unrihtwisa cyning Neron wolde hatan his agenne mægstre and his fosterfæder acwellan, þæs nama wæs Seneca; se wæs uðwita. Þa he þa onfunde þæt he dead beon sceolde, þa bead he ealle his æhta wið his feore. Þa nolde se cyning þæs onfon ne him his feores geunnan. Ða he þa þæt ongeat, þa geceas he him þone deað þæt him mon oflete blodes on þam earme, and þa dyde mon swa. ... Hwæt ealle men witon þæt se Seneca wæs Nerone and Papinianus Antonie þa weorðestan and þa leofestan and mæstne anweald hæfdon ge on hiora hirede ge buton, and þeah buton ælcere scylde wurdon fordone.[2]

> [We know that the unjust king Nero sought to order the death of his own teacher and foster-father, whose name was Seneca; he was a philosopher.

1 On the various passages concerning Nero in the Old English *Boethius*, see Paul E. Szarmach, "Alfred's Nero," 147–67.

2 Malcolm Godden and Susan Irvine, eds., *The Old English Boethius: An Edition of the Old English Versions of Boethius's "De consolatione philosophiae,"* 1:302–3 (B Text, ch. 29, lines 46–52, 55–8). The corresponding section in the C Text is Prose 15, lines 46–58. On the relationship between the two texts, see Godden and Irvine, *Old English Boethius*, 1:44–8. In this essay quotations will be from the B Text unless otherwise stated. Translations are based on those in Godden and Irvine, *Old English Boethius*, and in Susan Irvine and Malcolm R. Godden, eds., *The Old English Boethius with Verse Prologues and Epilogues Associated with King Alfred.*

> When he discovered that he was to die, he offered all his possessions in exchange for this life. Then the king would not accept that nor grant him his life. When he understood that, he chose to die by having someone let blood in the arm, and then that was done ... Indeed all men know that this Seneca was by Nero and Papinianus by Antoninus very greatly honoured and loved, and had very great power, both in their household and outside it, and yet they were destroyed without any guilt.]

The description of Seneca as Nero's "foster-father" is a curious one. Its pairing here with "mægstre" (teacher) may suggest that the author primarily has in mind Seneca's educative role.[3] But comparison with the Latin source gives a slightly enriched perspective. The word "fosterfæder," rather than simply acting as a synonym for "mægstre," seems to reflect the more personal relationship between Nero and Seneca implicit in the "familiarem" (companion) of Boethius's *De consolatione philosophiae* ("Senecam familiarem praeceptoremque suum" [his teacher and companion Seneca]).[4] The Old English passage as a whole emphasises the close bond between Nero and Seneca, adding independently of its source that Seneca was "very greatly honoured and loved" by Nero. Ultimately, however, the story of the relationship between foster-father and foster-son here is one of conflict, not of honour and love. Nero's implacable evil leads to his foster-father's untimely death. His villainy is all the more shocking in that he has ignored and transgressed a foster-familial bond.

This fascinating vignette of a foster-father betrayed offers in its context a stark lesson about the vagaries of powerful men, but its broader implications also deserve further exploration. To what extent is the passage representative of depictions of parent-child foster-relationships in Old English literary culture? Is there any distinction to be drawn between the foster-relationship, with its subtext of potential conflict, and the nature of relationships between biological parents and children in the Old English

3 The *DOE* defines *fostorfæder, fosterfæder* as "foster-father, guardian," and by extension "teacher, tutor," and translates the phrase *magister and fostorfæder* in the context of this passage as "teacher and tutor." Elsewhere in the Old English corpus, *fostorfæder* translates or glosses the Latin words *altor*, *alumnus*, and *nutritor* (for examples, see *DOE* s.v. *fostorfæder, fosterfæder*).

4 Ludwig Bieler, ed., *Anicii Manlii Severini Boethii philosophiae consolatio*, 3p5, 45. Cited below as *DCP*, followed by numbers of book and of prosa/metrum, and then by page number(s) where relevant. Translations from Latin and Old English are my own unless otherwise stated.

Boethius? Why might the *Boethius* author be so uncompromising about the ways that parents or children may distort or abuse bonds between them? This essay aims to show that the *Boethius* author makes provocative use of the dynamics of familial and foster-familial relationships and bonds to enhance the meanings of the work.

Conflict across Generations in Foster-Relationships: A Narrative Trope?

In depicting the foster-relationship as one potentially fraught with peril for one or other parties, the *Boethius* author may be building on a tradition found elsewhere in Old English literature, both poetry and prose. *Riddle* 9 ("cuckoo") in the Exeter Book, for example, builds up a picture of fosterage as life-giving and nurturing, only to undercut this in its final two lines:

Mec on þissum dagum deadne ofgeafun
fæder ond modor; ne wæs me feorh þa gen,
ealdor in innan. Þa mec an ongon,
welhold mege, wedum þeccan,
heold ond freoþode, hleosceorpe wrah
swa arlice swa hire agen bearn,
oþþæt ic under sceate, swa min gesceapu wæron,
ungesibbum wearð eacen gæste.
Mec seo friþe mæg fedde siþþan,
oþþæt ic aweox, widdor meahte
siþas asettan. Heo hæfde swæsra þy læs
suna ond dohtra, þy heo swa dyde. (*Riddle* 9, lines 1–12)[5]

[In these days my father and mother gave me up for dead; there was no life in me yet, no life within. Then someone began to cover me with clothes, a very loyal kinswoman protected and cherished me, and wrapped me with a protecting garment, just as generously as for her own child, until under that covering, as was my nature, I was endowed with a spirit amongst those unrelated to me. Afterwards the protecting kinswoman fed me until I grew up and could set out on wider journeys. She had fewer beloved sons and daughters because she did so.]

5 *The Exeter Book*, ASPR 3:185.

In this short poem the cuckoo chick describes how its foster-mother gave it the same quality of love and attention that she gave to her own children. But the riddle alludes at its close to a darker outcome, with the fosterling apparently responsible – albeit indirectly perhaps – for the death of its foster-siblings.[6] The fosterling abuses the power it attains through the foster-relationship, betraying its foster-parent just as Nero betrays his foster-father Seneca in the Old English *Boethius*.

The riddle hints at the possibility that the cuckoo and its foster-mother, unlike Nero and Seneca, may be related to each other by kinship as well as fosterage ("mege," line 4, and "friþe mæg," line 9).[7] In *Beowulf* too, the sometimes blurred lines between kinship and fosterage are exploited, contributing in this case to the poem's complex political landscape.[8] Implicit in the poet's depictions of foster-relationships is an acknowledgment of their destructive potential. We might look, for example, at Beowulf's description of how King Hrethel (his maternal grandfather) fostered him from the age of seven, giving him the same protection and love as he gave his own sons:

Ic wæs syfanwintre þa mec sinca baldor
freawine folca æt minum fæder genam;
heold mec ond hæfde Hreðel cyning,
geaf me sinc ond symbel, sibbe gemunde;
næs ic him to life laðra owihte,
beorn in burgum, þonne his bearna hwylc,
Herebeald ond Hæðcyn oððe Hygelac min. (*Beowulf*, lines 2428–34)[9]

[I was seven years old when the ruler of treasures, the lordly friend of peoples, took me from my father; King Hrethel protected and kept me, gave me treasure and feasts, remembered kinship; as a warrior in the strongholds, I was in no way more hateful than any of his sons, Herebeald, Hæðcyn, or my Hygelac, as long as he lived.]

6 See Dieter Bitterli, "The Survival of the Dead Cuckoo," 95–114; and Jennifer Neville, "Fostering the Cuckoo: Exeter Book Riddle 9," 431–46.

7 Paradoxically, "ungesibbum" in line 8 may seem to contradict this; on the possibility, however, that *ungesibbum* in line 8 of the poem might mean "in hostility" as well as "among those unrelated to me," see Shu-han Luo's essay in this volume.

8 See further Richard North's essay in this volume.

9 Robert D. Fulk, Robert E. Bjork, and John D. Niles, eds., *Klaeber's "Beowulf" and the Fight at Finnesburg*, 83 (cited hereafter as *Beowulf*).

Hrethel is depicted here as taking on the role of foster-father to Beowulf. The foster-relationship is mutually beneficial: Beowulf receives nurture and riches. For Hrethel Beowulf is "a warrior in the strongholds," and indeed Hrethel's power will eventually be transferred to Beowulf, whose foster-brothers (his biological uncles) all predecease him. This is apparently an ideal vision of fostering within a courtly environment, contrasting sharply with the negative behaviour of Nero to his foster-father in the Old English *Boethius*. But the positive depiction here is, as Jennifer Neville suggests, partly created through language that suggests the darker potential underlying such a relationship.[10] By remarking specifically that Hrethel "remembered kinship," the *Beowulf*-poet perhaps suggests that without that tie the foster-relationship might have turned out differently. And to say that Beowulf was "in no way more hateful" in Hrethel's life than his own sons subtly alludes to the potential for destructive competition among the various siblings and their (foster-)father, soon to be realised in the cycle of grief and revenge set off by Hæthcyn's killing of Herebeald.[11] This brief depiction of Beowulf's upbringing as a foster-son, despite the advantages it gives him, links closely with other strands of the poem, which depict a movement away from the honour and love that would ideally bind kin to one another.

Other vernacular depictions of fosterage similarly reflect a sense of uneasiness. For hagiographers, the characteristic role of foster-parents is to offer Christian teaching and strength to their fosterlings: so in the Old English *Martyrology*, for example, St Vitus is aligned with his foster-father St Modestus, against his pagan father who wishes to lure him away from Christ with presents, and St Marina (Margaret) is entrusted by her father, a pagan, to a Christian woman, later referred to as her "festermeder," for her education.[12] Even within the hagiographical tradition, however, the foster-relationship is not always a straightforward one. We might look, for example, at the Life of Benedict in Book II of the Old English *Dialogues* (based on Gregory the Great's *Dialogi*).[13] Here Benedict's transition from

10 Neville, "Fostering the Cuckoo," 437–8.

11 See *Beowulf*, lines 2435–40.

12 See Christine Rauer, ed. and trans., *The Old English Martyrology: Edition, Translation and Commentary*, 116 (entry for 15 June) and 132 (entry for 7 July).

13 Hans Hecht, ed., *Bischofs Wærferth von Worcester Übersetzung der Dialoge Gregors des Grossen*, 98. Ælfric offers another vernacular version of the Life of St Benedict (also based on Gregory's *Dialogi*) in his Second Series of *Catholic Homilies*: see Malcolm Godden, ed., *Ælfric's Catholic Homilies: The Second Series*, 92–109.

precocious child to a saint-in-waiting is delineated through his relationship to his nurturing and loving foster-mother. Benedict's sanctity from an early age is witnessed in two incidents of taking flight. In his first flight, away from the immoralities of his home city, he is followed by his foster-mother "forþon þe heo hine swyðe geornlice lufode" (because she loved him very deeply), and they take up residence at a place called Enfide.[14] When his foster-mother breaks a sieve she has borrowed, Benedict grieves for her distress and as a result of his prayers the sieve is made whole again. The sieve is then hung up at the church gate as a sign of Benedict's greatness. Wanting to avoid this fame, Benedict flees again, this time away from his foster-mother:

> Ac Benedictus gewilnode ma, þæt he þrowode þyses middaneardes yfel þonne þa herunga, and þæt he wære for Gode swyþur mid gewinnum geswænced, þonne he wære up ahafen on þam herungum þisses andweardan lifes. And he þa dygollice wæs fleonde þa his fostormoder and gesohte þa deogolnyssa þære westan stowe.[15]

> [But Benedict desired more to suffer earthly hardships than praises and to be further afflicted with struggles for God than to be exalted by the praises of this present life. And he then proceeded to flee secretly from his foster-mother and sought the seclusion of a desolate place.]

Benedict's bond with his foster-mother is both an opportunity for his sanctity to become known, and a threat to the more rigorous fulfilment of a saintly life. His affection for her is a sign of his goodness but at the same time she represents a tie to the human community that has the potential to distract him from his vocation. Her role is an ambivalent one. On the one hand, through nurturing Benedict she is linked to his sanctity, and this is reflected in their shared separation – moral and physical – from the immoralities of the worldly men in the city they leave behind. On the other hand, as the incident of the sieve reveals, she is also allied with the commitment to earthly values, which is inimical to Benedict's desire for sanctity, and for this reason his second flight is from her rather than with her – a flight that is all the harder because of the close bond between them. In the

14 Hecht, *Dialoge*, 96.
15 Ibid., 98.

Life of Benedict, the foster-mother is both the nurturer and paradoxically a potential threat to Benedict's sanctity.

The foster-mother also plays a morally ambivalent role in a very different kind of work, a secular narrative, probably composed in the eleventh century, known as the Old English *Apollonius of Tyre*.[16] At the beginning of the story, King Antiochus, inflamed by desire for his daughter, forces himself upon her and then leaves her in distress in her bedroom. When the girl's "fostormodor" (translating Latin "nutrix") comes in, not knowing who has committed this deed, she is puzzled that the girl hasn't gone to her father about it:

> Seo fostormodor cwæð: "Hwi ne segst þu hit þinum fæder?" Ðæt mæden cwæð: "Hwar is se fæder? Soðlice on me earmre is mines fæder nama reowlice forworden and me nu forðam deað þearle gelicað." Seo fostormodor soðlice þa ða heo gehyrde þæt þæt mæden hire deaðes girnde, ða cliopode heo hi hire to mid liðere spræce and bæd þæt heo fram þare gewilnunge hyre mod gewænde and to hire fæder willan gebuge, þeah ðe heo to geneadod wære.[17]
>
> [The foster-mother said: "Why don't you tell your father about it?" The maiden said: "Where is the father? Truly my father's name has cruelly perished as far as I'm concerned, wretched as I am, and therefore death seems highly desirable to me." Truly the foster-mother, when she heard that the maiden longed for her death, then called her with gentle speech to her, and begged that she would turn her mind from that desire and bow to her father's will, even though she was compelled to it.]

The focus of this passage is of course on the perversion of the role of father that Antiochus's behaviour represents. But the way in which the role of the father is perverted here is made to seem even more horrific by the response of the foster-mother. The foster-mother displays all the affection and desire to comfort that conventionally defines such a figure. But in order to save her foster-daughter's life, the foster-mother must persuade her to continue in an incestuous relationship with her father, a relationship

16 The vernacular version seems to have been a faithful translation of its Latin source, the *Historia Apollonii regis Tyri*; a collated version of the Latin text is printed alongside the Old English text by Peter Goolden, ed., *The Old English "Apollonius of Tyre."*

17 Ibid., 4.

whose moral inappropriateness is never left in doubt by the text. The ideal of nurture, bodily and spiritual, which is so closely tied up with the role of the foster-mother, is here undermined. Instead the foster-mother becomes linked with the conflict arising from the distortion of the paternal role in this text.

The ambivalence of perspective that is evident across a range of depictions of foster-relationships suggests that the Old English *Boethius* author, in describing Nero as Seneca's foster-father, may have had in mind a literary tradition of representing intergenerational foster-relationships as not only nurturing but also potentially tense. This subtext, as we shall see, may have informed the central relationship in the work, that between Wisdom and Mod (Mind). In this work, however, the depiction of parent-child relationships marked by conflict is by no means confined to a fostering context. The relationship between Wisdom and Mod is also enhanced by a sense in the Old English *Boethius* of the precarious nature of the bond between parents and children more generally.

Conflict in Biological Parent-Child Relationships

The *Boethius* author seems to have been under no illusion that the foster-relationship was any more destructive in its potential than biological parenting. In the Old English *Boethius* filial relationships more generally are seen as being areas in which love and loyalty can quickly disintegrate. Parent-child relationships are not straightforwardly symbiotic. The more positive side is seen in the example of Boethius's wife, daughter of Symmachus, whose unparalleled virtues are best described by saying that "heo is on ealum þeawum hiere fæder gelic" (she is in all her habits like her father),[18] and in Boethius himself, whose two sons, Wisdom suggests, have inherited the gifts and virtues of their father and grandfather:

> Hwæt wille we cweðan be þinum twæm sunum? Ða sind ealdormen and geðeahteras on þan is swiotol sio gifu and ealla þa duguþa hiora fæder and heora ealdran fæder, swa swa geonge men magon gelicoste beon ealdum monnum.[19]

18 Godden and Irvine, *Old English Boethius*, 1:259 (B Text, ch. 10, lines 30–1). Boethius's wife was called Rusticiana, but this information may not have been available to the author; see Susan Irvine, "Rewriting Women in the Old English *Boethius*," 2:488–501, at 491–2.

19 Godden and Irvine, *Old English Boethius*, 1:259 (B Text, ch. 10, lines 38–41).

[What will we say about your two sons? They are high officials and counsellors in whom the gift and all the virtues of their father and their grandfather are clear, as like old men as young men can be.]

In these cases, as in the Boethian original, the likeness between parent and child heaps credit on both generations. The *Boethius* author, though, very soon introduces a more sombre perspective than his source by explicitly alluding to the idea that either parent or child might die:

Hwæt ic wat þæt þæt is git deorwyrþre þonne monnes lif, forþam manegum men is leofre þæt he ær self swelte ær he geseo his wif and his bearn sweltende.[20]

[Indeed I know that those are still more precious than a man's life, because many a man would rather die himself than see his wife and children dying.]

The passage perhaps anticipates the subsequent chapter of the work in which the misery brought by having either no children, or children who are wicked or sickly, is used to exemplify the incompleteness of human fortune:

Manige habbað genog gesælilice gewifod ac for bearnleste eallne þone welan þe hi gegaderigað hi lætað fræmdum to brucanne, and hi beoþ for þam unrote. Sume habbað bearn genoge ac þa beoþ hwilum unhale oððe yfele and unweorþe oððe hraðe gefarað, þæt þa eldran for ðam gnorniað ealle heora woruld. Forþam ne mæg nan man on þys anweardan life eallunga gerad beon wið his wyrd.[21]

[Many have married felicitously enough but because of lack of children leave all the wealth that they gather to strangers to enjoy, and they are miserable for that reason. Some have children enough but those are sometimes unhealthy or wicked and worthless, or die early, so that the parents mourn for them all their lives. So no one can be wholly settled with his fate in this present life.]

20 Ibid., 1:259 (B Text, ch. 10, lines 44–7).
21 Ibid., 1:261 (B Text, ch. 11, lines 21–7).

Elsewhere too the *Boethius* author presents dysfunctional parent-child relationships, sometimes dwelling, independently of the Latin source, on the ways in which relationships across the generations may be subject to conflict and alienation. Nero's exultation at having his own mother (and various others close to him) put to death is stated more explicitly in the Old English *Boethius* than in its source (*DCP* 2m6):

> And eft he het ofslean ealle þa wisestan witan Romana, ge furðon his agene modor and his agene broðor; ge furðon his agen wif he ofslog mid sweorde, and for ðyllecum næs he nanwuht geunrotsod ac wæs þy bliþra and fagenode þæs.[22]

> [And afterwards he ordered all the wisest counsellors of the Romans to be killed, and even his own mother and his own brother, and he even killed his own wife with a sword, and for such deeds was not at all saddened but was the happier and rejoiced over it.]

Later in the work, Wisdom describes in much more detail than the Latin source the ways in which children may turn out to be tormentors of their parents:

> Swiðe gewunsum hit bið þæt mon wif hæbbe and bearn. Ac þeah manige bearn beoð gestryned to heora eldrena forwyrðe forþam þe manig wif swelt for hire bearne ær heo hit forðbringan mæge. And we leornodon eac þæt hwilum gebyrede swiðe ungewunelic and ungecyndelic yfel þæt ða bearn getreowedon betwuh him and sieredon ymbe þone fæder. Ge furðon þæt wyrse wæs, we geheordon geo geara on ealdum spellum þæt sum sunu ofsloge his fæder; ic nat humeta buton we witon þæt hit unmennisclic dæd wæs. Hwæt ælc mon mæg witan hu hefig sorg men beoð seo gemen his bearna. Ne þearf ic þe þeah þæt secgan forþam þu hit hæfst afunden bi þe selfum. Be þære hæfegan gemenne bearna cwæð min mægister Eurupides þæt hwilum gebyrede þam heardsælegum þæt him wære betere þæt he bearn næfde þonne he hæfde.[23]

22 Ibid., 1:276 (B Text, ch. 16, lines 153–7).
23 Ibid., 1:306–7 (B text, ch. 31, lines 16–29).

> [It is very pleasant for a man to have a wife and children. But yet many children are produced to the destruction of their parents, for many a woman dies for her child before she can bring it forth. And we have learned also that there sometimes happened a very strange and unnatural wickedness, in that the children conspired amongst themselves and plotted against the father. And indeed what was worse, we heard from long ago in old stories that a son killed his father; I do not know how but we know that it was an inhuman act. Truly, everyone can see how heavy a sorrow for a man is the responsibility for his children. I do not need to tell you that, for you have experienced it for yourself. About that burdensome responsibility for children my teacher Euripides said that sometimes it happened to the unfortunate that it was better for him not to have children than to have them.]

Although the idea here that children may become tormentors of their parents is in the Latin source, the three examples given to illustrate the point are the Old English author's independent addition: death in childbirth; children conspiring against parents; and a son killing his own father. The first, the death of a woman in childbirth, is, the passage implies, a common occurrence. For the second and third examples, the author uses the phrases "we leornodon" and "we geheordon," respectively, indicating an allusion in each case to a particular story or stories: the former perhaps to Brutus the first consul, whose sons plotted to deliver Rome back to Tarquin, and the latter to Oedipus's killing of his father.[24] The latter, however, may also invite us to draw a link with another example of a son killing his father recorded a couple of chapters earlier, Nero killing his foster-father Seneca. In any case the *Boethius* author is clearly alert to the destructive potential in relationships across generations. In an imperfect world, he implies, the normal symbiotic relationships between parent and child may become distorted only too easily.

Curiously, the potential for intergenerational conflict does not only manifest itself in children bringing grief to parents. At one point, Boethius (also referred to as Mod, "Mind") takes the point of view of a child, suggesting that he is being led astray and deluded as a child is:

24 See ibid., 2:365–6 for further discussion of what might have prompted these particular examples.

> Đa cwæð ic: "Me þyncð þæt ðu me dwelige and dyderie, swa mon cild deð, lætst me hider and þider on swa ðicne wudu þæt ic ne mæg ut aredian. Forþam ðu a ymbe sticce fehst eft on þa ilcan spræce þe þu ær sprace, and forlætst eft þa ær þu hi geendod habbe, and fehst on uncuðe."[25]
>
> [Then I said: "It seems to me that you are leading me astray and deluding me, as one does a child, leading me hither and thither in a wood so thick that I cannot find a way out. For you always after a time take up again the same speech that you spoke before, and leave it again before you have finished it, and begin on an unfamiliar one."]

The image of the child and the wood is not in the Latin *De consolatione philosophiae*, in which Boethius merely asks Philosophia: "Are you playing a game with me?" ("Ludisne … me?").[26] The implication of the Old English version, independently of the Latin, is that parenthood, from an educative perspective, is not always carried out in an entirely responsible way. The idea that this is just part of a game, as the Latin implies, does not carry over to the translation. Here the parent – or foster-parent – is cast in the role of someone who exploits his or her power to mislead, even if ultimately there is a way out that is not yet visible to the child.

The Relationship between Wisdom and Mod

Why might the author of the Old English *Boethius* be so uncompromising about the ways in which parents or children may distort or abuse the love, honour, and power implicit in the bond between them? The key to this, I think, lies in the relationship between Mod and Wisdom, the Old English equivalents of the Latin personae of Boethius and Philosophia, respectively. Wisdom is established early on in the work as Boethius's foster-mother. Wisdom first greets Boethius's mourning mind (which will become the figure of Mod) with a reminder that it has been nourished in Wisdom's school ("Hu ne eart ðu se mon þe on minre scole wære afed and gelæred?" [Are you not the man who was nourished and taught in my school?]), and proceeds to prompt Mod's memory by asking if it recognises its own foster-mother: "Adrigde þa mines modes eagan and hit fran bliðum wordum

25 Ibid., 1:334–5 (B Text, ch. 35, lines 153–7).
26 *DCP* 3p12, 62.

hwæðer hit oncneowe his fostermodor" (Then Wisdom dried my mind's eyes, and asked it with cheerful words whether it knew its foster-mother.)[27] In depicting Wisdom as the foster-mother of Mind (just as Philosophia is depicted as the "nutrix" of Boethius in the Latin original),[28] the Old English author presumably had in mind its figurative implications.[29] Vernacular precedent for a figurative interpretation of *fostormodor* may have prompted its use here: in the Old English *Pastoral Care* Patience is described as "sio fostermodur ælcre leornunga and ælces cræftes" (the foster-mother of all learning and every virtue).[30] In both cases, foster-motherhood is seen to be bound up closely with education ("gelæred" and "leornunga" in the *Boethius* and *Pastoral Care*, respectively).

The Old English *Boethius* apparently elides the role of foster-mother with that of mother. When the mind turns towards Wisdom, it recognises not its foster-mother, as we might expect, but its own mother:

> Mid þam þe ða þæt mod wið bewende, þa gecneow hit swiðe sweotele his agne modor, þæt wæs se wisdom ðe hit lange ær tyde and lærde.[31]
>
> [As soon as the Mind turned that way, it recognised clearly its own mother; that was Wisdom which had trained and taught it for a long time.]

---

27 Godden and Irvine, *Old English Boethius*, 1:245 (B Text, ch. 3, lines 3–4, 11–12).

28 *DCP* 1p3, 5.

29 On the use of feminine personal metaphors within medieval grammatical culture, see Ernst Robert Curtius, *European Literature and the Latin Middle Ages*, 131–2; and Clare Lees and Gillian Overing, "Pressing Hard on the 'Breasts' of Scripture: Metaphor and the Symbolic," 152–72. I am also grateful to Mercedes Salvador-Bello for sending me a copy of her paper "How Far Did the Influence of Anglo-Saxon Riddling Reach in the Continent?" in advance of its publication (delivered at the International Medieval Congress, University of Leeds, July 2016).

30 Henry Sweet, ed., *King Alfred's West-Saxon Version of Gregory's Pastoral Care*, 1:215–17 (where "fostermodur" again translates Latin "nutrix"). For another early vernacular example of a figurative rendering of the foster-relationship, see the Old English *Martyrology*, where Gregory, in the entry for 12 March, is described as "ure altor and we syndan his alumni; ðæt is ðæt he is ure festerfæder on Criste, and we syndon his festerbearn on fullwihte" ([He is] our *altor* and we are his *alumni*, which means that he is our foster-father in Christ and we are his foster-children in baptism): see Rauer, *Old English Martyrology*, 64.

31 Godden and Irvine, *Old English Boethius*, 1:245 (B Text, ch. 3, lines 12–14). "Lange ær" may alternatively be translated as "long before."

In referring to Wisdom as both foster-mother and mother, the author may, as Nicole Guenther Discenza has argued, be combining Boethius's presentation of Philosophia as a nurse ("nutrix") and the presentation of Wisdom as a mother in the Old Testament Wisdom Books.[32] This kind of conflation would fit too with the "complex games of identification and self-representation" that Malcolm Godden has noted elsewhere in the Old English *Boethius*.[33] The picture is further complicated, perhaps, by the allusion to Mod's "fæder eþele" (fatherland) from which, Wisdom tells us, Mod has moved away:

> Sona swa ic þe ærest on þisse unrotnesse geseah þus murciende ic ongeat þæt þu wære ut afaren of þines fæder eðele, þæt is of minum larum.[34]
>
> [As soon as I first saw you in this grief, lamenting in this fashion, I realised that you had departed from your fatherland, that is, from my teachings.]

The phrase "þines fæder eðele," corresponding to "patria" in the Latin source (*DCP* 1p5), is ambiguous in its wording, since *fæder* in this context could be identified with either God or Wisdom, or indeed both.[35] Wisdom here acts figuratively as a father-figure to Mod, adding to its roles as foster-mother and mother elsewhere.[36]

It is the trope of Wisdom as foster-parent which the Old English author subsequently chooses to develop. In chapter 7 Wisdom explains how its nurture has benefited Mod:

32 Nicole Guenther Discenza, *The King's English: Strategies of Translation in the Old English* Boethius, 89.

33 Malcolm Godden, "The Player King: Identification and Self-representation in King Alfred's Writings," 137–50, at 137.

34 Godden and Irvine, *Old English Boethius*, 1:247 (B Text, ch. 5, lines 4–6).

35 The *DOE*'s definition of *fæder eþel* as "the home of the Father, the true home of the righteous" (*DOE* s.v. *eþel*, sense 2.b.i.) is probably the relevant one here, though the more general sense of "fatherland, native country" (*DOE* s.v. *fædereþel*) may also underlie the usage. Elsewhere the Old English *Boethius* uses simply *eþel* to translate Latin *patria*: Godden and Irvine, *Old English Boethius*, 1:262 (B Text, ch. 11, line 44, cf. *DCP* 2p4, 24) and 1:340 (B Text, ch. 36, line 59, cf. *DCP* 4m1, 66).

36 The interchange of genders here perhaps reflects the use of masculine pronouns to refer to Wisdom throughout the Old English *Boethius* (in line with the grammatical gender of the word *wisdom* in Old English). For a recent discussion of the different facets of the representation of Wisdom in the work, see Nicole Guenther Discenza, "The Old English *Boethius*," 200–26, at 208–9.

Dysine and ungelæredne ic þe underfeng þa þu ærest to monnum become, and þa þe getydde and gelærde and þe þa snyttro on gebrohte þe þu þa woruldare mid begeate þe þu nu sorgiende anforlete.[37]

[I received you foolish and uneducated when you first came to mankind, and then I trained and instructed you and brought to you the wisdom with which you acquired the worldly prosperity that you have now sorrowfully lost.]

In the Boethian source for this passage (*DCP* 2p2), Philosophia assumes the persona of fickle Fortune, who reminds Boethius of the wealth she formerly bestowed on him. The Old English author reinterprets the passage so that Wisdom, now speaking as itself, takes responsibility for the learning and wisdom Mod attained, through which worldly prosperity was acquired.[38] The emphasis of the Old English, in other words, is on Mod's learning (which may indirectly bring material advantages) rather than the wealth itself. Wisdom as foster-parent is properly shown to be attending to its fosterling's spiritual rather than material welfare. The author of the Old English *Boethius* gives priority here to the role of the wise teacher, perhaps reflecting his own interest in the way the work might function in a learning context. Wisdom elaborates on its fostering role in chapter 8:

Ic þe giungne underfeng untydne and unlæredne and me to bearne genom and to minum tyhtum getyde.[39]

[I took you in when you were young (or, as a pupil?), untrained and uneducated, and adopted you as my child and trained you to my teachings.]

Reminding Mod that this was the time when it was "se gesælgesta" (most happy), Wisdom continues:

Þu me wære ær leof þonne cuð, and ær þon þe þu cuðest minne tyht and mine þeawas; and ic þe geongne gelærde swelce snytro swylce manegum oðrum

37 Godden and Irvine, *Old English Boethius*, 1:253–4 (B Text, ch. 7, lines 71–4).

38 See David Pratt, *The Political Thought of King Alfred the Great*, 284.

39 Godden and Irvine, *Old English Boethius*, 1:256 (B Text, ch. 8, lines 10–12).

ieldran gewittum oftogen is; and ic þe gefyrðrede mid minum larum to þon þæt þe mon to domere geceas.[40]

[You were beloved by me before you were well known, and before you knew my teachings and my customs; and I taught you when you were young such wisdom as is withheld from many other older intelligences; and I advanced you with my instruction to the point that you were chosen as a judge.]

Through its foster-mother's teaching, we hear, Mod attained an exceptional level of wisdom, and subsequently also benefited from the worldly advancement that wisdom made possible. Here again the Old English author has slightly reconfigured the Boethian source. In the corresponding passage in the Latin original (*DCP* 2p3), Philosophia describes how in his childhood Boethius was fostered and supported by high-ranking men. The Old English author instead uses this as an opportunity to develop the figurative interpretation of Wisdom itself as the foster-parent who adopts and teaches Mod in its youth. The combination of Mod's young age and its attainment of "such wisdom as is withheld from many other older intelligences" links it to the hagiographical motif of the *puer senex* (boy-old-man), the prematurely wise child.[41] By employing this motif, the Old English *Boethius* highlights the capacity of children to acquire wisdom from a young age. The crucial role of skilled teachers in developing that capacity is implied by the focus on Wisdom's pedagogic role in Mod's childhood.

Just as wisdom can be acquired in youth, so it can be lost with age, when power and wealth put it at risk. Mod, rather than being grateful for the gifts its foster-relationship with Wisdom brought, chafes at its loss of worldly honour. Only gradually does it come to acknowledge the sympathy and mutuality of interests that define the ideal foster-relationship. On numerous occasions Wisdom reproves Mod sharply for its wayward understanding – its devotion to the false and fleeting joys of the world, for example, and its failure to realise their true nature. Wisdom expresses astonishment that Mod is lamenting the loss of its gifts, rather than being

40 Ibid., 1:257 (B Text, ch. 8, lines 13–17). For discussion of the interpretative difficulties of this passage, see ibid., 2:286–7.

41 On this motif, see Curtius, *European Literature*, 98–101, and John A. Burrow, *The Ages of Man: A Study in Medieval Writing and Thought*, 96–102. I am grateful to Winfried Rudolf for helpful discussion on this and other aspects of the essay.

grateful for having had use of them: "Hwæt seofast þu wið me?" (Why do you sigh at me?), it asks.[42] The tension and conflict that emerge sometimes in the relationship between the two have an extra frisson because they build on the idea of a slightly recalcitrant fosterling rebelling against its foster-parent.

Although Mod, as the dialogue proceeds, does become fully reconciled with Wisdom's point of view, the Old English author develops elsewhere the potential for conflict within a foster-relationship to show the darker side of alienation from Wisdom's teaching. In the passage in which Wisdom first appears before Boethius and introduces itself as Mod's foster-mother, Mod asks why Wisdom's teaching is torn and broken (this is the equivalent of Philosophia's torn dress first mentioned in *DCP* 1p1). Wisdom explains that this is due to the folly of its pupils (or fosterlings) who think they "have it all" but in fact mistake partial for full understanding:

> Ac hit ongeat his lare swiðe totorenne and swiðe tobrocene mid dysigra hondum, and hine þa fran hu þæt gewurde. Þa andwyrde se wisdom him and sæde þæt his gingran hæfdon hine swa totorenne þæt þær hi teohhodon þæt hi hine eallne habban sceoldon. Ac hi gegaderiað monifeald dysig on ðære fortruwunga and on þam gilpe.[43]
>
> [But it [Mod] saw that its [Wisdom's] teaching was badly torn and broken up by the hands of fools, and asked it how that had happened. Then Wisdom answered it and said that its pupils had torn it in this way, wherever they had considered that they had it [Wisdom] complete; but they pile up much folly in that presumption and boast.]

The difference between the Old English *Boethius* and its source here is intriguing. In the Latin, Philosophia explains that those who tear her dress are wrongly assumed to be her servants ("meos esse familiares imprudentia rata" [ignorantly reckoned to be my servants]).[44] In the *Boethius*, however, those who tear its teaching actually *are* its "gingran" (disciples,

42 Ibid., 1:254 (B Text, ch. 7, line 76). The rendering of "violentorum … manus" (*DCP* 1p1, 2) by "dysigra hondum" may reflect glosses which "suggest heretics, pseudo-doctors or those of crooked understanding for *uiolentorum*" (ibid., 2:262).

43 Ibid., 1:245 (B Text, ch. 3, lines 14–19).

44 *DCP* 1p3, 5.

followers).[45] The *Boethius* presents this as a foster-relationship that has gone wrong. The author implies that Wisdom's fosterlings, if they fail to respect its teaching, violate Wisdom itself. Violence towards a foster-parent is a potent image for the ways in which people fail in the quest for wisdom. And here, perhaps, we see why the description of Seneca as Nero's foster-father has such a vivid resonance within the work – in offering a literal evocation of the destruction of a foster-parent it complements the metaphorical violence shown by Wisdom's "gingran."

This combination of the literal and metaphorical is characteristic of the Old English *Boethius*. Its author interprets abstract ideas in ways that makes them relevant to earthly existence, using terminology that can encompass both. The foster-relationship, with its literal and spiritual connotations, fits well with this technique. The transformative nature of wisdom – its potential to bring both earthly and spiritual wealth, power, and happiness – is evocatively conveyed through a foster-relationship that incorporates elements of its literal equivalent in human society yet always reaches beyond it.

Conclusion: Contemporary Contexts?

At various points in the depictions of fosterage in the Old English *Boethius*, a picture of an author keenly aware of the implications of fostering – in both its literal and metaphorical senses – for the education of the young has been seen to emerge. This perhaps allows us to speculate on what kinds of educative contexts the author might have had in mind. One context we might see reflected here is that of monastic learning, including that brought about by child oblation, where monks acted as spiritual fathers as well as teachers to their adopted children.[46] But we might also consider its resonance in relation to ideas of pedagogy associated with the Anglo-Saxon court around the end of the ninth century. Asser, in his *Life of King Alfred* written in AD 893, tells us that Alfred cherished his bishops and other clergy, along with his nobles and officials, personally giving

45 *DOE* s.v. *geong*, sense II.B.2.d., "Follower of a teacher, disciple." In its combination of ideas of teaching and youth, the word seems to emphasise the role of education in the acquisition of wisdom.

46 On child oblation, see Sally Crawford, *Childhood in Anglo-Saxon England*, 135–8; Sarah Foot, *Monastic Life in Anglo-Saxon England, c. 600–900*, 140–5; and Janet Nelson, "Parents, Children, and the Church in the Earlier Middle Ages,", 81–114, at 107–12.

"instruction in all virtuous behaviour and tutelage in literacy to their sons, who were being brought up in the royal household and whom he loved no less than his own children."[47] Whether or not the account is accurate – and its resemblance to Einhard's *Life of Charlemagne* may suggest that Asser's priority here is rather "writing Alfred up as a mirror-image of Charlemagne"[48] – this depiction of the way that wisdom disseminates from the king himself is clearly represented as an ideal. The patrimonial ruler, Alfred, like his Carolingian predecessors, is here being promoted as a fosterer: he is, as Peter Parkes points out, fitting into the idiom of the Christian monarch as *nutritor*, or nurturant "foster-father," of vassals, which stems from the early Carolingian era.[49] This idiom, I suggest, may conceivably be reflected in the foster-relationship between Wisdom and Mod in the Old English *Boethius*. To propose this is by no means to restrict the date of the work's composition to the Alfredian era:[50] there is no reason for thinking that the currency of the idiom ended with the death of Alfred. But an acknowledgment of the intersection more generally between the depiction of Wisdom as a nurturing foster-parent and the image of the king as a Christian ruler cherishing and nurturing his subjects and their children may enhance our understanding of the author's perspective on education.

Perhaps one other relationship underscored the concern of the *Boethius* author in calibrating so carefully his depictions of fostering, and that is the one between the author and the reader. Like the figure of Wisdom, the author assumes the role of a kind of foster-parent, nurturing his English-speaking readers through the provision of teaching in the vernacular. This

---

47 William H. Stevenson, ed., *Asser's Life of King Alfred together with the Annals of Saint Neots Erroneously Ascribed to Asser* (1904), 10 (ch. 76): "Filios quoque eorum, qui in regali familia nutriebantur, non minus propriis diligens, omnibus bonis moribus instituere et literis imbuere solus die noctuque inter cetera non desinebat"; the translation is from Simon Keynes and Michael Lapidge, eds., *Alfred the Great: Asser's* Life of King Alfred *and Other Contemporary Sources*, 91. Also see ch. 75. For the date of AD 893, see ch. 91.

48 Malcolm Godden, "Stories from the Court of King Alfred," 123–40, at 137.

49 Peter Parkes, "Celtic Fosterage: Adoptive Kinship and Clientage in Northwest Europe," 359–95, at 380.

50 Godden and Irvine, *Old English Boethius*, 1:146, work on the hypothesis that the Old English *Boethius* was "the work of an unknown writer of substantial learning, not necessarily connected with King Alfred or his court, but working some time in the period 890 to about 930, probably in southern England."

perspective is prominent in the verse preface to the prosimetrical version of the work, where we are told that Alfred desired to use poetry in order to reach out to the "selflicne secg" (the self-regarding man), a figure who serves as a variation on the recalcitrant foster-child motif found within the work itself.[51] Again the record of Alfred's input and motivation here may have little to do with historical reality. But the context of a paternalistic ruler wishing to disseminate wisdom among his subjects – his spiritual children – nevertheless informs the author-reader relationship of the Old English *Boethius*.

In developing the foster-relationship between Wisdom and Mod, the *Boethius* author takes full account not only of its sources but also of a range of literary traditions and historical contexts. The work confronts the potential tensions between foster-parents and foster-children, linking them to a broader picture of cross-generational conflicts. Set alongside the literal depiction of such relationships, and enhanced by them, is the figuratively resonant foster-relationship of Wisdom and Mod, itself the narrative and thematic pivot of the Old English *Boethius*. For the readers of this work, the attainability of spiritual wisdom is ultimately manifested through the reconciliation of a foster-parent and child.

51 Ibid., 1:384. On the relationship between this preface and the main work, see Susan Irvine, "The Protean Form of the Old English *Boethius*."

10 Hrothulf's Childhood and Beowulf's: A Comparison

RICHARD NORTH

The only time we see Hrothulf and Beowulf together is a third of the way into *Beowulf*, when Queen Wealhtheow compares one man with the other.[1] Grendel is dead and the Danes are in high spirits. With their hall in bunting, the "Lay of Finnsburh" is sung, a tribal epic on Scylding glory that the poet distils as a foreign queen's tragedy (lines 1071–80). Then Wealhtheow steps into the light before King Hrothgar, his nephew Hrothulf, and Unferth their *þyle* (speaker). She gives one speech in which she depreciates Beowulf and backs Hrothulf for regent after Hrothgar (lines 1178–87) and another in which she exhorts Beowulf to care for her boys in an advisory role (lines 1216–32).

A comparison between childhoods is encouraged in Wealhtheow's first speech, which refers to adoption.[2] After citing the Geats as gift-worthy en masse, she complains about Hrothgar's earlier offer to take Beowulf into his family. Hrothgar was clear enough at the time:

Nu ic Beowulf þec
secg betsta   me for sunu wylle
freogan on ferhþe;   heald forð tela
niwe sibbe.   (*Beowulf*, lines 946b–49a)

---

1 For all subsequent quotations and line references, see Bruce Mitchell and Fred C. Robinson, eds., "*Beowulf*": *An Edition with Relevant Shorter Texts*. For updated notes and discussions, I shall refer to Robert D. Fulk, Robert E. Bjork, and John D. Niles, eds., *Klaeber's "Beowulf" and the Fight at Finnsburg*.

2 *OED*, s.v., sense 1a, "The act of voluntarily taking into any relation: *esp*. of taking into sonship."

[Now Beowulf,
best of men, I will love you in heart
as a son to me; keep well from this time forth
a new kindred.]

In her speech Wealhtheow rehearses this offer negatively, without mentioning Beowulf by name:

Me man sægde þæt þu ðe for sunu wolde
hereri[n]c habban. (lines 1175–6a)

[It was said to me that for a son you would
have yourself a raiding man.]

Hereby she blocks Hrothgar's plan. Her words blame the old king for misjudgment, for she means that instead of matching gift to deed appropriately, as a man should do, he plans to give his kingdom to a stranger.[3] Her word "hererinc" is no cypher for "man" as "war-fighter" or "warrior,"[4] as its elements might recommend, but is here employed negatively. This is not only because *hererinc* elsewhere describes St Juliana's laughing pagan persecutor Eliseus (*Juliana*, line 189), as well as Boethius, whom Emperor Theodric takes to be a usurper as he calls on his men to arrest him (Old English *Boethius*, Metre 1).[5] More particularly, in its relation to Old English *here* (war-band) and *herian* (to plunder), Wealhtheow's

3 His daughter Freawaru, too, according to Richard North, *The Origins of "Beowulf": From Vergil to Wiglaf*, 101–15. On Wealhtheow's fears, see John M. Hill, "Beowulf and the Danish Succession: Gift Giving as an Occasion for Complex Gesture," 177–97, at 186–90; Gillian Overing, *Language, Sign and Gender in "Beowulf"*, 88–101, at 96; Scott Gwara, *Heroic Identity in the World of "Beowulf,"* 178–9. For the idea that Wealhtheow offers Beowulf a stake in the kingdom, see Stephanie Hollis, "*Beowulf* and the Succession," 39–54, esp. 44; and John M. Hill, *The Cultural World in "Beowulf,"* 103–5. For an idea that Wealhtheow's indirection is submissive, aiming "to deflect any impression that she is questioning her husband's judgment or authority," see Fulk, Bjork, and Niles, *Klaeber's "Beowulf,"* 192–3.

4 As glossed in Fulk, Bjork, and Niles, *Klaeber's "Beowulf,"* 395.

5 For *Juliana*, see *Beowulf and Judith*, ASPR 4. For the Old English *Boethius*, see Malcolm Godden and Susan Irvine, eds., *The Old English Boethius: An Edition of the Old English Versions of Boethius's "De consolatione philosophiae,"* 1:386 (C text, metre 1, line 71). The B Text, in prose, has no noun answering to Boethius in the same position; see ibid., 1:244 (B Text, ch. 1, lines 23–5).

hereri[n]c means "raiding man," i.e., "pirate." This term diminishes both Beowulf's rank and his deliverance of the Danes from Grendel, a true predator. The queen, moreover, with the words "me man sægde" (it was said to me), implies that Hrothgar lacked the courtesy to tell her of this plan himself. But we know how publicly Hrothgar announced his decision that morning, for it was "on stapole" (on a pillar, line 926a) that he did so, outside Heorot and with Wealhtheow and her ladies in attendance. It is after these mandarin words on Beowulf that Wealhtheow endorses Hrothulf as the next Danish ruler by referring to him as their truly adopted son (lines 1185b–87).

Nearly all of *Beowulf*'s surviving Norse analogues give Hrólfr and Bǫðvarr Bjarki as lifelong friends – one as the king, the other as his champion – and it can be argued that the English tradition before *Beowulf* had Hrothulf and Beowulf in similar roles.[6] But the poet of *Beowulf* keeps them apart, using Wealhtheow to make them rivals. The effect of the queen's two speeches is to portray Beowulf as an interloper, to silence Hrothgar concerning his offer of adoption and to safeguard her daughter's marriage with Ingeld as well as the Danish throne for Hrothulf. By the time she refers to her adoption of Hrothulf at the end of her speech about not adopting Beowulf, we know enough about both men to compare their childhoods. This essay will attempt to do this and then show why it matters.

Hrothulf's Childhood

The poet briefly alludes to Hrothulf's birth not long into the poem, by way of his genealogical reference to Halga as "til" (excellent, virtuous, line 61). This line-final moral agnomen might be passed over in silence, were it not for the unwittingly immoral turn of events in Scandinavian analogues in which King Helgi begets Hrólfr on his own daughter. The oldest source for the story is preserved in Arngrímur Jónsson's 1596 Latin abstract or adaptation of a large but now-lost vernacular fragment of *Skjǫldunga saga*, a history of the Scyldings (ca. 1190).[7] Here, after early adventures

6 North, *Origins of "Beowulf,"* 45–57. For the analogues in English, see George N. Garmonsway and Jacqueline Simpson, *"Beowulf" and Its Analogues.*

7 Bjarni Guðnason, ed., *Danakonunga sögur: Skjǫldunga saga, Knýtlinga saga, Ágrip af sǫgu danakonunga.* Also edited in Jakob Benediktsson, ed., *Arngrimi Jonae opera Latine conscripta I–IV.*

that include a childhood on the run with his brother Roas (Hróarr, i.e., Hrothgar), as well as a more grown-up encounter with Yrsa's mother, it is said that

> Helgo deinde Daniæ Rex ad rapinam et piracticam reversus Sveco bellum intulit, vicit: Reginam Yrsam surripuit secumqve avexit in Daniam, ignarusqve pater cum filia nuptias celebrat, etiam contra voluntatem et consilium fratris Roæ, qvi suam agnoscere se dicebat ex vultu consangvineam; his filius natus Rolfo, postea cognomento Krag.[8]

> [King Helgo of Denmark later turned back to plundering and piracy, made war on Sweden, and was victorious; he snatched the queen Yrsa, carried her back with him to Denmark, and thus while ignorant did a father wed his own daughter, even if contrary to the will and advice of his brother Roas, who said he knew her from her features to be kin to them in blood; the son born to them was Rolfo, later nicknamed *Krag*.]

Further on, we learn that "Helgo post qvinqvennium in bello occubuit" (Helgo five years later died in battle, chapter 11). The author reiterates the tale when Rolfo becomes king:

> Rolfo cognomento Krake vel Krag Danicè (est nomen, qvo cornice marem notamus) ex tali concubitu natus, cæso Helgoni patri avoqve eidem octennis successit. Roas patruus Rolfonis Paulo post à patruelibus Ræerico et Frodone Ingialldi filiis occisus est.[9]

> [Rolfo, nicknamed Krake, or, in Danish, Krag (the name by which we know the sea-crow), born of such cohabitation that Helgo was at once his father and grandfather, succeeded at eight years old. Not long after, Roas, Rolfo's uncle, was slain by his own first cousins, Rærricus and Frodo, sons of Ingialldus.]

Before we go on, a defence of *Beowulf*'s Norse analogues is in order, since the essentials of these often fill gaps in the poem's narrative. The analogues, for example, have already told us that Halga is Hrothulf's father

8 *Skjǫldunga saga*, ed. Bjarni, 25.
9 *Skjǫldunga saga*, ed. Bjarni, ch. 12, 26.

– the poem does not. Arngrímur's digest descends through *Skjǫldunga saga* from a story associated with a genealogy, the *Langfeðgatal* (List of Forefathers), which was probably created by the Icelander Sæmundr "inn fróði" (the learned) Sigfússon (1056–1133) in ca. 1120.[10] It is thought that Sæmundr's great-grandson, bishop Páll Jónsson of Skálholt, fleshed out this genealogy in *Skjǫldunga saga* in ca. 1190.[11] The remaining analogues descend from a related but less learned tradition. The oldest of these is *Bjarkamál in fornu* (the old lay of Bjarki), which portrays King Hrólfr's (i.e., Hrothulf's) last stand in his hall in Lejre. The king's champion is called variously *Bjarki* (little bear), *bǫðvar-Bjarki* (battle Bjarki) or *bǫðvarr Bjarki* (battle-ready Bjarki), or just Bǫðvarr. Bjarki is the Norse analogue of *Bēo-wulf*, whose "bee-wolf" name is, by the simplest determination, a kenning for "bear" and whose cognate epithet "beadwe heard" (battle-hard, line 1539), in the fight with Grendel's Mother, aligns him even closer with Bǫðvarr.[12] *Bjarkamál* may be as old as the tenth century; it survives in three forms: a translation by Saxo Grammaticus, canon of Lund, into Latin hexameters towards the end of the twelfth century in his *Gesta Danorum* (deeds of the Danes);[13] two Old Norse stanzas quoted in Snorri's *Óláfs saga Helga* (saga of St Óláf), ca. 1230;[14] and an Icelandic prose paraphrase that is to be found in chapters 32–3 of *Hrólfs saga kraka* (saga of pole-ladder Hrólfr).[15] Saxo's *Gesta*, a work that was influenced in ca. 1200 by a text of *Skjǫldunga saga*, is itself an analogue of *Beowulf*.[16] So is *Hrólfs saga*, from a text that existed in ca. 1200, but which is now fully extant only in a seventeenth-century manuscript, albeit the text itself is datable to ca. 1400.[17] There is lastly an incomplete ballad, *Bjarkarímur*

10 Bjarni Guðnason, *Um Skjöldungasögu*, lii–vii.

11 Bjarni, *Um Skjöldungasögu*, 158–61.

12 Jakob Benediktsson, "Icelandic Traditions of the Scyldings," 48–66, esp. 56. For a theory that his name derives from *bēow-wulf* (barley-wolf) as a mythological analogue of Freyr's little servant *Byggvir* (barley-man, cf. Old Icelandic *bygg*, "barley") in *Lokasenna*, see Fulk, Bjork, and Niles, *Klaeber's "Beowulf,"* xlviii–li, as well as Robert D. Fulk and Joseph Harris, "Beowulf's Name," 98–100.

13 K. Friis-Jensen, ed., and P. Fisher, trans., *Saxo Grammaticus: Gesta Danorum: The History of the Danes*, 122–42 (ii.7.4–27).

14 Bjarni Aðalbjarnarson, ed., *Snorri Sturluson: Heimskringla II*, 361.

15 Desmond Slay, ed., *Hrólfs Saga Kraka*, ch. 33, 98–100.

16 Bjarni, *Um Skjöldungasögu*, 63–8.

17 Jakob, "Icelandic Traditions of the Scyldings," 48–52.

(rhymes of Bjarki), which was created partly out of *Hrólfs saga* in the fifteenth century.[18]

Patchy and late as these varied prose and verse Skjǫldung narratives are, their narrative outlines have much in common with *Beowulf*.[19] The prose analogues, in this case, tally with Wealhtheow's statement that she and Hrothgar brought up Hrothulf "umborwesendum" (when he was a child, line 1187). Arngrímur's Latin version of the lost *Skjǫldunga saga* lets us work out that Roas has looked after Rolfo for three years: between Helgo's death (when Rolfo is five) and Roas's (when Rolfo is eight). The moral charge of Halga's *til*-agnomen (*Beowulf*, line 61) might therefore tell us that the poet has the same story but omits most of it as distasteful, protesting only that Halga was both father and grandfather to Hrothulf through no fault of his own.

Wealhtheow alludes to Hrothulf's childhood when she draws attention to Hrothgar's death as soon likely and to the possibility that Hrothulf, his nephew, might succeed him:

Ic minne can
glædne Hroþulf, þæt he þa geogoðe wile
arum healdan gyf þu ær þonne he,
wine Scildinga, woruld oflætest. (1180b–83)

[I know my
gracious Hrothulf, that these youths he will
keep in favours, if you, sooner than he,
friend of Scyldings, leave the world.]

With the words "þa geogoðe" (these youths), Wealhtheow refers to her sons with Hrothgar, whose names are later given as Hrethric and Hrothmund (line 1189). The definite article in her construction defines these boys as the "magum" (kinsmen) to whom she has just reminded Hrothgarto bequeath his kingdom (line 1178). The poet uses Wealhtheow's

18 Edited in Finnur Jónsson, ed., *Hrólfs saga Kraka og Bjarkarímur*.

19 Raymond W. Chambers, *"Beowulf": An Introduction to the Study of the Poem*, 427; Jakob, "Icelandic Traditions of the Scyldings," 55; Andy Orchard, *A Critical Companion to "Beowulf,"* 100–14, esp. 113.

construction "arum healdan" (keep in favours) later for Beowulf's regency over his own young cousin Heardred on the death of Hygelac, Heardred's father and his uncle: "freondlarum heold / estum mid are oð ðæt he yldra wearð" (with friend's teaching he kept him / kindly in favour until he grew older, lines 2377b–78). Wealhtheow's words thus show that she creates an obligation for Hrothulf to be regent to her boys, should they still be minors when Hrothgar dies:

wene ic þæt he mid gode gyldan wille
uncran eaferan gif he þæt eal gemon,
hwæt wit to willan ond to worðmyndum
umborwesendum ær arna gefremedon. (lines 1184–7)

[I expect that he will repay our heirs
with advantage, if he remembers all the
favours that we two for his will and honour
performed for him before when he was a child.]

From these words we may infer a story that was better known to the audience, whose knowledge of Scylding tales is given as an expectation in lines 1–3 of the poem. It appears from what Queen Wealhtheow says that she and Hrothgar have brought up Hrothulf in the Danish court because Hrothulf lost both parents when he was a child. With her word "gyldan" (repay), Wealhtheow redefines the "arna" (favours) that she and Hrothgar then showed him as an advance payment for the favours which she now tells him to be ready to show her children. If there were evidence that Hrothulf had been groomed for this role, we might even call this "long-term reciprocity." To emphasise her point at the end of the fitt (no. XVII), Wealhtheow faces Beowulf who is seated alongside Hrethric and Hrothmund, "be þæm gebroðrum twæm" (by those brothers, line 1191).

The seating seems contrived to make Beowulf into a new son of Hrothgar – although not for much longer, since the queen's speech thwarts Hrothgar's plan to adopt him. In her view, King Hrothgar's offer brings with it Beowulf's succession to the Danish throne. By backing Hrothulf for immediate successor instead, to be regent to Hrethric and Hrothmund should Hrothgar predecease their majority, Wealhtheow keeps her sons' hopes of power alive for the future. In doing so, she represents Hrothulf's adopted childhood as something both happy and secure.

Beowulf's Childhood

Although Beowulf's birth does not come about through incest, like Hrothulf's, his childhood trajectory seems similar. With his father either dead or missing, Beowulf is adopted, in his case by his grandfather (on the turmoil affecting Beowulf's uncles, see below). When we first see him in the poem, Beowulf appears *in medias res*, a man on a mission with fourteen followers (lines 205–9), but the poet still alludes to his childhood early on. We learn something of this through Beowulf's words about his father to the Danish coast guard:

Wæs min fæder folcum gecyþed
æþele ordfruma Ecgþeow haten,
gebad wintra worn ær he on weg hwurfe
gamol of geardum; hine gearwe geman
witena welhwylc wide geond eorþan. (lines 262–6)

[My father became famous to the peoples,
front-line noble captain, Ecgtheow by name,
endured a great many winters before he passed on,
old, from his dwellings; he is readily recalled
by every wise man widely across the earth.]

For the picture of a parent honoured in old age, this one is hard to match. Its positivity compares well with the poet's *til*-epithet for the unfortunate Halga, but there the resemblance ends. If Beowulf's statement is true and his father died as an old man, Ecgtheow must have fathered him late, for Beowulf is young when we meet him. Wealhtheow calls him "hyse" (lad, line 1217). To Heorot's doorman Wulfgar, who has come to request Beowulf's entry, King Hrothgar reveals a story that predates the period of Grendel's attacks:

Ic hine cuðe cnihtwesende,
wæs his ealdfæder Ecgþeo haten
ðæm to ham forgeaf Hreþel Geata
angan dohtor. (lines 372–5)

[I knew him when he was a boy,
his late father was called Ecgtheow

to whom at home Geatish Hrethel gave
his only daughter.]

That is, Ecgtheow brought Beowulf to Denmark twelve or more years earlier. Beowulf's age on this visit may be put at a bit younger than seven, because it was at this age that his grandfather adopts him (line 2428), so we may deduce that Beowulf is presently aged between eighteen and his mid-twenties.

To those in the poet's assumed audience who know Beowulf's story less well than they do the stock of Scylding tales, Hrothgar's words in lines 372–5 make it possible to place Beowulf as Hygelac's sister's son, with a blood-link to the Geatish royal house on his mother's side. There is evidence within the poem that Beowulf's maternal connection makes him inferior by birth: the poet calls the Geatish "lond" (lands) and "eard eðelriht" (homeland by right of inheritance) "swiðor" (more strongly) Hygelac's than Beowulf's, referring to Hygelac as "selra" (higher ranking, lines 2196–9); Hrothgar avows or reveals ignorance of Beowulf's mother's name when he says that "swa hwylc mægða" (whichever maid, line 943) bore this young man, she may say that God blessed her in childbirth; and Hrothgar, when he says that a king may say "þæt ðes eorl wæs / geboren betera" (that this gentleman was born for higher rank, lines 1702–3), shows that Beowulf's eligibility for kingship does not speak for itself. Outside the poem, there is historical evidence that the usual requirement for succession was a paternal link to the royal line.[20]

Ecgtheow, moreover, as Hrothgar makes clear to Wulfgar, and a little later to Beowulf himself, is not a Geat but a foreign interloper, and more infamous than famous. Beowulf is introduced as Hygelac's thane (lines 194 and 261), not as Ecgtheow's son. The wildness of Ecgtheow's record emerges in Hrothgar's reply to Beowulf's offer to help him. Halfway through Beowulf's opening pitch it is already clear that he takes the king's leave to fight Grendel for granted. This assumption the king answers with mocking ambiguity when he says that it is "f[or w]erefyhtum" (for manly fighting) and "for arstafum" (for kindness) that Beowulf has sought him

20 David N. Dumville, "The Ætheling: A Study in Anglo-Saxon Constitutional History," 1–33, at 26–7, 32; Karen L. Maund, "'A Turmoil of Warring Princes': Political Leadership in Ninth-Century Denmark," 29–47, at 41 and n. 63.

out (lines 457 and 458).[21] If we, perhaps like the young hero, first believe that the old king means these qualities to be Beowulf's, we receive a check in his following lines, which establish the fighting as Ecgtheow's, the kindness as his own:

Gesloh þin fæder fæhðe mæste,
wearþ he Heaþolafe to handbonan
mid Wilfingum; ða hine *Wede*ra cyn [MS *gara* (of spears)
for herebrogan habban ne mihte.
Þanon he gesohte Suð-Dena folc
ofer yða gewealc. (lines 459–64a)

[Your father by killing began the greatest feud,
with his hands he was the bane of Heatholaf
among the Wylfings; then the Weather-Geatish kin
for terror of raids could not keep him.
Thence he sought Danish folk southwards
over rolling of waves.]

So it seems that the itinerant Ecgtheow stopped in Geatland just long enough to marry the princess and to be a father to their son. Then his past catches up with him. Having to light out for Denmark with Beowulf, Ecgtheow reveals two things to us: one is that Beowulf's mother, not caring for Beowulf in Ecgtheow's absence, is probably dead (in childbirth?); the other is a record for reckless violence that may work against his son in later years. It is even possible that Wealhtheow, a Wylfing herself (if we connect her Helming family in line 620 with King Helm in *Widsith*, line 29), purposely leaves Beowulf's welcome to the last in her round of Heorot in lines 620–4.[22]

The next stage in Beowulf's childhood is revealed by the man himself fifty years later, before his fight with the Dragon, when he tells his bodyguard that his grandfather, King Hrethel of the Geats, took him from Ecgtheow at the age of seven (line 2428). If this was because of death, it

21 MS *fere fyhtum* is read as "Fore †fyhtum" in Fulk, Bjork, and Niles, *Klaeber's "Beowulf,"* 144–5, although without translation, because "[p]recisely what is intended here cannot be determined."

22 North, *Origins of "Beowulf,"* 128–9.

is unlikely that Ecgtheow's passing was as peaceful as Beowulf presents it to the coast guard in lines 262–6. Even if Ecgtheow died years later, he emerges as a liability, an unknown force. His apparently barehanded dispatch of Heatholaf anticipates Beowulf's technique not only with Grendel but also years later with Dæghrefn, Hygelac's Frankish or Alemannic slayer whom Beowulf hugs to death on the beach in Frisia (lines 2501–2 and 2506–8). If we take into account the analogues, Ecgtheow's style fits with the fate of Bjarki's father in *Bjarka þáttr* (Bjarki's tale), in the middle of *Hrólfs saga* (chs. 17–24), where Bjǫrn (bear), as he is called, is forced to haunt the margins as a real bear. His pregnant peasant wife, Bera (bear), having been made to eat of his flesh, gives birth to three sons of whom Bjarki (chs. 18–20) is the third; Bjarki (little bear) projects a mighty bear spirit to ravage Hrólfr's enemies outside the hall during their last stand in Lejre (ch. 33). Nor in *Beowulf* can the hero's great height (lines 247–50), his strength of thirty men (lines 379–81), his wrenching of Grendel's arm from the shoulder (lines 815–18), and his long-distance swim from Frisia to Geatland (lines 2367–8) be regarded as entirely human in the case of a man whose name may be read as a kenning for "bear."[23] This aspect appears to be what Beowulf inherits from Ecgtheow.

Ecgtheow's foreign status and physical legacy allow Beowulf less integration with his mother's family than he admits in his final speech to the honour guard (lines 2428–34). Unferth, a trusted adviser of King Hrothgar, seizes on Beowulf's exclusion when he puts down Beowulf over an incident from his youth. His discrediting story is about Beowulf's rowing or swimming race with an opponent named Breca.[24] Indicating that he got this from Breca himself, Unferth says that both boys went in for "dolgilpe" (mad boasting, line 509), followed by "sorhfullne sið" (a venture bringing sorrow, line 512);[25] and that Breca beat Beowulf, completing the distance in Norway, from where he returned to his "swæsne eþel,/

---

23 Chambers, *"Beowulf": An Introduction*, 365–81. Jakob, "Icelandic Traditions of the Scyldings," 56.

24 Probably rowing: Andrew T. Cooper, "Literary Perspectives on the Case for Beowulf's Rowing Adventure with Breca," 16–20. The case for "swam" in *reon* is preferred in *Klaeber's "Beowulf,"* ed. Fulk, Bjork, and Niles, 152, because Beowulf is later in the water and because "the adversaries must not be imagined to have held swords in their hands as they rowed"; but swimmers need both arms, and a sword can be stowed in a boat.

25 Translation in Gwara, *Heroic Identity*, 113.

leof his leodum" (beloved homeland, a man dear to his people) and to the "freoðoburh fægere þær he folc ahte / burh ond beagas" (fair protecting fortress where he had a tribe, township and rings, lines 520–1 and 522–3). A "Breoca" is named king of the Brondings in the poem *Widsith* (line 25) and furthermore it seems that *Beowulf*'s Breca, son of Beanstan, is not far from becoming king of his own land. Unferth, however, cites Breca's advantages in order to present them as things that Beowulf does not have. By citing them just before he says that Breca fulfilled his vow to Beowulf (lines 523–4), thus winning the contest, Unferth gives Beowulf to be a troublemaking boy without family.

Nor does the poet contradict him. After Beowulf gives his version of events, claiming (with himself as sole witness) that he stayed with Breca for five days until the current drove them apart, the poet makes Beowulf look more isolated by saying nothing. Initially Beowulf averts the disputed outcome with a disclaimer, saying that he and Breca swore to compete in this way "cnihtwesende" (when we were boys, line 535) and that they only made vows to do this because "wæron begen þa git / on geogoðfeore" (we were both still youths at this time, lines 536–7). But by the end of his riposte, despite showing personal force, Beowulf has vindicated Breca by treating him as Unferth's ally. When he says that "ne gehwæðer incer" (neither of you) could perform such a feat, his dual pronoun for Unferth and Breca divides him from his friend. As neither man is Beowulf's equal, it is true that he stands out from them, but his words reveal a youth in isolation.

Fifty years later Beowulf represents his childhood as fulfilled (lines 2428–34), but by then we know that it was filled with misery. Soon after Beowulf's return, his reunion with Hygelac, his mother's brother, and his elevation to the rank of ealdorman, the poet flies back to the hero's childhood following his adoption by King Hrethel:

Hean wæs lange
swa hyne Geata bearn godne ne tealdon
ne hyne on medobence micles wyrðne
drihten We*dera* gedon wolde; [MS *wereda* (of hosts)
swyðe wendon þæt he sleac wære,
æðeling unfrom. Edwenden cwom
tireadigum men torna gehwylces. (lines 2183b–89)

[Long was the scorn,
such that children of Geats reckoned him

no good, nor of much on mead-bench did
the Weather-lord wish to make him worthy;
very much they supposed he was a slouch,
a prince without prospects. A reversal
of each grief came to the glorious man.]

This allusion also accounts for a time in Beowulf's life after his vagrant earlier childhood and before the ungoverned youth that may be inferred from his friendship with churls and from his rowing (or swimming) race with Breca. The "drihten" (lord) in question cannot be Hæthcyn or Hygelac, given their own youth, the former's brief reign, and the latter's welcoming attention (lines 1992–8), but must be Hrethel, Beowulf's grandfather. So startling is this passage that its relevance to Beowulf has prompted widely different interpretations: Eliason reads it on little evidence and for even less purpose as a reference to the younger Hygelac, whereas Tripp, associating the passage with Beowulf, nonetheless aligns it with "his later and altruistic refusal to accept Queen Hygd's offer of the throne after Hygelac's death."[26]

However, the timing of this "edwenden" (reversal) defines its miserable earlier subject as Beowulf. The poet places it just before Hygelac rewards Beowulf with full honours, with Hrethel's sword, seven thousand hides, and a princely seat (lines 2190–6). As Fred Biggs says, the passage "praises the system that allows the best-suited member of a kin-group to advance,"[27] but its typology also shows the teen Beowulf to have been seen as a slacker who became a hero suddenly, by rising to a challenge. The *sleac*-descriptor accords with the typology of the *coal-biter* or *ash-lad* archetype of thirteenth-century Norse legend, for which two prominent examples are the orphaned Starkaðr Stórvirksson in *Gautreks saga* and the fatherless half-Norwegian Víga-Glúmr Eyjólfsson in *Víga-Glúms saga*.[28] And so

26 Norman E. Eliason, "Beowulf's Inglorious Youth," 101–8. Raymond Tripp Jr, "Did Beowulf have an 'Inglorious Youth'?," 129–43, esp. 130.

27 Frederick M. Biggs, "The Politics of Succession in *Beowulf* and Anglo-Saxon England," 709–41, esp. 725–6.

28 Guðni Jónsson and Bjarni Vilhjálmsson, eds., *Fornaldarsögur norðurlanda*, 3:12–29 (ch. 7); Hermann Pálsson and Paul Edwards, trans., *Seven Viking Romances*, 145–59, Gabriel Turville-Petre, eds., *Víga-Glúms Saga*, 10–11 (ch. 6) and 13 (ch. 7); George Johnston, trans., *The Schemers and Víga-Glúm: Bandamanna Saga & Víga-Glúms Saga*, 93–101.

now we see Beowulf through doubting relatives' eyes.[29] Hygelac says that he tried to stop Beowulf going (lines 1992–5). However, the poet says that wise churls encouraged him (lines 202–4, 415–16), and now Hrothgar has given him honours. Up to this moment of "edwenden" in their eyes, the poet gives his hero a history of exclusion: how Beowulf spent his youth outside; how his parentless childhood was full of griefs ("torna"); how, at least to start with, other children despised him; how his father made him a charge on his relatives; how his link to the house through his mother defined him socially as an inferior; how even Hrethel seems to have regretted adopting him. In short, it seems that Beowulf's adopted childhood has been neither happy nor secure.

Hrothulf's Response to His Childhood

Like Beowulf, Hrothulf is adopted by a kinsman after the loss of his father, but unlike Beowulf, he appears to have been shown "to willan ond to worðmyndum / umborwesendum ær arna" (favours before, for his will and honour, when he was a child, lines 1186–7). It has been suggested that Wealhtheow's if-clause construction, in "gif he þæt eal gemon" (if he remembers all that, line 1185), casts doubt on her nephew's gratitude,[30] but there is no doubt that he is feted in Heorot just for being there. Hrothulf has his family to thank for social inclusion, as the alliterative link between his name and Hrothgar's shows, not only in *Beowulf* (line 1017), but also in *Widsith* (line 45). At the start of victory celebrations, says the poet, when the Danes settle down with their guests to the most splendid carousal, never did a greater army behave more decorously before their giver of treasure (lines 1011–12). The longevity of Hrothgar, his adoptive father, has given Hrothulf a period of security stretching into the narrative present:

Bugon þa to bence   blædagende,
fylle gefægon;   fægere geþægon
medofull manig   magas þara
swiðhicgende   on sele þam hean
Hroðgar ond Hroþulf.   Heorot wæs

29 Haruko Momma, "The Education of Beowulf and the Affair of the Leisure Class," 163–82, esp. 170.

30 Gwara, *Heroic Identity*, 149–50.

freondum afylled; nalles facenstafas
þeod-Scyldingas þenden fremedon. (lines 1013–19)

[Moved then to bench magnificent nobles,
rejoiced in their fill; exquisitely partaking
of many a mead-cup were their kinsmen,
thinking valiant thoughts in that high hall,
Hrothgar and Hrothulf. Heorot was
filled up with friends; not at all were criminal acts
as yet practised by nation-Scyldings.]

With this, the first of only three references to Hrothulf by name, comes an example of the poet's tendency to balance light with dark: "freondum" (friends) with two or more "facenstafas" (criminal acts, line 1018), which are committed by two or more Scyldings. The adverb "þenden" may mean also "then" or "at that time," as Mitchell notes when he reads these lines as "a restatement of the 'noble savage' theme" by which the old heroes are praised as better than people of today.[31] On the other hand, Orchard points out that "þenden" here is both stressed and carries alliteration "in a way that is unusual, to say the least."[32] Mitchell, like Sisam and Morgan, generalises the passage in order to preserve the moral integrity of the Scyldings, but this tribe is no more idealised than the others in *Beowulf*.[33] Elsewhere we see a family insurrection among Swedes (lines 2381–4), some questionable spear-aiming and then family turmoil among Geats (lines 2435–43), and a big breach of contract followed by slaughter in the case of earlier Scyldings in Frisia (lines 1146–58).[34] Against this background it seems more likely that "þenden" here means "as yet," and that both this adverb and the poet's later named reference to Hrothulf hint at imminent discord.

Widsith gives a glimpse of the Scylding story as it was before *Beowulf*. *Widsith*, a working verse catalogue of names for Germanic and other tribes and their kings in the Exeter Book, shows some stability in the

---

31 Bruce Mitchell, "Literary Lapses: Six Notes on *Beowulf* and Its Critics," 1–17, esp. 11.

32 Orchard, *Critical Companion*, 246. Disputed, on the basis of Kuhn's Laws, in Fulk, Bjork, and Niles, *Klaeber's "Beowulf,"* 177 and 324.

33 Kenneth Sisam, *The Structure of "Beowulf,"* 33–43. Gerald Morgan, "The Treachery of Hrothulf," 23–39, esp. 33–8.

34 Richard North, "Tribal Loyalties in the *Finnsburh Fragment* and Episode," 13–43, esp. 28–32.

Anglo-Saxon Scylding narrative, which is in any case inferrable from the later Scandinavian texts in Latin and Old Norse. *Widsith* contains five lines on Hrothgar and Hrothulf that bear comparison with Wealhtheow's hypermetric passage in *Beowulf*, lines 1162b–68.[35] *Widsith*'s dates may be various, dependent on all the unknown stages of composition, but since the Geats but neither Beowulf nor Hygelac are named in *Widsith*, and since *Beowulf* would have been too big for *Widsith* to ignore, it is reasonable to suppose that any resemblance between the poems is owed to their descent from a common tradition.[36] In this case *Widsith*'s notice about Hrothwulf may reflect the source from which *Beowulf*'s Hrothulf derives:

Hroþwulf ond Hroðgar heoldon lengest
sibbe ætsomne suhtorfædran,
siþþan hy forwræcon wicinga cynn
ond Ingeldes ord forbigdan,
forheowan æt Heorote Heaðobeardna þrym. (*Widsith*, lines 45–9)

[Hrothwulf and Hrothgar kept most closely
kindred together, uncle and nephew,
when they drove off the tribe of pirates
and crushed Ingeld's front line,
cut down the Heathobards' glory at Heorot.]

The adverbial superlative "lengest" means either "most closely" (from *lenge*, "near, close at hand," as in *Beowulf*, line 83), or "for the longest time" (from *long*, "long," as in "Sigehere lengest Sædenum weold" [Sigehere ruled the Sea-Danes for the longest time, *Widsith*, line 28]). The former meaning is supported by the usage in *Beowulf*, line 83, in that the poet there says "ne wæs hit lenge þa gen" (nor was it yet close at hand) that the newly built Heorot would burn to the ground. Since this "lenge" refers to the same Heathobard raid that follows the word "lengest" in *Widsith*, line 45, it might be thought to arise from the common source. With either meaning, however, "most closely" or "for the longest time," *Widsith* implies that the Scylding family unity ends soon after King Ingeld attacks Heorot. It cannot be right, as Mitchell implies, that Hrothgar's long friendship with his nephew begins in *Beowulf* after the attack, for Hrothgar is

35 Mitchell and Robinson, *Beowulf*, 198.
36 North, *Origins of "Beowulf,"* 134–5.

already an old king in this poem.[37] The force of the subordinating temporal conjunction "siþþan" (*Widsith*, line 47), is not "after" but "when," for it highlights Ingeld's raid as the beginning of Danish change. In this case we have the outline of a story in *Beowulf* in which the Scylding concord ends with the death of King Hrothgar, not long after Ingeld's defeat.

In *Beowulf* Hrothulf grows up at court where he comes to share the challenges of his uncle's kingship, whether the day-to-day rule of Denmark or the raid from Ingeld, which is set for the near future. As we have seen in Wealhtheow's words to Hrothulf in lines 1181–2, after Hrothgar's death a regency rather than outright rule will be offered him. The queen's following words to Beowulf underline the arrangement that she has set in place. Exhorting Beowulf to act in the interest of her sons, as their adviser, Wealhtheow tells him that the Danish court is united under her:

Her is æghwylc eorl   oþrum getrywe
modes milde   mandrihtne hold,
þegnas syndon geþwære,   þeod ealgearo,
druncne dryhtguman   doð swa ic bidde.   (*Beowulf*, lines 1228–31)

[Here each gentleman is true to the other,
generous of heart, loyal to his beloved master,
thanes are in harmony, the nation fully prepared,
men of the retinue, having drunk, do as I ask.]

In keeping with this vision of good queenly governance, the import of the Danes' status as "þeod ealgearo" (a nation fully prepared, line 1230) is that they are ready for Hrothgar to die and for Hrothulf to take over.

Ominously for Wealhtheow, however, we have already heard the wording of her declaration of stability in the poet's assessment of Heorot, just before she speaks to King Hrothgar:

Þa cwom Wealhþeo forð
gan under gyldnum beage,   þær þa godan twegen
sæton suhtergefæderan.   Þa gyt wæs hiera sib ætgædere,
æghwylc oðrum trywe.   Swylce þær *U*nferþ þyle   [MS *Hunferþ*
æt fotum sæt frean Scyldinga.   Gehwylc hiora his ferhþe treowde,

37 Mitchell, "Literary Lapses," 12.

þæt he hæfde mod micel, þeah þe he his magum nære
arfæst æt ecga gelacum. (lines 1162b–68a)

[Then came Wealhtheow forth
walking beneath a golden necklace to where the two generous men
were sitting, uncle and nephew. Still at this time was their kindred together,
each man true to the other. Likewise there Unferth the man who speaks
sat at the feet of the Scylding lord. Each of them trusted his spirit,
that he had great courage, though to his kinsmen he may not have been
kind in the play of blades.]

The fact that these six lines are hypermetric, as the first and longest of only three such sustained passages in *Beowulf* (the others are in lines 1705–7 and 2995–6), tells us that the poet is making a point about the Danish *sib* ("kindred" rather than "peace"),[38] which he describes. The poet implies that Heorot's great show of loyalty is about to end, in some way because all three royals have co-opted Unferth into their family despite his history as a fratricide: his fraternal jealousy will become Hrothulf's.

Beowulf, in his riposte to Unferth earlier (lines 529–607), tells us that a legend of Unferth has spread. Beowulf knows not only his name (line 530) and patronymic "sunu Ecglafes" (Ecglaf's son, line 590), but also that "ðu þinum broðrum to banan wurde / heafodmægum" (you became a slayer to your brothers, the head members of your family, lines 587–8). The term *hēafodmǣg* does not mean "close kinsman," as Mitchell and Robinson recommend, or "near relative," as is similarly suggested by the editors of *Klaeber's Beowulf*,[39] but literally "head kinsman," for Beowulf uses it to name his uncle Hygelac as his one authority when he comes home (line 2151). Likewise Beowulf means that Unferth's brothers were ranked above Unferth. So, when the poet introduces Wealhtheow's speech in lines 1162b–68a, saying that her "sib" (kindred) is still united despite trusting Unferth, he means that Unferth will help make it disunited. Unferth is known for having killed his higher-ranking brothers. With "þa gyt" (still at this time, line 1164), the poet implies that not long from

38 *Pace* Morgan, "The Treachery of Hrothulf," 35.
39 Mitchell and Robinson, *Beowulf*, 268. Fulk, Bjork, and Niles, *Klaeber's "Beowulf,"* 392.

now he will advise Hrothulf to kill his higher-ranking adoptive brothers, the boys Hrethric and Hrothmund.[40]

Where Hrothulf's later regency for his cousins is concerned, Saxo's translation of *Bjarkamál*, in which Rolvo is famed for killing Røricus, gives reason to believe that in the future King Hrothulf does kill a man by the name of Hrethric.[41] Moreover, the plural in "facenstafas" (criminal acts, line 1018) might tell us that Hrothmund is murdered by his cousin as well. The Norse analogues give no cousin relationship between the leading cognates, Hrólfr and Hrœrekr or Hrókr, but the slaying of at least Hrethric by Hrothulf is plausibly a detail held in common. The issue with Hrothulf is not his loyalty to Hrothgar, which we are told is beyond question (lines 1164–5).[42] It is rather how Unferth influences Hrothulf against his adoptive brothers when Hrothgar is dead. Hrothulf's role in *Beowulf* is to darken the Danish future. By killing, if he does, his younger cousin or cousins for whom he is asked to rule as regent, Hrothulf responds to his childhood with treachery.

Beowulf's Response to His Childhood

Beowulf's words on his childhood conflict with the poet's. The context of his version is important, for he is then speaking to his retinue before leaving them so that he may fight the Dragon alone. Beowulf must convince these hand-picked Geatish warriors that he belongs to a family with experience in war: first there is King Hrethel, who held off the Swedes until his death (lines 2472–4); then there are Hæthcyn and Hygelac, who repaid the

40 Proposed by William W. Lawrence, *"Beowulf" and the Epic Tradition*, 73–9; Adrien Bonjour, *The Digressions in "Beowulf,"* 30–1, 60–1; Arthur G. Brodeur, *The Art of "Beowulf,"* 153; Tom A. Shippey, *Beowulf*, 30–3; Sam Newton, *The Origins of "Beowulf" and the Pre-Viking Kingdom of East Anglia*, 83–7; and Orchard, *Critical Companion*, 245–7. Disputed by Sisam, *Structure of "Beowulf,"* 34–43, 81; Morgan, "The Treachery of Hrothulf," 35; and repeatedly Bruce Mitchell: review of Kenneth Sisam, *The Structure of "Beowulf,"* 190–1; review of Edward B. Irving Jr, *A Reading of "Beowulf,"* 202–4; review of Alvin A. Lee, *The Guest-Hall of Eden: Four Essays on the Design of Old English Poetry*, 195–6, esp. 195; "Literary Lapses," 10–14. No preference is advised in Fulk, Bjork, and Niles, *Klaeber's "Beowulf,"* 177.

41 Friis-Jensen, *Gesta Danorum*, 128–9 (ii.7.11).

42 *Pace* Morgan, "The Treachery of Hrothulf," 28–9; and Mitchell, "Literary Lapses," 13.

subsequent Swedish incursions until Hæthcyn died in battle and Hygelac avenged him (lines 2479–86). Beowulf celebrates his grandfather, saying that for him "on geogoðe" (in his youth, line 2426) he survived many a battle-charge in times of war. Then he gives the saintly age at which his military training began:

Ic wæs syfanwintre þa mec sinca baldor
freawine folca æt minum fæder genam,
heold mec ond hæfde Hreðel cyning,
geaf me sinc ond symbel, sibbe gemunde;
næs ic him to life laðra owihte
beorn in burgum þonne his bearna hwylc
Herebeald ond Hæðcyn oððe Hygelac min. (lines 2428–34)

[I was seven winters when the prince of treasures,
lordly friend of peoples, took me from my father,
when Hrethel the king kept and held me,
gave me treasure and feasting, remembered kinship;
nor was I in any way to his life a more tiresome
trooper in the forts than any one of his children,
Herebeald and Hæðcyn, or my own Hygelac.]

Beowulf's bluff words are at odds with the poet's earlier story of misery and dishonour, for he recalls his childhood being the very picture of good "sibbe" (kinship), with treasures and public honours and a place alongside Hrethel's three sons. That Hrethel "mec … æt minum fæder genam" (took me from my father, lines 2428–9) even suggests that it was Beowulf's young promise, rather than Ecgtheow's death or delinquency, which made the king bring up the "beorn" – "trooper," by etymology "bear" – with his own "bearna" (children) who, unlike Beowulf, were royal on their father's side. This spin from King Beowulf is the prelude to his encomium on his uncle Hygelac, and how he gave Beowulf treasures and land and placed him at the head of his army. In context, therefore, Beowulf's words on Hrethel are a face-saving construction in which the rosy picture of adoption would better fit Hrothgar's care of young Hrothulf at about the same time. His words might even be read as a sublimation of Hrothgar's offer (lines 946–9) to adopt him fifty years earlier.

In Denmark, Beowulf seems to see the risk that Hrothulf poses to his cousins. When he takes his leave of King Hrothgar, he tries vainly to get the older boy out:

Gif him þonne Hreþric to hofum Geata
geþingeð þeodnes bearn, he mæg þær fela
freonda findan. (lines 1836–38a)

[If in this case Hrethric to the Geatish court
takes his business, a king's son, he in that place
will be able to find a great many friends.]

About Beowulf the poet tells us later, just before his revelation of the hero's childhood in shame (line 2183), that he did not knock down drunks nor was there "hreoh sefa" (a cruel sensibility, line 2180) in him. So it seems that his offer to foster Hrethric is really one to save him – should the father only see it – from his cousin. After Hygelac's death, Beowulf resists Queen Hygd's and the Geats' offer of the Geatish throne precisely because this would compromise his bond with his own cousin:

No ðy ær feasceafte findan meahton
æt ðæm æðelinge ænige ðinga,
þæt he Heardrede hlaford wære,
oððe þone cynedom ciosan wolde. (lines 2373–5)

[No sooner for this could the destitute ones find
in that prince any terms or conditions
by which he might be a lord to Heardred,
or might wish to choose that kingship.]

Thereafter Beowulf's friendly counsel to Heardred, as John M. Hill says, "befits an older kinsman and eventual subordinate."[43] Before dying some fifty years later, Beowulf appears to justify his refusal to rule Heardred when he rejoices that the Lord need not rebuke him for "morðorbealo maga" (murderous slaughter of kinsmen, line 2742). Earlier in the poem this formula describes Hildeburh's loss of her son and brother at Finnsburh (line 1079), anticipating a similar bereavement for Wealhtheow. Retrospectively with these words Beowulf appears to contrast the initial survival of his maternal cousin Heardred with the early destruction of Hrethric, paternal cousin of Hrothulf. By supporting rather than killing

43 Hill, *The Cultural World in "Beowulf,"* 106.

his own younger cousin, for whom he prefers to rule as regent, Beowulf responds to his childhood with loyalty.

Conclusion

A comparison between Hrothulf's childhood and Beowulf's is invoked as soon as Wealhtheow raises both men's adoption in her speech to King Hrothgar in Heorot. As a boy, each man sees little of his father, growing up in the care of kin, but Hrothulf, unlike Beowulf, reaches manhood with the advantage of being royally descended on the father's side. His claim to rule the Danes is ideologically stronger than Beowulf's to rule the Geats, or indeed the Danes, and is reconfirmed by the fact that his Scylding father, Halga, is also his grandfather. Beowulf, on the other hand, Geatish only through his mother, has a lower birth, which blights both his candidacy for adoption in Denmark and his kingship back home.[44] The irony is that Hrothulf, granted full rights in a childhood completely secure, grows up to betray the family that loves him, whereas Beowulf never fails to help the family that marginalised him when he was a child. For Hrothulf childhood feeds a resentment, whereas Beowulf's upbringing makes him wiser to Danish family dynamics than either Wealhtheow or Hrothgar, as well as careful not to override the right of his own younger cousin to rule. The *Beowulf*-poet encourages this comparison, the better to contrast Hrothulf's kingship with Beowulf's in later years. His view of childhood in the meantime is that the child, not the father, is father to the man.

44 See North, "Gold and the Heathen Polity in *Beowulf*" (forthcoming).

11 Of Boys and Men: Anglo-Saxon Literary Adaptations of the Book of Daniel

DANIEL ANLEZARK

Representations of childhood are not uncommon in the Bible, but they are relatively rare in Old English biblical poetry.[1] This essay will look at childhood and adolescence as they are represented in a group of Anglo-Saxon texts based on the Book of Daniel, and explore the ways in which ideas of age and youth are enhanced and developed by the various authors. The longest and fullest of these treatments is found in the Old English poem *Daniel*, which survives in manuscript Oxford, Bodleian Library Junius 11, a collection of mostly Old Testament Old English narrative verse. The Old English *Daniel* (apart from a seventy-nine-line historical introduction)[2] is based on the first five chapters of the book of the prophet Daniel, and in the poem both the eponymous hero, but especially the three figures Azarias, Ananias, and Misahel, become representatives of the Israelite nation in their youthful holiness, a theme borne out in their salvation in Nebuchadnezzar's Babylonian furnace.[3] Their innocence and sanctity are contrasted with the sins of their elders in Jerusalem who had wickedly

1 The other major treatment of childhood is found in *Genesis A*, in the protracted story of Abraham's desire for an heir, and especially in the relationship between Sarah and Hagar, and Isaac and Ishmael, which comes to a climax in the expulsion of Hagar and Ishmael (lines 2772–806) and the sacrifice of Isaac (lines 2850–936); *The Junius Manuscript*, ASPR 1:3–87.

2 See David A. Jost, "Biblical Sources of Old English *Daniel* 1–78," 257–63; Samantha Zacher, *Rewriting the Old Testament in Anglo-Saxon Verse: Becoming the Chosen People*, 96–9.

3 See Robert E. Bjork, "Oppressed Hebrews and the Song of Azarias in the Old English *Daniel*," 213–26.

and wilfully turned away from a life of holiness, a failure that has led to national calamity. A much shorter version of the encounter between the Chaldean king and the three youths is found in the closely related poem *Azarias* in the Exeter Book, where the significance of the age of the three youths is developed in similar ways to those found in *Daniel*, though with some important differences. The three holy boys, who were universally regarded as proto-martyrs in the early Christian church, were also included beside the prophet Daniel by Aldhelm in both the prose and poetic versions of his *De virginitate*. In Aldhelm's two versions of the *De virginitate*, but also in *Daniel*, we find authors modifying the ambiguous biblical text to emphasise the fact that the three youths are indeed young when thrown into the furnace for refusing to worship Nebuchadnezzar's idol, as narrated in Daniel chapter 3. This reflects both the authors' own thematic interests and also the influence of traditions around the youths in the liturgy of the church. I will discuss the ways in which the age of the three holy youths is defined and emphasised in the texts, examine the relationships between them, and finally explore the ways in which their story and its treatment resonate with the idea of generational change and reform in Anglo-Saxon England.

Aldhelm's *De virginitate*

The *De virginitate* by Aldhelm (died AD 709) was dedicated to Abbess Hildelith and the sisters of Barking Abbey.[4] Two versions of this treatise on virginity were made, first in prose and later in verse. Aldhelm's list of historic virgins begins in the poetic version, as also in the prose, with four of the Old Testament prophets: first Elijah, then Elisha and Jeremiah, and finally Daniel. The discussion of Daniel makes no reference to the prophet's age. After Daniel we find the last of the Old Testament examples, the three youths:[5]

4 Michael Lapidge and Michael Herren, trans., *Aldhelm: The Prose Works*, 51. On Aldhelm's life and intellectual development, see Michael Lapidge, "The Career of Aldhelm," 15–69.

5 For the following quotations of Aldhelm's works, see Rudolf Ehwald, ed., *Aldhelmi opera omnia*, 368–9; Michael Lapidge and James L. Rosier, trans., *Aldhelm: The Poetic Works*, 111.

Sic quoque virgineis redolentes floribus olim
Tres pueri pariter servarunt jura pudoris
Aurea spernentes stolidi simulacra tyranni.
Qui turmas vulgi surdum mutumque metallum
Imperio terrente iubet venerarier omnes:
Tum tuba raucisonis reboat clangoribus alte,
Fistula cum citharis reclamans aethera pulsat,
Sambuca salpicibus respondet musica crebris,
Vt genibus flexis et curvo poplite plebes
Aurea per campos orarent idola regis;
Sed tamen Hebraea spernens ludibria pubes
Cernua non flectit simulacris colla nefandis.
Impius idcirco fornacis torre minatur
Puberibus castis ut cultum suggerat ardor,
Dum furibunda pios nodarent vincla lacertos.
Extemplo nexus combussit flamma feroces,
Sed sacra sanctorum non quibat membra cremare.
O mirum dictu, pueros quod flamma camini
Torribus innocuis diro sub carcere coxit,
Verum virginitas sprevit tormenta rogorum,
Scintillante fide dum fervent corda virorum.
Angelus ignicomis nam sanctus scandit ab astris
Torrida cum gelidis sedans incendia flabris
Carbonumque globos exstinguens imbre superno. (*De virginitate*, lines 367–90)

[In a similar way the three boys, redolent of the flowers of chastity, had once preserved the rights of decency in spurning the golden image of the stolid tyrant who, by a threatening command, ordered all the multitudes to venerate a deaf and dumb image of metal [Dan. 3:1–11]. A trumpet with hoarse-sounding blasts resounded from on high; the reed-pipe resounding with the cithara reached the skies; the sambuca responded to the frequent blasts of the trumpet so that, genuflecting with bended knee, the people throughout the fields would pray to the king's golden idol. But the Hebrew youths, scorning this folly, refused to bow their heads to the heinous image. The sacrilegious king therefore threatened the chaste youths with the heat of the furnace, in order that the fire might induce worship, while hostile bonds would bind their holy arms [Dan. 3:21]. Fire immediately consumed the cruel bonds, but could not burn the blessed limbs of those saintly boys. It is wondrous to speak of: that the flame of the furnace should harass the boys in the dreadful prison with harmless firebrands; but chastity rejected the torments of the furnace while the hearts of these men burned with glowing faith. For a blessed angel descended from the fiery stars to quench the burning fire with icy winds and to extinguish the red-hot lumps of coal with heavenly showers.]

It is striking that in a poem listing virgins by name, the names of the three holy youths are not included by Aldhelm – with the probable implication that the author assumes his readers will know who they are by his reference to their youthfulness and their story: the refusal to bow to Nebuchadnezzar's idol and their miraculous preservation in the furnace. Such knowledge would not be surprising in the monastery at Barking or any monastic context; the canticle sung by the three youths formed part of the office of the church and the monastic liturgy. Also noteworthy is the association of pagan persecution with youthful chastity in this story of proto-martyrs; this is a recurrent motif in Christian martyrdom accounts where young virgins refuse marriage to pagan suitors. The lines of emphasis and outright opposition in this simple telling of the story – the three holy youths versus the wicked pagan king – are shared with the Old English poem *Azarias*, but not with the poem *Daniel*, in which the king's characterisation is far more complex. While here defiance of the ironically *impius* king by pious youths is an important theme, as we shall see, in *Daniel* the emphasis is on the role of youths in converting the king. In the poetic *De virginitate* idolatry is presented as if it is a threat to the boys' chastity, so that the heat of the furnace becomes an image of unchastity and of passion. The imagery of martyrdom lends spice to the account, seen in the emphasis on their bodies in opposition to the flames, freedom from bonds, and the idea that they are in "prison." Their youthfulness anticipates that of martyrs like the youthful Agnes (thirteen years old) later in *De virginitate*,[6] and their imprisonment anticipates that of Christian martyrs. This imagery of the fire of passion is maintained throughout the episode of the three holy youths in Aldhelm's poetic version.

The verse telling differs in emphasis from its prose source; the poem in fact only takes up the last section of the prose version, with the imagery of the fires of passion and the opposition to the king, neither of which dominate in the prose version, which is more interested in the nature of their

6 Ehwald, *Aldhelmi opera*, 433, line 1928.

chastity. The emphases of the prose resonate (together with the preceding description of the prophet Daniel) with monastic life and discipline:[7]

> Ea tempestate etiam tres pueri avita Ebraeorum stirpe progeniti et in transmigratione Babiloniae ad Chaldeos abducti nequaquam carnalis copulae voluptatibus operam dedisse leguntur, sed in arto spontaneae virginitatis proposito permansisse memorantur, quamvis importuna Iudaeorum garrulitas fribula falsitatis deleramenta confingat asserens, nequaquam eosdem puberes aut praefatum collegam externae peregrinationis participem ultroneos castitatis caelibes, sed invitos spadones exstitisse, qui secundo eunuchorum gradui evangelica veritatis astipulatione deputatur. Hi denique in tantum paternae traditionis regulam et divinae sanctionis censuram servasse scribuntur, ut etiam ad obtinendam integritatis et continentiae gloriam opulentas regalium ferculorum delicias et principalis alimoniae pulmentum in tenerrima pubertate contempserint; vilibus tantum leguminibus vitam sustentare contenti lascivam iuventutis petulantiam refrenarunt. Quamobrem inorme Chaldaici regnatoris simulacrum, quod colosi sublimitatem centenis ac septenis pedibus in alto porrectam bis tricena cubitorum proceritate vincebat, licet horrendus salpicum clangor increpuerit et musica sambucorum armonia persultans insonuerit simulque flammivoma camini incendia naptarum fomite sarmentorumque nutrimine succensa terribiliter torruerint, flexis poplitibus suspicere refragabantur et pro inflexibili rigidae mentis constantia angelico fulti suffragio ambustas malleoli machinas crepitantesque clibani globos fide invicta vicerunt.
>
> [Also at that time three boys born of the ancestral race of the Hebrews and carried off to the Chaldeans in the transmigration to Babylon, are read to have in no wise devoted themselves to the pleasures of carnal copulation, but are said to have persisted in the strict resolve of voluntary virginity, even though the troublesome chattering of the Jews fabricates frivolous absurdities of falsehood, asserting that in no way were these youths, or their aforementioned fellow [Daniel], the sharer of their journey into foreign lands, voluntary devotees of chastity, but rather unwilling eunuchs – who are (accordingly) assigned to the second rank of eunuchs by the evangelical affirmation of truth [Matt. 19:12]. These (youths) in fact are recorded as having kept the rule of their paternal tradition and the law of divine sanction to such an extent,

7 Ehwald, *Aldhelmi opera*, 252, lines 1–18; Lapidge and Herren, *Aldhelm: The Prose Works*, 78.

that for (the purpose of) obtaining the glory of integrity and continence they even spurned the opulent delights of regal feasts and the sauces of princely food in their tenderest youth; content to sustain their life merely with humble pulse, they curbed the playful high spirits of their youth. As a result of this, they refused to behold on bended knees the enormous statue of the Chaldean tyrant – which exceeded the height of the Colossus of Rhodes, lifted 170 feet high with its (immense) stature of sixty cubits – even though the horrendous blaring of trumpets thundered and the musical harmony of psalteries echoed resoundingly, and at the same time the flame-belching volcano of the furnace, stoked up with the kindling of naphtha and the fuel of firewood, blazed fearfully; and, supported by angelic assistance because of the constancy of their fixed resolve, they conquered with unconquerable faith the scorching engines of the incineration and the crackling flames of the furnace.]

The prose account focuses more than the verse on the renunciation of the pleasures of the flesh – including fine food. Youth is a time of high spirits, and a plain diet can help curb these, much as it would in a monastery. This discipline – monastic by association – is implicitly part of the discipline that gives the three the power to resist idolatry, again aligned with sexuality, in the shape of the enormous idol. The emphasis on music in both the poetic and prose versions of the *De virginitate* must recall the music of liturgy in which the youths' own canticle was repeated – the familiar association of the youths for readers of *De virginitate* was primarily liturgical and musical in the weekly cycle of the Office;[8] Nebuchadnezzar's worship is a Satanic perversion of the liturgy.

Aldhelm's vocabulary describing the age of the three across the two texts is generally consistent. In the prose their age is described with the following terms: "pueri," "puberes," "pubertate," and "iuventutis." In the verse, based on the prose, the reference to their *iuventus* is gone, replaced by a reference to them as *viri* ("virorum," line 387); this does not change their age – a *puer* can be a *vir* (male), though a man (*vir*) cannot be a *puer* (boy). The characterisation remains that they are young, either boys (*pueri*) or young men (*pubes*): "pueri" (line 368), "pubes" (line 377), "puberibus" (line 380), "pueros" (line 384). It is difficult to know exactly what age Aldhelm has in mind for the three in relation to the terms he uses, and the scheme expounded by Isidore of Seville in his *Etymologiae* (ch. XI.ii,

8 See Jesse D. Billett, *The Divine Office in Anglo-Saxon England, 597–c. 1000*, 16–19.

De aetatibus hominum) offers only little help.[9] Among the six ages Isidore outlines are *pueritia* (from eight to fourteen years), *adolescentia* (fifteen to twenty-eight years), and *iuventus* (twenty-nine to forty-nine years). Isidore does not include *pubes*, and there is no obvious indication that Aldhelm attaches the same significance to the terms he uses that Isidore does. In Antiquity *pubes* denoted a man who had reached puberty (at fourteen years), but could just as easily be applied to one who had just reached it, or had done so many years before.[10] What is most significant, though, is that Aldhelm here almost entirely avoids the Vulgate's term *vir*, which more obviously means "adult male."[11]

The book of Daniel speaks about these three characters in different ways in the two episodes in which they appear. In Daniel chapter 1, the three are clearly identified with the other youths at court (1:13, "puerorum"; 1:15 "pueris"; 1:17 "pueris"), but in the episode in chapter 3, where they refuse to worship the king's idol and are cast into the furnace, the biblical narrative drops all reference to their youth and only calls them "viri" (men, 3:12):[12]

> sunt ergo viri iudaei quos constituisti super opera regionis Babyloniae Sedrac Misac et Abdenago; viri isti contempserunt rex decretum tuum.
>
> [Now there are certain men of the Jews, whom you have set over the works of the province of Babylon, Sidrach, Misach, and Abdenago: these men, O king, have slighted your decree.]

Vir is the only term used in this episode to describe their age (Dan. 3:21, 23, 91–2, 94). The text of the Book of Daniel is highly problematic in various places, including at this point, and in addition we also find here a name change to Sidrach, Misach, and Abdenago, from the earlier Ananias,

9 Isidore, *Etymologiae*, ed. Lindsay, 1: n.p.

10 Charlton T. Lewis and Charles Short, *A Latin Dictionary*, s.v. *pubes*.

11 Lewis and Short, *Latin Dictionary*, s.v. *vir*.

12 The text of the Vulgate cited is Robert Weber, ed., *Biblia sacra iuxta latinam Vulgatam versionem*, with minimal punctuation added; the translation is informed by the revised Douay Rheims text, Richard Challoner, ed., *The Holy Bible Translated from the Latin Vulgate*.

Misahel, and Azarias.[13] Aldhelm, who gives the youths no names at all, is clearly choosing to diverge from the biblical account of the furnace episode in his presentation of their age.[14] In relation to the biblical text it is possible to imagine that in chapter 3 they are older than they were in chapter 1, but in his telling Aldhelm not only maintains their youth, but ties their youth and holiness together. One likely impetus behind this decision is the fact that for a monastic audience, such as the one he is writing for, the three youths were best known for the canticle they sang in the furnace (Dan. 3:57–88), which was sung at Lauds on Sundays throughout the year.[15] The title given the canticle is the *Canticum trium puerorum* (Canticle of the Three Boys, now more often called the *Benedicite*), one used in Anglo-Saxon England, creating a popular characterisation of the three youths that could not easily be ignored, and which probably influenced both Aldhelm's characterisation and, as we shall see, that of the poet of the Old English *Daniel.*

Daniel

In the Old English *Daniel* it is the same sinful pleasures of the flesh emphasised by Aldhelm in the *De virginitate* that bring undone the kingdom of the Israelites at the beginning of the poem. These sins are implicitly equated with a rejection of the Law and covenant, a rejection which will be reversed by the youths' obedience to the Law later in the poem:[16]

13 Dan. 1:6, 1:11, 1:19; see 1:7, where Jerome's Vulgate supplies both sets of names in an effort to avoid confusion; "Azarias" is reverted to at 3:25, 49, in the context of his canticle in the furnace.

14 Aldhelm was undoubtedly aware of the two sets of names, and probably (and ironically) for the sake of their clear identification, has omitted names altogether.

15 See, e.g., Sherman Kuhn, ed., *The Vespasian Psalter*, 156; James L. Rosier, ed., *The Vitellius Psalter*, 382. There is no doubt that Aldhelm wrote for monastic readers, but the origins of *Daniel* and *Azarias* are unknown, as are the many readers who might have known the poem across the Anglo-Saxon period. It is more than likely that literacy and knowledge of vernacular verse would imply some familiarity with the Office, as it did for King Alfred when he was a child; see William H. Stevenson, ed., *Asser's Life of King Alfred together with the Annals of Saint Neots Erroneously Ascribed to Asser*, chs. 23–4.

16 The edition used for all subsequent quotations is R.T. Farrell, ed., *Daniel and Azarias*, though I have occasionally changed the punctuation and in places preferred the text of *Daniel* in *Junius Manuscript*, ASPR 1:111–32. The translations of *Daniel* and *Azarias* are my own, *Old Testament Narratives*.

oðþæt hie wlenco anwod   æt winþege
deofoldædum,   druncne geðohtas.
Þa hie æcræftas   ane forleton,
metodes mægenscipe,   swa no man scyle
his gastes lufan   wið gode dælan.   (*Daniel*, lines 17–21)

[until pride invaded them with devilish deeds at the feast, drunken thoughts. Then at once they abandoned the power of the Law, the Creator's majesty, as no man should cut off his spirit's love from God.]

The idea of keeping the Law, or not, is an important theme in both *Daniel* and *Azarias*. The holy youths' elders had given up the power of the Law ("æcræftas," line 19), but had used the sacred vessels according to the Law (line 750) before their fall, while the three youths are "æfæst" (fixed on the Law), both before the furnace (line 89) and inside it (lines 248, 272). While the youths are "æfæst," Daniel on the other hand is "æcræftig" (powerful in the Law, lines 550, 741) in his interpretations of signs and wonders. Nebuchadnezzar lives in ignorance of the Law (line 106), while the youths wish to fulfil God's "æ" in the furnace (line 219). There is no direct mention of the Law in the biblical source, let alone any development of its thematic emphasis that is found in *Daniel*, and also in *Azarias*.[17] Seth Lerer has argued that the outline of Daniel's character in Aldhelm's *De virginitate* has influenced the *Daniel*-poet's presentation of the prophet as learned in grammar and rhetoric, suggesting that Aldhelm, and the poet, "realign the prophet in the context of an English monastic education."[18] This monastic context also informs both texts' treatment of the three youths. The youths' concerns over their food in Dan. 1:8–19 can obviously be interpreted as a concern with dietary laws, a connection that is in fact made by Aldhelm, who in his prose *De virginitate* extends this concern beyond food and understands it as representing their great love of the Law as a whole: "These [youths] in fact are recorded as having kept the rule of their paternal tradition and the law of divine sanction ["paternae traditionis regulam et divinae sanctionis censuram"] to such an extent, that for [the purpose of] obtaining the glory of integrity and continence they

17 On the character of the Latin text behind the poem, see Paul G. Remley, *Old English Biblical Verse: Studies in Genesis, Exodus, and Daniel*, 231–333.

18 Seth Lerer, *Literacy and Power in Anglo-Saxon Literature*, 126–57, at 128; Lerer does not discuss the treatment of the three youths either by Aldhelm or in *Daniel* and *Azarias*.

even spurned the opulent delights of regal feasts and the sauces of princely food in their tenderest youth." Aldhelm's *De virginitate* was read widely in monastic circles in Anglo-Saxon England, and his originality in placing an emphasis on the boys' keeping of the Law has quite likely influenced the characterisation of the Law-fast youths in *Daniel*, where the dietary discussion has disappeared, while the emphasis on the zealous keeping of the Law remains.

This does not mean that the *Daniel*-poet leaves out all reference to desires of the flesh. In response to the Hebrews' sinfulness, God sends prophets to turn the people from their drunken thoughts and forgetfulness of Law and covenant:

Hie þære snytro soð gelyfdon
lytle hwile, oðþæt hie langung beswac
eorðan dreamas eces rædes,
þæt hie æt siðestan sylfe forleton
drihtnes domas, curon deofles cræft. (*Daniel*, lines 28–32)

[For a little while they believed in the truth of that wisdom, until passion, the joys of the earth, deprived them of eternal counsel, so that they themselves eventually abandoned the Lord's decrees, chose the craft of the devil.]

These older Israelites who have given in to their passions and appetites are the very opposite of the abstemious youths described by Aldhelm, who discusses these passions in a way not found in the biblical source. The poet takes up the theme present in Aldhelm's version, but not in the Bible, and it is the same Law-fast youths, free of wayward passions, who will later repent on behalf of the sinful nation banished into exile.[19] In the Old English *Daniel* these youths are selected from among the exiles at the command of Nebuchadnezzar:

Het þa secan sine gerefan
geond Israela earme lafe,
hwilc þære geogoðe gleawost wære
boca bebodes, þe þær brungen wæs.
Wolde þæt þa cnihtas cræft leornedon,

19 See Graham D. Caie, "The Old English *Daniel*: A Warning Against Pride," 1–9, at 6.

þæt him snytro on sefan secgan mihte,
nales ðy þe he þæt moste oððe gemunan wolde
þæt he þara gifena gode þancode
þe him þær to duguðe drihten scyrede. (*Daniel*, lines 79–87)

[Then he commanded his officials to seek throughout the wretched remnant of the Israelites, for those of the youth that had been brought there who were wisest in the books of the Law. He intended that the young men should learn skill, so that he could tell them the wisdom in his mind, not at all for the reason that he could or would remember that he should thank God for the gifts which the Lord allotted him there for his benefit.]

The poet's wordplay on *duguð* is careful, and develops the dual meaning of *duguð* as either "trained group of warriors" (often in contrast with *geogoþ*, "untried warriors"), or alternatively, "benefit."[20] Earlier in the passage the king has called for a selection of boys ("cnihtas")[21] from among the "young troop," the *geogoð*, and they indeed will become part of his own court, but ironically despite his own best efforts, the youths will benefit him more than his older troop. The wordplay, emphasising the ironic fact that the youths will prove better counsellors than the older troop, is completed at one of the rhetorical climaxes of the episode in the furnace:

Wæs heora blæd in Babilone, siððan hie þone bryne fandedon;
dom wearð æfter duguðe gecyðed, siððan hie drihtne gehyrdon.
Wæron hyra rædas rice, siððan hie rodera waldend,
halig heofonrices weard, wið þone hearm gescylde. (*Daniel*, lines 454–7)

[Glory was theirs in Babylon, after they passed the test in the fire, their honor was made known among the seasoned troop (*duguðe*), after they had obeyed the Lord. Their counsels were potent, after the Ruler of the skies, the holy Guardian of the heavenly kingdom, shielded them against harm.]

20 *DOE* s.v. *duguð*, senses 3, 4a., 4a.i. The term *duguð* implies a membership that is older than that of *geogoð*, rather than states it; the experience required to be counted among the *duguð*, and the assumption that wisdom can only come with experience over time, is best articulated in *The Wanderer*, lines 65–72; see *The Exeter Book*, ASPR 3:133–6.

21 *DOE* s.v. *cniht*, sense 1. "male child; boy; young man"; *cniht* also glosses Latin *pubes* (see sense 1.d.).

This is the only other occasion on which the word *duguð* is used in the poem, and it is followed immediately by the intervention of the king's *ræswa*, or leading advisor, now enlightened by the wise and faithful *geogoð*. The poet develops the thematic importance of the age of the boys in the context of contrastive relationship to their elders in Jerusalem, but also more subtly in their Babylonian exile.

These young men, unlike their elders, are chosen by the Babylonians because they are fixed on the Law:

Þa hie þær fundon þry freagleawe
æðele cnihtas and æfæste,
ginge and gode in godsæde;
an wæs Annanias, oðer Azarias,
þridda Misael, metode gecorene. (*Daniel*, lines 88–92)

[Then they discovered there three young men, nobly-wise, princely and fixed on the Law, young and good among the divine stock; one was Ananias, the second Azarias, the third Misahel, chosen by the creator.]

The choice of the youths is not, of course, the Babylonians', but God's. As well as being "æfæst," the youths are chosen ("gecorene"), of divine stock ("in godsæde," perhaps a recollection of the biblical phrase "de semino regio" in Dan. 1:3),[22] and will later be called royal ("cynegode," lines 196a, 432a). Not only are they contrasted with their elders who failed to keep the Law and chose the ways of the devil in their drunken feasting and surrender to passion, but also with the similarly characterised pagan king Nebuchadnezzar, who "did not keep the Law" (line 106). He is proud and foolish, the boys single-minded in their wisdom:

Þa þry comon to þeodne foran,
hearde and higeþancle, þær se hæðena sæt,
cyning corðres georn, in Caldea byrig.
Þa hie þam wlancan wisdom sceoldon,
weras Ebrea, wordum cyðan,
higecræft heane, þurh halig mod. (*Daniel*, lines 93–8)

22 See Zacher, *Rewriting the Old Testament*, 99.

[These three came before the prince, steadfast and thoughtful, where the pagan sat, a king eager for pomp, in the city of the Chaldeans. Then the men of the Hebrews had to make known wisdom in words to the proud one, high intelligence through a holy mind.][23]

When the king commands that they be cared for by the court officials, the *Daniel*-poet does not show even the residual interest that Aldhelm has in Jewish concerns about their diet, and the refusal to eat food from the pagan king's table; this fact in itself points to the logic of the emphasis on the youths' adherence to the Law in *Daniel* having its origin in the prose *De virginitate*. The scene in the poem does not appear in the Bible, which simply reports that the youths are chosen to be instructed in the learning of the Chaldeans (Dan. 1:4).

The relationship between the king and the youths is radically altered from the Bible and expanded in the poem – they become his instructors,[24] in anticipation of their role in the later conflict that develops when they refuse to worship his idol. The opening of this scene has been lost from Junius 11 (see line 177), and probably also from *Azarias* in the Exeter Book. When the king has established his idol, the whole populace falls in worship (lines 178–87), though there are three who do not, in another substantial addition to the biblical narrative:

Þær þry wæron   on þæs þeodnes byrig,
eorlas Israela,   þæt hie a noldon

23 The seemingly anomalous "weras" (men, line 97), carries the alliteration in a formulaic line (repeated at line 215), and should not be given much weight when determining the age of the three. Compare also *Judith*, line 241, "weras Ebrisce." The reference to the youths' holiness (lines 98, 280) is not in the poem's biblical source, but is the whole point of Aldhelm's treatise; see the verse *De virginitate*, line 383, "sacra sanctorum."

24 The motif of youth instructing their elders (and rulers) was not unfamiliar in the early medieval classroom. In the popular early medieval Latin dialogue *Adrian and Epictitus*, Epictitus the *iuvenis homo* instructs the emperor Hadrian; see Walter Suchier, ed., *Das mittellateinische Gespräch Adrian und Epictitus nebst verwandten Texten (Joca monachorum)*, 11. The Old English dialogue of *Adrian and Ritheus* forms part of this tradition; see James E. Cross and Thomas D. Hill, eds., *The Prose Solomon and Saturn and Adrian and Ritheus*, 7–13. One source of inspiration for this tradition is likely to be the account of Christ as a youth (or child) instructing the doctors in the Temple in Luke 2:46–8. In his commentary on the episode, Bede refers to Jesus as *puer* and *parvulus*; see Bede, *In Lucae evangelium expositio*, ed. Hurst, 72–3, lines 2085–115.

hyra þeodnes dom þafigan onginnan,
þæt hie to þam beacne gebedu rærde,
ðeah ðe ðær on herige byman sungon.
Ða wæron æðelum Abrahames bearn,
wæron wærfæste, wiston drihten
ecne uppe, ælmihtigne.
Cnihtas cynegode cuð gedydon,
þæt hie him þæt gold to gode noldon
habban ne healdan, ac þone hean cyning,
gasta hyrde, ðe him gife sealde.
Oft hie to bote balde gecwædon
þæt hie þæs wiges wihte ne rohton,
ne hie to þam gebede mihte gebædon
hæðen heriges wisa, þæt hie þider hweorfan wolden,
guman to þam gyldnan gylde, þe he him to gode geteode.

(*Daniel*, lines 188–205)

[There were three in that prince's city, noblemen of the Israelites, who would in no way begin to accept the prince's edict, that they should lift up prayers to that token, even though the trumpets sounded there at the idol. These were by noble descent sons of Abraham, they were faithful to the covenant, they knew the Lord, eternally on high, the Almighty. The royal youths made it known that they would neither have nor hold that gold as their god, but rather the high king, the shepherd of souls, who gave them grace. In addition, they often boldly said that they did not care at all for that idol, nor could that pagan people's guide command them to pray, that they should turn there, the men towards the golden idol, which he had set up as a god for them.]

This statement of their position, including that they are children of Abraham, replaces the biblical scene in Dan. 3:13–18 where the three are summoned before the king to explain their refusal to worship his idol:

tunc Nabuchodonosor in furore et in ira praecepit ut adducerentur Sedrac Misac et Abdenago qui confestim adducti sunt in conspectu regis. pronuntiansque Nabuchodonosor rex ait eis verene Sedrac Misac et Abdenago deos meos non colitis et statuam auream quam constitui non adoratis. nunc ergo si estis parati quacumque hora audieritis sonitum tubae fistulae et citharae sambucae psalterii et symphoniae omnisque generis musicorum prosternite vos et adorate statuam quam feci quod si non adoraveritis eadem hora mittemini in fornacem ignis ardentem et quis est Deus qui eripiat vos de manu mea.

respondentes Sedrac Misac et Abdenago dixerunt regi Nabuchodonosor non oportet nos de hac re respondere tibi. ecce enim Deus noster quem colimus potest eripere nos de camino ignis ardentis et de manibus tuis rex liberare. quod si noluerit notum tibi sit rex quia deos tuos non colimus et statuam auream quam erexisti non adoramus.

[Then Nebuchadnezzar in fury and in wrath commanded that Sidrach, Misach, and Abdenago should be brought, who immediately were brought before the king. And Nebuchadnezzar the king spoke to them, and said: "Is it true, O Sidrach, Misach, and Abdenago, that you do not worship my gods, nor adore the golden statue that I have set up? Now therefore if you are ready at whatsoever hour you shall hear the sound of the trumpet, flute, harp, sackbut, and psaltery, and symphony, and of all kind of music, prostrate yourselves, and adore the statue which I have made, but if you do not adore, you shall be cast at the same hour into the furnace of burning fire, and who is the God that shall deliver you out of my hand?" Sidrach, Misach, and Abdenago answered and said to king Nebuchadnezzar: "We have no occasion to answer you concerning this matter. For behold our God, whom we worship, is able to save us from the furnace of burning fire, and to deliver us out of your hands, O king. But if he will not, be it known to you, O king, that we will not worship your gods, nor adore the golden statue which you have set up."]

In the biblical version the conflict that is established is between the power of the two gods, the God of the Israelites and the Chaldean idol. The youths in the biblical version directly defy the king – an encounter perhaps deemed inappropriate for *Daniel*'s Anglo-Saxon audience. Their role in the poem, along with the miracle of their salvation in the fire, is to serve the king by bringing about his conversion.[25] As such they are asserted as his most loyal followers, rather than being the few who defy him. They are his *geogoð* – the loyal young troop serving his benefit.

Another significant modification to the biblical narrative comes with the poet's choice to treat the three as youths (*cnihtas*). The poet chooses to call them "boys" in the very place where the source presents them as

25 See Robert E. Finnegan, "The Old English *Daniel*: The King and His City," 194–211; Claire Fanger, "Miracle as Prophetic Gospel: Knowledge, Power and the Design of the Narrative in *Daniel*," 123–35; Gillian R. Overing, "Nebuchadnezzar's Conversion in the Old English *Daniel*: A Psychological Portrait," 3–14; Roberta B. Bosse and Jennifer L. Wyatt, "Hrothgar and Nebuchadnezzar: Conversion in Old English Verse," 257–71; Antonina Harbus, "Nebuchadnezzar's Dreams in the Old English *Daniel*," 489–508.

men.[26] In doing so the poet is informed by a long Christian tradition, the same one that informs Aldhelm's characterisation, found in the popular title of the canticle sung by the three men in the Book of Daniel, excerpted and adapted as the *Canticum trium puerorum*. It would be impossible to determine whether or not Aldhelm's own choice to characterise the youths in the same way has influenced the *Daniel*-poet, though given the likelihood that *De virginitate* has exerted influence on the texts in other ways, the shared treatment is probably related.

The boys' defiance, reported to the king, enrages him, and is reasserted, again without any description of a direct encounter here between the king and the "young ones" ("gingum"), and he orders the furnace kindled (lines 224–9). Their youth is emphasised when they are ordered to be shoved into the fire (lines 225 "cnihta," 230 "hyssas," and 231 "beornas geonge"). In the furnace under the angel's protection the "hyssas" (youths, line 251)[27] maintain their nobility ("eorlas Ebrea," line 256).[28] The protection of the holy boys ("halgan cnihton," line 266) is attributed to their attachment to the Law:

Hyssas hale hwurfon   in þam hatan ofne,
ealle æfæste ðry;   him eac þær wæs an on gesyhðe,
engel ælmihtiges.   (*Daniel*, lines 271–73a)

[The youths roamed safely in the hot oven, all three who kept the Law; there was another one visible there with them, the angel of the Almighty.]

It is in this furnace that Azarias sings the first of the two canticles. While the second praises God in creation, the first represents a national repentance, led, significantly, by the holy and sinless Azarias:[29]

26 The instance of *eorl*, "nobleman," at line 189 in the context of their heroic defiance is more likely to imply "warrior" than either "man" or "nobleman"; see *DOE* s.v. *eorl*, senses 1., 1a., 1b.

27 BT, s.v. *hyse*, "young man."

28 On some of the textual difficulties of this episode, see Harry J. Solo, "The Twice-Told Tale: A Reconsideration of the Syntax and Style of the Old English *Daniel*, 245–429," 347–64.

29 On the significance of the poet's emphasis on Azarias's sinlessness, see John Bugge, "Virginity and Prophecy in the Old English *Daniel*," 127–47, at 135. On the idea of the youths as representing a faithful remnant, see Phyllis Portnoy, "'Remnant' and Ritual: The Place of *Daniel* and *Christ and Satan* in the Junius Epic," 408–21.

Ða Azarias ingeþancum
hleoðrade halig þurh hatne lig,
dæda geornful, drihten herede,
wer womma leas, and þa word acwæð:
"Metod alwihta, hwæt, þu eart mihtum swið
niðas to nergenne. Is þin nama mære,
wlitig and wuldorfæst ofer werðeode." (*Daniel*, lines 279–85)

[Then holy Azarias spoke from his inner thoughts through the hot flame, eager for deeds, praised the Lord, the man without taint, and spoke these words: "Maker of all things, listen! You are ready in might to save men. Great is your name, beautiful and glorious over the nations."]

The afflictions of exile and national calamity have been caused specifically by the sins of *user yldran*, our elders:

"We ðæs lifgende
worhton on worulde, eac ðon wom dyde
user yldran. For oferhygdum
bræcon bebodo burhsittende,
had oferhogedon halgan lifes." (*Daniel*, lines 295b–99)

["Living in the world we brought this about, and our elders also did evil; in arrogance the citizens broke the commandments, despised the calling of holy life."]

In the furnace this disobedience of the fathers is undone by the radical obedience of the sons, who renew the covenant long ago made with the three patriarchs Abraham, Isaac, and Jacob (lines 313–14), which promises innumerable offspring (lines 315–24). Azarias pleads that this promise of offspring be fulfilled now in the three youths (line 326) for the benefit of the onlooking Chaldeans (lines 326–32). The logic is double – these boys are Abraham's sons, aligned with their youth; and from the Christian perspective the promise to Abraham was to be fulfilled in the salvation of the pagans.[30]

30 The *locus classicus* of this displacement theology is Galatians 3. Zacher, *Rewriting the Old Testament*, 88–119, argues that the transfer of divine election is an important theme running through *Daniel.*

Paul Remley has established that the Latin text underlying the *Canticum trium puerorum* section of the Old English poem is an Old Latin liturgical version of the canticle, which would later be modified by the Old English *Azarias* poet, whose vernacular version of the *Canticum* varies in its appropriation and incorporation by the poets of the *Daniel* tradition.[31] Remley suggests a date of around the middle of the tenth century for this poet's activity, but it can now be established on the evidence of a recently unearthed inscription on a small metal object (possibly a clasp) from Lincolnshire, which presents in runes the opening lines of the Old English canticle (*Daniel*, lines 362–4; *Azarias*, lines 73–5), that the source poem was already in existence by ca. AD 825, and perhaps was composed by as early as ca. AD 725.[32] The date of *Daniel* is not certain, though the version we have was copied into Junius 11 between ca. AD 960 and ca. 990.[33] The canticle, which praises God in creation, concludes with a return to the theme of sonship – "the children of men love you in their hearts" (line 390) – and an evocation of the Son of God in the Christianizing doxology, which was appended to the canticle under the influence of its liturgical use:

"We þec bletsiað,
frea folca gehwæs, fæder ælmihtig,
soð sunu metodes, sawla nergend,
hæleða helpend, and þec, halig gast,
wurðiað in wuldre, witig drihten." (*Daniel*, lines 399b–403)

["We bless you, Lord of all nations, Father almighty, true Son of the Creator, Saviour of souls, help of heroes, and you, Holy Spirit, we worship you in your glory, wise Lord."][34]

---

31 Paul G. Remley, "*Daniel*, the *Three Youths* Fragment and the Transmission of Old English Verse," 81–140, at 90–3; see also his earlier study, Remley, *Old English Biblical Verse*, 334–447.

32 See John Hines, "The *Benedicite* Canticle in Old English Verse: An Early Runic Witness from Southern Lincolnshire," 257–77, at 272, Treasure no. 2012T295. The fact that this text is closer to the version in *Azarias* would suggest the more faithful transmission of some of the earliest text in this poem's line of descent. The dating is Hines's, on runic and linguistic grounds; see Remley, "*Daniel*, the *Three Youths* Fragment," 137.

33 See Leslie Lockett, "An Integrated Re-examination of the Dating of Oxford, Bodleian Library, Junius 11," 141–73.

34 Compare the doxology Latin text of the *Canticum* in the Vitellius Psalter (ed. Rosier, 384): "Benedicamus patrem et filium cum sancto spiritu laudemus et superexaltemus eum in secula."

For the Christian this son is Christ, the promised seed of Abraham who would bring salvation to the nations, and who by this miracle will bring Nebuchadnezzar to a realization of the true God. But this only comes about through a contemplation of the three youths (line 420 "gingum gædelingum" [young companions]), as is pointed out by a royal advisor, one of the poet's most radical additions to the biblical narrative:

"Ongyt georne hwa þa gyfe sealde
gingum gædelingum. Hie god herigað,
anne ecne, and ealles him
be naman gehwam on neod sprecað,
þanciað þrymmes þristum wordum,
cweðað he sie ana ælmihtig god,
witig wuldorcyning, worlde and heofona.
Aban þu þa beornas, brego Caldea,
ut of ofne. Nis hit owihtes god
þæt hie sien on þam laðe leng þonne þu þurfe." (*Daniel*, lines 420–9)

["Understand clearly who has granted that grace to these young companions. They are praising God, the One everlasting, and call on him by each and every name in necessity, they thank him for victory with bold words, they say that he is alone almighty God, wise King of glory, of the world and heavens. Summon the men, prince of the Chaldeans, out of the furnace. It is not at all good that they should be in your hate longer than you need."]

When they are summoned out of the fire, their youth is again emphasized:

Het þa se cyning to him cnihtas gangan.
Hyssas hearde hyrdon lare,
cyrdon cynegode swa hie gecyðde wæron,
hwurfon hæleð geonge to þam hæðenan foran. (*Daniel*, lines 430–3)

[Then the king ordered the young men to come to him. The tough youths obeyed the instruction, the noblemen turned as they were taught, the young heroes went before the pagan.]

These "hyssas" (line 444) praise the true God before the pagan nation, to the point where the king accepts the truth of their words, and understands how the "hyssas þry" (line 461) have been saved, and by whom. The king himself then makes a speech to the nation affirming the same truth (lines 473–4): "We saw that he sheltered the youths against death in the oven." The treatment of the relationship between the youths and their elders in *Daniel* represents a significant enhancement of the biblical source. In the biblical text Azarias sings a song of national repentance, with the young articulating a correction of the sins of their elders, but in the context of the poem's seventy-nine-line introduction we have a full explanation of what these sins were – sins of passion and lawlessness, more usually associated with the young. The youths in the biblical source are chosen to receive instruction from the Chaldeans, but in a significant addition in *Daniel*, they are summoned to instruct the king. This redefined relationship with the king nuances the episode of the furnace, where the king is converted by the miracle of the boys' preservation. In the poem the role of the boys themselves – as much as that of God or his angel – is emphasized as bringing about the king's change of heart. In both these sets of relationships in the poem *Daniel* – the three boys with their elders, and the three boys with the king – we find the young correcting the faults of their elders, significantly altering the biblical text, which presents the three as adults in the furnace episode. We can ask why the poet would make such radical alterations in favour of the young, but it must certainly have something to do with the poem's original audience, which was in all likelihood monastic. If the poem was directed at boys in monastic life it can only have had the intention of encouraging in them the life of holiness embodied by the three holy youths whose canticle they themselves gave voice to every Sunday at Lauds.

Azarias

Azarias is a much shorter poem than *Daniel*, and as it stands in the Exeter Book presents only the furnace episode from Daniel chapter 3. Codicological evidence points strongly to the conclusion that the poem is acephalous, and that in all likelihood, though the poem copied into the Exeter Book was never as long as *Daniel* (which covers Daniel 1–5), *Azarias* nevertheless did originally tell a full story of the idol and the furnace based on Daniel chapter 3.[35] The text of *Azarias* increasingly diverges from that witnessed by *Daniel*, and indeed by the biblical source. There is no reason to presume *Daniel* is the immediate source of *Azarias*, but the two poems together, copied in the later tenth century, with their divergent

35 Remley, "Daniel, the *Three Youths* Fragment," 116.

texts, point to a wide and sustained interest in elements of this poetic tradition across a considerable length of time.

As it survives, *Azarias* begins with the briefest of introductions to the first of the two canticles in the furnace:

> Him þa Azarias ingeþoncum
> hleoþrede halig þurh hatne lig,
> dreag dædum georn, dryhten herede,
> wis in weorcum, ond þas word acwæð. (*Azarias*, lines 1–4)

> [Then holy Azarias spoke from his inner thoughts through the hot flame, carried on eager for deeds, praised the Lord, wise in works, and spoke these words.]

In this version Azarias is still "holy" (line 2, "halig"; cf. *Daniel*, line 280), but the reference to his sinlessness found in *Daniel* is replaced here by praise of his wisdom (line 4; *Daniel*, line 281, "wer womma leas"). This variation omits, incidentally, the reference to Azarias as a *wer* (man), perhaps pointing to an ongoing awareness in the tradition of the poems that the biblical source could be ambivalent about the age of Azarias and his companions, and perhaps to a desire to suppress any vocabulary that might suggest the three were anything other than youths. The text lost from the head of the poem means that the first reference to the youth of the three boys comes much later in the poem, though the content of Azarias's song is substantially the same – expressing repentance by the young for the sins of their elders, though here without the fuller historical context given to this by the *Daniel* poet.

The texts of the *Canticum trium puerorum* in the two poems show many minor and some major disagreements, which have been meticulously examined by Paul Remley.[36] One significant difference is found in the macaronic phrase "lux et tenebre" at *Azarias*, line 100, which Remley argues cannot represent a reversion to the Latin of the canticle underlying *Daniel*, line 373, "leoht and þeostro," because the Latin *Romanum* text of the *Canticum* does not have this word order, whereas the Gallican version, following the Vulgate text, does. This Latin intrusion into the text of *Azarias* probably represents the effort of a scribe reconstructing a

36 Remley, "Daniel, the *Three Youths* Fragment," 95–6.

damaged text by deploying a memorized phrase, a set of words he knows from the version of the Latin canticle familiar to him. Significantly, the widespread use of the Gallican version of the *Canticum* was associated with the Benedictine Reform of the tenth century, and in all likelihood this textual intervention points to a date of composition for this version of *Azarias* some time perhaps not far removed from its copying in the Exeter Book, which was made between ca. AD 960 and ca. 980.[37]

The major and more thematically significant differences between *Azarias* and *Daniel* come at the end of the second canticle, with a thirty-line narrative conclusion (lines 161–91) that falls into two roughly equal parts. The poetic narrator first observes that the pagans had come to understand that they could not kill "the law of the youths" ("acwellan cnyhta æ," line 165) because Christ shielded them. *Daniel* has no corresponding comment, despite that poem's interest in Law; like the youths in the furnace in *Daniel*, here they also hold fast to the Law (*Azarias*, line 58). This interest in the Law in both poems is significant given the two texts' divergence, and it suggests that their attachment to the Law was an important part of their characterisation across the vernacular poems' tradition, indicating a shared early debt in the Old English poetic tradition to Aldhelm's prose *De virginitate*. The first reference to the age of the boys also means that *Azarias* agrees with both Aldhelm and *Daniel* in breaking with the authority of the text of the Vulgate version of Daniel chapter 3. The reference to their age comes in a brief passage (lines 161–5) establishing the opposition between them and God on one side, and the heathen nation and God's enemies (lines 162–3) on the other. The heathen could not harm the boys because God did not will it. After this, a "fierce-minded nobleman" ("eorl acolmod," line 167) returns to the hall to report to the king what has taken place – in this version Nebuchadnezzar seems not to be a direct observer of the action in the furnace, and the retainer describes here the observations that the king makes both in the biblical source (Dan. 3:92–3) and in the poem *Daniel* (lines 411–15). Only the first four lines of the two speeches in *Daniel* and *Azarias* show any substantial agreement. Significantly, the nobleman reports to the "duguð" (trained group of warriors, *Azarias*, line 168) what has taken place. He reports the wonder that three "geonge cniehtas" (young boys, line 172) had been thrown into the fire, where now

37 Remley, "Daniel, the *Three Youths* Fragment," 98; Richard Gameson, "The Origin of the Exeter Book of Old English Poetry," 135–85, at 166.

four are seen. Their youth is as significant a part of the discourse here as in *Daniel*; the reference to them as "men" (line 174) seems to mean nothing more than "people."

This thematic emphasis is confirmed in the second movement of the closing narrative, when the king travels to the blaze, and commands the "lifgende bearn" (living children, line 182), to come out. The king, by contrast, is characterised simply as an "arrogant prince" ("anhydig eorl," line 181), and there is no hint that he is to undergo anything like the transformation (however temporary its effects) found in *Daniel*, which itself builds on the change of heart the king has in the biblical source. In this way the encounter as it is presented in *Azarias* – even the headless poem as we have it in the Exeter Book – recalls the emphasis in Aldhelm's *De virginitate*, and especially the prose, where the point of the episode is the victory of sanctity over sin as an end in itself. In *Azarias* the Law of the boys is not killed (line 165), "but with spiritual love they crushed sin" ("ac he mid gæstlufon synne geswencton," lines 188–9), and "through prudence escaped the fire" ("þurh foreþoncas fyr gedygdon," line 191). The "gæstlufon" (spiritual love) used by the youths to crush sin evokes the power of virginity and the rejection of the opposite kind of love, the pleasures of "carnal copulation" ("carnalis copulae"), in the terms used to describe the three youths by Aldhelm in the prose *De virginitate*; this has no basis in the biblical text. The poem's conclusion echoes Aldhelm's own in the prose *De virginitate*, though in less flowery terms:

> et pro inflexibili rigidae mentis constantia angelico fulti suffragio ambustas malleoli machinas crepitantesque clibani globos fide invicta vicerunt.
>
> [supported by angelic assistance because of the constancy of their fixed resolve, they conquered with unconquerable faith the scorching engines of the incineration and the crackling flames of the furnace.]

The framing of this conclusion, and its expression, points to the direct influence of the *De virginitate* on the casting of the story of the three youths in *Azarias*.

Conclusion

In this examination of four different literary treatments of the three holy youths in Anglo-Saxon England a number of shared features have emerged. The most striking of these is their unanimous agreement, against the biblical text of Daniel chapter 3, that in the furnace there were three youths or boys, not three men. The most likely influence on all these texts was the traditional title given to the canticle sung by the three of them in the furnace: *Canticum trium puerorum*. It would be impossible to say if Aldhelm's prose and verse *De virginitate* had any subsequent influence on the youthful characterisation of the three in the tradition of the vernacular poem, to which both *Daniel* and *Azarias* belong, as an Old English poet would also be familiar with the canticle. It would, however, be surprising if Aldhelm, himself a teacher, abbot, and bishop, and aware of his debts to his own teachers,[38] had not established a template that might influence other English authors writing creatively from the same biblical material. There is a close alignment in Aldhelm's two versions and the Old English *Azarias* between the chastity of the youths and their defeat of evil paganism, and also their direct opposition to the pagan king Nebuchadnezzar. The reference in *Azarias* to the power of the boys' "gæstlufon" (spiritual love) in conquering sin presents either a remarkable coincidence with Aldhelm's *De virginitate*, or more likely points to the influence of this treatise on the *Azarias*-poet's presentation of his chaste holy youths. The treatment of the youths in the Old English *Daniel* presents similarities and differences. The young age of the three is foregrounded in the poem *Daniel* through frequent repetition of words emphasising their youth, and the opposition between youth and age, fathers and sons, elders and heirs. Their youth emerges as the paradoxical key to the conversion of Nebuchadnezzar at the end of the furnace episode. This is emphasised at two key moments of the poem by play on the words and ideas of the *geogoð* and *duguð* – the wise youth of the children brings the king to his senses. It is this paradoxical wisdom of youth and folly of age that envelops the furnace episode in *Daniel*, repairing not only the damage done in Jerusalem by the boys' elders, but the folly of idolatry in Babylon.

38 In his Letter to Leuthere (no. 1), Aldhelm discusses how he had to return to the status of a student to relearn aspects of *computus*, citing Jerome's comment in his Preface to Daniel on his own similar experience: "qui mihi videbar scolius, rursus coepi esse discipulus?" (Shall I begin again to be a student, who thought myself learned?). In a Letter to his former teacher Hadrian (no. 2), Aldhelm greets him: "Reverentissimo patri meaeque rudis infantiae venerando praeceptori Hadriano" (To the most reverend father Hadrian, venerable teacher of my rough infancy); see Lapidge and Herren, *Aldhelm: The Prose Works*, 152–3; Ehwald, *Aldhelmi opera*, 475, 478. Lapidge and Herren translate *infantia* in a literal sense as "ineloquence," and Aldhelm would seem to be playing on the various senses of the word.

The emphasis on the three youths' close adherence to the Law also points to Aldhelm's influence on the Old English poem, representing as it does one of the few features he chooses to draw out and expand from the biblical narrative. Aldhelm's verse and prose *De virginitate* were originally written for a monastic community, and the Old English poems that take up one small episode in his treatise strongly savour of a monastic environment. The two poems are built around a canticle sung in the monastic liturgy, and emphasise the importance of a holy life lived in community. In the case of the poem *Daniel* this holy life is lived for the benefit of others, both king and nation. Malcolm Godden has commented that "one can only guess at the circumstances" in which a poem like *Daniel* might have developed, telling the story that it does of fleeting human power and heathen captivity.[39] It is notable that at the heart of both *Daniel* and *Azarias* is the song of Azarias, lamenting the wickedness and decline of the past that has led to national calamity. This sentiment is a familiar trope in Anglo-Saxon writing, and was expressed more famously and in slightly different terms by King Alfred in his Preface to the translation of Gregory the Great's *Cura pastoralis* as he embarked on and sought to justify his educational program, looking back at a past in which learning and prosperity had given way to decay through neglect.[40] This was also a trope taken up by the monastic reformers of the tenth century, who positioned themselves as inheritors of a decayed church, in their great reform document, the *Regularis concordia*, written sometime between AD 970 and 973:[41]

> Comperto etenim quod sacra coenobia diuersis sui regiminis locis diruta ac paene Domini nostri Ihesu Christi seruitio destituta neglegenter tabescerent, Domini compunctus gratia, cum magna animi alacritate festinando ubicumque locorum decentissime restaurauit; eiectisque neglegentium clericorum spurcitiis non solum monachos uerum etiam sanctimoniales, patribus matribusque constitutes, ad Dei famulatum ubique per tantam sui regni amplitudinem deuotissime constituit, bonisque omnibus locupletans gratulabundus ditauit.

39 Malcolm Godden, "Biblical Literature: The Old Testament," 206–26, at 224.

40 Henry Sweet, ed., *King Alfred's West-Saxon Version of Gregory's Pastoral Care*, 1:1–7.

41 Thomas Symons, ed., *Regularis Concordia: The Monastic Agreement of the Monks and Nuns of the English Nation*, 1–2; see Joyce Hill, "The Benedictine Reform and Beyond," 154–61, at 153. The monastic reform led to a return in popularity of Aldhelm's treatise across the tenth century; see Scott Gwara, "Manuscripts of Aldhelm's *Prosa de Virginitate* and the Rise of Hermeneutic Literacy in Tenth-Century England," 101–59.

> [When therefore he (Edgar) learned that the holy monasteries in all quarters of his kingdom, brought low, and almost wholly lacking in service of our Lord Jesus Christ, were wasting away and neglected, moved by the grace of the Lord he most gladly set himself to restore them everywhere to their former good estate. Wherefore he drove out the negligent clerks with their abominations, placing in their stead for the service of God, throughout the length and breadth of his dominations, not only monks but also nuns, under abbots and abbesses; and these, out of gratitude to God, he enriched with all good things.]

The opposition of past and present, the contrasting conduct of old and new, and the role of secular power in reflecting and enacting the divine will, characterise both *Daniel* and *Azarias*, copied into their respective manuscripts at the very time this reform was being implemented, and it is of course possible that the displacement and reform motif found in the biblical text of Daniel also influenced monastic reformers. The Old English *Daniel* itself, emerging from a monastic milieu, appealing to monastic readers, treating the subjects of the rise and fall of kingdoms, appeals to the young as the rising generation and driving force behind change and renewal, with these processes grounded in ascetic discipline and holiness. These boys are the ones who will overturn the sins of "our elders," those who "despised the calling of the holy life" (*Daniel*, lines 295–9). Whenever the poems of the *Daniel* tradition were first created, their appeal undoubtedly continued wherever the young looked in their turn to replace the old.

12 "Sharper than a Serpent's Tooth": Parent-Child Litigation in Anglo-Saxon England

ANDREW RABIN

Early in the reign of Edward the Elder, a minor nobleman asked the king to confirm a judgment handed down by Alfred the Great twenty years earlier, a petition now referred to as the "Fonthill Letter." In framing his request, the author asks, "when will any suit be resolved if one can end it neither with payment nor with an oath? And if one wishes to change every judgment which King Alfred gave, when shall we have finished disputing?" ("hwonne biþ engu spæc geendedu gif mon ne mæg nowðer ne mid feo ne mid aða geedigan? Oððe gif mon ælcne dom wile onwendan ðe Ælfred cing gesette hwonne habbe we ðonne gemotad?").[1] Traditionally, this passage has been read as a reminder to Edward of the threat posed by unending appeals to the cohesiveness of royal authority;[2] however, the next few lines suggest that these questions may have been intended to evoke another association as well. The author relates that a fellow petitioner, hoping to gain the king's favour, "sought your father's body and retrieved the seal" ("gesahte he ðines fæder lic ⁊ brohte insigle").[3] Like the author's questions, the petitioner's actions remind Edward of the origin

1 Text taken from Nicholas Brooks, *Charters of Christ Church, Canterbury*, no. 104, 2:852–62, at 853.

2 See, for instance, Simon Keynes, "The Fonthill Letter," 76–7; Andrew Rabin, "Testimony and Authority in Old English Law: Writing the Subject in the *Fonthill Letter*," 147–71, at 170–1; Scott Thompson Smith, "Of Kings and Cattle Thieves: The Rhetorical Work of the Fonthill Letter," 447–67, at 455–6.

3 Brooks, *Charters of Christ Church, Canterbury*, 2:854. For a particularly insightful discussion of this passage, see Nicole Marafioti, "Seeking Alfred's Body: Royal Tomb as Political Object in the Reign of Edward the Elder," 202–28.

of his authority, yet here the reminder takes the form of a token from "your father's body" ("ðines fæder lic"), emphasising Edward's identity as Alfred's son as well as his successor. Paired in this way, the address to the king and the symbolic homage to the king's father locate the source of Edward's power in his biological, as much as his legal, descent. Although not all families had to reckon with the dynamics of royal succession, this passage nonetheless provides a useful illustration of the extent to which early notions of legal authority overlapped with Anglo-Saxon views of the parent-child relationship. That early medieval writers (including the author of the Fonthill Letter) understood these concepts as linked reflects the fact that the institutions of law and family both developed in response to two essential communal priorities: first, the need to ensure the coherence of society in the present through the administration of property and the formalization of social hierarchies; and second, the desire to secure the coherence of society in the future by dictating the suitable means by which both property and authority were handed down to the next generation.[4] For the author of the Fonthill Letter, overturning Alfred's judgment threatens the integrity of both the legal and familial hierarchy: if a son will not heed the judgment of his father and a king the judgment of his predecessor, "when shall we have finished disputing?"

As the Fonthill Letter indicates, Anglo-Saxon concepts of legal authority were closely intertwined with contemporary views concerning biological descent and filial obligation.[5] Yet, even as studies of pre-Conquest kinship ties have become more common over the past decade, scholarship on the treatment of children and their parents in pre-Conquest law remains notably absent. In particular, the significance early lawmakers attached to childhood as a category encompassing both physical immaturity and legal incapacity has yet to be fully explored. Although Pauline Stafford pointed out as far back as 2001 that the charters and laws of early medieval England have a "potential still not fully realized" to shed light on Anglo-Saxon views of the parent-child relationship, the most complete treatment of this topic remains Ernest Young's useful, if outdated,

4 On this point, see especially R. Howard Bloch, *Etymologies and Genealogies: A Literary Anthropology of the French Middle Ages*, 64–91.

5 On the contrast between biological parenthood and godparenthood in Anglo-Saxon law, see Joseph H. Lynch, *Christianizing Kinship: Ritual Sponsorship in Anglo-Saxon England*, esp. 135–51 and 189–205.

study "The Anglo-Saxon Family Law" from 1876.[6] One goal of this chapter, then, must be to fill in at least a few of the gaps in our understanding of how both parenthood and childhood were construed under the laws of the Anglo-Saxons.

Yet it must be observed at the outset that law complicates as much as it reveals. The evidence provided by Anglo-Saxon royal legislation is often inconsistent or contradictory. Moreover, the surviving records of early English lawsuits suggest that the prescriptions of royal law often proved inadequate when confronted with the chaotic reality of inheritance disputes, family feuds, and the competing demands of crown, church, and regional aristocracy. Of course, discrepancies between legal practice and legal statute have been the subject of considerable critical head-scratching since Patrick Wormald's groundbreaking 1977 essay "*Lex scripta* and *verbum regis*"; however, the challenges are particularly acute when it comes to the study of the relations between parents and children.[7] As minors lacking full legal personhood, children fell under the *mund* (protection) of their legal guardians.[8] Although often discussed merely as a form of benevolent custodianship, the institution of *mund* represented one facet of a complex societal response to the problem of legal incapacity, that is, the inability to fulfil the responsibilities and exercise the rights of a fully realized legal

---

6 Pauline Stafford, "Parents and Children in the Early Middle Ages," 257–71, at 260; Ernest Young, "The Anglo-Saxon Family Law," 121–82. For broader discussions of parent-child relations in Anglo-Saxon culture, see Sally Crawford, *Childhood in Anglo-Saxon England*; Mathew S. Kuefler, "'A Wryed Existence': Attitudes toward Children in Anglo-Saxon England," 823–34; Joseph H. Lynch, *Godparents and Kinship in Early Medieval Europe*; Lynch, *Christianizing Kinship*; Robin D. Smith, "Anglo-Saxon Maternal Ties," 106–17; Eric G. Stanley, "The *Familia* in Anglo-Saxon Society," 37–64. Discussions of early English notions of childhood within a broader European context can be found in Albrecht Classen, ed., *Childhood in the Middle Ages and the Renaissance: The Results of a Paradigm Shift in the History of Mentality*; Rob Meens, "Children and Confession in the Early Middle Ages," 53–65; Janet L. Nelson, "Parents, Children, and the Church in the Earlier Middle Ages," 81–114; Bronagh Ni Chonaill, "Child-Centred Law in Medieval Ireland"; Shulamith Shahar, *Childhood in the Middle Ages*.

7 Patrick Wormald, "*Lex scripta* and *verbum regis*: Legislation and Germanic Kingship, from Euric to Cnut," 1–43.

8 On the definition of *mund*, its etymology, and its use in Germanic and Anglo-Saxon law, see BT, s.v. *mund*; Ferdinand Holthausen, *Altenglisches Etymologisches Wörterbuch*, s.v. *mund*; Felix Liebermann, ed., *Die Gesetze Der Angelsachsen*, v. II, s.v. *mund*; Jan Frederik Niermeyer, Co van de Kieft, and J.W.J. Burgers, eds., *Mediae Latinitatis Lexicon Minus*, s.v. *mund*.

subject. Those kept via *mund* – children, women, the physically or mentally incapable – and those such as servants or slaves who were viewed as similarly incapable all fell under the category of persons deemed *alieni iuris* (under the jurisdiction of another), individuals subject to the extraordinary protection and constraint of the *patria potestas* (power of the father).[9] For persons deemed *alieni iuris*, the full exercise of legal power or agency was unavailable. Rather, as Janet Nelson has suggested, such individuals instead sought to achieve "some room for manoeuvre in shaping the future for [them]selves, [their] property and other persons in [their] social network."[10] However, although recent scholarship has shown that many of those considered *alieni iuris* achieved substantial success when seeking "room for manoeuvre," scholars of early medieval law have yet to consider the problems raised when the interests of different marginalized subjects came into conflict; in other words, when the exceptional legal constraints placed on those *alieni iuris* meant that the expansion of one subject's "room for manoeuvre" necessarily involved the contraction of another's. This is a problem particularly relevant to the study of Anglo-Saxon childhood, for as we shall see, children's attempts to assert their prerogatives often placed their legal interests at odds with those of another category of persons deemed *alieni iuris* – their mothers. Disputes between parents and children thus have the potential to reveal the range of strategies used by marginalized subjects seeking a degree of legal agency in pre-Conquest society.

This chapter examines how the treatment of parent-child relations in pre-Conquest law sheds light on early English concepts of legal agency. As I will argue, the view of children under the law as individuals *alieni iuris* reflected

---

9 Carole A. Hough, "The Widow's 'Mund' in Æthelberht 75 and 76," 1–16, at 1–4; Anne L. Klinck, "'To Have and to Hold': The Bridewealth of Wives and the *Mund* of Widows in Anglo-Saxon England," 231–46, at 241–2; Thomas Kuehn, *Law, Family, and Women: Toward a Legal Anthropology of Renaissance Italy*, 212–13; Lynch, *Christianizing Kinship*, 200; Jo Ann McNamara and Suzanne Wemple, "The Power of Women through the Family in Medieval Europe, 500–1100," 83–101, at 83; Julie Mumby, "The Descent of Family Land in Later Anglo-Saxon England," 399–415, at 410; David Pelteret, *Slavery in Early Mediaeval England*, 138; Theodore John Rivers, "Widows' Rights in Anglo-Saxon Law," 208–15, at 208–9.

10 Janet Nelson, "The Wary Widow," 82–113, at 83. For further discussion of Nelson's argument, see Andrew Rabin, "Female Advocacy and Royal Protection in Tenth Century England: The Legal Career of Queen Ælfthryth," 261–88, at 261–2; Victoria Thompson, "Women, Power, and Protection in Tenth- and Eleventh-Century England," 1–17, at 1–3.

broader notions of legal capacity and ethical responsibility. Yet if placing children under the explicit protection of the *patria potestas* was a way to ensure their protection, well-being, and right of inheritance, it also placed their legal interests in potential conflict with those of their female relations and caregivers. For wives, mothers, and especially widows – all of whom were likewise defined as subjects *alieni iuris* – oversight of their children's person and property served as a means of carving out a space of agency within a male-dominated legal system. Accordingly, this chapter considers not just childhood per se, but also the implications of a child's transition to adulthood. As children matured and sought to assume more control over their affairs, the interests of parent and child frequently came into conflict. The manner in which this conflict of interest played out in surviving legal disputes reveals the negotiations and strategies available to marginalized subjects when trying to secure their own "room for manoeuvre."

Children and Their Parents in Anglo-Saxon Law

Before addressing problems of agency, it is necessary first to define the parameters of legal childhood; however, this task is more difficult than it first appears. Early English legislation offers little consistency in identifying childhood's beginning or end. Concerning its beginning, from a legal standpoint the recognition of childhood status appears to have preceded birth, since the *Laws of Alfred* – the only legislation to address the subject – specify that an unborn child carried a wergild half that of its father.[11] It is unclear, however, whether wergild attached at conception or at some later point. Likewise, the absence of analogues means we cannot gauge the extent to which this single clause reflects widely held legal beliefs or practices.[12] The end of childhood is equally problematic. Despite Sally Crawford's assertion that "an examination of the surviving Anglo-Saxon law-codes leaves no room for doubt that there existed a traditionally

11 *Alfred* 9. Anglo-Saxon legislation is cited according to Liebermann, *Gesetze*, vol. 1.

12 The absence of clauses relating to the legal status of the unborn extends not just to crimes against foetuses but also to medical procedures such as abortions. Although abortion is mentioned three times in surviving Old English penitentials – one of which does distinguish between early- (before the first forty days, when the child is "ensouled") and late-term abortions – there is no evidence of these prescriptions influencing either legislation or legal practice. On this point, see Marianne Elsakkers, "The Early Medieval Latin and Vernacular Vocabulary of Abortion and Embryology," 377–414.

accepted age of transition from childhood to adulthood," the laws themselves are somewhat less clear on the point.[13] The seventh-century Kentish *Laws of Hlothhere and Eadric* decree that childhood ended at ten as do the West Saxon *Laws of Ine*.[14] Æthelstan's earlier *Laws* end childhood at twelve, yet by the end of his reign he had raised the age of adulthood to fifteen.[15] Cnut lowered the age of transition back to twelve, though this appears to have been similarly temporary since Anglo-Norman legal texts date the age of transition to between fifteen and twenty-one.[16] The freedom Anglo-Saxon lawmakers appear to have felt in revising the age of transition upwards or downwards suggests that the age at which childhood ended was seen as relatively fluid. This fluctuation indicates a certain flexibility in the definition of childhood itself, whereby changing views of transition to adulthood reflected evolving social norms and shifting familial practices.[17]

More revealing than the precise age at which childhood was deemed to have begun and ended were the criteria used to determine those boundaries. The traditional view, articulated by Young and still frequently cited in current scholarship by Stafford, Crawford, and others, was that accession to legal adulthood corresponded with a female child's ability to bear children and a male child's ability to bear arms.[18] There are several problems with this assertion, though: first, neither criteria for adulthood occurs in surviving legislation (Young's claim rests primarily on the evidence of continental analogues, in particular Tacitus's *Germania* and the thirteenth-century *Sachsenspiegel*); second, concerning the bearing of children, while the age at which girls reached reproductive maturity during the early

13 Crawford, *Childhood in Anglo-Saxon England*, 52.

14 *Hlothhere and Eadric* 6; *Ine* 7.2.

15 *II Æthelstan* 1; *VI Æthelstan* 1.1, 12.1.

16 *II Cnut* 20, 21. These sorts of fluctuations appear to have been common in early medieval law across different cultures. See, for instance, Kuefler, "'A Wryed Existence,'" 826; Ni Chonaill, "Child-Centred Law"; Theodore John Rivers, *Laws of the Salian and Ripuarian Franks*, 65–6; Stafford, "Parents and Children," 261–2; Young, "The Anglo-Saxon Family Law," 160–1.

17 Though we can only speculate, it is also possible that the varying ages at which childhood was a practical necessity reflecting the limited government bureaucracy of early medieval England: an individual's precise age may often have been difficult to determine prior to the introduction of formal birth or baptismal certificates.

18 Young, "The Anglo-Saxon Family Law," 157 and 159–63. See also Crawford, *Childhood in Anglo-Saxon England*, 52; Stafford, "Parents and Children," 261–2.

Middle Ages remains the subject of some dispute, it almost certainly was not as young as ten or twelve;[19] and third, regarding the bearing of arms, while weapons occur as grave goods in the burials of individuals between the ages of fifteen and twenty-one, they are found only very rarely in the burials of those between ten and fifteen.[20] This is not to suggest that Young's criteria did not inform broader Anglo-Saxon views of the transition between childhood and adulthood; however, Anglo-Saxon lawmakers appear to have had different standards in mind when determining the qualifications for legal adulthood.

Setting aside Young's criteria, royal legislation appears to establish two principal conditions by which childhood is characterized: first, the inability to administer property, and second, an inadequate sense of ethical responsibility. Regarding the first, the *Laws of Hlothhere and Eadric* specify that a child must yield "its property to guardianship until it is ten years old" ("his feoh to healdenne oþ þæt he x wintra sie").[21] Likewise, *II Cnut* decrees that at the age of twelve a child must be enrolled in a hundred in order to receive the rights of a freeperson and establish any claims to land or property.[22] *II Cnut* also declares that if a man's property has been free of litigation or competing claims of ownership during his lifetime, his children will not be required to defend their ownership during the period of their minority nor can their inheritance be seized because of crimes committed by their relatives.[23] Taken together, these clauses suggest that Anglo-Saxon lawmakers not only viewed the capacity to manage property as a prerequisite for full legal personhood but that they understood the state to have a compelling interest in ensuring guardianship of property owned by those incapable of administering it themselves.

Equally if not more important was a child's inability to comprehend the ethical consequences of his or her actions. Thus, the *Laws of Ine* decree

---

19 S.M.P.F. de Muinck Keizer-Schrama and D. Mul, "Trends in Pubertal Development in Europe," 287–91, at 288; J.B. Post, "Ages at Menarche and Menopause: Some Mediaeval Authorities," 83–7.

20 Nick Stoodley, "From the Cradle to the Grave: Age Organization and the Early Anglo-Saxon Burial Rite," 99–107, at 460. On this point, see also Heinrich Härke, "'Warrior Graves'?: The Background of the Anglo-Saxon Weapon Burial Rite," *Past & Present* 126 (1990): 22–43, at 35–7; Härke, "Early Anglo-Saxon Social Structure," 125–60, at 129–30.

21 *Hlothhere and Eadric* 6.

22 *II Cnut* 20.

23 *II Cnut* 72 and 76.2.

that a child cannot be considered an accessory to theft before the age of ten.[24] Similarly, Æthelstan initially ruled that only those over the age of twelve could be put to death as thieves, though he later revised this to fifteen, "because it seemed too cruel to him to execute those so young and for so little" ("þæt him to hreowlic þuhte þæt man swa geonge man cwealde oððe eft for swa lytlan").[25] Underlying such clauses is a view of children as lacking sufficient moral cognizance or legal agency to be held fully culpable for capital crimes.[26] This understanding of childhood is made more explicit in the *Laws of Cnut*, which identify the public acceptance of ethical responsibility as the central feature of the transition to legal adulthood. *II Cnut* requires that every person over the age of twelve be enrolled in a hundred and swear an oath declaring that he "will be neither a thief nor a thief's accomplice" ("nyle ðeof beon ne ðeofes gewita").[27] Taking this oath in the presence of the hundred court serves as the ritual transition to legal adulthood; the court's acceptance of the oath signifies that the new adult has been deemed "worthy of the right of exculpation and of wergild" ("lade wyrðe beon oððe weres wyrðe").[28] At the same time, the law also condemns those who would treat a child "as if it were culpable and entirely aware" ("ealswa scyldigne ⁊ hit gewittig wære").[29] In short, then, to be an adult before the law entailed the ability to understand not just wrongdoing but crime, that is, wrongdoing against society. Significantly, the fact that the crime specified in each of the relevant clauses was theft highlights once again the centrality of property ownership and administration to the

24 *Ine* 7.2.

25 *VI Æthelstan* 12.1. For the clauses setting the minimum age of execution to twelve, see *II Æthelstan* 1 and *VI Æthelstan* 1.1. It should be noted that, despite these clauses, there is little evidence that the execution of children as young as twelve was a common practice during this period. See Andrew Rabin, "Capital Punishment and the Anglo-Saxon Judicial Apparatus: A Maximum View?," 181–200, at 189–90.

26 A similar view of childhood appears in penitential literature, in which children were characterised as lacking the moral awareness necessary to commit sinful acts. See Meens, "Children and Confession," 55; Janet L. Nelson, "Parents, Children, and the Church," 86–7.

27 *II Cnut* 21.

28 *II Cnut* 20.

29 *II Cnut* 76.2. Similar injunctions can also be found in early medieval Irish law, which marks the transition from foolishness to sensibility as one of the stages on the path to legal adulthood. See Daniel A. Binchy, ed., *Corpus iuris Hibernici*, 4:1265, lines 4–6.

determination of legal adulthood.[30] One must not only be able to manage property, one must also have the capacity to understand the ethical dimensions of possession and transaction.

Significantly, these two criteria – the inability to manage property and the lack of fully developed ethical awareness – are also those used to identify other categories of persons subject to the *mund* of the head of household. The *Laws of Alfred*, for instance, note that special guardianship is required for those "born mute or deaf" ("dumb oððe deaf geboren") and anyone else who "cannot refute [accusations] or confess wrongdoing" ("ne mæge synna onsecggan ne geandettan").[31] Exceptional penalties are then assigned for guardians who steal the property or otherwise violate the rights of "unmagan" (persons without means, dependent ones), a term Felix Liebermann and F.L. Attenborough argue encompasses children as well as the physically or mentally infirm.[32] Similar stipulations occur in *VI Æthelred*, which decrees that "one must act with moderation and carefully distinguish in both spiritual penance and worldly punishment between age and youth, wealth and poverty, health and impairment, and each social rank" ("man sceal medmian ⁊ gescadlice toscadan ge on godcundan scriftan ge on woroldcundan steoran ylde ⁊ geogoþe, welan ⁊ wædle, hæle ⁊ unhæle, ⁊ hada gehwilcne").[33] The need for these distinctions, the text continues, stems from the different degree of agency available to those held to be dependent or otherwise legally incompetent: "he who commits a misdeed out of compulsion is always worthy of protection and lighter penalties because he acted involuntarily" ("se þe nydwyrhta bið þæs þe he misdeð se bið gebeorhges ⁊ þy beteran domes symle wyrðe þe he nydwyrhta wæs þæs þe he worhte").[34] Clauses such as these indicate that the view of childhood in Anglo-Saxon legislation should be understood

30 Patrick Wormald has pointed out that theft frequently serves as the paradigmatic "socially disruptive" crime in royal legislation due to the threat that the violation of property rights posed to the coherent social order which the king claimed to guarantee. See Patrick Wormald, "'*Inter cetera bona ... genti suae*': Law Making and Peacekeeping in the Earliest English Kingdoms," 179–99, at 194.

31 *Alfred* 14.

32 *Alfred* 17. For commentary on this clause, see Frederick L. Attenborough, ed. and trans., *The Laws of the Earliest English Kings*, 195; Liebermann, *Gesetze*, 3:55.

33 *VI Æthelred* 52.

34 *VI Æthelred* 52.1. Nearly identical clauses occur at *II Cnut* 68.1b–1c. Cf. Stefan Jurasinski, "Madness and Responsibility in Anglo-Saxon England," 99–120, at 100–1; Pelteret, *Slavery in Early Mediaeval England*, 90–1.

within the broader context of legal capacity and guardianship. As marginal subjects with limited agency, children were only one of a range of persons held to require special protection. Although different from other types of dependents in that one eventually ceased to be a child while femininity, physical infirmity or impairment, and enslavement were all potentially permanent conditions, childhood nonetheless shared an assumption of legal incompetence that limited both the subject's degree of responsibility and capacity for action.

Perhaps the most important of those with whom children shared protected status were their female caregivers, especially their mothers. Within the context of the household, women, like their children, were subject to the *patria potestas* of their husbands, fathers, or other male relatives. Consequently, like children, women's ability to own property was strictly circumscribed and, in the absence of a husband, their interests were overseen by a male guardian. Space does not permit a full survey of the statutes concerning women's property rights in Anglo-Saxon royal legislation – a topic dealt with in far more detail elsewhere[35] – yet it is worth noting the extent to which laws concerning women coincide with those concerning children. As Julia Crick has shown, women typically held land only in *usufruct* – that is, with a lifetime interest only and without the capacity to sell or exchange it – and their real property (that over which they exercised full rights of ownership) was largely limited to movable goods.[36] Although a woman did receive a *morgengifu* (morning-gift) of either land or chattel upon marriage, even this was not fully in her control: possession of the

35 See, for instance, Anne L. Klinck, "Anglo-Saxon Women and the Law," 107–21; Marc A. Meyer, "Land Charters and the Legal Position of Anglo-Saxon Women," 57–82; Marc A. Meyer, "The Queen's 'Demesne' in Later Anglo-Saxon England," 75–113; Andrew Rabin, "Anglo-Saxon Women before the Law: A Student Edition of Five Old English Lawsuits," 33–56; Rabin, "Female Advocacy," 261–88; Pauline Stafford, "Women and the Norman Conquest," 221–49; Thompson, "Women, Power and Protection," 1–17; Christine E. Fell, *Women in Anglo-Saxon England*; Fell, "A 'friwif locbore' Revisited," 157–66; Hough, "The Widow's 'Mund,'" 1–16; Carole A. Hough, "Two Kentish Laws Concerning Women: A New Reading of Æthelberht 73 and 74," 554–78; and Hough, "Women and the Law in Seventh-Century England," 207–30; Mary P. Richards and B. Jane Stanfield, "Concepts of Anglo-Saxon Women in the Laws," 89–99.

36 Julia Crick, "Women, Posthumous Benefaction, and Family Strategy in Pre-Conquest England," 399–422; Crick, "Men, Women, and Widows: Widowhood in Pre-Conquest England," 24–36. Discussions of the implications of Crick's argument can be found in Rabin, "Female Advocacy," 278–9.

morgengifu was held jointly by the wife and her husband, its contents (whether property or goods) were not distinguished from the couple's other holdings, and its management fell primarily to the male head-of-household.[37] Moreover, a wife's potential to alienate or capitalise on the *morgengifu* was strictly limited since, as the *Laws of Æthelberht* stipulate, women's property ultimately was to be inherited by her children or, if she was without issue, to pass into the holdings of her new husband and his kindred.[38] Although widows exercised slightly more autonomy than other categories of women, even their ability to manage property was limited by their status as dependents of either their male relatives or, in the absence of family, of the king or church.[39] The relationship between women's dependent status and the claims of their guardians particularly emerges in the statutes concerning compensation and legal redress. Royal legislation consistently rules that women could not directly receive compensation for injury – this was paid either to a male relation, the church, or the crown – since violence against a woman was deemed to be principally a violation of her guardian's *mund*.[40] Implicitly, then, the same protected status that restricted a woman's ability to own property likewise limited her rights as a legal subject: insofar as responsibility for both her financial and physical well-being lay with her guardian, that guardian's prerogatives necessarily constrained her ability to achieve full agency under the law.

Although the laws do not treat women's ethical awareness as they do children's – upon reaching adulthood, a woman was understood to be fully aware of the morality of her actions – royal legislation does distinguish

37 As, for instance, in the will of the reeve Æthelnoth; see Agnes J. Robertson, ed., *Anglo-Saxon Charters*, no. 3, 4. This text is catalogued as S 1500 in P.H. Sawyer, *Anglo-Saxon Charters: An Annotated List and Bibliography*. On the relation between morning-gifts and other property, see Meyer, "Land Charters," 62–3.

38 *Æthelberht* 81. On this clause, see Meyer, "Land Charters," 62. There are cases, as in the will of Wynflæd (S 1539), in which women are able to pass on some or all of their property; however, as Julia Crick has shown, these sort of benefactions occur only in special instances in which other constraints on female property ownership (in particular, the presence of male guardians or direct heirs) are absent. See Crick, "Women, Posthumous Benefaction, and Family Strategy," 416–18, and "Men, Women, and Widows," 28–9.

39 Rolf H. Bremmer Jr, "Widows in Anglo-Saxon England," 58–88; Hough, "The Widow's 'Mund,'" 1–16; Klinck, "Bridewealth of Wives," 231–45; Rivers, "Widows' Rights in Anglo-Saxon Law," 208–15.

40 See, for instance, *Alfred* 8 and 18, *I Edmund* 4, *V Æthelred* 21, *VI Æthelred* 12.1 and 39, *I Cnut* 7.1, and *Cnut 1020* 16. On this point, see Rabin, "Anglo-Saxon Women before the Law," 38.

between the degree of culpability assignable to the head of a household on one hand and that to his wife and children on the other. Wihtred, for instance, exempts a wife from punishment if her husband engages in devil worship without her knowledge ("butan wifes wisdome").[41] The *Laws of Ine* take this exemption further, noting that a wife cannot be held culpable for participating in her husband's crimes "since she must obey her lord" ("forðon hio sceal hire ealdore hieran").[42] *II Cnut* decrees that a woman can only be considered a participant in her husband's thefts if the stolen goods are found in the rooms, chests, or cupboards to which she has a key; nevertheless, it also concedes that "no wife can forbid her husband from putting anything he wishes into his house" ("ne mæg nan wif hire bundan forbeodan þæt he ne mote into his cotan gelegian þæt þæt he wille").[43] At issue in the *Laws* of Ine and Cnut is not women's ethical awareness per se, but rather the ability to translate that awareness into action. Significantly, contemporary lawsuit records indicate that the awareness of women's limited agency influenced the progress of legal disputes as well: a charter of ca. AD 980 × 987 exonerates a widow because her guardian had "compelled her [to agree] to forcibly seize a set of disputed estates" ("genedde þæt hy brucan ðara land on reaflace").[44] The legal position of women within a household thus bore notable similarities to that of their children: both were defined by their dependent status, which limited their capacity to exercise property rights and limited the degree to which they could be held responsible for their actions. As such, although it would be too much to claim that the status of women was identical to that of children, it is important to recognize that, in the words of Marc Meyer, "a married woman was legally bound to her husband in much the same way as a minor to a father."[45]

---

41 *Wihtred* 11. On this clause, see Lisi Oliver, *The Beginnings of English Law*, 171.

42 *Ine* 57.

43 *II Cnut* 76.1a–1b. On these clauses, see Klinck, "Anglo-Saxon Women and the Law," 111; Pauline Stafford, *Unification and Conquest: A Political and Social History of England in the Tenth and Eleventh Centuries*, 164.

44 S 1457, ed. in Robertson, *Anglo-Saxon Charters*, no. 59, 122.

45 Meyer, "Land Charters," 61. For a reiteration of this point in a different context, see Marc A. Meyer, "Early Anglo-Saxon Penitentials and the Position of Women," 47–61, at 55. As Neil McLeod has shown, the parallel between mothers and children appears to have been a common one in early medieval insular law. See Neil McLeod, ed., *Early Irish Contract Law*, 71.

However, if a woman's legal status was comparable to that of a child, her role as caregiver, particularly if her husband was absent or deceased, still afforded her an otherwise unattainable degree of agency. In part, this agency derived from increased financial wherewithal: the *Laws of Æthelberht*, for instance, specify that a woman caring for her children following her husband's death was entitled to half of his goods; if she did not have a child, though, her inheritance and dowry (the so-called morning-gift) reverted to her paternal kindred. If she did have offspring, yet married again, her entitlement was reduced to no more than that reserved for any one of her children.[46] Likewise, the *Laws of Ine* decree that a widow caring for her children must receive "six shillings [per year] for their upkeep, a cow in summer and an ox in winter" ("vi scill. to fostre, cu on sumera, oxan on wintra"), though this entitlement ends once the children reach maturity.[47] Equally important was the power a widow exercised as caregiver: the *Laws* of Æthelberht, Hlothere and Eadric, Ine, and Cnut all specify that the guardianship of fatherless children was to be held by their mother, rather than their paternal kindred.[48] Clauses such as these indicate that the status of caregiver or, in the event of her husband's death, guardian offered women a modicum of flexibility: the legal right to oversee her children's interests – in other words, to place them under such protection – enabled women to assume at least some of the prerogatives of a *mundbora*.[49] Although it is doubtful that the real authority available to women was as extensive as these laws suggest – more likely, these clauses were intended to safeguard a child's inheritance by establishing a checks-and-balances system to ensure that neither side of the family could exploit property held in trust without infringing on the rights of the other[50] – they nonetheless open up a space of agency for women within the legal constraints of the Anglo-Saxon household.

46 *Æthelberht* 78–81. On these clauses, see Carole A. Hough, "The Early Kentish 'Divorce Laws': A Reconsideration of Æthelberht, Chs. 79 and 80," 19–34; Oliver, *Beginnings*, 112–13.

47 *Ine* 38.

48 *Æthelberht* 79, *Hlothhere and Eadric* 6, *Ine* 38, and *II Cnut* 70.1 and 72.

49 Hough, "The Widow's 'Mund,'" 10–11. On this point, see also Fell, *Women in Anglo-Saxon England*, 75; Smith, "Anglo-Saxon Maternal Ties," 110.

50 A similar suggestion has been raised by Pauline Stafford, who observes, "there must be a strong suspicion that these women are often doing little more than implementing arrangements made by husbands and fathers." Stafford, *Unification and Conquest*, 175.

At the same time, these clauses also illustrate the potential for conflict between the legal interests of mothers and those of their children. The *Laws* of Æthelberht, Hlothere and Eadric, Ine, and Cnut each limit the financial benefits of maternal guardianship to the child's minority: female caregivers may receive fosterage support and exercise control over their children's property only "until [the child] reaches maturity" ("oð ðæt hit gewintred sie").[51] Accordingly, insofar as mothers' legal agency relied upon their children's dependent status, it was in a woman's interest to prevent her child's transition to legal adulthood as long as possible in order to retain control over money or property. An example of the type of dispute that ensued can be found in the record of an eighth-century lawsuit between a newly installed abbess and her mother:

> [B]ecause this [daughter] was still underage, custody of the charter of the recorded estates as well as the governance of the monastery had been entrusted to the girl's mother, a married woman, until she reached maturity. When the daughter requested that the charter be returned, her mother, not wishing to return it, responded that it had been stolen."[52]

For the unnamed mother, surrendering the disputed charters meant yielding both legal agency and financial control, hence the somewhat desperate (and ultimately futile) attempt to claim that the documents had been stolen.[53] This brief episode illustrates the issues confronting mothers of maturing children: as Jo Ann McNamara and Suzanne Wemple have written, "the protecting mother was all too often found to be simultaneously acting the wicked stepmother."[54] For a woman in pre-Conquest

---

51 *Ine* 38.

52 S 1429, ed. in Walter de Gray Birch, ed., *Cartularium Saxonicum: A Collection of Charters Relating to Anglo-Saxon History*, no. 156, 1:25–7: "Sed quia hæc in parvula adhuc ætate erat posita cartulam conscripti agri necnon et omnem monasterii procurationem quo adusque illa ad maturiorem pervenisset ætatem matri illius maritatæ conservandam injunxit. Quæ cum cartulam reddi poposcisset illa reddere nolens, furtu hanc sublatam respondit." For a full discussion of this dispute, see Andrew Rabin, "Courtly Habits: Monastic Women's Legal Literacy in Early Anglo-Saxon England," 289–305.

53 Claims that disputed documents had been lost or stolen seem to have been a relatively common stratagem for women during this period. For a continental analogue, see Sarah Foot, *Veiled Women: Female Religious Communities in England, 871–1066*, 1:57.

54 McNamara and Wemple, "Power of Women," 91.

England, the role of caregiver offered both increased financial independence and, insofar as she functioned as guardian to her husband's children, leverage in any negotiations with his surviving kindred. Yet, as her children matured, her capacity to exercise her agency decreased – or, to borrow Nelson's language, as her children's "room to manoeuvre" expanded, her own grew smaller.

Recognising the extent to which the legal definition of childhood overlapped with that of other dependents under the jurisdiction of the *mundbora* helps clarify the relationship between agency and capacity in pre-Conquest law. The emergence of *mund* as an institution acknowledged that certain categories of person required extraordinary protection and oversight; however, to be subject to a guardian's *mund* also entailed strict constraints on the individual's ability to pursue his or her legal interests independently. The intermediate position occupied by women within the household – as both dependents and potential guardians – offered them a path to greater agency even as it raised the possibility of conflict between their legal interests and those of their children. As the following case study illustrates, the progress of such conflicts when they broke out and the means by which they were resolved cast into high relief the underlying assumptions and inconsistencies behind the parent-child relationship in pre-Conquest law.

Mothers and Sons in Conflict

The stakes involved in the conflict between the claims of children and their mothers become clearer if we turn from royal legislation to the charters, writs, and wills in which are preserved the records of Anglo-Saxon dispute resolution. The litigation recorded in these texts indicates both the frequency with which familial disputes came to law as well as the strategies employed by the claimants in pursuing their interests.[55] The remainder of this chapter will focus on one such dispute between a mother and her son that offers a useful case study of the ways in which the law dealt with conflicts of this sort. The only account of the dispute survives in the charter designated S 1462, a short text of approximately 350 words transcribed

55 See Wormald, "A Handlist of Anglo-Saxon Lawsuits," 265–75.

in an early eleventh-century hand at the end of the Hereford Gospels.[56] The text records that Edwin, son of Enniaun, appeared before the shire-meeting at Aylton during the reign of Cnut to demand a series of estates that he claimed his mother was withholding from him. As no one in the court was familiar with the claims involved, Thurkil the White, husband of one of the widow's kinswomen, dispatched a delegation to take her testimony. Furious over her son's accusation, the widow summoned Leofflaed, Thurkil's wife, and, in the presence of the court's representatives, both swore to her own rightful ownership and dispossessed her son in favour of her kinswoman. The court subsequently found in her favour and Thurkil rode quickly to Hereford Cathedral to ensure that his wife's inheritance would be documented. Presumably, the surviving text is the original record commissioned by Thurkil.

In examining the various legal manoeuvres employed by the claimants, it is important to bear in mind the limitations of S 1462 as an entry in the history of Anglo-Saxon legal agency. As is often the case with Old English dispute records, S 1462's narrative was composed by a victorious litigant who was either literate himself or had sufficient financial resources to commission a scribe.[57] The purpose of such records was not strict accuracy; rather, it was to represent the past in such a way as to serve the present and future needs of their compositors. In shaping the memory of a dispute – both the manner in which it was resolved and the personalities of those involved – the documentary record served as a form of preventative law designed to limit the possibility of future litigation.[58] As such, in S 1462 it is Thurkil's voice as well as his interests that are foregrounded in the narrative. The litigants – especially Edwin's unnamed mother and Leofflaed – are viewed only through the perspective of a male interlocutor with a vested interest in the disposition of the disputed estates. S 1462 thus

56 Hereford, Cathedral Library, MS P. 1.2, fol. 134r–v. Modern editions of the text include Henry Adams, ed., *Essays in Anglo-Saxon Law*, 365–7; Robertson, *Anglo-Saxon Charters*, no. 78, 150–3; Benjamin Thorpe, ed., *Diplomatarium Anglicum Ævi Saxonici: A Collection of English Charters from the Reign of King Æthelberht of Kent to That of William the Conqueror*, 336–8. The discussion here will be based on the edition found in Rabin, "Anglo-Saxon Women before the Law," 48–50, revised in Andrew Rabin, Lisi Oliver, and Stefan Jurasinski, *Old English Law: A Reader*.

57 Wormald, "Charters," 292–4; Wormald, "A Handlist of Anglo-Saxon Lawsuits," 281–3.

58 Warren Brown, "Charters as Weapons: On the Role Played by Early Medieval Dispute Records in the Disputes They Record," 227–48, at 230; Sarah Foot, "Reading Anglo-Saxon Charters: Memory, Record, or Story?," 39–67, at 40–1; Paul R. Hyams, "The Charter as a Source for the Early Common Law," 173–89, at 173–4.

illustrates, as Nancy Partner has written in a different context, that "in far too many ways, the women whom medieval historians have to study are the imaginative constructs of men."[59]

However, if S 1462 cannot be read as an objective account of either events or people, it nonetheless offers a useful illustration of the rhetorical conditions of agency. That is, the record's success in fulfilling its preventative function depends upon the extent to which the narrative it records is acceptable to potential readers. In other words, the charter must tell its story in such a way as to encourage the reader to acquiesce to the court's judgment.[60] Accordingly, even though we lack an objective, unmediated account of the dispute and its participants, the narrative strategies employed by Thurkil and his scribe have the potential to illuminate the ways in which legal agency – especially that of subjects on the margins of the legal community – could be characterized in such a way as to meet the expectations and acceptance of an early eleventh-century reader.

Viewed in this light, it is striking that the narrative justifies the unusual alienation of family land – unusual both because it occurred and because it was initiated by a woman – as the direct result of Edwin's violation of proper family relations. The case begins with the son's appearance before the court, where, as the text relates, "he spoke there against his own mother" ("he spæc þær on his agene modor"). The adjective *agen* (own) interrupts the typically economical syntax of this passage, highlighting the extent to which the son's suit represented a departure from the conventional parent-child bond. As Christine Fell points out, "the wording suggests a sense of shock in the scribe making the record."[61] The importance of "agene" in this context is further indicated by its recurrence later in the charter, when the widow emphasises that she leaves "to my own son, not a thing" ("minon agenan suna næfre nan þingc"). Edwin's violation of familial norms also appears to underlie the court's surprised reaction to his claims:

> Þa acsode se bisceop hwa sceolde andswerian for his moder. Þa andsweorode Þurcil Hwita ⁊ sæde þæt he sceolde gif he ða talu cuðe. Þa he ða talu na ne cuðe, ða sceawode man þreo þegnas of þam gemote [ridan] þær ðær heo wæs.

---

59 Nancy F. Partner, "No Sex, No Gender," 419–43, at 423.

60 Andrew Rabin, "Law and Justice," 85–98, at 94–6.

61 Fell, *Women in Anglo-Saxon England*, 78. See also Crawford, *Childhood in Anglo-Saxon England*, 117.

[Then the bishop asked who should answer for the mother. Then Thurkil the White responded and said that he should, if he was familiar with the claim. As he was not familiar with the claim, three thegns were selected from the court to ride to where (the mother) was.]

Edwin's maternal kindred (including Thurkil himself) appear nonplussed by his suit, while his paternal relations, even if present, go entirely unmentioned. It is unclear how seriously the reader should take the claims of ignorance by Thurkil and company: it is possible that they truly had no knowledge of Edwin's case, yet it is equally likely that their protestations represent, in the words of Clare Lees and Gillian Overing, "sheer opportunism or even good strategy."[62] It was not uncommon for victorious litigants both to portray themselves as the innocent victims of an opposing claimant's unscrupulousness and to find reasons to omit evidence from the dispute record that might contradict their version of events.[63] Whatever the truth may have been, the scribe's depiction of the court's confusion in the face of the son's claim, the professed unfamiliarity of his maternal relations concerning the reasons behind the suit, and the omission from the record of any supporters from his paternal kin group all serve to isolate Edwin and diminish the validity of his claim. Accordingly, as depicted in the charter, any right Edwin might have had to his mother's land has been negated by his rejection of his family – a rejection highlighted by their apparent absence from court and seeming ignorance of his suit – and his violation of the obligations a pious son owes his mother.

Read in this way, the charter's emphasis on the irregular features of Edwin's claim offers rhetorical justification for the widow's unusual response. Upon learning of her son's suit, the text records that "gebealh heo

62 Clare Lees and Gillian R. Overing, *Double Agents: Women and Clerical Culture in Anglo-Saxon England*, 74.

63 Rabin, "Testimony and Authority," 158–9; Rabin, "Law and Justice," 95–6; Rabin, "Courtly Habits," 303–4. In this context, it may be significant that this charter is unique in the records of Anglo-Saxon dispute resolution for its depiction of a lawsuit brought before a court in which one of the parties professes to be entirely ignorant, not only of the claims of the other, but even of the other's intention to go to law. One might contrast the omissions of S 1462 with the detailed record of a land transaction untainted by dispute in S 1469, the charter transcribed immediately after S 1462 in the Hereford Gospels.

swiðe eorlice wið hire sunu," a phrase typically rendered as "she became extremely angry" or "was strongly incensed with her son."[64] However, the translation of this sentence is complicated by the otherwise unattested adverb "eorlice," possibly a Mercian dialectal variant of *irlice* (angrily) but also resembling the adjective *eorlic* (noble, masculine).[65] Although "angrily" must be considered the more plausible translation, the anomalous occurrence of a Mercian spelling in a text composed in literary West Saxon nonetheless suggests the possibility of an alternate reading that lends the widow's response a gender-inappropriate undertone: "[the widow] swelled manfully against her son."[66] If the use of "eorlice" is indeed a slight play on words, it would be in line with other examples of what Wormald described as scribes "exploiting the implications of literacy" to shape the reception of dispute narratives.[67] In context, the widow's masculine anger explains her unfeminine response to Edwin's suit: the disinheritance of her son and the alienation of her property, legal manoeuvres typically inappropriate for female landholders. Significantly, the charter further underscores the widow's masculine, aristocratic behaviour with the use of a parallel adverb just a few words later: just as the widow has "gebeah eorlice," she orders the thegns recording her response to "doð þegnlice" ("act thegnly") in reporting it to the court. Within the rhetorical world of the text, Edwin's failure to observe conventional parent-child relations releases his mother from the conventional limitations placed upon her as woman, mother, and widow. This is not to suggest that Edwin's suit necessarily violated conventional parent-child bonds in actuality – indeed, the commonality of such cases among surviving pre-Conquest lawsuits suggests that inheritance disputes of this sort occurred with some frequency[68] – nor should

64 The former translation can be found in Dorothy Whitelock, ed., *English Historical Documents, Volume I: c. 500–1042*, 603. The latter occurs in Robertson, *Anglo-Saxon Charters*, 153.

65 Dorothy Whitelock, ed., *Sweet's Anglo-Saxon Reader in Prose and Verse*, 247, n. to line 19. See also BT, s.v. *eorlic* and *eorlisc*; *DOE*, s.v. *eorlic* and *eorlisc*.

66 Lees and Overing note that the *eorlice/irlice* parallel is "highly suggestive of a masculine gendering of anger and class in a woman's voice." Lees and Overing, *Double Agents*, 86.

67 Wormald, "Charters," 303. Pauline Stafford likewise suggests that "we can suspect an editing of claims on the land to emphasise her freedom to give, a wider range of arguable family claims than the document admits." Stafford, "Women and the Norman Conquest," 242 and n. 82.

68 Cf. Bremmer, "Widows," 67. For a discussion of an analogous lawsuit, see Andrew Rabin, "Courtly Habits," 300–5.

the text be understood to imply that the widow truly acquired the rights and prerogatives of a man; rather, references to traditional expectations concerning parent-child behaviour here function as a means of legitimising the widow's departure from established tenurial custom. Implicitly, the widow's violation of conventional gender norms and legal practices assumes a degree of legitimacy because of Edwin's violation of his filial duty. The widow's room for manoeuvre can thus expand even as her son's contracts.

At the same time, it is important to recognise the extent to which this room to manoeuvre was strictly circumscribed. The charter's culmination appears to offer a vivid illustration of female legal agency: filled with (manly?) rage, the widow enlists the court's representatives as witnesses and produces a new will in the form of an oral testament that replaces her male offspring with a female relation as her principle heir.[69] Yet the narrative also ensures that the widow's agency has its boundaries: though seemingly an individual of some substance – the property at stake is not insignificant – the widow nonetheless remains nameless and no information about her is offered beyond her relationship with Edwin and Thurkil's wife, Leofflæd. Although this is often attributed to the tendency in Anglo-Saxon legal records to relegate women to the background, it likely has as much to do with Thurkil's need to erase, insofar as possible, the history of the disputed lands' prior ownership.[70] As other charters indicate, the conversion of property from *folcland* to *bocland* or the composition of new charters often involved omitting the property's prior owners in order to limit those who might dispute the rights of the present owner. This is not to say that the widow's gender plays no role in her erasure; rather, that it serves as a useful instrument for the text's author. On one hand, exploiting her maternity enables him to justify her gift of the land to Leofflæd, yet at the same time her gender also makes it easier for him to omit her name, thereby ensuring that the memory of her ownership will not be preserved. Revealingly, when the disputed property later comes to be entered

69 On the widow's statement as a form of oral will, see Bremmer, "Widows," 67; Lees and Overing, *Double Agents*, 73–4; Stafford, "Women and the Norman Conquest," 241–3.

70 Lees and Overing, *Double Agents*, 76–83; Stafford, "Women and the Norman Conquest," 241. In this context, it may be significant that the text was transcribed in a gospel book, thus bestowing the Church's sanction on Thurkil's version of events and validating any apparent manipulation of the record. These books and their legal additions were often accessible to the Anglo-Saxon public.

in the Domesday Book, it is listed as a holding of the family of Thurkil the White.[71] In short, though the widow appeared to bestow the land on her female relative Leofflæd, it ultimately entered into the paternal inheritance of Thurkil's kin group.[72]

The Herefordshire dispute reveals the potential for conflict underlying the treatment of parent-child relations in pre-Conquest law. The charter's depiction of the widow and her son illustrates the ways in which the shared status of mothers and their children as persons under the *mund* of their male relatives informed the processes through which disputes were both adjudicated and recorded for future readers. In a broader sense, it reminds us that the pursuit of "room for manoeuvre" under early English law necessarily involved negotiation, conflict, and compromise. The legal definition of childhood may have emerged as a way of protecting children's rights and securing their place in the social order, yet the extent to which it overlapped with those of others deemed *alieni iuris* meant that even close relatives could find themselves wrestling for the limited avenues of agency available under the law. A mother cannot keep her children young forever ... but sometimes it may have been in her best interest to try.

71 Stafford, "Women and the Norman Conquest," 243. Interestingly, Leofflæd herself is one of the few women mentioned in Domesday Book as a landholder, although (despite the evidence of S 1462) the Wellington and Cradley estates are not among her possessions. Instead, the lands, which had passed into the possession of the Norman Hugh l'Asne, are listed as having been among the holdings of Thurkil and his family. Ann Williams and H.G. Martin, eds., *Domesday Book: A Complete Translation*, 516–17.

72 The precise date at which the disputed lands came to be understood as Thurkil's rather than Leofflæd's is unknown, though the fact that Domesday Book explicitly associated them with Thurkil himself (who presumably had died long before the Domesday survey was compiled) suggests that this transfer took place relatively soon after the lawsuit had been settled.

Bibliography

Adams, Henry, ed. *Essays in Anglo-Saxon Law*. Boston: Little Brown and Company, 1876.

Alexander, Michael. *The Earliest English Poems*. Berkeley: University of California Press, 1966.

Alford, Richard D. *Naming and Identity: A Cross-Cultural Study of Personal Naming Practices*. New Haven, CT: HRAF Press, 1988.

Allen, L., V. Brown, L. Dickinson, and K.C. Pratt. "The Relation of First Name Preferences to their Frequency in the Culture." *Journal of Social Psychology* 14 (1941): 279–93.

Anlezark, Daniel, ed. and trans. *The Old English Dialogues of Solomon and Saturn*. Woodbridge, Suffolk, UK; Rochester, NY: D.S. Brewer, 2009.

– ed. and trans. *Old Testament Narratives*. Dumbarton Oaks Medieval Library. Cambridge, MA: Harvard University Press, 2011.

Ardener, Edwin. "Belief and the Problem of Women." In *Perceiving Women*, edited by Shirley Ardener, 1–17. London: Malaby Press, 1975.

Ariès, Philippe. *Centuries of Childhood: A Social History of Family Life*. Translated by Robert Baldick. New York: Knopf, 1962. Reprinted London: Random House, 1996.

– *L'enfant et la vie familiale sous l'Ancien Régime*. Paris: Plon, 1960. Reprinted Paris: Seuil, 1973.

Assmann, Bruno, ed. *Angelsächsische Homilien und Heiligenleben*. Bibliothek der angelsächsischen Prosa 3. Kassel, 1889. Reprinted with a supplementary introduction by Peter Clemoes. Darmstadt: Wissenschaftliche Buchgesellschaft, 1964.

Aðalbjarnarson, Bjarni, ed. *Snorri Sturluson: Heimskringla II*. Íslenzk fornrit 27. Reykjavík: Hið Íslenzka Fornritafélag, 1945.

Atkinson, Clarissa W. *The Oldest Vocation: Christian Motherhood in the Middle Ages.* Ithaca, NY: Cornell University Press, 1991.

Attenborough, Frederick L., ed. and trans. *The Laws of the Earliest English Kings.* Cambridge: Cambridge University Press, 1922.

Augustine. *City of God*, 7 vols., edited and translated by William M. Green. Cambridge, MA: Harvard University Press, 1957–72.

– *Confessions.* Translated by Henry Chadwick. Oxford: Oxford University Press, 2009.

– *Treatises on Marriage and Other Subjects.* Translated by Charles T. Wilcox, edited by Roy J. Deferrari. The Fathers of the Church 27. 1955. Reprinted with corrections, Washington, DC: Catholic University of America Press, 1969.

Bächtold-Stäubli, Hanns, Eduard Hoffmann-Krayer et al., eds. *Handwörterbuch des deutschen Aberglaubens.* 10 vols. Berlin and Leipzig: de Gruyter, 1927–42.

Bäck, Hilding. *The Synonyms for "Child," "Boy," "Girl" in Old English. An Etymological-Semasiological Investigation.* Lund: Gleerup, 1934.

Bammesberger, Alfred. "Wealhtheow's Address to Beowulf (*Beowulf*, Lines 1226b–7)." *N&Q* 57 (2010): 455–7.

Barley, Nigel F. "Structure in the Cotton Gnomes." *NM* 78 (1977): 244–9.

Barney, Stephen, W.J. Lewis, J.A. Beach, and Oliver Berghof, trans. *The Etymologies of Isidore of Seville.* Cambridge: Cambridge University Press, 2006.

Barry, Herbert, III, and Aylene S. Harper. "Feminization of Unisex Names from 1960 to 1990." *American Name Society* 41 (1993): 228–38.

Bassett, S.R. "A Probable Mercian Royal Mausoleum at Winchcombe, Gloucestershire." *Antiquaries Journal* 65 (1985): 82–100.

Baxter, Jane Eva. *The Archaeology of Childhood: Children, Gender and Material Culture.* Walnut Creek, CA: Altamira Press, 2005.

Bayless, Martha. "Alcuin's *Disputatio Pippini* and the Early Medieval Riddle Tradition." In *Humour, History and Politics in Late Antiquity and the Early Middle Ages*, edited by Guy Halsall, 157–78. Cambridge: Cambridge University Press, 2002.

– "The *Collectanea* and Medieval Dialogues and Riddles." In *Collectanea Pseudo-Bedae*, edited by Martha Bayless and Michael Lapidge, 12–24. Scriptores Latini Hiberniae 14. Dublin: School of Celtic Studies, Dublin Institute of Advanced Studies, 1998.

Bazire, Joyce, and James E. Cross, eds. *Eleven Old English Rogationtide Homilies.* King's College London Medieval Studies IV. Exeter: Short Run Press, 1989.

Beda. *The Complete Works of Venerable Bede: Ecclesiastical History*, edited by J.A. Giles. London, 1843.

– *De temporum ratione. Bedae opera didascalica*, pars 2, edited by Charles W. Jones. CCSL 123B. Turnhout: Brepols, 1977.

– *In Lucae evangelium expositio. In Marci evangelium expositio. Bedae opera exegetica* 3, edited by David Hurst. CCSL 120. Turnhout: Brepols, 1960.

Benediktsson, Jakob, ed. *Arngrimi Jonae opera Latine conscripta I–IV.* Editiones Arnamagnæanæ IX–XII. Copenhagen: Munksgaard, 1950–7.

– "Icelandic Traditions of the Scyldings." *Saga-Book* 15 (1957–61): 48–66.

Bergamin, Manuela, ed. and trans. *Aenigmata Symposii: La fondazione dell'enigmistica come genere poetico.* Per Verba. Testi mediolatini con traduzione 22. Florence: SISMEL Ed. del Galluzzo, 2005.

Bethurum, Dorothy, ed. *The Homilies of Wulfstan.* Oxford: Clarendon Press, 1957.

Bieler, Ludwig, ed. *Anicii Manlii Severini Boethii philosophiae consolatio.* Turnhout: Brepols, 1957.

Biggs, Frederick M. "The Politics of Succession in *Beowulf* and Anglo-Saxon England." *Speculum* 80 (2005): 709–41.

Billett, Jesse D. *The Divine Office in Anglo-Saxon England, 597–c. 1000.* Henry Bradshaw Society Subsidia 7. London: Boydell, 2014.

Binchy, Daniel A., ed. *Corpus Iuris Hibernici.* 6 vols. Dublin: Dublin Institute for Advanced Studies, 1978.

Birch, Walter de Gray, ed. *Cartularium Saxonicum: A Collection of Charters Relating to Anglo-Saxon History.* London: Whiting and Company, 1885–93.

Bitterli, Dieter. "Alkuin von York und die angelsächsische Rätseldichtung." *Anglia* 128 (2010): 4–20.

– "Exeter Book Riddle 15: Some Points for the Porcupine." *Anglia* 120 (2003): 461–87.

– *Say What I Am Called: The Old English Riddles of the Exeter Book and the Anglo-Latin Riddle Tradition.* Toronto: University of Toronto Press, 2009.

– "The Survival of the Dead Cuckoo: Exeter Book Riddle 9." In *Riddles, Knights and Cross-Dressing Saints: Essays on Medieval English Language and Literature*, edited by Thomas Honegger, 95–114. Bern; New York: Peter Lang, 2004.

Bjork, Robert E. "Oppressed Hebrews and the Song of Azarias in the Old English *Daniel.*" *Studies in Philology* 77 (1980): 213–26.

Björkman, Erik. *Nordische Personennamen in England in alt- und frühmittelenglischer Zeit: ein Beitrag zur englischen Namenkunde.* Halle: M. Niemeyer, 1910.

Bland, Dave. "The Formation of Character in the Book of Proverbs." *Restoration Quarterly* 40 (1998): 221–37.

Bloch, R. Howard. *Etymologies and Genealogies: A Literary Anthropology of the French Middle Ages.* Chicago: University of Chicago Press, 1983.

Bloomfield, Morton. "Understanding Old English Poetry." *Annuale Mediaevale* 9 (1968): 5–25.

Bond, C. James. "Hawking and Wildfowling." In *The Wiley-Blackwell encyclopedia of Anglo-Saxon England*, 2nd ed., edited by Michael Lapidge, John Blair, Simon Keynes, and Donald Scragg, 236. Chichester: Wiley Blackwell, 2014.

Bonjour, Adrien. *The Digressions in "Beowulf."* Oxford: Blackwell, 1950.

Bosse, Roberta Bux, and Jennifer Lee Wyatt. "Hrothgar and Nebuchadnezzar: Conversion in Old English Verse." *Papers on Language and Literature* 23 (1987): 257–71.

Boswell, John. *The Kindness of Strangers: The Abandonment of Children in Western Europe from Late Antiquity to the Renaissance*. Chicago: University of Chicago Press, 1998.

Bosworth, Joseph, *An Anglo-Saxon Dictionary. Based on the Manuscript Collections of the Late Joseph Bosworth*. Edited by Thomas Northcote Toller and Alistair Campbell. Oxford: Oxford University Press, 1838–1972 (London: Longman, 1838; ed. Toller, 1882–98; Toller's Supplement, 1921; reprinted 1966; Campbell's *Enlarged Addenda and Corrigenda to the Supplement*, 1972).

Boyle, Angela, Anne Dodd, David Miles, and Andrew Mudd. *Two Oxfordshire Anglo-Saxon Cemeteries: Beringsfield and Didcot*. Thames Valley Landscapes Monograph 8. Oxford: Oxford Archaeological Unit, 1995.

Brady, Lindy. "Death and the Landscape of *The Fortunes of Men*." *Neophilologus* 98 (2014): 325–36.

Bremmer, Rolf H., Jr. "Widows in Anglo-Saxon England." In *Between Poverty and the Pyre: Moments in the History of Widowhood*, edited by Jan Bremmer and Lourens van den Bosch, 58–88. London: Routledge, 1995.

Briggs, Elizabeth. "Nothing But Names: The Original Core of the Durham *Liber Vitae*." In *The Durham Liber Vitae and Its Context*, edited by David Rollason, A.J. Piper, Margaret Harvey, and Lynda Rollason, 63–85. Woodbridge: Boydell, 2004.

Brodeur, Arthur Gilchrist. *The Art of "Beowulf."* Berkeley: University of California Press, 1959.

Brooks, Nicholas. "The Career of St Dunstan." In *St Dunstan: His Life, Times and Cult*, edited by Nigel Ramsay, Margaret Sparks, and Tim Tatton-Brown, 1–23. Woodbridge: Boydell, 1992.

– *Charters of Christ Church, Canterbury*. Anglo-Saxon Charters 18. 2 vols. Oxford: Oxford University Press, 2013.

– "English Identity from Bede to the Millennium." *Haskins Society Journal* 14 (2003): 33–51.

Brown, George H. *A Companion to Bede*. Woodbridge: Boydell, 2009.

Brown, Marjorie. "The Feast Hall in Anglo-Saxon Society." In *Food and Eating in Medieval Europe*, edited by Martha Carlin and Joel Rosenthal, 1–13. London and Rio Grande: Continuum, 1998.

Brown, Warren. "Charters as Weapons: On the Role Played by Early Medieval Dispute Records in the Disputes They Record." *Journal of Medieval History* 28 (2002): 227–48.

Bugge, John. "Virginity and Prophecy in the Old English *Daniel.*" *English Studies* 87 (2006): 127–47.

Bullough, Donald A. *Alcuin: Achievement and Reputation.* Education and Society in the Middle Ages and Renaissance 16. Leiden: Brill, 2014.

– "The Missions to the English and the Picts and their Heritage (to *c.*800)." In *Die Iren und Europa im früheren Mittelalter*, 2 vols., edited by Heinz Löwe, 1:80–98. Stuttgart: Klett-Cotta, 1982.

Burrow, John. *The Ages of Man: A Study in Medieval Writing and Thought.* Oxford: Clarendon Press, 1986.

Caie, Graham D. "The Old English *Daniel*: A Warning Against Pride." *English Studies* 59 (1978): 1–9.

Cameron, Angus, Ashley Crandell Amos, Antoinette diPaolo Healey, et al. *The Dictionary of Old English.* Toronto: Dictionary of Old English Project, 1980–.

Cavill, Paul. *Maxims in Old English Poetry.* Cambridge: D.S. Brewer, 1999.

Chadwick, H. Munro. *The Heroic Age*. Cambridge: Cambridge University Press, 1912.

Challoner, Richard, ed. *The Holy Bible Translated from the Latin Vulgate.* Baltimore: John Murphy Co., 1899.

Chambers, Raymond W. *Beowulf*: *An Introduction to the Study of the Poem.* 3rd ed., with a supplement by Charles L. Wrenn. Cambridge: Cambridge University Press, 1959.

Chardonnens, László Sándor. *Anglo-Saxon Prognostics 900–1100: Study and Texts*. Leiden: Brill, 2007.

Clark, Cecily. "English Personal Names ca. 650–1300." *Medieval Prosopography* 8 (1987): 31–60.

– "Onomastics." In *The Cambridge History of the English Language*, vol. 1: *The Beginnings to 1066*, edited by Richard M. Hogg, 452–89. Cambridge: Cambridge University Press, 1992.

Clark, Gillian. "The Fathers and the Children." In *The Church and Childhood: Papers Read at the 1993 Summer Meeting and the 1994 Winter Meeting of the Ecclesiastical History Society*, edited by Diana Wood, 1–27. Oxford; Cambridge, MA: Published for the Ecclesiastical History Society by Blackwell Publishers, 1994.

Clarke, John. "The Origins of Childhood: In the Beginning …" In *Key Issues in Childhood and Youth Studies*, edited by Derek Kassem, Lisa Murphy, and Elizabeth Taylor, 3–13. New York: Routledge, 2010.

Classen, Albrecht. "Phillipe Ariès and the Consequences: History of Childhood, Family Relations, and Personal Emotions: Where do we stand today?" In *Childhood in the Middle Ages and the Renaissance: The Results of a Paradigm Shift in the History of Mentality*, edited by Albrecht Classen, 1–65. Berlin: de Gruyter, 2005.

– ed. *Childhood in the Middle Ages and the Renaissance: The Results of a Paradigm Shift in the History of Mentality*. Berlin: de Gruyter, 2005.

Clayton, Mary. "An Edition of Ælfric's Letter to Brother Edward." In *Early Medieval English Texts and Interpretations: Studies Presented to Donald G. Scragg*, edited by Elaine Treharne and Susan Rosser, 263–83. Medieval and Renaissance Texts and Studies 252. Tempe, AZ: ACMRS Press, 2002.

Clayton, Mary, and Hugh Magennis, ed. and trans. *The Old English Lives of St Margaret*. Cambridge Studies in Anglo-Saxon England 9. Cambridge: Cambridge University Press, 1994.

Clements, Jill Hamilton. "Sudden Death in Early Medieval England and the Anglo-Saxon *Fortunes of Men*." In *Dealing with The Dead: Mortality and Community in Medieval and Early Modern Europe*, edited by Thea Tomaini. Leiden: Brill, forthcoming.

Clements, Ronald E. "Wisdom and Old Testament Theology." In *Wisdom in Ancient Israel: Essays in Honour of J. A. Emerton*, edited by John Day, Robert Gordon, and H.G.M. Williamson, 269–86. Cambridge: Cambridge University Press, 1995.

Clemoes, Peter. *Rhythm and Cosmic Order in Old English Christian Literature; An Inaugural Lecture*. Cambridge: Cambridge University Press, 1970.

– "King Alfred's Debt to Vernacular Poetry: The Evidence of *ellen* and *cræft*." In *Words, Texts and Manuscripts: Studies in Anglo-Saxon Culture Presented to Helmut Gneuss on the Occasion of his Sixty-Fifth Birthday*, edited by Michael Korhammer with Karl Reichl and Hans Sauer, 213–38. Cambridge, D.S. Brewer, 1992.

Cockayne, Thomas Oswald, ed. *Leechdoms, Wortcunning and Starcraft of Early England*. 3 vols. Rolls Series. London: The Holland Press, 1961.

Colgrave, Bertram, ed. *Felix's Life of St Guthlac*. Cambridge: Cambridge University Press, 1956.

– ed. *The Life of Bishop Wilfrid by Eddius Stephanus*. Cambridge: Cambridge University Press, 1927.

– ed. *Two Lives of Saint Cuthbert: A Life by an Anonymous Monk of Lindisfarne and Bede's Prose Life. Texts, Translation, and Notes*. Cambridge: Cambridge University Press, 1940.

Colgrave, Bertram, and Roger A.B. Mynors, eds. and trans. *Bede's Ecclesiastical History of the English People*, Oxford: Oxford University Press, 1969.

Colman, Fran. *The Grammar of Names in Anglo-Saxon England: The Linguistics and Culture of the Old English Onomasticon*. Oxford: Oxford University Press, 2014.

Cooper, Andrew T. "Literary Perspectives on the Case for Beowulf's Rowing Adventure with Breca." BA dissertation, Stockholm University, 2009.

Crawford, Sally. "Age Differentiation and Related Social Structure: A Study of Earlier Anglo-Saxon Mortuary Ritual." DPhil thesis, University of Oxford, 1991.

– "The Archaeology of Play Things: Theorizing a Toy Stage in the 'Biography' of Objects." *Childhood in the Past* 2 (2009): 55–70.

– *Childhood in Anglo-Saxon England*. Stroud: Sutton, 1999.

– "Children, Death, and the Afterlife in Anglo-Saxon England." In *The Archaeology of Anglo-Saxon England: Basic Readings*, edited by Catherine E. Karkov, 339–53. New York: Routledge, 1999.

– *Daily Life in Anglo-Saxon England.* Oxford: Greenwood, 2009.

– "The Disposal of Dead Infants in Anglo-Saxon England from c. 500–1066: An Overview." In *(Re)Thinking the Little Ancestor: New Perspectives on the Archaeology of Infancy and Childhood.* BAR International Series 2271, edited by Mike Lally and Alison Moore, 75–84. Oxford: Archaeopress, 2011.

– "Food, Fasting and Starvation: Food Control and Body Consciousness in Early Anglo-Saxon England." In *Intersections: The Archaeology and History of Christianity in England, 400–1200: Papers in Honour of Martin Biddle and Birthe Kjølbye-Biddle*, edited by Martin Henig and Nigel Ramsay, 99–107. Oxford: Archaeopress, 2010.

– "Medieval and Anglo-Saxon Childhoods." *Oxford Bibliographies.* http://www.oxfordbibliographies.com/view/document/obo-9780199791231/obo-9780199791231-0091.xml.

– "Spinning Yarns and Weaving Futures: Female and Juvenile Spaces in Early Anglo-Saxon Settlements." In *Lebenswelten von Kindern und Frauen in der Vormoderne. Archäologische und anthropologische Forschungen in memoriam Brigitte Lohrke.* PAST Paläowissenschaftliche Studien Band 4, edited by Raimar Kory, 111–22. Berlin: curach bhán publications, 2015.

– "When Do Anglo-Saxon Children Count?" *Journal of Theoretical Archaeology* 2 (1991): 17–24.

Crawford, Sally, and Carenza Lewis. "Childhood Studies and the Society for the Study of Childhood in the Past." *Childhood in the Past* 1 (2008): 5–16.

Crenshaw, James L. "Prolegomena." In *Studies in Ancient Israelite Wisdom*, edited by James L. Crenshaw, 1. New York: Ktav, 1976.

– *Old Testament Wisdom: An Introduction.* 3rd ed. Louisville, KY: Westminster John Knox Press, 2010.

Crick, Julia. "Men, Women, and Widows: Widowhood in Pre-Conquest England." In *Widowhood in Medieval and Early Modern Europe*, edited by Sandra Cavallo and Lyndan Warner, 24–36. London: Routledge, 1999.

– "The Wealth, Patronage and Connections of Women's Houses in Late Anglo-Saxon England." *Revue Benedictine* 109 (1999): 154–85.

– "Women, Posthumous Benefaction, and Family Strategy in Pre-Conquest England." *The Journal of British Studies* 38 (1999): 399–422.

Cronan, Dennis. "Poetic Words, Conservatism, and the Dating of Old English Poetry." *ASE* 33 (2004): 23–50.

Cross, James E. *Cambridge Pembroke College MS 25: A Carolingian Sermonary Used by Anglo-Saxon Preachers*. King's College London Medieval Studies 1. Exeter: Short Run Press, 1987.

– "The Conception of the Old English Phoenix." *Old English Poetry: Fifteen Essays*, edited by Robert P. Creed, 129–52. Providence: Brown University Press, 1967.

– "Source and Analysis of Some Ælfrician Passages." *NM* 72 (1971): 446–53.

Cross, James E., and Thomas D. Hill, eds. *The Prose Solomon and Saturn and Adrian and Ritheus.* Toronto: University of Toronto Press, 1982.

Cubitt, Catherine. "Memory and Narrative in the Cult of Early Anglo-Saxon Saints." In *The Uses of the Past in the Early Middle Ages*, edited by Yitzhak Hen and Matthew Innes, 29–66. Cambridge: Cambridge University Press, 2000.

Curtius, Ernst Robert. *European Literature and the Latin Middle Ages.* Translated by Willard R. Trask. London: Routledge & Kegan Paul, 1953.

Damico, Helen. *Beowulf and the Grendel-kin: Politics and Poetry in Eleventh-Century England*. Morgantown: West Virginia University Press, 2015.

De Mause, Lloyd. "The Evolution of Parent-Child Relationships as a Factor in History." In *The History of Childhood*, edited by Lloyd de Mause, 1–71. New York: Psychohistory Press, 1974.

– ed. *The History of Childhood.* New York: Psychohistory Press, 1974.

de Muinck Keizer-Schrama, S.M.P.F., and D. Mul. "Trends in Pubertal Development in Europe." *Human Reproduction Update* 7 (2001): 287–91.

Deshman, Robert. *The Benedictional of Æthelwold.* Princeton, NJ: Princeton University Press, 1995.

Dickinson, Emily. "To Make a Prairie." In *The Poems of Emily Dickinson: Variorum Edition*, vol. 3, edited by Ralph W. Franklin, 1521. Cambridge, MA: Harvard University Press, 1999.

Dickinson, Tania. "Overview: Mortuary Ritual." In *The Oxford Handbook of Anglo-Saxon Archaeology*, edited by Helena Hamerow, David Hinton, and Sally Crawford, 221–37. Oxford: Oxford University Press, 2011.

Diekstra, Frans N.M. "The Physiologus, the Bestiaries and Medieval Animal Lore." *Neophilologus* 69 (1985): 142–55.

Dieterich, Albrecht. *Mutter Erde: Ein Versuch über Volksreligion.* 2nd ed. Leipzig and Berlin: Teubner, 1913.

DiNapoli, Robert. "Close to the Edge: *The Fortunes of Men* and the Limits of Wisdom Literature." In *Text and Transmission in Medieval Europe*, edited by Chris Bishop, 127–47. Newcastle: Cambridge Scholars, 2007.

Dobbie, Elliott van Kirk, ed. *The Anglo-Saxon Minor Poems.* Anglo-Saxon Poetic Records 6. New York: Columbia University Press, 1942.

Dockray-Miller, Mary. *Motherhood and Mothering in Anglo-Saxon England.* Basingstoke and London: MacMillan Press Ltd, 2000.

Drout, Michael D.C. "*The Fortunes of Men* 4a: Reasons for Adopting a Very Old Emendation." *Modern Philology* 96 (1998): 184–7.

Dumitrescu, Irina A. "Violence, Performance, and Pedagogy in Ælfric Bata's Colloquies." *Exemplaria* 23 (2011): 67–91.

Dümmler, Ernst, ed. *Alcuini carmina.* MGH, Poetae Latini Aevi Carolini 1. Berlin: Weidmann, 1880.

– ed. *Alcuini epistolae.* MGH, Epistulae 4. Berlin: Weidmann, 1888.

– ed. *Theodulfi carmina*. MGH, Poetae Latini Aevi Carolini 1. Berlin: Weidmann, 1881.

Dumville, David N. "The Anglian Collection of Royal Genealogies and Regnal Lists." *ASE* 5 (1976): 23–50.

– "The Ætheling: A Study in Anglo-Saxon Constitutional History." *ASE* 8 (1979): 1–33.

– "The Northumbrian Liber Vitae: London, British Library, MS. Cotton Domitian A.vii, Folios 15–24 & 25–45, the Original Text." In *Anglo-Saxon Essays, 2001–2007*, edited by David N. Dumville, 109–82. Aberdeen: Centre for Anglo-Saxon Studies, 2007.

Ehwald, Rudolf, ed. *Aldhelmi opera omnia.* MGH Auctores Antiquissimi 15. Berlin: Weidmann, 1919.

Eliason, Norman E. "Beowulf's Inglorious Youth." *Studies in Philology* 76 (1979): 101–8.

Elsakkers, Marianne. "The Early Medieval Latin and Vernacular Vocabulary of Abortion and Embryology." In *Science Translated: Latin and Vernacular Translations of Scientific Treatises in Medieval Europe*, edited by Michéle Goyens, Pieter De Leemans, and An Smets, 377–414. Leuven: Leuven University Press, 2008.

Fanger, Claire. "Miracle as Prophetic Gospel: Knowledge, Power and the Design of the Narrative in *Daniel*." *English Studies* 72 (1991): 123–35.

Farrell, R.T., ed. *Daniel and Azarias.* Methuen's Old English Library. London: Methuen; New York: Barnes & Noble, 1974.

Fehr, Bernhard, ed. *Die Hirtenbriefe Ælfrics.* Bibliothek der angelsächsischen Prosa 9. Hamburg, 1914. Reprinted with supplement by Peter Clemoes. Darmstadt: Wissenschaftliche Buchgesellschaft, 1966.

Fell, Christine E. "A 'friwif locbore' Revisited." *ASE* 13 (1984): 157–66.

– *Women in Anglo-Saxon England*. Bloomington: Indiana University Press, 1984.

Finnegan, Robert E. "The Old English *Daniel*: The King and His City." *NM* 85 (1984): 194–211.

Frank, Roberta. "The Unbearable Lightness of Being a Philologist." *JEGP* 96 (1997): 486–513.

Frantzen, Allen. *Food, Eating and Identity in Early Medieval England.* Woodbridge: Boydell, 2014.

Folkerts, Menso. *Die älteste mathematische Aufgabensammlung in lateinischer Sprache: Die Alcuin zugeschriebenen 'Propositiones ad acuendos iuvenes': Überlieferung, Inhalt, kritische Edition.* Österreichische Akademie der Wissenschaften, mathematisch-naturwissenschaftliche Klasse, Denkschriften 116.6. Vienna: Springer, 1978.

– "Die Alkuin zugeschriebenen *Propositiones ad acuendos iuvenes.*" In *Science in Western and Eastern Civilization in Carolingian Times*, edited by Paul Leo Butzer and Dietrich Lohrmann, 273–81. Basel: Birkhäuser, 1993.

Foot, Sarah. "The Making of the *Angelcynn*: English Identity before the Norman Conquest." *Transactions of the Royal Historical Society* 6 (1996): 25–49.

– *Monastic Life in Anglo-Saxon England, c. 600–900*. Cambridge: Cambridge University Press, 2006.

– "Reading Anglo-Saxon Charters: Memory, Record, or Story?" In *Narrative and History in the Early Medieval West*, edited by Elizabeth M. Tyler and Ross Balzaretti, 39–67. Turnhout: Brepols, 2006.

– *Veiled Women: Female Religious Communities in England, 871–1066.* 2 vols. Aldershot: Ashgate, 2000.

Forsyth, Ilene H. "Children in Early Medieval Art: Ninth through Twelfth Centuries." *Journal of Psychohistory* 4 (1976): 31–70.

Fowler, Roger. "A Late Old English Handbook for the Use of a Confessor." *Anglia* 83 (1965): 1–34.

– ed. *Wulfstan's Canons of Eadgar.* EETS os 266. London: Oxford University Press, 1972.

Friis-Jensen, Karsten, ed., and Peter Fisher, trans. *Saxo Grammaticus: Gesta Danorum: The History of the Danes*, 2 vols. Oxford: Oxford University Press, 2015.

Fulk, Robert D. *A History of Old English Meter*. Philadelphia: University of Pennsylvania Press, 1992.

Fulk, Robert D., and Joseph Harris. "Beowulf's Name." In *Beowulf: A Verse Translation*, translated by Seamus Heaney and edited by Daniel Donoghue, 98–100. New York: Norton, 2002.

Fulk, Robert D., and Christopher M. Cain. *A History of Old English Literature.* Malden, MA: Blackwell, 2003.

Fulk, Robert D., Robert E. Bjork, and John D. Niles, eds. *Klaeber's "Beowulf" and the Fight at Finnesburg.* 4th ed. Toronto: University of Toronto Press, 2008.

Galtung, Johan. "Struktur, Kultur und intellektueller Stil. Ein vergleichender Essay über sachsonische, teutonische, gallische und nipponische Wissenschaft." In *Das Fremde und das Eigene. Prolegomena zu einer interkulturellen Germanistik*, edited by Alois Wierlacher, 151–96. Munich: Iudicium, 1985.

Gameson, Richard. *The Earliest Books of Canterbury Cathedral: Manuscripts and Fragments to c. 1200.* London: The Bibliographical Society, 2008.

– "The Origin of the Exeter Book of Old English Poetry." *ASE* 25 (1996): 135–85.

Garmonsway, George N., ed. *Ælfric's Colloquy*. Rev. ed. Exeter: University of Exeter Press, 1978.

Garmonsway, George N., and Jacqueline Simpson, trans., with notes by Hilda E. Davidson. *"Beowulf" and Its Analogues.* London: Dent, 1968.

Garrison, Mary. "An Aspect of Alcuin: 'Tuus Albinus': Peevish Egotist or Parrhesiast?" In *Ego Trouble: Authors and Their Identities in the Early Middle Ages*, edited by Richard Corradini, Rosamond McKitterick, Matthew Brian Gillis, and Irene van Renswoude, 137–51. Vienna: Verlag der Österreichischen Akademie der Wissenschaften, 2010.

– "The Emergence of Carolingian Latin Literature and the Court of Charlemagne (780–814)." In *Carolingian Culture: Emulation and Innovation*, edited by Rosamond McKitterick, 111–40. Cambridge: Cambridge University Press, 1994.

– "The English and the Irish at the Court of Charlemagne." In *Charlemagne and his Heritage: 1200 Years of Civilization and Science in Europe*, vol. 1, edited by Paul Leo Butzer, Max Kerner, and Walter Oberschelp, 97–123. Turnhout: Brepols, 1997.

– "The Library of Alcuin's York." In *The Cambridge History of the Book in Britain. Volume 1: c.400–1100*, edited by Richard Gameson, 633–64. Cambridge: Cambridge University Press, 2012.

– "The Social World of Alcuin: Nicknames at York and at the Carolingian Court." In *Alcuin of York: Scholar at the Carolingian Court*, Germania Latina III, edited by Luuk Houwen and Alasdair MacDonald, 59–79. Groningen: Egbert Forsten, 1998.

Gavin, Adrienne E. *The Child in British Literature: Literary Constructions of Childhood, Medieval to Contemporary.* New York: Palgrave Macmillan, 2012.

Geake, Helen. *The Use of Grave Goods in Conversion-Period England, c. 600–850.* BAR British Series 261. Oxford: Archaeopress, 1997.

Geary, Patrick. "Ethnic Identity as a Situational Construct in the Early Middle Ages." *Mitteilungen der anthropologischen Gesellschaft in Wien* 113 (1983): 15–26.

Gilchrist, Roberta. "Archaeological Biographies: Realizing Human Lifecycles, Courses and Histories." *World Archaeology* 31 (2000): 325–28.

Gneuss, Helmut. *Handlist of Anglo-Saxon Manuscripts: A List of Manuscripts and Manuscript Fragments Written or Owned in England up to 1100.* Tempe, AZ: ACMRS Press, 2001.

– "The Old English Language." In *The Cambridge Companion to Old English Literature*, 2nd ed., edited by Malcolm Godden and Michael Lapidge, 19–49. Cambridge: Cambridge University Press, 2013.

– "Origin and Provenance of Anglo-Saxon Manuscripts: The Case of Cotton Tiberius A.III." In *Of the Making of Books. Medieval Manuscripts, Their Scribes and Readers: Essays Presented to M.B. Parkes*, edited by Pamela Robinson and Rivkah Zim, 13–48. Aldershot: Ashgate, 1997.

Gneuss, Helmut, and Michael Lapidge. *Anglo-Saxon Manuscripts: A Bibliographical Handlist of Manuscripts and Manuscript Fragments Written or Owned in England up to 1100.* Toronto Anglo-Saxon Series. Toronto: University of Toronto Press, 2015.

Godden, Malcolm, ed. *Ælfric's Catholic Homilies: Introduction, Commentary and Glossary.* EETS ss 18. Oxford: Oxford University Press, 2000.

– *Ælfric's Catholic Homilies: The Second Series Text.* EETS ss 5. London: Oxford University Press, 1979.

– "Biblical Literature: The Old Testament." In *The Cambridge Companion to Old English Literature*, edited by Malcolm Godden and Michael Lapidge, 206–26. Cambridge: Cambridge University Press, 1991.

– "The Player King: Identification and Self-representation in King Alfred's Writings." In *Alfred the Great: Papers from the Eleventh-Centenary Conferences*, edited by Timothy Reuter, 137–50. Aldershot: Ashgate, 2003.

– "The Sources of Ælfric Lives 17 (On Auguries) (Cameron C.B.1.3.18)." *Fontes Anglo-Saxonici: World Wide Web Register.* http://fontes.english.ox.ac.uk/, accessed July 2016.

– "Stories from the Court of King Alfred." In *Saints and Scholars: New Perspectives on Anglo-Saxon Literature and Culture in Honour of Hugh Magennis*, edited by Stuart McWilliams, 123–40. Cambridge: D.S. Brewer, 2012.

Godden, Malcolm, and Susan Irvine, eds. *The Old English Boethius: An Edition of the Old English Versions of Boethius's* De consolatione Philosophiae, with a chapter on the Metres by Mark Griffith and contributions by Rohini Jayatilaka. 2 vols. Oxford: Oxford University Press, 2009.

Goolden, Peter, ed. *The Old English* Apollonius of Tyre. London: Oxford University Press, 1958.

Gowland, Rebecca. "Ageing the Past: Examining Age Identity from Funerary Evidence." In *Social Archaeology of Funerary Remains*, edited by Rebecca Gowland and Christopher Knuesel, 143–55. Oxford: Oxbow, 2006.

Greenfield, Stanley B., and Daniel G. Calder. *A New Critical History of Old English Literature.* With a Survey of the Anglo-Latin Background by Michael Lapidge. New York: New York University Press, 1986.

Greenleaf, Barbara. *Children through the Ages: A History of Childhood.* New York: Barnes & Noble Books, 1978.

Grocock, Christopher, and Ian N. Wood, eds. *Abbots of Wearmouth and Jarrow.* Oxford: Oxford University Press, 2013.

Gropp, Harald. "*Propositio de lupo et capra et fasciculo cauli* – On the History of River-Crossing Problems." In *Charlemagne and His Heritage: 1200 Years of Civilization and Science in Europe: Karl der Grosse und sein Nachwirken: 1200 Jahre Kultur und Wissenschaft in Europa*, vol. 2: *Mathematical Arts*, edited by P. Butzer et al., 31–41. Turnhout: Brepols, 1998.

Groves, Sara, Charlotte Roberts, Sam Lucy, Graham Pearson, Darren Gröcke, Geoff Nowell, Colin Macpherson, and Graeme Young. "Mobility Histories of 7th–9th Century AD People Buried at Early Medieval Bamburgh, Northumberland, England." *American Journal of Physical Anthropology* 151 (2013): 462–76.

Guenther Discenza, Nicole. *The King's English: Strategies of Translation in the Old English* Boethius. Albany: State University of New York Press, 2005.

– "The Old English Boethius." In *A Companion to Alfred the Great*, edited by Nicole Guenther Discenza and Paul E. Szarmach, 200–26. Leiden and Boston: Brill, 2015.

Gundry-Volf, Judith M. "The Least and the Greatest." In *The Child in Christian Thought*, edited by Marcia J. Bunge, 29–60. Cambridge: W.B. Eerdmans, 2001.

Guðnason, Bjarni. *Um Skjöldungasögu.* Reykjavík: Menningarsjóður, 1963.

– ed. *Danakonunga Sögur: Skjǫldunga saga, Knýtlinga saga, ágrip af sǫgu Danakonunga.* Íslenzk fornrit 35. Reykjavík: Hið Íslenzka Fornritafélag, 1982.

Gwara, Scott. "Anglo-Saxon Schoolbooks." In *The Cambridge History of the Book in Britain*, edited by Richard Gameson, 507–25. Cambridge: Cambridge University Press, 2012.

– *Heroic Identity in the World of "Beowulf."* Medieval and Renaissance Authors and Texts 2. Leiden: Brill, 2008.

– "Manuscripts of Aldhelm's *Prosa de virginitate* and the Rise of Hermeneutic Literacy in Tenth-Century England." *Studi Medievali* 35 (1994): 101–59.

Haddan, A.W., and W. Stubbs, eds. *Councils and Ecclesiastical Documents Relating to Great Britain and Ireland.* 3 vols. Oxford: Clarendon Press, 1869–78.

Hadley, Dawn, and Hemer, Katie. "Introduction: Archaeological Approaches to Medieval Childhood, c. 500–1500." In *Medieval Childhood: Archaeological Approaches*, Childhood in the Past Monograph Series 3, edited by Dawn Hadley and Katie Hemer, 1–25. Oxford: Oxbow, 2014.

– "Microcosms of Migration: Children and Early Medieval Population Movement." *Childhood in the Past* 4 (2011): 63–78.

Hadley, John, and David Singmaster. "Problems to Sharpen the Young: An Annotated Translation of *Propositiones ad acuendos iuvenes,* the Oldest Mathematical Problem Collection in Latin, Attributed to Alcuin of York." *Mathematical Gazette* 76 (1992): 102–26.

Hall, Mark. "'Merely Players'? Playtime, Material Culture and Medieval Childhood." In *Medieval Childhood: Archaeological Approaches*, Childhood in the Past Monograph Series 3, edited by Dawn Hadley and Katie Hemer, 39–56. Oxford: Oxbow, 2014.

Hanawalt, Barbara A. "Medievalists and the Study of Childhood." *Speculum* 77 (2002): 440–60.

– *The Ties that Bound: Peasant Families in Medieval England.* Oxford: Oxford University Press, 1986.

Hansen, Elaine Tuttle. *The Solomon Complex: Reading Wisdom in Old English Poetry.* Toronto: University of Toronto Press, 1988.

Harbus, Antonina. "Nebuchadnezzar's Dreams in the Old English *Daniel.*" *English Studies* 75 (1994): 489–508.

Härke, Heinrich. "Early Anglo-Saxon Social Structure." In *The Anglo-Saxons from the Migration to the Eighth Century*, edited by John Hines, 125–60. Woodbridge: Boydell, 1997.

– "'Warrior Graves'?: The Background of the Anglo-Saxon Weapon Burial Rite." *Past & Present* 126 (1990): 22–43.

Harris, Stephen. *Race and Ethnicity in Anglo-Saxon Literature.* Medieval History and Culture 24. New York: Routledge, 2003.

Hatcher, John. *Plague, Population and the English Economy 1348–1530.* Studies in Economic and Social History. London and Basingstoke: Macmillan Press, 1977.

Hecht, Hans, ed. *Bischofs Waerferth von Worcester Übersetzung der Dialoge Gregors des Grossen.* Bibliothek der angelsächsischen Prosa 5. Leipzig: Wigand, 1900.

Herlihy, David. In *Essays on Medieval Civilization*, edited by Richard E. Sullivan, Bede K. Lackner, and Kenneth R. Philip, 109–41. Austin: University of Texas Press, 1978.

– *Medieval Households.* Cambridge, MA: Harvard University Press, 1985.

Hill, John M. "*Beowulf* and the Danish Succession: Gift Giving as an Occasion for Complex Gesture." *Medievalia et Humanistica* 11 (1982): 177–97.

– *The Cultural World in "Beowulf."* Anthropological Horizons 6. Toronto: University of Toronto Press, 1995.

Hill, Joyce. "Authorial Adaptation: Ælfric, Wulfstan and the Pastoral Letters." In *Text and Language in Medieval English Prose: A Festschrift for Tadao Kubouchi*, edited by Akio Oizumi, Jacek Fisiak and John Scahill, 63–76. Frankfurt: Peter Lang, 2005.

– "The Benedictine Reform and Beyond." In *A Companion to Anglo-Saxon Literature*, edited by Phillip Pulsiano and Elaine Treharne, 154–61. Malden: Blackwell, 2008.

Hill, Thomas D. "Hæthcyn, Herebeald, and Archery's Laws: *Beowulf* and the *Leges Henrici Primi.*" *Medium Ævum* 81 (2012): 210–21.

Hines, John. "The Becoming of the English: Identity, Material Culture, and Language in Early Anglo-Saxon England." *Anglo-Saxon Studies in Archaeology and History* 7 (1994): 49–59.

– "The *Benedicite* Canticle in Old English Verse: An Early Runic Witness from Southern Lincolnshire." *Anglia* 133 (2015): 257–77.

– *The Scandinavian Character of Anglian England.* Oxford: British Archaeological Reports, 1984.

Hollis, Stephanie. *Anglo-Saxon Women and the Church: Sharing a Common Fate.* Woodbridge: Boydell, 1992.

– "*Beowulf* and the Succession." *Parergon* n.s. 1 (1983): 39–54.

Holthausen, Ferdinand. *Altenglisches etymologisches Wörterbuch.* 2nd ed. Heidelberg: Winter, 1963.

Honegger, Thomas, ed. *Riddles, Knights, and Cross-Dressing Saints: Essays on Medieval English Language and Literature.* Bern; New York: Peter Lang, 2004.

Hough, Carole A. "The Early Kentish 'Divorce Laws': A Reconsideration of Aethelberht, Chs. 79 and 80." *ASE* 23 (1994): 19–34.

– "Towards an Explanation of Phonetic Differentiation in Masculine and Feminine Personal Names." *Journal of Linguistics* 36 (2000): 1–11.

– "Two Kentish Laws Concerning Women: A New Reading of Æthelberht 73 and 74." *Anglia* 119 (2001): 554–78.

– "The Widow's 'Mund' in Æthelberht 75 and 76." *JEGP* 98 (1999): 1–16.

– "Women and the Law in Seventh-Century England." *Nottingham Medieval Studies* 51 (2007): 207–30.

Howe, Nicholas. "Fabling Beasts: Traces in Memory." *Social Research* 62 (1995): 641–59.

– *The Old English Catalogue Poems.* Anglistica 23. Copenhagen: Rosenkilde and Bagger, 1985.

Howell, Wilbur Samuel, ed. and trans. *The Rhetoric of Alcuin and Charlemagne: a Translation, with an Introduction, the Latin Text, and Notes.* New York: Russell and Russell, 1965.

Hull, Bradley, and Tamsin O'Connell. "Diet: Recent Evidence from Analytical Chemical Techniques." In *The Oxford Handbook of Anglo-Saxon Archaeology*, edited by Helena Hamerow, David Hinton, and Sally Crawford, 667–87. Oxford: Oxford University Press, 2011.

Hutcheson, Bellenden R. *Old English Poetic Metre*. Cambridge: D.S. Brewer, 1995.

Hyams, Paul R. "The Charter as a Source for the Early Common Law." *Journal of Legal History* 12 (December 1991): 173–89.

Insley, John. "Pre-Conquest Personal Names." *Reallexikon der germanischen Altertumskunde* 23 (2003): 367–96.

Insley, John, and David Rollason, with P. McClure. "English Dithematic Names." In *The Durham Liber Vitae: London, British Library, MS Cotton Domitian A.VII*, vol II, edited by David Rollason and Lynda Rollason, 81–165. London: British Library, 2007.

Irvine, Susan. "Rewriting Women in the Old English *Boethius.*" In *New Windows on a Woman's World: Essays for Jocelyn Harris*, 2 vols., Otago Studies in English 9, edited by Colin Gibson and Lisa Marr, 2:488–501. Department of English: University of Otago, 2005.

– "The Protean Form of the Old English *Boethius.*" In *The Legacy of Boethius in Medieval England*, edited by Joey McMullen and Erica Weaver. Tempe, AZ: ACMRS, forthcoming.

Irvine, Susan, and Malcolm R. Godden, eds. *The Old English Boethius with Verse Prologues and Epilogues Associated with King Alfred.* Dumbarton Oaks Medieval Library. Cambridge, MA: Harvard University Press, 2012.

Isaacs, Neil D. "Up a Tree: To See the Fates of Men." In *Anglo-Saxon Poetry: Essays in Appreciation for John C. McGalliard*, edited by Lewis E. Nicholson and Dolores Warwick Frese, 363–75. Notre Dame, IN: University of Notre Dame Press, 1975.

Isidore. *Isidori hispalensis episcopi Etymologiarum sive Originum libri XX.* Edited by Wallace M. Lindsay. 2 vols. Oxford: Clarendon Press, 1911.

Jackson, Peter, and Michael Lapidge. "The Contents of the Cotton-Corpus Legendary." In *Holy Men and Holy Women: Old English Prose Saints' Lives and Their Contexts*, edited by Paul E. Szarmach, 131–46. Albany: State University of New York Press, 1996.

Jacob, Marni L., and Eric A. Storch. "Postpartum Anxiety Disorders." *Asian Pacific Journal of Reproduction* 2 (2013): 63–8.

James, Edward. "Childhood and Youth in the Early Middle Ages." In *Youth in the Middle Ages*, edited by Peter J.P. Goldberg and Felicity Riddy, 11–24. York: York Medieval Press, 2004.

Johnson, David F., and Winfried Rudolf. "More Notes by Coleman." *Medium Ævum* 79 (2010): 113–25.

Johnston, George, trans. *The Schemers and Víga-Glúm: Bandamanna saga & Víga-Glúms saga.* Erin, ON: The Porcupine's Quill, 1999.

Jónsson, Finnur, ed. *Hrólfs saga Kraka og Bjarkarímur.* Samfund til udgivelse af gammel nordisk litteratur 35. Copenhagen: Møller, 1904.

Jónsson, Guðni, and Bjarni Vilhjálmsson, eds. *Fornaldarsögur Norðurlanda.* 3 vols. Reykjavík: Bókaútg. Forni, 1944.

Jost, David A. "Biblical Sources of Old English Daniel 1–78." *English Language Notes* 15 (1978): 257–63.

Jullien, Marie-Hélène, and Françoise Perelman. *Clavis des auteurs latins du moyen âge (territoire français, 735–987). II. Alcuin.* Turnhout: Brepols, 1999.

Jurasinski, Stefan. "Caring for the Dead in *The Fortunes of Men.*" *Philological Quarterly* 86 (2007): 343–63.

– "Madness and Responsibility in Anglo-Saxon England." In *Peace and Protection in the Middle Ages*, edited by Thomas B. Lambert and David Rollason, 99–120. Toronto: Pontifical Institute of Mediaeval Studies, 2009.

Kamp, Kathryn. "Where Have All the Children Gone? The Archaeology of Childhood." *Journal of the History of Childhood and Youth* 3 (2001): 1–34.

Kendall, Calvin B. "Bede and Education." In *The Cambridge Companion to Bede*, edited by Scott DeGregorio, 99–112. Cambridge: Cambridge University Press, 2010.

Ker, Neil R. *A Catalogue of Manuscripts Containing Anglo-Saxon.* Oxford: Clarendon Press, 1957.

Keynes, Simon. "The Fonthill Letter." In *Words, Texts, and Manuscripts: Studies in Anglo-Saxon Culture Presented to Helmut Gneuss on the Occasion of His Sixty-Fifth Birthday*, edited by Michael Korhammer with Karl Reichl and Hans Sauer, 53–97. New York: D.S. Brewer, 1992.

Keynes, Simon, and Michael Lapidge, eds. *Alfred the Great: Asser's* Life of King Alfred *and Other Contemporary Sources.* Harmondsworth: Penguin, 1983.

Kirby, David P. "Bede, Eddius Stephanus and the 'Life of Wilfrid'." *English Historical Review* 98 (1983): 101–14.

– "The Genesis of a Cult: Cuthbert of Farne and Ecclesiastical Politics in Northumbria in the Late Seventh and Early Eighth Centuries." *Journal of Ecclesiastical History* 46 (1995): 383–97.

Klinck, Anne L. "Anglo-Saxon Women and the Law." *Journal of Medieval History* 8 (1982): 107–21.

– "'To Have and to Hold': The Bridewealth of Wives and the *Mund* of Widows in Anglo-Saxon England." *Nottingham Medieval Studies* 51 (2007): 231–45.

– ed. *The Old English Elegies: A Critical Edition and Genre Study.* Montreal: McGill-Queen's University Press, 1992.

Kline, Daniel T. Review of *Childhood in the Middle Ages and the Renaissance: The Results of a Paradigm Shift in the History of Mentality*, edited by Albrecht Classen. H-Childhood, H-Net Reviews. October, 2008.

Krapp, George Philip, ed. *The Junius Manuscript.* Anglo-Saxon Poetic Records 1. New York: Columbia University Press, 1931.

Krapp, George Philip, and Elliott van Kirk Dobbie, eds. *The Exeter Book.* Anglo-Saxon Poetic Records 3. New York: Columbia University Press, 1936.

Krugman, Scott D. "Parent-Infant Bedsharing Is Not Recommended." *JAMA Pediatrics* 168 (2014): 386–7.

Kuefler, Mathew. "'A Wryed Existence': Attitudes toward Children in Anglo-Saxon England." *Journal of Social History* 24 (1991): 823–34.

Kuehn, Thomas. *Law, Family, and Women: Toward a Legal Anthropology of Renaissance Italy*. Chicago: University of Chicago Press, 1991.

Kuhn, Sherman, ed. *The Vespasian Psalter.* Ann Arbor: University of Michigan Press, 1965.

Lapidge, Michael. *The Anglo-Saxon Library*. Oxford: Oxford University Press, 2005.

– "The Archetype of *Beowulf.*" *ASE* 29 (2000): 5–41.

– "The Career of Aldhelm." *ASE 36* (2007): 15–69.

– ed. and trans. *Byrhtferth of Ramsey: The Lives of St Oswald and St Ecgwine.* Oxford: Clarendon Press, 2009.

Lapidge, Michael, and Michael Herren, trans. *Aldhelm: The Prose Works.* Cambridge: D.S. Brewer, 1979.

Lapidge, Michael, and James L. Rosier, trans. *Aldhelm: The Poetic Works.* Cambridge: D.S. Brewer, 1985.

Lapidge, Michael, and Michael Winterbottom, eds. *Wulfstan of Winchester: The Life of St Æthelwold.* Oxford: Clarendon Press, 1991.

Larrington, Carolyne. *A Store of Common Sense: Gnomic Theme and Style in Old Icelandic and Old English Wisdom Poetry.* Oxford: Clarendon Press, 1993.

Lawrence, William W. *"Beowulf" and the Epic Tradition.* Harvard, 1928. Reprinted New York: Hafner, 1961.

Leary, Timothy J., ed. and trans. *Symphosius, The "Aenigmata:" An Introduction, Text, and Commentary.* London: Bloomsbury, 2014.

Lee, Christina. *Feasting the Dead: Food and Drink in Anglo-Saxon Burial Rituals.* Woodbridge: Boydell, 2007.

Lees, Clare. "The 'Sunday Letter' and the 'Sunday Lists'." *ASE* 14 (1985): 129–51.

Lees, Clare, and Gillian R. Overing. *Double Agents: Women and Clerical Culture in Anglo-Saxon England.* Philadelphia: University of Pennsylvania Press, 2001.

Lemke, Andreas. "*Puer* and *pueritia* in Bede's *Historia ecclesiastica gentis Anglorum.*" *JML* 24 (2014): 153–69.

Lerer, Seth. *Children's Literature: A Reader's History, from Aesop to Harry Potter.* Chicago: University of Chicago Press, 2008.

– *Literacy and Power in Anglo-Saxon Literature.* Lincoln: University of Nebraska Press, 1991.

Lewis, Carenza. "Children's Play in the Later Medieval English Countryside." *Childhood in the Past* 2 (2009): 86–108.

Lewis, Charlton T., and Charles Short. *A Latin Dictionary.* Oxford: Clarendon Press, 1879.

Lewis, Mary. *The Bioarchaeology of Children: Perspectives from Biological and Forensic Anthropology.* Cambridge: Cambridge University Press, 2007.

Liebermann, Felix, ed. *Die Gesetze der Angelsachsen.* 3 vols. Halle: Niemeyer, 1903.

Lieberson, Stanley. "What's in a Name? ... Some Sociolinguistic Possibilities." *International Journal of the Society of Language* 45 (1984): 77–88.

Lieberson, Stanley, and Eleanor O. Bell. "Children's First Names: An Empirical Study of Social Taste." *American Journal of Sociology* 98 (1992): 511–54.

Lieberson, Stanley, Susan Dumais, and Shyon Baumann. "The Instability of Androgynous Names: The Symbolic Maintenance of Gender Boundaries." *American Journal of Sociology* 105 (2000): 1249–87.

Lillehammer, Grete. "A Child Is Born: The Child's World in an Archaeological Perspective." *Norwegian Archaeological Review* 22 (1989): 91–105.

Liuzza, Roy M., ed. *Anglo-Saxon Prognostics: An Edition and Translation of Texts from London, British Library, MS Cotton Tiberius A.iii.* Cambridge: D.S. Brewer, 2011.

Lockett, Leslie, "An Integrated Re-examination of the Dating of Oxford, Bodleian Library, Junius 11." *ASE* 31 (2002): 141–73.

Love, Rosalind C., ed. and trans. *Three Eleventh-Century Anglo-Latin Saints' Lives: Vita S. Birini, Vita et miracula S. Kenelmi and Vita S. Rumwoldi.* Oxford: Clarendon Press, 1996.

– ed. and trans. *Goscelin of Saint-Bertin: The Hagiography of the Female Saints of Ely.* Oxford: Clarendon Press, 2004.

Lucy, Sam. "Gender and Gender Roles." In *The Oxford Handbook of Anglo-Saxon Archaeology*, edited by Helena Hamerow, David Hinton, and Sally Crawford, 688–703. Oxford: Oxford University Press, 2011.

Lucy, Sam, Richard Newman, Natasha Dodwell, and Catherine Hills. "Burial of a Princess? The Anglo-Saxon Cemetery at Westfield Farm, Ely." *Antiquaries Journal* 89 (2009): 81–141.

Lynch, Joseph H. *Christianizing Kinship: Ritual Sponsorship in Anglo-Saxon England.* Ithaca, NY: Cornell University Press, 1998.

– *Godparents and Kinship in Early Medieval Europe*. Princeton, NJ: Princeton University Press, 1986.

Maass, Ernest. "Integration and Name Changing among Jewish Refugees from Central Europe in the United States." *Names* 6 (1958): 129–71.

Mackie, William S. *The Exeter Book: Part II: Poems IX–XXXII.* EETS, os 194. London: Trübner 1934.

Magennis, Hugh. *Images of Community in Old English Poetry.* Cambridge: Cambridge University Press, 1996.

Maitland, Frederic W. *Domesday Book and Beyond*. Cambridge: Cambridge University Press, 1897. Reprinted 1907.

Malone, Kemp. *The Literary History of Hamlet*. Heidelberg: Winter, 1923.

Marafioti, Nicole. "Seeking Alfred's Body: Royal Tomb as Political Object in the Reign of Edward the Elder." *Early Medieval Europe* 23 (2015): 202–28.

Matter, E. Ann. "Alcuin's Question-and-Answer Texts." *Rivista di storia della filosofia* 4 (1990): 645–56.

Maund, Karen L. "'A Turmoil of Warring Princes': Political Leadership in Ninth-Century Denmark." *Haskins Society Journal* 6 (1994): 29–47.

McCulloch, John M. "Jewish Ritual Murder: William of Norwich, Thomas of Monmouth, and the Early Dissemination of the Myth." *Speculum* 72 (1997): 698–740.

McLaughlin, Mary Martin. "Survivors and Surrogates; Children and Parents from the 9th to the 13th Centuries." In *The History of Childhood*, edited by Lloyd de Mause, 101–82. New York: Psychohistory Press, 1974. Reprinted in *Medieval Families: Perspectives on Marriage, Household, and Children*, edited by Carol Neel, 20–124. Toronto: University of Toronto Press, 2004.

McLeod, Neil, ed. *Early Irish Contract Law*. Sydney: University of Sydney Press, 1992.

McNamara, Jo Ann, and Suzanne Wemple. "The Power of Women through the Family in Medieval Europe, 500–1100." In *Women and Power in Medieval Europe*, edited by Mary Erler and Maryanne Kowaleski, 83–102. Athens: University of Georgia Press, 1988.

Meens, Rob. "Children and Confession in the Early Middle Ages." In *The Church and Childhood*, edited by Diane Wood. Studies in Church History, 53–65. Oxford: Blackwell, 1994.

Meyer, Marc A. "Early Anglo-Saxon Penitentials and the Position of Women." *Haskins Society Journal* 2 (1990): 47–61.

– "Land Charters and the Legal Position of Anglo-Saxon Women." In *The Women of England from Anglo-Saxon Times to the Present*, edited by Barbara Kanner, 57–82. Hamden, CT: Archon Books, 1979.

– "The Queen's 'Demesne' in Later Anglo-Saxon England." In *The Culture of Christendom: Essays in Medieval History in Commemoration of Denis L.T. Bethell*, ed. Marc A. Meyer, 75–113. London: Hambledon and London, 1993.

– "Women and the Tenth Century English Monastic Reform." *Revue Bénédictine* 87 (1977): 34–61.

Millekin, William, and Char Meredith. *Tough Love.* Old Tappan, NJ: Revell Press, 1968.

Miller, Edward, and John Hatcher. *Medieval England: Rural Society and Economic Change 1086–1348*. Social and Economic History of England. London and New York: Longman, 1978.

Miller, Thomas, ed. *The Old English Version of Bede's Ecclesiastical History of the English People*. EETS os 95. London, 1890–8. Reprinted London: Oxford University Press, 1959.

Mitchell, Bruce. "Literary Lapses: Six Notes on *Beowulf* and Its Critics." *RES* 43 (1992): 1–17.

– Review of *A Reading of "Beowulf,"* by Edward B. Irving Jr. *RES* 20 (1969), 202–4.

– Review of *The Guest-Hall of Eden. Four Essays on the Design of Old English Poetry*, by Alvin A. Lee. *RES* 24 (1973), 195–6.

– Review of *The Structure of "Beowulf,"* by Kenneth Sisam. *RES* 17 (1966), 190–1.

Mitchell, Bruce, and Fred C. Robinson, eds. *Beowulf: An Edition with Relevant Shorter Texts.* Oxford: Blackwell, 1998.

Mize, Britt. *Traditional Subjectivities: The Old English Poetics of Mentality.* Toronto: University of Toronto Press, 2013.

Momma, Haruko. "The Education of Beowulf and the Affair of the Leisure Class." In *Verbal Encounters: Anglo-Saxon and Old Norse Studies for Roberta Frank*, edited by Antonia Harbus and Russell Poole, 163–82. Toronto: University of Toronto Press, 2005.

Morgan, Gerald. “The Treachery of Hrothulf.” *English Studies* 53 (1972): 23–39.
Muir, Bernard J. *The Exeter Anthology of Old English Poetry.* 2 vols., 2nd rev. ed. Exeter: Exeter University Press, 2000.
Müller, Rudolf. *Untersuchungen über die Namen des nordhumbrischen Liber Vitae.* Berlin: Mayer & Müller, 1901.
Mumby, Julie. “The Descent of Family Land in Later Anglo-Saxon England.” *Historical Research* 84 (2011): 399–415.
Murphy, Patrick J. *Unriddling the Exeter Riddles.* University Park: Pennsylvania State University Press, 2011.
Murphy, Roland E. “The Proverbs” and “Wisdom.” In *Harper's Bible Dictionary*, edited by Paul J. Achtemeier, 1135–6. New York: Harper Collins, 1985.
– *The Tree of Life. An Exploration of Biblical Wisdom Literature.* New York: Doubleday, 1996.
– “Wisdom Literature and Biblical Theology.” *Biblical Theology Bulletin* 24 (1994): 4–7.
Napier, Arthur S., ed. “Ein altenglisches Leben des heiligen Chad.” *Anglia* 10 (1888): 131–56.
– *Wulfstan: Sammlung der ihm zugeschriebenen Homilien nebst Untersuchungen über ihre Echtheit.* Dublin, 1883. Reprinted with a bibliographical supplement by K. Ostheeren. Dublin. Weidmann, 1967.
Neckel, Gustav, ed. *Edda: Die Lieder des Codex Regius nebst einigen verwandten Denkmälern.* 2 vols. Heidelberg: Winter, 1914.
Neidorf, Leonard. “Beowulf before *Beowulf*: Anglo-Saxon Anthroponymy and Heroic Legend.” *RES* 64 (2013): 553–73.
– “The Dating of *Widsið* and the Study of Germanic Antiquity.” *Neophilologus* 97 (2013): 165–83.
– “Lexical Evidence for the Relative Chronology of Old English Poetry.” *SELIM* 20 (2013): 7–48.
– “Germanic Legend, Scribal Errors, and Cultural Change.” In *The Dating of “Beowulf”: A Reassessment*, edited by Leonard Neidorf, 37–57. Cambridge: D.S. Brewer, 2014.
– “Philology, Allegory, and the Dating of *Beowulf*.” *Studia Neophilologica* 88 (2016): 97–115.
– “On the Epistemology of Old English Scholarship.” *Neophilologus* 99 (2015): 631–46.
– “Scribal Errors of Proper Names in the *Beowulf* Manuscript.” *ASE* 42 (2013): 249–69.
Neidorf, Leonard, and Rafael J. Pascual. “The Language of *Beowulf* and the Conditioning of Kaluza's Law.” *Neophilologus* 98 (2014): 657–73.

Nelson, Janet. "Parents, Children, and the Church in the Earlier Middle Ages (Presidential Address)." In *The Church and Childhood: Papers Read at the 1993 Summer Meeting and the 1994 Winter Meeting of the Ecclesiastical History Society*, edited by Diana Wood, 81–114. Oxford: Blackwell, 1994.

– "The Wary Widow." In *Property and Power in the Early Middle Ages*, edited by Wendy Davies and Paul Fouracre, 82–113. Cambridge: Cambridge University Press, 1995.

Nelson, Marie. "Old English Riddle 15: The 'Badger': An Early Example of Mock Heroic." *Neophilologus* 59 (1975): 447–50.

Neville, Jennifer. "Fostering the Cuckoo: Exeter Book Riddle 9." *RES* 58 (2007): 431–46.

– *Representations of the Natural World in Old English Poetry.* Cambridge; New York: Cambridge University Press, 1999.

The New English Bible. 2nd ed. Oxford: Oxford University Press, 1970.

Newton, Sam. *The Origins of "Beowulf" and the Pre-Viking Kingdom of East Anglia*. Cambridge: D.S. Brewer, 1993.

Ni Chonaill, Bronagh. "Child-Centred Law in Medieval Ireland." In *The Empty Throne: Childhood and the Crisis of Modernity*, edited by R. Davis and T. Dunne. Cambridge: Cambridge University Press, forthcoming.

Niermeyer, Jan Frederik, Co van de Kieft, and Jan W.J. Burgers, eds. *Mediae Latinitatis lexicon minus*. 2 vols. Leiden: Brill, 2002.

North, Richard. "Gold and the Heathen Polity in *Beowulf*." Forthcoming.

– *Heathen Gods in Old English Literature*. Cambridge Studies in Anglo-Saxon England 22. Cambridge: Cambridge University Press, 1997.

– *The Origins of "Beowulf": From Vergil to Wiglaf.* Oxford: Oxford University Press, 2006.

– "Tribal Loyalties in the *Finnsburh Fragment* and Episode." *Leeds Studies in English*, N.S. 21 (1990): 13–43.

O'Brien O'Keeffe, Katherine. *Stealing Obedience: Narratives of Agency and Identity in Later Anglo-Saxon England.* Toronto: University of Toronto Press, 2012.

Oliver, Lisi. *The Beginnings of English Law*. Toronto: University of Toronto Press, 2002.

Orchard, Andy. *A Critical Companion to "Beowulf."* Cambridge: D.S. Brewer, 2003.

– "Enigma Variations: The Anglo-Saxon Riddle Tradition." In *Latin Learning and English Lore: Studies in Anglo-Saxon Literature for Michael Lapidge*, 2 vols., edited by Katherine O'Brien O'Keeffe and Andy Orchard, 1:284–304. Toronto: University of Toronto Press, 2005.

– "Reconstructing 'The Ruin'." In *(Inter)Texts: Studies in Early Insular Culture Presented to Paul E. Szarmach*, edited by Helene Scheck and Virginia Blanton, 47–70. Tempe, AZ: MRTS, 2008.
– "Wish You Were Here: Alcuin's Courtly Verse and the Boys Back Home." In *Courts and Regions in Medieval Europe*, edited by Sarah Rees Jones, Richard Marks, and Alastair J. Minnis, 21–43. Woodbridge: York Medieval Press, 2000.
– ed. and trans. *The Anglo-Saxon Riddle Tradition.* Dumbarton Oaks Medieval Library. Cambridge, MA: Harvard University Press, forthcoming.
– *The Anglo-Saxon Riddle Tradition: Notes and Commentary.* Dumbarton Oaks Medieval Library Commentary Series. Washington, DC: Dumbarton Oaks, forthcoming.
Orme, Nicholas. *Medieval Children.* New Haven, CT: Yale University Press, 2001.
Overing, Gillian R. *Language, Sign and Gender in "Beowulf."* Carbondale: Southern Illinois University Press, 1990.
– "Nebuchadnezzar's Conversion in the Old English *Daniel*: A Psychological Portrait." *Papers on Language and Literature* 20 (1984): 3–14.
Pálsson, Hermann, and Paul Edwards, trans. *Seven Viking Romances.* Harmondsworth: Penguin, 1985.
Parkes, Peter. "Celtic Fosterage: Adoptive Kinship and Clientage in Northwest Europe." *Comparative Studies in Society and History* 48 (2006): 359–95.
Partner, Nancy F. "No Sex, No Gender." *Speculum* 68 (1993): 419–43.
Patrologia Latina, edited by J.-P. Migne. Paris, 1815–75.
Pelteret, David. *Slavery in Early Mediaeval England.* Woodbridge: Boydell, 1995.
Pohl, Walther. "Ethnic Names and Identities in the British Isles." In *The Anglo-Saxons from the Migration Period to the Eighth Century: An Ethnographic Perspective*, edited by John Hines, 7–40. Woodbridge: Boydell, 1997.
Pollock, Linda. *Forgotten Children: Parent-Child Relations from 1500–1900.* Cambridge: Cambridge University Press, 1983.
Pope, John C., ed. *Homilies of Ælfric: A Supplementary Collection.* 2 vols. EETS os 259/260. Oxford: Oxford University Press, 1967–8.
Portnoy, Phyllis. "'Remnant' and Ritual: The Place of *Daniel* and *Christ and Satan* in the Junius Epic." *English Studies* 75 (1994): 408–21.
Post, J.B. "Ages at Menarche and Menopause: Some Mediaeval Authorities." *Population Studies* 25 (1971): 83–7.
Pratt, David. *The Political Thought of King Alfred the Great.* Cambridge: Cambridge University Press, 2007.
Priebsch, Robert, "The Chief Sources of Some Anglo-Saxon Homilies." *Otia Merseiana* 1 (1899): 129–47.

Privat, Karen, Tamsin O'Connell, and Michael Richards. "Stable Isotope Analysis of Human and Faunal Remains from the Anglo-Saxon Cemetery at Berinsfield, Oxfordshire: Dietary and Social Implications." *Journal of Archaeological Science* 29 (2002): 779–90.

Rabin, Andrew. "Anglo-Saxon Women before the Law: A Student Edition of Five Old English Lawsuits." *Old English Newsletter* 41 (2008): 33–56.

– "Capital Punishment and the Anglo-Saxon Judicial Apparatus: A Maximum View?" In *Capital and Corporal Punishment in Anglo-Saxon England*, edited by Jay Paul Gates and Nicole Marafioti, 181–200. Woodbridge: Boydell, 2014.

– "Courtly Habits: Monastic Women's Legal Literacy in Early Anglo-Saxon England." In *Nuns' Literacies in Medieval Europe: The Kansas City Dialogue*, edited by Virginia Blanton, Veronica O'Mara, and Patricia Stoop, 179–89. Turnhout: Brepols, 2015.

– "Female Advocacy and Royal Protection in Tenth Century England: The Legal Career of Queen Ælfthryth." *Speculum* 84 (2009): 261–88.

– "Law and Justice." In *The Blackwell Handbook of Anglo-Saxon Studies*, edited by Jacqueline Stodnick and Renee Trilling, 85–98. Oxford: Blackwell, 2012.

– "Old English *Forespeca* and the Role of the Advocate in Anglo-Saxon Law." *Mediaeval Studies* 69 (2007): 223–55.

– "Testimony and Authority in Old English Law: Writing the Subject in the 'Fonthill Letter'." In *Law and Sovereignty in the Middle Ages and the Renaissance*, edited by Robert Sturges, 147–71. Tempe, AZ: ACMRS, 2011.

Rabin, Andrew, Lisi Oliver, and Stefan Jurasinski. *Old English Law: A Reader.* Old English Publications. Tempe: ACMRS, forthcoming.

Raith, Josef, ed. *Die altenglische Version des Halitgar'schen Bussbuches.* Bibliothek der angelsächsischen Prosa 13. Hamburg, 1933. Reprinted Darmstadt: Wissenschaftliche Buchgesellschaft, 1964.

Rauer, Christine, ed. and trans. *The Old English Martyrology: Edition, Translation and Commentary.* Cambridge: D.S. Brewer, 2013.

Redin, Mats. *Studies on Uncompounded Personal Names in Old English.* Uppsala: Edv. Berling, 1919.

Remley, Paul G. "Daniel, the *Three Youths* Fragment and the Transmission of Old English Verse." *ASE* 31 (2002): 81–140.

– *Old English Biblical Verse: Studies in Genesis, Exodus, and Daniel.* Cambridge Studies in Anglo-Saxon England 16. Cambridge: Cambridge University Press, 1996.

Reuschel, Helga. "Kenningar bei Alcuin. Zur 'Disputatio Pippini cum Albino'." *Beiträge zur Geschichte der deutschen Sprache und Literatur* 62 (1938): 143–55.

Richards, Mary P., and B. Jane Stanfield. "Concepts of Anglo-Saxon Women in the Laws." In *New Readings on Women in Old English Literature*, edited by Helen Damico and Alexandra Hennessey Olsen, 89–99. Bloomington: Indiana University Press, 1990.

Ridyard, Susan J. "*Condigna veneratio*: Post-Conquest Attitudes to the Saints of the Anglo-Saxons." In *Proceedings of the Battle Conference 1986*, edited by R. Allen Brown, 179–206. Woodbridge: Boydell, 1987.

– *The Royal Saints of Anglo-Saxon England.* Cambridge: Cambridge University Press, 1988.

Riese, Alexander. "Die Sueben." *Rheinisches Museum für Philologie* 44 (1889): 331–46.

Rivers, Theodore John. *Laws of the Salian and Ripuarian Franks*. New York: AMS Press, 1986.

– "Widows' Rights in Anglo-Saxon Law." *American Journal of Legal History* 19 (1975): 208–15.

Roberts, Jane, Christian Kay, and Lynne Grundy. *A Thesaurus of Old English*. 2 vols. London: King's College, Centre for Late Antique and Medieval Studies, 1995.

Robertson, Agnes Jane, ed. *Anglo-Saxon Charters*. 2nd ed. Cambridge: Cambridge University Press, 1956.

Rollason, David W. "The Cults of Murdered Royal Saints in Anglo-Saxon England." *ASE* 11 (1983): 1–22.

– *Saints and Relics in Anglo-Saxon England.* Oxford: Blackwell, 1989.

Rollason, David W., and Lynda Rollason, eds. *The Durham Liber Vitae: London, British Library, MS Cotton Domitian A.VII*. 3 vols. London: British Library, 2007.

Rollason, Lynda. "History and Codicology." In *The Durham Liber Vitae: London, British Library, MS Cotton Domitian A.VII*, vol. I, edited by David Rollason and Lynda Rollason, 5–42. London: British Library, 2007.

Rosier, James L., ed. *The Vitellius Psalter.* Ithaca, NY: Cornell University Press, 1962.

Rowley, Sharon M. "Bede in Later Anglo-Saxon England." In *The Cambridge Companion to Bede*, edited by Scott DeGregorio, 216–28. Cambridge: Cambridge University Press, 2010.

Rudolf, Winfried. "Riddling and Reading: Iconicity and Logogriphs in Exeter Book *Riddles* 23 and 45." *Anglia* 130 (2012): 499–525.

– "The Source and Textual Identity of 'Homily' Napier XXXI – Ælfric and the *Munuccild* of Saint-Maurice d'Agaune." *RES* 57 (2006): 607–22.

Rushforth, Rebecca. "Cambridge, Pembroke College 25: The Manuscript and Its Historical Context.", 1–27. www.stoa.org/Pembroke25/Website-tv/essays/Rushforth.pdf, accessed September 2015.

– *Saints in English Kalendars before A.D. 1100.* Henry Bradshaw Society 117. London: Henry Bradshaw Society, 2008.

Russell, Josiah Cox. *British Medieval Population.* Albuquerque: University of New Mexico Press, 1948.

Salvador-Bello, Mercedes. "How Far did the Influence of Anglo-Saxon Riddling Reach in the Continent?" Paper presented at the International Medieval Congress, Leeds, July 2016.

– *Isidorean Perceptions of Order: the Exeter Book Riddles and Medieval Latin Enigmata.* Medieval European Studies 17. Morgantown: West Virginia University Press, 2015.

Sawyer, P.H. *Anglo-Saxon Charters: An Annotated List and Bibliography.* London: Royal Historical Society, 1968.

Sayer, Duncan. "'Sons of Athelings Given to the Earth': Infant Mortality within Anglo-Saxon Mortuary Geography." *Medieval Archaeology* 58 (2014): 83–109.

Schabram, Hans. "Bemerkungen zur Etymologie von ae. *umbor* 'Kind'." In *Florilegium Linguisticum. Festschrift für Wolfgang P. Schmid zum 70. Geburtstag*, edited by Eckhardt Eggers et al., 403–14. Frankfurt: Lang, 1999.

Schmitt, Jean-Claude. *The Holy Greyhound: Guinefort, Healer of Children since the Thirteenth Century.* Cambridge: Cambridge University Press, 1983.

Schofield, Philip. "Medieval Diet and Demography." In *Food in Medieval England: Diet and Nutrition*, edited by Christopher Woolgar, Dale Serjeantson, and Tony Waldron, 239–53. Oxford: Oxford University Press, 2006.

Schönfeld, Moritz. *Wörterbuch der altgermanischen Personen- und Völkernamen.* Heidelberg: Winter, 1911.

Schultz, James A. *The Knowledge of Childhood in the German Middle Ages, 1100–1350.* Philadelphia: University of Pennsylvania Press, 1995.

Scragg, Donald G., ed. *The Vercelli Homilies and Related Texts.* EETS os 300. Oxford: Oxford University Press, 1992.

Seymour, Michael C., et al., eds. *On the Properties of Things: John Trevisa's Translation of Bartholomaeus Anglicus De proprietatibus rerum.* 3 vols. Oxford: Clarendon Press, 1975–88.

Shahar, Shulamith. *Childhood in the Middle Ages.* Translated by Chaya Galai. London; New York: Routledge, 1990.

Shippey, Thomas A. *Beowulf.* London: Arnold, 1978.

– "Names in *Beowulf* and Anglo-Saxon England." In *The Dating of "Beowulf": A Reassessment*, edited by Leonard Neidorf, 58–78. Cambridge: D.S. Brewer, 2014.

– *Poems of Wisdom and Learning in Old English.* Cambridge: D.S. Brewer, 1976.

Shorter, Edward. *The Making of the Modern Family.* London: Collins, 1976.

Singmaster, David. "The History of Some of Alcuin's Propositions." In *Charlemagne and His Heritage: 1200 Years of Civilization and Science in Europe: Karl der Grosse und sein Nachwirken: 1200 Jahre Kultur und Wissenschaft in Europa.* vol. 2: *Mathematical Arts*, edited by Paul Leo Butzer, Max Kerner, and Walter Oberschelp, 11–29. Turnhout: Brepols, 1998.

Sisam, Kenneth. "Marginalia in the Vercelli Book." In *Studies in the History of Old English Literature*, edited by Kenneth Sisam, 109–18. Oxford: Clarendon Press, 1953.

– *The Structure of "Beowulf."* Oxford: Clarendon Press, 1965.

Skambraks, Tanja. *Das Kinderbischofsfest im Mittelalter.* Florence: SISMEL/ Edizioni de Galluzzo, 2014.

Skeat, Walter W., ed. and trans. *Ælfric's Lives of Saints.* 2 vols. EETS os 76 and 114. London: Trübner, 1881–1900.

Slay, Desmond, ed. *Hrólfs saga Kraka.* Editiones Arnamagnæanæ, Series B, 1. Copenhagen: Munksgaard, 1960.

Smith, Anthony D. "The Myth of the 'Modern Nation' and the Myths of Nations." *Ethnic and Racial Studies* 11 (1988): 1–25.

Smith, Robin D. "Anglo-Saxon Maternal Ties." In *This Noble Craft ...: Proceedings of the Xth Research Symposium of the Dutch and Belgian Teachers of Old and Middle English and Historical Linguistics, Utrecht, 19–20 January, 1989*, edited by Erik Kooper, 106–17. Amsterdam: Editions Rodopi, 1991.

Smith, Sally. "The Spaces of Late Medieval Peasant Childhood: Children and Social Reproduction." In *Medieval Childhood: Archaeological Approaches*, Childhood in the Past Monograph Series 3, edited by Dawn Hadley and Katie Hemer, 57–74. Oxford: Oxbow, 2014.

Smith, Scott Thompson. "Of Kings and Cattle Thieves: The Rhetorical Work of the Fonthill Letter." *JEGP* 106 (2007): 447–67.

Smyth, Alfred P. "The Emergence of English Identity: 700–1000." In *Medieval Europeans: Studies in Ethnic Identity and National Perspectives in Medieval Europe*, edited by Alfred P. Smyth, 24–52. New York: St Martin's Press, 1998.

Sofaer Derevenski, Joanna. "Material Culture Shock: Confronting Expectations in the Material Culture of Children." In *Children and Material Culture*, edited by Joanna Sofaer Derevenski, 3–16. London and New York: Routledge, 2000.

Sofaer, Joanna, and Budden, Sandy. "Many Hands Make Light Work: Embodied Knowledge at the Bronze Age Tell at Szazhalombatta." In *Embodied Knowledge*, edited by Marie Louise Stig Sørensen and Katharina Rebay-Salisbury, 117–27. Oxford: Oxbow, 2012.

Solo, Harry Jay. "The Twice-Told Tale: A Reconsideration of the Syntax and Style of the Old English *Daniel*, 245–429." *Papers on Language and Literature* 9 (1973): 347–64.

Sorrell, Paul. "Alcuin's 'Comb' Riddle." *Neophilologus* 80 (1996): 311–18.
– "Oaks, Ships, Riddles and the Old English *Rune Poem*." *ASE* 19 (1990): 103–16.
Southern, Richard W., ed. *The Life of St Anselm Archbishop of Canterbury by Eadmer.* London: Thomas Nelson, 1962.
Spindler, Robert, ed. *Das altenglische Bussbuch (sog. Confessionale Pseudo-Egberti).* Leipzig: Tauchnitz, 1934.
Stafford, Pauline. "Parents and Children in the Early Middle Ages." *Early Medieval Europe* 10 (2001): 257–71.
– "Queens, Nunneries and Reforming Churchmen: Gender, Religious Status and Reform in Tenth- and Eleventh-Century England." *Past and Present* 163 (1999): 3–35.
– "Sons and Mothers: Family Politics in the Early Middle Ages." In *Medieval Women*, edited by Derek Baker, 79–100. Oxford: Blackwell, 1978.
– *Unification and Conquest: A Political and Social History of England in the Tenth and Eleventh Centuries.* London: Edward Arnold, 1989.
– "Women and the Norman Conquest." *Transactions of the Royal Historical Society* 4 (1994): 221–49.
Stanley, Eric. "The *Familia* in Anglo-Saxon Society." *Anglia* 126 (2008): 37–64.
– "*Staþol*: A Firm Foundation for Imagery." In *Text, Image, Interpretation: Studies in Anglo-Saxon Literature and Its Insular Context in Honour of Éamonn Ó Carragáin*, edited by Alastair Minnis and Jane Roberts, 319–32. Turnhout: Brepols, 2007.
Stenton, Frank M. "Personal Names in Place Names." In *Introduction to the Survey of English Place-Names*, edited by Allen Mawer and Frank M. Stenton, 165–89. Cambridge: Cambridge University Press, 1924.
Stevenson, William H., ed. *Asser's Life of King Alfred together with the Annals of Saint Neots Erroneously Ascribed to Asser.* 1904, reissued with an article on recent work on Asser's *Life of Alfred* by Dorothy Whitelock. Oxford: Clarendon Press, 1959.
Stone, Lawrence. *The Family, Sex and Marriage in England 1500–1800*. London: Weidenfeld & Nicolson, 1977.
Stoodley, Nick. "Burial Rites, Gender and the Creation of Kingdoms: The Evidence from Seventh Century Wessex." *Anglo-Saxon Studies in Archaeology and History* 10 (1999): 99–107.
– "From the Cradle to the Grave: Age Organization and the Early Anglo-Saxon Burial Rite." *World Archaeology* 31 (2000): 456–72.
Suchier, Walther, ed. "Disputatio Pippini cum Albino." In *Die Altercatio Hadriani Augusti et Epicteti philosophi, nebst einigen verwandten Texten*, edited by Lloyd William Daly and Walter Suchier, 134–46. Urbana: University of Illinois Press, 1939.

– ed. *Das mittellateinische Gespräch Adrian und Epictitus nebst verwandten Texten (Joca monachorum).* Tübingen: Max Niemeyer, 1955.

Sweet, Henry, ed. *King Alfred's West-Saxon Version of Gregory's Pastoral Care.* EETS os 45, 50. London: Oxford University Press, 1871.

Swenson, Karen. "Death Appropriated in 'The Fates of Men'." *Studies in Philology* 88 (1991): 123–39.

Symons, Thomas, ed. *Regularis concordia: The Monastic Agreement of the Monks and Nuns of the English Nation.* London: Nelson, 1953.

Szarmach, Paul E. "Alfred's Nero." In *Sources of Wisdom: Old English and Early Medieval Latin Studies in Honour of Thomas E. Hill*, edited by Charles Darwin Wright, Frederick M. Biggs, and Thomas N. Hall, 147–67. Toronto: University of Toronto Press, 2007.

Taylor, Archer. "Riddles Dealing with Family Relationships." *Journal of American Folklore* 51 (1938): 25–37.

Taylor, Charles. *Modern Social Imaginaries.* Durham, NC: Duke University Press, 2004.

Thacker, Alan. "Wilfrid, His Cult and His Biographer." In *Wilfrid: Abbot, Bishop, Saint*, edited by Nicholas J. Higham, 1–16. Donington: Shaun Tyas, 2013.

Thompson, Victoria. *Dying and Death in Later Anglo-Saxon England.* Cambridge: Boydell, 2004.

– "Women, Power, and Protection in Tenth- and Eleventh-Century England." In *Medieval Women and the Law*, edited by Noël James Menuge, 1–17. Woodbridge: Boydell, 2000.

Thorpe, Benjamin, ed. *Diplomatarium Anglicum ævi Saxonici: A Collection of English Charters from the Reign of King Æthelberht of Kent to That of William the Conqueror.* London: Macmillan and Co., 1865.

Timofeeva, Olga. "Anglo-Latin Bilingualism before 1066: Prospects and Limitations." In *Interfaces between Language and Culture in Medieval England. A Festschrift for Matti Kilpiö*, edited by Alaric Hall, Olga Timofeeva, Ágnes Kiricsi, and Bethany Fox, 1–36. Leiden: Brill, 2010.

Tripp, Raymond, Jr. "Did Beowulf have an Inglorious Youth?" *Studia Neophilologica* 61 (1989): 129–43.

Turville-Petre, Gabriel, ed. *Víga-Glúms saga.* 2nd ed. Oxford: Clarendon Press, 1960.

Wallach, Luitpold. *Alcuin and Charlemagne: Studies in Carolingian History and Literature.* Ithaca, NY: Cornell University Press, 1959.

Wallis, Faith, trans. *Bede: The Reckoning of Time: Translated with Introduction, Notes and Commentary.* Translated Texts for Historians 29. Liverpool: Liverpool University Press, 2004.

Ward, Benedicta. "The Spirituality of St Cuthbert." In *St Cuthbert, His Cult and His Community to AD 1200*, edited by Gerald Bonser, David Rollason and Clare Stancliffe, 65–76. Woodbridge: Boydell, 1989.

Wasyliw, Patricia Healy. *Martyrdom, Murder, and Magic: Child Saints and Their Cults in Medieval Europe*. Studies in Church History 2. New York: Peter Lang, 2005.

Watkins, Susan Cotts, and Andrew S. London. "Personal Names and Cultural Change: A Study of the Naming Patterns of Italians and Jews in the United States in 1910." *Social Science History* 18 (1994): 169–209.

Webber, Teresa. "The Diffusion of Augustine's Confessions in England during the Eleventh and Twelfth Centuries." In *The Cloister and the World: Essays in Medieval History in Honour of Barbara Harvey*, ed. John Blair and Brian Golding, 29–45. Oxford: Clarendon Press, 1996.

Weber, Robert, ed. *Biblia sacra iuxta Latinam Vulgatam versionem*, 4th ed. Stuttgart: Deutsche Bibelgesellschaft, 1994.

Wendrich, Willeke, ed. *Archaeology and Apprenticeship: Body Knowledge, Identity, and Communities of Practice.* Tucson: University of Arizona Press, 2012.

Westgard, Joshua. "Bede in the Carolingian Age and Beyond." In *The Cambridge Companion to Bede*, edited by Scott DeGregorio, 201–15. Cambridge: Cambridge University Press, 2010.

Whatley, E. Gordon, ed. *The Saint of London: The Life and Miracles of St Erkenwald. Text and Translation.* Binghamton: Centre for Medieval and Early Renaissance Studies, State University of New York, 1989.

Whitelock, Dorothy, ed. *Sermo Lupi ad Anglos*. New York: Appleton-Century-Crofts, 1966.

– ed. *English Historical Documents, Volume I: c. 500–1042*. 2nd ed. New York: Oxford University Press, 1979.

– ed. *Sweet's Anglo-Saxon Reader in Prose and Verse*. 15th ed. Oxford: Oxford University Press, 1967.

William of Malmesbury. *Saints' Lives: Lives of SS. Wulfstan, Dunstan, Patrick, Benignus and Indract*, edited and translated by M. Winterbottom and Rodney M. Thomson. Oxford Medieval Texts. Oxford: Oxford University Press, 2002.

Williams, Ann, and H.G. Martin, eds. *Domesday Book: A Complete Translation*. New York: Penguin, 1992.

Williamson, Craig, ed. *A Feast of Creatures: Anglo-Saxon Riddle Songs.* Philadelphia: University of Pennsylvania Press, 2011.

– *The Old English Riddles of the Exeter Book*. Chapel Hill: University of North Carolina Press, 1977.

Winterbottom, Michael, and Michael Lapidge, eds. and trans. *The Early Lives of St Dunstan.* Oxford: Clarendon Press, 2012.

Wood, Diana, ed. *The Church and Childhood: Papers Read at the 1993 Summer Meeting and the 1994 Winter Meeting of the Ecclesiastical History Society.* Oxford; Cambridge, MA: Published for the Ecclesiastical History Society by Blackwell Publishers, 1994.

Wood, Ian. *The Most Holy Abbot Ceolfrid.* Jarrow Lecture: Jarrow, 1995.

Wood, Michael. "The Making of King Aethelstan's Empire: An English Charlemagne?" In *Ideal and Reality in Frankish and Anglo-Saxon Society: Studies Presented to J.M. Wallace-Hadrill*, edited by Patrick Wormald with Donald Bullough and Roger Collins, 250–72. Oxford: Blackwell, 1983.

Woolf, Henry Bosley. *The Old Germanic Principles of Name-Giving*. Baltimore: Johns Hopkins University Press, 1939.

Wormald, Patrick. "*Beowulf*: The Redating Reassessed." In *The Times of Bede: Studies in Early English Christian Society and Its Historian*, edited by Stephen Baxter, 71–81, 98–105. Malden: Blackwell, 2006.

– "Charters, Law, and the Settlement of Disputes in Anglo-Saxon England." In *Legal Culture in the Early Medieval West: Law as Text, Image, and Experience*, edited by Patrick Wormald, 289–312. London: The Hambledon Press, 1999.

– "*Engla lond*: the Making of an Allegiance." *Journal of Historical Sociology* 7 (1994): 1–24.

– "A Handlist of Anglo-Saxon Lawsuits." In *Legal Culture in the Early Medieval West: Law as Text, Image, and Experience*, edited by Patrick Wormald, 253–88. London: The Hambledon Press, 1999.

– "'*Inter cetera bona … genti suae*': Law Making and Peacekeeping in the Earliest English Kingdoms." In *Legal Culture in the Early Medieval West: Law as Text, Image, and Experience*, edited by Patrick Wormald, 179–99. London: The Hambledon Press, 1999.

– "*Lex scripta* and *verbum regis*: Legislation and Germanic Kingship, from Euric to Cnut." In *Legal Culture in the Early Medieval West: Law as Text, Image, and Experience*, edited by Patrick Wormald, 1–43. London: The Hambledon Press, 1999.

Yorke, Barbara. "Aethelmaer, the Foundation of the Abbey at Cerne and the Politics of the Tenth Century." In *The Cerne Abbey Millennium Lectures*, edited by Katherine Barker, 15–25. Cerne Abbas: The Cerne Abbey Millennium Committee, 1988.

Young, Ernest. "The Anglo-Saxon Family Law." In *Essays in Anglo-Saxon Law*, edited by Henry Adams, 121–82. Boston: Little, Brown and Company, 1876.

Zacher, Samantha. *Rewriting the Old Testament in Anglo-Saxon Verse: Becoming the Chosen People.* London and New York: Bloomsbury, 2013.

Contributors

Daniel Anlezark is Associate Professor in the Department of English at the University of Sydney.

Sally Crawford is Senior Research Fellow at the Institute of Archaeology, Oxford University.

Joyce Hill is Emeritus Professor of Medieval Literature at the University of Leeds.

Susan Irvine is Quain Professor of English Language and Literature at University College London.

Stacy S. Klein is Associate Professor of English at Rutgers University, State University of New Jersey.

Andreas Lemke completed his PhD at the University of Göttingen in 2014.

Shu-han Luo is currently studying for a PhD in Old and Middle English literature at Yale University.

Leonard Neidorf is Professor of English at Nanjing University.

Richard North is Professor of English Language and Literature at University College London.

Andy Orchard is Rawlinson-Bosworth Professor of Anglo-Saxon at the University of Oxford.

Andrew Rabin is Associate Professor at the Department of English, University of Louisville.

Winfried Rudolf is Professor of Medieval English Language and Literature at the University of Göttingen.

Index

Toronto Anglo-Saxon Series

1 *Preaching the Converted: The Style and Rhetoric of the Vercelli Book Homilies,* Samantha Zacher

2 *Say What I Am Called: The Old English Riddles of the Exeter Book and the Anglo-Latin Riddle Tradition*, Dieter Bitterli

3 *The Aesthetics of Nostalgia: Historical Representation in Anglo-Saxon Verse,* Renée Trilling

4 *New Readings in the Vercelli Book*, edited by Samantha Zacher and Andy Orchard

5 *Authors, Audiences, and Old English Verse*, Thomas A. Bredehoft

6 *On Aesthetics in "Beowulf" and Other Old English Poems*, edited by John M. Hill

7 *Old English Metre: An Introduction*, Jun Terasawa

8 *Anglo-Saxon Psychologies in the Vernacular and Latin Traditions*, Leslie Lockett

9 *The Body Legal in Barbarian Law*, Lisi Oliver

10 *Old English Literature and the Old Testament*, edited by Michael Fox and Manish Sharma

11 *Stealing Obedience: Narratives of Agency and Identity in Later Anglo-Saxon England*, Katherine O'Brien O'Keeffe

12 *Traditional Subjectivities: The Old English Poetics of Mentality*, Britt Mize

13 *Land and Book: Literature and Land Tenure in Anglo-Saxon England*, Scott T. Smith

14 *Writing Women Saints in Anglo-Saxon England*, edited by Paul E. Szarmach

15 *Anglo-Saxon Manuscripts: A Bibliographical Handlist of Manuscripts and Manuscript Fragments Written or Owned in England up to 1100*, Helmut Gneuss and Michael Lapidge

16 *The King's Body: Burial and Succession in Anglo-Saxon England*, Nicole Marafioti

17 *From Lawmen to Plowmen: Anglo-Saxon Legal Tradition and the School of Langland*, Stephen Yeager

18 *The Politics of Language: Byrhtferth, Ælfric, and the Multilingual Identity of the Benedictine Reform*, Rebecca Stephenson

19 *Weaving Words and Binding Bodies: The Poetics of Human Experience in Old English Literature*, Megan Cavell

20 *Joinings: Compound Words in Old English Literature*, Jonathan Davis-Secord

21 *Imagining the Jew in Anglo-Saxon Literature and Culture*, edited by Samantha Zacher

22 *Latinity and Identity in Anglo-Saxon Literature*, edited by Rebecca Stephenson and Emily Thornbury

23 *Inhabited Spaces: Anglo-Saxon Constructions of Place*, Nicole Guenther Discenza

24 *England in Europe: English Royal Women and Literary Patronage, c.1000 – c.1150*, Elizabeth M. Tyler

25 *Undoing Babel: The Tower of Babel in Anglo-Saxon Literature*, Tristan Major

26 *Compelling God: Theories of Prayer in Anglo-Saxon England*, Stephanie Clark

27 *Biblical Epics in Late Antiquity and Anglo-Saxon England:* Divina in Laude Voluntas, Patrick McBrine

28 *Childhood and Adolescence in Anglo-Saxon Literary Culture*, edited by Susan Irvine and Winfried Rudolf

www.ingramcontent.com/pod-product-compliance
Lightning Source LLC
LaVergne TN
LVHW090149080826
844660LV00013B/732/J

* 9 7 8 1 4 8 7 5 0 2 0 2 7 *